THE
WIZARD
OF
LIES

Also by Diana B. Henriques

A First-Class Catastrophe:
The Road to Black Monday, the Worst Day in Wall Street History

The White Sharks of Wall Street:
Thomas Mellon Evans and the Original Corporate Raiders

Fidelity's World:
The Secret Life and Public Power of the Mutual Fund Giant

The Machinery of Greed:
Public Authority Abuse and What to Do About It

THE WIZARD OF LIES

BERNIE MADOFF AND THE DEATH OF TRUST

DIANA B. HENRIQUES

ST. MARTIN'S GRIFFIN
NEW YORK

www.stmartins.com

Design by Meryl Sussman Levavi

The Library of Congress has cataloged the Henry Holt edition as follows:

Henriques, Diana B.
  The wizard of lies : Bernie Madoff and the death of trust / Diana B. Henriques.—1st ed.
    p. cm.
  Includes bibliographical references and index.
  ISBN 978-0-8050-9134-2
  1. Madoff, Bernard L.   2. Swindlers and swindling—United States—Biography.
3. Ponzi schemes—United States.   4. Commercial crimes—United States.   I. Title.
  HV6692.M33 H46 2011
  364.16'3092 B—dc22

2011011332

ISBN 978-1-250-00743-8 (trade paperback)

Originally published in hardcover format by Times Books,
an imprint of Henry Holt and Company

D 20 19 18 17

For my colleagues at *The New York Times*,
yesterday, today, and tomorrow;
and for Larry,
forever

CONTENTS

CAST OF CHARACTERS

THE MADOFF FAMILY

Bernie Madoff, founder of Bernard L. Madoff Investment Securities
Ruth Madoff (née Alpern), his wife
Mark Madoff, their elder son, born 1964
Andrew Madoff, their younger son, born 1966

Peter Madoff, Bernie Madoff's younger brother
Shana Madoff, his daughter
Roger Madoff, his son

Ralph Madoff, Bernie Madoff's father
Sylvia Madoff (née Muntner), Bernie Madoff's mother

AT BERNARD L. MADOFF INVESTMENT SECURITIES

Eleanor Squillari, Bernie Madoff's secretary
Irwin Lipkin, Madoff's first employee
Daniel Bonventre, the director of operations
Frank DiPascali, the manager on the seventeenth floor
Annette Bongiorno ⎫
JoAnn "Jodi" Crupi ⎭ his colleagues

Jerome O'Hara, a computer programmer

George Perez, his coworker and officemate

David Kugel, an arbitrage trader

THE ACCOUNTANTS

Saul Alpern, Ruth Madoff's father

Frank Avellino, Alpern's colleague and successor

Michael Bienes, Avellino's longtime partner

Jerome Horowitz, an early Alpern partner and Madoff's accountant

David Friehling, Horowitz's son-in-law and successor

Paul Konigsberg, a Manhattan accountant

Richard Glantz, a lawyer and the son of an early Alpern associate

INDIVIDUAL INVESTORS
AND "INTRODUCERS"

Martin J. Joel Jr., a stockbroker in New York

Norman F. Levy, a real estate tycoon in New York

Carl Shapiro, a philanthropist in Palm Beach

Robert Jaffe, his son-in-law

Jeffry Picower, a secretive New York investor

William D. Zabel, his longtime attorney

Mendel "Mike" Engler, a stockbroker in Minneapolis

Howard Squadron, a prominent Manhattan attorney

Fred Wilpon, an owner of the New York Mets baseball team

MAJOR U.S. FEEDER FUNDS

Stanley Chais, a Beverly Hills investor

Jeffrey Tucker, a cofounder of Fairfield Greenwich Group

Walter Noel Jr., his founding partner

Mark McKeefry, the general counsel at Fairfield Greenwich

Amit Vijayvergiya, the chief risk officer at Fairfield Greenwich

J. Ezra Merkin, a prominent Wall Street investor

Victor Teicher, his former adviser

Sandra Manzke, a pension fund specialist

Robert I. Schulman, her onetime partner

INTERNATIONAL INVESTORS AND PROMOTERS

Jacques Amsellem, a French investor

Albert Igoin, a secretive financial adviser in Paris

Patrick Littaye, a French hedge fund manager

René-Thierry Magon de la Villehuchet, his partner

Sonja Kohn, a prominent Austrian banker and founder of Bank Medici

Carlo Grosso, a manager of the Kingate fund, based in London

Rodrigo Echenique Gordillo, a Banco Santander director in Madrid

COHMAD SECURITIES

Maurice J. "Sonny" Cohn, Bernie Madoff's partner in this firm

Marcia Beth Cohn, his daughter

WHISTLE-BLOWERS

Michael Ocrant, a writer for an elite hedge fund newsletter

Erin Arvedlund, a freelance writer for *Barron's* magazine

Harry Markopolos, a quantitative analyst in Boston

SECURITIES AND EXCHANGE COMMISSION (SEC)

Christopher Cox, chairman from August 2005 to January 2009

Mary Schapiro, his successor as chairman

H. David Kotz, their independent inspector general

Grant Ward, a regional official in Boston

Ed Manion, his coworker

Lori Richards, a senior official in Washington

Eric Swanson, a lawyer in Washington

Andrew Calamari, a senior regional official in New York

Meaghan Cheung, a lawyer in the New York office

Simona Suh, her colleague

William David Ostrow, an examiner in the New York office

Peter Lamore, his colleague

Lee S. Richards III, a New York lawyer in private practice, appointed as receiver for Madoff's firm

FAMILY LAWYERS

Ira Lee "Ike" Sorkin, defense lawyer for Madoff

Daniel J. Horwitz

Nicole De Bello } Madoff's defense team

Mauro Wolfe

Peter Chavkin, lawyer for Ruth Madoff

Martin Flumenbaum, lawyer for Mark and Andrew Madoff

FEDERAL BUREAU OF
INVESTIGATION (FBI)

Ted Cacioppi, special agent

B. J. Kang, his colleague

FEDERAL PROSECUTORS
IN MANHATTAN

Preet Bharara, U.S. attorney for the Southern District of New York

William F. Johnson, chief of the Securities and Commodities Fraud Task Force

Marc Litt, the lead prosecutor in the Madoff case

Lisa Baroni, his colleague

SECURITIES INVESTOR PROTECTION CORPORATION (SIPC)

Irving H. Picard, the trustee for the Madoff bankruptcy case

David J. Sheehan, his chief legal counsel at Baker & Hostetler

FEDERAL JUDGES IN MANHATTAN

Douglas Eaton
Gabriel W. Gorenstein } magistrate judges
Ronald Ellis

Louis L. Stanton, a district court judge

Burton R. Lifland, a bankruptcy court judge

Denny Chin, a district court judge

Richard J. Sullivan, a district court judge

Jed S. Rakoff, a district court judge

VICTIMS' ADVOCATES

Helen Davis Chaitman, a lawyer in New Jersey

Lawrence R. Velvel, a law school dean in Massachusetts

PROLOGUE

Glimpsed through the glass double doors at the end of a long prison hall-way, he is not recognizable as the impassive hawk-faced man who was marched incessantly across television screens around the world less than two years ago. He seems smaller, diminished—just an elderly man in glasses talking deferentially to a prison official and looking a little anxious as he waits for the locked doors ahead of him to click open.

Escorted by an associate warden, he steps from the sunshine of the prison's sealed courtyard into the dim, cheaply paneled visiting room. The room would have fit easily into a corner of his former penthouse in Manhattan. Its furnishings consist entirely of faded plastic lawn furniture—red armless chairs around low tan tables—and it is illuminated today only by light from one large window and a row of vending machines.

On most of his occasional visits to this room, it had been filled with prisoners and their families. But as he enters with his escort on this Tuesday morning, the room is empty except for his lawyer, a guard, and the visitor he has finally agreed to see. As the rules require, he sits facing the guard's desk, where the associate warden settles down to wait. He unfolds a single sheet of ruled paper; it appears to be some handwritten notes and a few questions for his lawyer. He spreads the sheet out on the table in front of him.

The creases in his tan short-sleeved shirt and trousers are knife-sharp, despite the humidity of this late summer morning. His hair is shorter, but it suits his slimmer frame. His black leather sneakers are gleaming. Aside from a small spot where the brass plating on his belt buckle has worn away, he is as carefully groomed as ever. Even though he does not much resemble the heavier, better-dressed man shown so often in the news reports after his arrest, he still has a quiet magnetism that draws the eye.

For more than two hours, he answers questions, sometimes with a direct gaze and sometimes with eyes that shift to the empty patio outside the window beside him. He is soft-spoken and intense, with occasional flashes of wit. He loses his composure just once, when he talks about his wife. Throughout, he seems unfailingly candid, earnest, and trustworthy.

But then, he always does—even when he is lying. That is his talent and his curse. That is what enabled him to pull off the largest Ponzi scheme on record. That is what will enable him to spin the facts and obscure the truth about his crime for as long as he lives, if he chooses to do so.

Bernard L. Madoff—Inmate Number 61727054—is the best-known prisoner currently held at the sprawling Federal Correctional Complex on the outskirts of Butner, North Carolina.

The Butner-Creedmore exit on Interstate 85 does not announce that the prison is located here. There are no clearly marked signs within the little hamlet, just a few narrow black-and-white painted pointers at inter-sections, old-fashioned and easy to miss. The prison is not on the local map in the telephone book, so visitors have to ask the motel clerks for directions.

The twisting route from the interstate involves urban-sounding byways like Thirty-third Street and E Street but is lined mostly with vine-blanketed trees and weed-strewn fields. The prison complex looms suddenly out of the pine woods on the right. It consists primarily of four large buildings set in a floodlit clearing among the lowland forests and fields.

To the right, set slightly apart on the eastern edge of the property, is a minimum-security prison, the color of manila folders and distinctively free of walls or fences. Almost hidden from view behind a thick stretch of trees to the left is a large modern prison hospital, whose separate entrance is farther along the two-lane road that meanders past the complex. And just visible up on a small wooded hill at the center of the complex is a multistory medium-security prison clad in corrugated gray stone.

Madoff is housed in a fourth facility on the Butner grounds, another medium-security prison to the left of the main entrance, down a short drive lined with flowering white crepe myrtle trees. The low gray-stone building is laid out like a giant game of dominoes. Except for its entry-way, it is completely surrounded by a double row of towering chain-link fences taller than the building itself. The encircling fences are lined with shimmering swirls of shiny razor wire. A watchtower stands at one corner of the large, nearly treeless exercise yard, and guards cruise the narrow roads winding through the complex, constantly alert for wandering prisoners or too-curious visitors.

The unit's cinder-block entryway is a low-ceilinged maze of security screening equipment, lockers for visitors' belongings, pay phones, and offices. A set of locked doors leads into a sort of double airlock; the rear doors of each section are sealed before the doors ahead swing open. The last pair of doors opens into a wide white hallway leading to the visiting room. The corridor is immaculately clean and decorated, incongruously, with black-and-white Ansel Adams posters of big skies and wide-open spaces.

The sense of impenetrable isolation descends as soon as the last set of doors thud shut. Cell phones are out of reach, left in the lockers by the entryway. No written messages can be handed to the prisoner, who is constantly watched during visits. Without permission, not even a notebook can be carried into the visiting room; no tape recorders are allowed. Like laboratory rats or ants in a glass-walled colony, these prisoners are under constant scrutiny in a way few Americans can fathom. Phone calls—collect calls only—are rationed and monitored. Letters are opened and read. Every human interaction is policed, regulated, constrained, limited, fettered—including this one.

All media visits require the prisoner's invitation and the warden's approval. After nearly a month of paperwork, the green light from the warden came with barely a week's notice. The time allowed is limited, and that limit is politely enforced. (A follow-up visit will be authorized in February 2011. In the interval, Madoff will send along a note promising to mail his responses to any additional questions. He keeps his promise, sending several lengthy handwritten letters over the next few months and arranging to send short messages via the restricted and closely monitored prisoner e-mail system.)

Until today, Madoff's only visitor, apart from lawyers, has been his wife. Until now, he has not answered any independent questions about his crime except when standing in a courtroom, responding to a judge.

Amid that continued silence and mystery, Madoff's time in prison has been the subject of several speculative magazine and television specials—the latest one will air this week, in fact. In it, a former prisoner will claim that the guards here act "starstruck" around their infamous prisoner from Wall Street, although there is no sign of that today. That television program will also portray Butner as "Camp Fluffy," a gentle white-collar jail compared with harsher state prisons that house murderers and other violent criminals. Madoff's victims may feel that he deserves nothing more comfortable than a Vietcong tiger cage; if so, they will be disappointed at the roomlike two-man cells, the exercise equipment, and the television rooms available here.

But Madoff is unquestionably in a medium-security prison. It is not a steel jungle of brutal, barely restrained violence and depravity, but neither does it resemble a comfortable "Club Fed" with a golf course and tennis courts and casual visits from friends and family. These inmates do not wander beyond the towering razor-wire fences for a leisurely smoke. With his 150-year sentence, Madoff will live and die under lock and key.

It is unwise to trust the information about Madoff that leaks out of this sealed world. Besides an early tabloid report that he was dying of pancreatic cancer, there have been other reports, in more credible venues, that he was beaten up in an argument with another inmate. One report said he told a visitor he "didn't give a shit" about his sons. *New York* magazine reported that, after being provoked by an inmate, Madoff blurted out, "Fuck my victims." And the *New York Post* reported that he told unidentified inmates that he had hidden away billions of dollars during the course of his long-running crime.

What is the truth? The prison firmly denies that Madoff, who is now seventy-two years old, has pancreatic cancer or any fatal disease—he concurs, and he shows no sign of illness today. The prison and Madoff also deny that he was ever attacked or involved in a fight; the minor injuries that prompted the rumor were sustained when he fell after becoming dizzy from some blood-pressure medication. And Madoff denies that he ever said anything contemptuous about his sons or his victims or claimed to have a secret fortune stashed away. On those last points, someone in this self-contained world of lies is telling the truth. It might be him.

Bernie Madoff's name is recognized and vilified around the world, a universal shorthand for a selfish, shameful era. He has been deplored in Switzerland, discussed on radio programs in Australia, whispered about in China, fretted over in the Persian Gulf. His face has been in every newspaper in the country, slapped onto the covers of magazines in a half-dozen languages, caricatured in editorial cartoons everywhere.

Even in an age of hyperbole, the story was beyond belief: a multibillion-dollar Ponzi scheme that lasted for decades, stretched around the globe, and ensnared some of the richest, wisest, and most respected people in the world. Thousands of ordinary people were caught in Madoff's web, too, and were utterly ruined.

In the aftermath of the economic meltdown of 2008, with dishonesty and chicanery exposed throughout the world of finance, no villain put a human face on the collapse the way Madoff did, perhaps because his crime encompassed far more than just the financial crisis. It was a timeless drama in itself, a morality play as ancient as human greed, as poignant as human trust.

The Madoff scandal struck a chord deep in that part of our imagination that responds to folktales and endows them with so much emotional power. A staple of such tales is instant transformation. In the blink of an eye, the ugly frog is a handsome prince. With one kiss, a sleeping princess is awakened, still beautiful after a century. With the sweep of a magic wand, a rolling pumpkin and a half-dozen scurrying mice become a golden coach and six gray horses.

Instant change was the core experience of Madoff's downfall. Suddenly, rich people were poor, admired people were scorned, smart people were exposed as fools, reasonable people were consumed with rage. The handsome prince became an ugly toad. This one man, Bernie Madoff, had made the life savings of tens of thousands of overly trusting people all around the world disappear in an instant. Thousands of times over, people were shattered by that stroke-of-midnight moment. Just an eyeblink, and it was all gone—their money, their status, their easy confidence in the future, the first-class travel, the secure retirement, the college fund, the peaceful sleep, the charitable pledges. In a single moment in their busy lives, while they were sleeping or having their hair cut or driving home from a meeting or waiting in line for a movie, their wealth simply vanished.

And there stood Bernie Madoff, the evil wizard who had waved his hand and, in one broken heartbeat, taken it all away.

For decades, Bernie Madoff lived at the center of an expanding web of lies.

In his long silence after his arrest, parts of that web became hopelessly knotted with misinformation and malicious gossip. In the pages ahead, many of those knots will be untangled, with the help of fresh information and new analysis about his relationships with his family and with key investors, and their relationship to his crimes.

More significantly, the chapters ahead will explore parts of his original skein of lies that have never been made public. They can be detailed here, for the first time, because Bernie Madoff himself agreed to meet with me in prison and talk with me about them, the first on-the-record media interviews he granted since his shattering arrest.

He deflected my numerous earlier requests with flattery and promises. "I have followed your distinguished career and reporting for many years," he said in a letter from prison in September 2009. "I will certainly consider your request at the appropriate time, which could only be after the open litigation and inquiries are concluded. You can rest assured you are at the top of my list. I know you will continue to be the professional journalist you have always been and understand my position."

When he finally sat down to talk with me for the first time, the conversation lasted more than two hours and ranged from family history to Wall Street foibles. His view of the fallout from his vast crime was shocking—another strand in his spidery web of illusion. He knew that some of his early victims had managed to withdraw more from his Ponzi scheme than they originally invested; the rest did not, but he knew that they would share in whatever assets the massive Madoff bankruptcy case produced. Looking at those two facts, he predicted—beyond all logic— that "people who were with me will make out better than if they'd been in the market" during the meltdown of 2008.

Madoff also disclosed details of his early life and business career that have been hidden in the shadows until now. From those details, it is clear that his habit of deceit began earlier than we knew. As early as 1962, by his own admission, he covered up huge losses he inflicted on his clients when he improperly invested their savings in high-risk newly issued stocks. The falsely inflated profits burnished his reputation and brought in more business. By the late 1980s, he acknowledged, he was using arcane strategies to help his biggest clients sidestep income taxes and evade foreign currency controls, drifting even further toward the gray edges of fraud. After the 1987 market crash, he was swamped by withdrawals from some longtime investors, familiar names whose ties to him can now be seen in a new light. He said he began covering those unwelcome withdrawals with cash that had just started to pour in from new hedge fund clients—and his Ponzi scheme, the classic fraud of "robbing Peter to pay Paul," was born.

By 1992, he was undoubtedly falsifying whole portfolios of stocks, options, and bonds. At the end, his defrauded clients included giant institutional investors around the world—from Banco Santander in Spain to the government of Abu Dhabi, from hedge funds in the Cayman Islands to private banks in Switzerland—and the scale of his theft was unprecedented. On the day of his arrest, he was supposed to be managing roughly $64.8 *billion* of other people's money. If he had actually possessed that money, he would have ranked as the largest investment manager in the world—50 percent bigger than the banking giant JPMorgan Chase, twice as big as Goldman Sachs, and more than three times bigger than funds organized by the legendary global investor George Soros.

But very little of that money was actually there. He was faking everything, from customer account statements to regulatory filings, on a scale that dwarfed every other Ponzi scheme in history.

"By 1998, I realized I was never going to get out of this," he said in one prison interview. "That's when I acknowledged the fact to myself that the ax was going to fall on me eventually."

When it was clear that he would never climb out of the hole he was in, why didn't he flee with his remaining millions and seek refuge beyond the reach of American justice? "There were lots of things I could have tried to do over the years [to escape], but I didn't," he said in August. "There was never a thought to run away and hide my money. . . . It never entered my mind to do that."

So he stayed on, cultivating the trust and reputation that sustained his expanding fraud—living a life that had become "a charade" of honesty and respectability, he said.

Of course, there will always be mysteries about Madoff. In the months and years ahead, government investigators may yet turn up evidence that will expand or cast doubt on some of what seems plausible today. And intense skepticism must always be employed when assessing Madoff's own memories and descriptions of his crimes—he tells the truth as gracefully as he tells lies, and the border between the two shifts from moment to moment. With that caveat, this book will map out the shadowy route Madoff followed on his long journey toward destruction and clarify what still remains beyond the borders of the map today.

Madoff's construction of the biggest Ponzi scheme in history was enabled by the Wall Street he had helped to build. He played a prominent role in shaping the modern market, from computerized NASDAQ trading to the mystique of hedge funds to the proliferation of specious derivatives. He spotted the trends, saw the opportunities, helped write the rule book, and abetted the weaknesses that we all live with, even now. And he was a creature of the world he helped create, a world that was greedy for riskless gain, impatient with regulation, arrogantly certain of success, woefully deluded about what could go wrong, and selfishly indifferent to the damage done to others.

That his life was woven so tightly into Wall Street's story surely helped him sustain his crime for as long as he did. To understand the Madoff scandal, we must understand the changing shape of the marketplace he helped build for the rest of us, a market that became increasingly crucial to our personal financial security just as it was becoming exponentially more difficult for most of us to understand. Madoff was reassuringly fluent in a new market language we all wished we could learn or pretended we already knew. He seemed warmly comfortable in a strange new place that left us feeling cold and anxious.

If he was an evil wizard, his power was vastly enhanced by the fact that we all moved into the castle with him.

THE
WIZARD
OF
LIES

1

AN EARTHQUAKE
ON WALL STREET

He is ready to stop now, ready to just let his vast fraud tumble down around him.

Despite his confident posturing and his apparent imperviousness to the increasing market turmoil, his investors are deserting him. The Spanish banking executives who visited him on Thanksgiving Day still want to withdraw their money. So do the Italians running the Kingate funds in London, and the managers of the fund in Gibraltar and the Dutch-run fund in the Caymans, and even Sonja Kohn in Vienna, one of his biggest boosters. That's more than $1.5 billion right there, from just a handful of feeder funds. Then there's the continued hemorrhaging at Fairfield Greenwich Group—$980 million through November and now another $580 million for December.

If he writes a check for the December redemptions, it will bounce.

There's no way he can borrow enough money to cover those withdrawals. Banks aren't lending to anyone now, certainly not to a midlevel wholesale outfit like his. His brokerage firm may still seem impressive to his trusting investors, but to nervous bankers and harried regulators today, Bernard L. Madoff Investment Securities is definitely not "too big to fail."

Last week he called a defense lawyer, Ike Sorkin. There's probably not much that even a formidable attorney like Sorkin can do for him at this point, but he's going to need a lawyer. He made an appointment for

11:30 AM on Friday, December 12. He's still unsure of what to do first and when to do what, but a Friday appointment should give him enough time to sort things out.

In his nineteenth-floor office on this cold, blustery Monday, Bernie Madoff starts going through the motions. Around him, the setting is incongruously serene: black lacquer furnishings against silvery carpets and darker gray walls, a graceful staircase in the center. His firm occupies the eighteenth and nineteenth floors of the Lipstick Building, a distinctive oval tower on Third Avenue at East Fifty-third Street. Around the curving walls of windows on each floor, slabs of glass hang from the ceiling to form bright offices and conference rooms. Hidden behind locked doors on the seventeenth floor is a bland set of cluttered offices that Madoff also rents, connected to the rest of the firm only by the building's main elevators and fire escapes. It is down there, far from Madoff's light-filled office, that his fraud is invisibly but inexorably falling apart.

A little before lunch, he talks on the phone with Jeffrey Tucker at Fairfield Greenwich. They've known each other for almost twenty years.

Madoff's controlled frustration sounds fierce over the phone lines. What the hell is this, $1.2 billion in withdrawals in just over a month? Hadn't the executives at Fairfield Greenwich been promising since June that they would "defend" against these redemptions? They're even taking money from their own insider funds! Some defense.

He threatens: Fairfield Greenwich has to replace the redemptions already piling up for December 31, or he will close its accounts. He will kill the goose supplying all those golden eggs for Tucker and his wife, for his younger partners, and for the extended family of Tucker's cofounder Walter Noel Jr.

He bluffs: "My traders are tired of dealing with these hedge funds," he says. Plenty of institutions could replace that money, and have been offering to do so for years. But he has "remained loyal" to Fairfield Greenwich, he reminds Tucker.

As calm as a losing litigator, Tucker assures Madoff that he and Noel are working on a brand-new fund, the Greenwich Emerald fund, that will be a little riskier but will produce better returns. It will sell easily, when the markets settle down.

Madoff scoffs at the notion that Tucker and Noel will ever raise the $500 million they hope for—even though the partners are putting millions of dollars of their own money into it already. They'd better focus on hanging on to the money they are losing right now, Madoff says, or he is going to cut them off.

A shaken Jeffrey Tucker writes an e-mail to his partners a few minutes later. "Just got off the phone with a very angry Bernie," he tells them, repeating the threats. "I think he is sincere."

He isn't. The Fairfield Sentry fund will shut down before December 31, but it won't be because Tucker and his partners aren't "defending" against their redemptions. It will be because they have stifled their skepticism for twenty years, determined to believe that their golden nest eggs were safe with Madoff.

Sometime today, people down on the seventeenth floor who work for Madoff's right-hand man, Frank DiPascali, will get the paperwork done so that Stanley Chais, one of Madoff's backers since the 1970s, can withdraw $35 million from one of his accounts. Chais has been loyal to Madoff a lot longer than the Fairfield Greenwich guys.

Around 4:00 PM, friends and clients start to arrive for a meeting of the board of the Gift of Life Bone Marrow Foundation, which helps find bone marrow matches for adults with leukemia. Bernie and his wife, Ruth, support the group because their nephew Roger succumbed to the disease and their son Andrew had a related illness, a form of lymphoma. In ones and twos, the board members show up, climbing the oval stairway from the reception area on the eighteenth floor, where the firm's administrative staff is housed.

At the head of the stairs, they turn right and head for the big glass-walled conference room between Madoff's office and his brother Peter's office. Ruth Madoff arrives and joins them. Eleanor Squillari, Bernie's secretary, has arranged some soft drinks, bottled water, and snacks on the credenza near one of the doors.

Jay Feinberg, the foundation's executive director and a leukemia survivor himself, sits down at one end of the long stone table with a few of his staff members and his elderly father, a board member. Bernie is at the other end, with Ruth on his right. There are people here who were woven into every decade of Madoff's life—Ed Blumenfeld, his buddy and the co-owner of his new jet; Fred Wilpon, an owner of the New York Mets baseball team and a friend since their kids were growing up together in Roslyn, Long Island; Maurice "Sonny" Cohn, his partner in Cohmad

Securities since the mid-1980s, a friend who has shared so many jokes with him over the years and now shares his office space.

Ezra Merkin, the financier and conduit to so many Jewish charities, arrives and settles his bulk into the square black leather chair next to Ruth. The elegant stockbroker Bob Jaffe, the son-in-law of Madoff's long-time Palm Beach investor Carl Shapiro and a broker with Cohmad, sits nearby. A few other board members or volunteers find seats at the table. There is a little trouble with the phone, but finally they manage to link in Norman Braman, the genial former owner of the Philadelphia Eagles football team, who presumably is in Florida.

At this moment, most of the people around this table are Madoff's friends, his admirers, his clients. In a few days they, and thousands like them, will become his victims. Their wealth will be diminished and their reputations questioned. Their lives will become a nightmare merry-go-round of lawyers, litigation, depositions, bankruptcy claims, and court-room battles. They will all profoundly regret that they ever trusted the genial silver-haired man seated at the head of the table.

With Ruth taking notes, Madoff turns to the agenda—fund-raising efforts and plans for the big annual dinner in the spring. A fund-raising committee is needed. "Who will take this on?" Madoff asks. Fred Wilpon agrees to do so. The rest of the discussion is routine, except that some members recall Feinberg passing around copies of the foundation's conflict-of-interest policy and getting a signed copy from each member for the file.

By six o'clock, they are done. Madoff escorts his wife and friends through the private nineteenth-floor exit. They head out into the winter night.

TUESDAY, DECEMBER 9, 2008

Things are starting to slip. Madoff has planned to meet with the son of his friend J. Ira Harris, one of the wise lions of Wall Street and now a genial philanthropist in Palm Beach, but the visit is canceled.

Instead, Madoff sits down with his older son, Mark, and explains that, despite the recent meltdown in the market, he's had a very strong year with his private investment advisory business. He's cleared several hundred million dollars, and he wants to distribute bonuses to some employees a little earlier than usual. Not in February—now, this week. He tells Mark to draw up a list of the trading desk employees who should get checks.

Troubled, Mark consults his brother, Andrew. The two men have seen their father tense up a little more every day as the market crisis has wrung them all out. Just a little liquidity strain on the hedge fund side, he told them last month. But he is clearly more than just worried; they've never seen him like this. And now he wants to pay out millions in early bonuses—it doesn't make sense. Shouldn't he be conserving cash, with things as rocky as they are? He should wait to see how things look in two months, when bonus season arrives. But Bernie Madoff is an autocrat—he is in charge, and he brooks no opposition. Still, the brothers decide they must talk with their father on Wednesday about their concerns.

After the markets close and the firm starts to empty out, Madoff walks across the oval area where the secretaries sit and enters Peter's office. Peter has aged and pulled inward in the two years since his only son died. He still carries Roger's photo in his wallet, one taken after leukemia had already left its stamp on his once-handsome face. For decades before that bereavement, Peter had been Bernie's right hand, his confidant, the technological guru of the firm, the "kid brother."

If Peter has not previously known about his brother's crime—his lawyers will insist later that he did not—he is going to learn about it now. Bernie takes a deep breath and asks his brother if he had "a moment to talk." Peter nods, and Bernie closes the door.

"I have to tell you what's going on," he says.

People speak glibly about "life-changing" moments. Some truly qualify. You propose marriage and are accepted. You hear "You're hired" or "You're fired," and your future shifts instantly. The doctor says "malignant," and everything is different. But anyone who has ever lived through it will tell you: It is profoundly shattering to learn, in one instant, that everything you thought was true about a loved one is actually a lie. The world rocks on its axis; when it is finally steady again, you are in a strange place that resembles but is totally unlike the place you were in just a moment earlier.

So if this is the moment Peter Madoff learns of his brother's crime, it seems unlikely that he immediately contemplates the ruin of his career and his family's fortune, or worries about the chain saw of civil lawsuits and criminal investigations that will chew through the years ahead. Those thoughts will surely come. But if this news has hit him from out of the blue, it is far more likely that his mind just stops and tries to rewind an entire lifetime in a split second, to get back to something real and true.

Peter is a lawyer and the firm's chief compliance officer—they've always been too casual about job titles here, and now it matters. He listens as Bernie explains that he's going to distribute the bonuses and send redemption checks to those closest to him—to make whatever amends he can before he turns himself in. He needs just a few days more, he says. He's already made a date with Ike Sorkin for Friday.

Perhaps still waiting for the world to stop rocking, Peter blurts out, "You've got to tell your sons."

Mark and Andrew had both talked with their uncle Peter about how worried they were about their father, who had grown increasingly preoccupied in recent weeks. They kept asking, "Is Dad all right?" They are frightened, Peter says. Again, he tells Bernie, "You have to tell them."

He would, he would. He just couldn't decide when.

WEDNESDAY, DECEMBER 10, 2008

Sometime during the morning, Eleanor Squillari sees Ruth Madoff make a quick visit to the office. On Bernie's instructions, she is withdrawing $10 million from her Cohmad brokerage account and moving the cash into her bank account at Wachovia so she can write checks on it if he needs the money. It would not be surprising if she thought her husband needed cash to help cover redemptions from his hedge fund—perhaps she remembers the run on Bear Stearns in February and fears that Bernie is in the same kind of trouble. The distress in the market is apparent to everyone.

Madoff has been at his desk since about nine o'clock, quietly working on what looks like a bunch of figures. In fact, he is probably signing three dozen of the one hundred checks DiPascali prepared last week—checks totaling $173 million, made out to friends, employees, and relatives, cashing out their accounts.

Peter Madoff comes in early, pressing him again to share his dreadful news with his sons. Bernie agrees that he will, but he still isn't certain about when to do it. Tonight is the office holiday party. Perhaps it's not the right moment. Once he tells them, they will need time to get their bearings. Maybe the weekend would be better.

He calls Ike Sorkin and asks to reschedule their appointment until 10:00 AM next Monday, December 15. Sorkin says, "Sure," and changes his calendar.

But the timing is taken out of his hands.

At midmorning, Mark and Andrew Madoff walk past Squillari's desk and enter their father's office. According to her, Peter Madoff goes in, too, and sits on the sofa beside the desk. Legs crossed and arms folded, Peter looks limp—"as if the air has been sucked out of him," she will recall. Mark and Andrew sit in front of the desk, their backs to the door.

Madoff's sons are not accustomed to challenging their father's decisions about running the business. It is entirely his, after all; he owns every share of it. If their father wants to fire them today, he can. But they have to say something. Mark raises the issue of the bonuses, saying that he and Andrew agree that they are premature and unwise.

Madoff initially tries to reassure them. It's just as he told them: he has had a good year, he has made profits through his money management business, and he thinks this is a good time to distribute the money.

The sons stand firm; they challenge their father's explanation. Wouldn't it be wiser to hang on to any windfall in case they need to replenish the firm's capital? As they persist, their father grows more visibly upset. He rises from his chair, glances past them to the oval area beyond. His office is a fishbowl. How can a man with so much to hide wind up without a single spot in his office where he can talk to his sons in private?

He tells his sons that he isn't going to be able to "hold it together" any longer. He needs to talk with them alone, and he asks them to come with him to his apartment on East Sixty-fourth Street. He calls Ruth to tell her that he and their sons are heading over.

Memories of their departure are illogically jumbled, shaken to fragments by the events that followed. Eleanor Squillari recalls asking Bernie where they were going and being told, "I'm going out." Her memory is that Mark whispers something about Christmas shopping. One of the sons gets Madoff's coat from the nearby closet and helps him into it. He turns its collar up, as if he is heading into a storm. Squillari thinks it is only about 9:30 AM when she calls down to the seventeenth floor for one of the drivers to go for a car. But the driver later recalls it took nearly ninety minutes to return with the sedan. It seems unlikely that father and sons stood in their winter coats and waited for the car for an hour and a half when they could have hailed a cab or walked to the apartment in less than twenty minutes. It is a detail no one will remember.

Finally, they climb into the big black sedan. Madoff, shaken and close to tears, slides into the back seat and sits between his two worried sons. They ride uptown, silence and fear filling the car. They reach the apartment and take the elevator to the penthouse.

Ruth meets them, and they all file into the study that Madoff loves so much, a dark refuge of rich burgundy leather and tapestry fabric, with vintage nautical paintings on the wood-paneled walls and cluttered bookcases embracing the windows.

Madoff breaks down as he talks with his wife and sons; as he begins to weep, they do, too. He tells them that the whole investment advisory business was a fraud, just one enormous lie, "basically, a giant Ponzi scheme." He is finished. He has "absolutely nothing" left. The business—the family business, where his sons had worked all their lives and where they expected to spend the rest of their careers—is insolvent, ruined. He says the losses from the fraud could run to $50 billion. None of them can take in a sum like that, but they know that millions were entrusted to him by his own family, by generations of Ruth's relatives, by their employees, by most of their closest friends.

Madoff assures them that he has already told Peter about the fraud and intends to turn himself in within a week. And he actually does have several hundred million dollars left, he says; that bit is true. Before he gives himself up, he plans to pay that money out to certain loyal employees, to family members and friends.

Ruth and her sons seem to be in shock. She asks her weeping husband, "What's a Ponzi scheme?" Mark is speechless with fury. Andrew is prostrate, slumping to the floor in tears. At one point, he wraps his arms around his father with a tenderness that sears itself into Madoff's memory. When Andrew's world stops rocking, he will say that what his father has done is "a father-son betrayal of biblical proportions."

The brothers leave the apartment and tell the driver to wait for their father, stumbling through an excuse about going to lunch. They agree they must report this shattering confession, but neither knows how to do that.

Mark thinks of calling his wife's stepfather, Martin London, a retired partner at the New York law firm of Paul, Weiss, Rifkind, Wharton & Garrison. London directs them to the Beekman Tower Hotel, where he and his wife are living temporarily. London is a formidable litigator and a much-honored lawyer. He is also one of the people who trusted Bernie Madoff. On Mark's advice, he has invested with the family genius.

The sons tell him what the family genius has just revealed to them. London is stunned, too, but his legal instincts kick in. He immediately tries to reach a younger colleague at Paul Weiss named Martin Flumenbaum, one of the top trial lawyers in Manhattan.

Flumenbaum, a short, rotund man with a beaming face, is several hours away, at the federal courthouse in Hartford, Connecticut. Following courthouse rules, he had handed over his cell phone when he went through courthouse security this morning. He retrieves it and sees the urgent messages from New York.

At about 1 p.m., Flumenbaum calls and learns about the surreal confession Bernie Madoff has made to his sons. He tells London he can't get to the Beekman until 3 p.m., and Mark decides to wait at his downtown loft apartment. Andrew returns to the firm and waits, dazed and alone, in his glass-walled office.

The Art Deco facade of the Beekman is lost in the drizzling winter twilight when Mark's driver pulls up in front of the building. Mark joins Andrew in London's suite. The driver waits, but after about ninety minutes, Mark calls and tells him to go on to the office party.

Flumenbaum and an associate arrive promptly. As they settle down to talk, Mark and Andrew repeat the story of their shocking day, adding a few explanatory details. Madoff's money management business operates from a small office on a separate floor, they said. It has always seemed successful—they know he has a lot of big hedge fund clients, has turned rich potential clients away—but their father has kept it very private, virtually under lock and key. Dozens of family members have let Bernie manage their savings, trust funds, retirement accounts. Mark and Andrew know he hasn't used their trading desk to buy or sell investments for his private clients—he's always said he used "European counterparties." He has a London office and spends time there, so it made sense.

Now nothing makes sense. Their father, a man they have looked up to all their lives, has plunged them instantly from wealth to ruin. He is not the financial genius and Wall Street statesman they always believed he was; he is a crook, a thief, a con artist of almost unimaginable dimensions. How could they have been so deceived about their own father?

These are not Marty Flumenbaum's immediate concerns. Madoff has made it clear to his sons that he intends to continue his criminal behavior for one more week, distributing what prosecutors will soon be calling "ill-gotten gains" to his relatives, employees, and friends. This vast crime isn't over; it is a work in progress. Madoff's sons have no choice, Flumenbaum tells his new clients. They must report this conversation—this confession—to the federal authorities immediately.

Flumenbaum knows very senior people at the U.S. Attorney's Office in Manhattan and at the New York office of the Securities and Exchange Commission. He makes some calls. When he reaches his contact at the SEC, he sketches out the afternoon's events, the Ponzi scheme allegations, the estimate from Bernie himself that the losses could reach $50 billion.

There is a pause at the other end of the line, then the taut question: Is that *billion*, with a *B*?

Yes. *Billion*, with a *B*.

The investigative machinery grinds into motion. The FBI musters its financial crime team. The SEC, not for the first time, opens a case file labeled "Madoff, Bernard L."

∽

It's not precisely clear how Madoff spends the rest of this day, the last day he will be able to go anywhere unrecognized. He recalls returning to the office; he remembers Andrew being there and telling him that he and Mark would be consulting a lawyer. As Eleanor Squillari remembers the afternoon, he does not return to his office on the nineteenth floor; she recalls trying to reach him on his cell phone numerous times but getting only his voice mail.

Mismatched memories also distort what happens on the rest of this bizarre day. For Bernie Madoff and his family, today is already etched in acid in their minds, in their hearts—but for the drivers and other junior office employees, it is simply the day of the annual office Christmas party. For them, its devastating significance will not emerge for another twenty-four hours. So, inevitably, some pieces of this puzzle simply won't fit.

Still, Squillari feels sure she would have seen her boss if he had returned to his own office. There is a hand-delivered letter waiting for him there from Jeffrey Tucker at Fairfield Greenwich. In it, Tucker apologizes for not keeping Madoff better informed about pending redemptions and promises to do better in the future. "You are our most important business partner and an immensely respected friend. . . . Our mission is to remain in business with you and to keep your trust," the letter says.

Perhaps Madoff simply goes directly from the lobby to the seventeenth floor, where Frank DiPascali and some of his small crew are working on the checks Madoff plans to distribute.

ço

After the long meeting with Flumenbaum, Andrew Madoff returns to his sleek, airy apartment on the Upper East Side. Without even removing his coat, he lies motionless on his bed for hours—waiting, perhaps, for his world to stop reeling.

It never occurs to Mark or Andrew to attend the Christmas party already under way at Rosa Mexicano, a cheery Mexican restaurant where the firm held last year's party. Tonight's party is happening in the world they used to live in. They can't get there from the world they live in now.

It does not occur to Bernie and Ruth *not* to attend the party. They are on autopilot, trying just to function. What possible explanation could they give for not showing up? Neither of them could even phone in their regrets without breaking down. Perhaps attending the party is simply the path of least resistance, the only option that will keep reality at bay for a few more hours, a few more days.

Like the images of the day, the memories of this evening's party will collide and conflict, shift and shatter.

One person recalls that Madoff surprised the staff by holding the party a week earlier than usual. But it is being held the same week, almost on the same date, as last year's—and not even Bernie could commandeer a popular restaurant on short notice during the holidays.

Some say Madoff never says a word tonight, just huddles silently with Ruth at a corner of the bar and avoids the crowd. Others say he has "a look of death on his face," with "that thousand-yard stare," and seems stunned, very tense, "out of it." But Squillari remembers the Madoffs as their normal selves, "as if they didn't have a care in the world." Two other guests and longtime friends agree, except they say Madoff seems maybe a little more emotional, hugging and kissing family members and friends a little more than usual. Ruth chats with a few employees, too, going awkwardly through the familiar party rituals. But it must be a strain—after a half hour or so, she is ready to leave. Madoff recalls that they stay on "for a couple of hours."

Everyone recalls "a taco station, a guacamole station, a buffet bar, and waiters walking around with frozen pomegranate margaritas, two of which could put a person out for the night"—and one of which could put clear, orderly memories of this ephemeral evening out of reach forever.

Besides the food and drinks, there is one other thing everyone agrees on: Andrew and Mark Madoff are expected to attend the party, and neither ever arrives.

As he and his wife head home, Bernie Madoff clearly does not expect events to spin out of his control as quickly as they will. His sons had ample time that afternoon to turn him in, yet no one has shown up at the office or the apartment to arrest him. No one has called to demand he come in for questioning. He feels confident that he still has several days to settle matters before he turns himself in.

THURSDAY, DECEMBER 11, 2008

At about 7:30 on this rainy morning, FBI special agent Ted Cacioppi and his partner, B. J. Kang, drive up to Madoff's apartment building at the corner of East Sixty-fourth Street and Lexington Avenue. Cacioppi, a powerfully built young man with close-cropped brown hair, has been up since 4:00 AM, discussing the delicate nature of this assignment with his superiors, federal prosecutors, and SEC attorneys.

There is no indictment. There is no hard evidence of a fraud—just the say-so of Madoff's two sons. A precipitous arrest could derail the investigation. But if the FBI delays making an arrest, Madoff might flee, perhaps taking whatever money is left. Finally, it is decided that the FBI agents will pay a visit and politely ask if Madoff has anything to say about his sons' story.

Leaving two other agents in the car, Cacioppi and Kang show their badges to the doorman and take the elevator to the penthouse, as the startled doorman calls ahead.

Madoff had been about to get dressed for work in his spacious closet on the floor below the duplex penthouse's entrance. Alerted by the doorman, he climbs upstairs and opens the apartment door, wearing a light blue bathrobe over his pajamas. The agents step into the apartment's entry hall, with its glowing carriage lamp and towering grandfather clock. Ruth, jolted by the doorman's call, throws on some jeans and a polo shirt and joins them in the foyer.

Madoff is surprised, but he tells them, "I know why you're here."

Cacioppi says, "We're here to find out if there's an innocent explanation."

"There is no innocent explanation," Madoff answers.

Cacioppi asks if there is somewhere they can sit down and talk. Madoff leads the two agents to his study, where he gathered his wife and sons less than twenty-four hours earlier. He takes a chair and invites the agents to sit on the leather sofa across from him. Agent Kang silently takes notes as Cacioppi poses questions and Madoff answers them.

Speaking without visible emotion, Madoff confirms what he told his brother and sons: He has been operating a Ponzi scheme, paying returns to investors with "money that wasn't there"—in reality, money taken from other investors. He is broke, insolvent. He knows it cannot go on. He expects to go to jail.

In the absence of a formal indictment, Cacioppi is not sure he will be making an arrest this morning. He steps into a nearby bathroom and calls his office on his cell phone, explaining what has happened. He is directed to bring Madoff in "on probable cause."

Madoff excuses himself to get dressed, choosing expensive gray slacks, a soft navy blazer, and a crisp navy-striped white shirt, open at the neck. He has been briefed by the agents on the wardrobe restrictions that go with being arrested: no belt, no shoelaces, no tie, no jewelry.

During this time—perhaps as Madoff is dressing, perhaps earlier—Ruth calls the office and asks Squillari if Mark or Andrew has arrived yet. They haven't. Squillari hears Ruth say to someone else, probably Bernie, "They're not there."

When Madoff is dressed, the agents get ready to take him downtown. He tells Ruth to try to reach Ike Sorkin, shrugs into his dark gray twill raincoat, and is handcuffed. He and the two agents ride down in the elevator, walk quickly through the small dark lobby, and step out into the rainy morning. Madoff is tucked into the rear passenger seat of the waiting car. Kang gets in behind the driver, and the car pulls away.

Cacioppi heads toward Rockefeller Center to meet Madoff's sons at their lawyer's office so he can craft the affidavit he will file with the court to start the process rolling.

Peter Madoff arrives at the office unusually early. When Squillari first notices him, he is meeting with some strangers in a small conference room on the eighteenth floor. The receptionist says they identified themselves only as "lawyers." Then a brusque man in a trench coat arrives to join them, flashing a badge—perhaps an FBI agent, joining a team already there from the SEC and FINRA, the financial industry's self-regulatory agency.

Adding it all up, and throwing in Ruth's early call asking about her sons, Squillari first thinks that someone has been kidnapped. Or maybe it's an extortion plot. Madoff still hasn't shown up.

Frank DiPascali and his longtime colleague Annette Bongiorno come up separately from the seventeenth floor, each asking Peter what's going on. Peter tells them: Bernie has been arrested for securities fraud. Each leaves, subdued, with no further questions, according to Squillari. Others think they see DiPascali weeping with a group of employees outside Sonny Cohn's office, throwing up in the men's room, and sharing a comforting hug with a colleague. Unseen by them, DiPascali also tries to delete sensitive information from the computers on the seventeenth floor.

Madoff is driven downtown to the FBI offices at 26 Federal Plaza, the forty-two-story office building that forms the western edge of Foley Square, the hub of the judicial and law enforcement machinery in Manhattan. Unable to find a parking space, the driver takes Madoff and Kang to an employee entrance next to a small playground. They hurry through the busy lobby to the line of bulletproof doors protecting the FBI's separate set of elevators.

When they reach the FBI offices on the twenty-third floor, Madoff is taken to Room 2325, a small windowless space about the size of a suburban walk-in closet. It contains a table, two chairs, and a telephone. Madoff sits down, and Kang removes the handcuff from one of his wrists and clicks it around the arm of the chair. Madoff is allowed to use the telephone on the table to call his lawyer. He dials Ike Sorkin's cell phone number.

Ruth hasn't yet been able to reach Sorkin because he went to Washington on business the previous day and is taking advantage of a free morning to take his granddaughter to her nursery school class in the Maryland suburbs.

When his cell phone rings, he checks it, sees an unfamiliar Manhattan number, and answers.

"Ike, this is Bernie Madoff." He quickly explains that he is handcuffed to a chair in the FBI offices; he's under arrest.

"Bernie, don't say another thing," Sorkin hastily advises him, whispering as the children around him follow the teacher's lead and mimic the sounds of various farm animals. He hurries out of the classroom, noticing the fading battery on his phone. He tells Madoff to put one of the FBI men on the phone and then firmly tells the agent not to question his client further until one of his partners gets there. Then he calls his longtime secretary Maria Moragne and asks her to track down his partner Daniel J. Horwitz.

Dan Horwitz, a boyish-looking man in his forties with horn-rimmed glasses and a thatch of brown hair, is at a political breakfast at his father-in-law's Midtown law firm. Before going to work with Sorkin, he was one of "Morgy's boys," the aggressive assistant district attorneys trained by the near-legendary Manhattan district attorney Robert Morgenthau. Like Sorkin, Horwitz knows the criminal processing routine inside and out.

Maria reaches Horwitz on his cell phone. One of Ike's clients has been arrested, she tells him—the room is noisy and he doesn't catch the name. He steps into the hall and asks her to repeat it: Bernie Madoff. Horwitz has met Madoff a few times at charity events. Maria tells him that Ike says to call Peter Madoff and get back to the office immediately.

En route across Manhattan, Horwitz tries unsuccessfully to call Sorkin, whose cell phone battery has finally given out. When Horwitz reaches the office, he immediately calls William F. Johnson, the formidable chief of the Securities and Commodities Fraud Task Force at the U.S. Attorney's Office in Manhattan. The unit is one of the premier white-collar crime teams in the country, and one of the oldest—established in 1960, long before Justice Department officials elsewhere recognized the need for special fraud prosecution skills. Horwitz has known Bill Johnson for years, and his call is put through quickly.

It is a brief conversation—the prosecutors still have nothing to go on but Madoff's own words, spoken either to them or to his sons. But whatever information Bill Johnson can share with Horwitz surely isn't encouraging: his client has made a lot of statements to the FBI, and those statements are obviously very damaging.

Horwitz learns that Madoff is still at the FBI office downtown, where he is now on the twenty-sixth floor being photographed and fingerprinted. The FBI agents expect to walk Madoff across Foley Square to the federal courthouse for processing by the U.S. Marshals fairly soon.

Rapidly rearranging his day, Horwitz enlists his young and accomplished colleague Nicole De Bello, a stately blonde who has been part of Sorkin's team for six years. They head downtown to the new federal courthouse at 500 Pearl Street, towering behind the classic hexagonal state courthouse on the east side of Foley Square. At the security screening, they hand in their cell phones—courthouse orders. The rest of the day, they will rely on pay phones to navigate between Sorkin, en route from Washington; their own offices uptown; Ruth Madoff, back at the apartment; and a car service.

They hurry to the Pretrial Services office on the fifth floor, where Madoff is waiting. They need to learn as much as they can about the case against Madoff and get him released on bail.

Madoff is sitting alone in a small, windowless conference room. He quietly reports what has happened, how he wound up in that room.

They quiz him as politely as they can. What is the evidence against you? What did you say to your sons? What have you told the government? The interview continues through the lunch hour. One of them finds a pay phone and calls Ruth, asking her to meet them at the Pretrial Services office and explaining how to find it.

Ruth Madoff is already dressed: jeans, a white blouse, and a blazer. She has been ready since Bernie was taken away, although the intervening hours have probably been a blur. As she leaves the apartment, she grabs a small red paisley scarf and pulls on a dark olive quilted coat. She heads out into the rain.

Meanwhile, the Madoff offices are in turmoil. Battalions of accountants and investigators from the FBI, the SEC, and FINRA have arrived in force—the SEC alone has sent in more than a dozen people—while squadrons of other government lawyers have headed off to court for permission to seize control of the Madoff brokerage firm and put it into receivership.

Still, there is a legitimate business going on all around them, a trading desk where shaken employees are fielding calls and taking orders from some of the largest firms on Wall Street. Trades have to be wrapped up, trading has to stop, clearinghouses must be informed, bank accounts must be frozen. The legal complexities of the next twenty-four hours are staggering, even in retrospect.

Who in this chaotic office is innocent? Who can tell? The employees all seem dazed and distressed. Peter Madoff and his daughter, Shana, also a lawyer at the firm, struggle with questions and offer simple directions: those files are here, the computers are there, Bernie's investment advisory business was downstairs, on the seventeenth floor.

Another of Ike Sorkin's young colleagues, Mauro Wolfe, has been assigned to help Peter Madoff with the regulatory crisis engulfing the firm. At around eleven o'clock that morning, Sorkin's secretary alerts Wolfe that someone named Andrew Calamari from the SEC has called. Wolfe, a former SEC lawyer, knows him well and promptly calls him back. Calamari puts him on a speakerphone.

"We want to give you a heads-up," Calamari says, his voice tense and hard. Madoff Securities is a billion-dollar trading firm. There is a serious fraud going on. The SEC is going to seek a court order to take control of the firm and freeze all trades and financial transactions. The SEC lawyers are trying to line up a judge to conduct a hearing immediately via conference call—will Wolfe be available to handle it?

Of course.

Wolfe calls Peter Madoff—one of countless conversations he will have with Peter or Shana that day. The questions from Peter are obvious: What should the company be doing? What should it tell its clients? Wolfe no doubt tells him that the SEC is getting a court order to suspend its trading operation and freeze its assets.

Within a few hours, the forty-eight-year-old firm called Bernard L. Madoff Investment Securities has been seized by regulators, who will shut it down and dismantle it.

Sometime on this day, federal investigators remove a thick stack of checks from Bernie Madoff's office. Made out at DiPascali's direction and signed yesterday by Madoff, they total $173 million, payable to various family members and friends. Madoff told his sons he intended to distribute between $200 million and $300 million; this was the first installment.

As investigators and accountants race to keep this leaking ship afloat until they can get it secured in port, its captain is downtown calmly answering his lawyers' questions about how much he can afford to post as bail. There is the equity in the penthouse, the beach house in Montauk, Long Island, the Florida home—all owned free and clear. Madoff had Ruth move money from her investment account into her bank account, so she can write checks. What will the prosecutors demand?

Horwitz doesn't know yet. Sometime after 1:00 PM, he finds a phone and calls the prosecutor's office to check on the status of the formal paperwork. Until that's ready, nothing can happen—no hearing, no magistrate's ruling on bail, no release.

Marc Litt, a quiet-spoken assistant U.S. attorney, was already busy with a major insider trading investigation when he was assigned the Madoff case. He takes Horwitz's call and listens as the defense attorney makes a case for releasing Madoff on his own recognizance. The prosecutors have no evidence, except Madoff's confession. In effect, he turned himself in by confessing to his sons. To Horwitz, a personal recognizance bond seems perfectly appropriate.

The bargaining begins. Nothing Horwitz proposes satisfies Litt—not the personal recognizance bond or the pledge of the $7 million apartment in Manhattan or Ruth Madoff as a cosigner with her husband. "I need more," he says.

Okay, how about his wife and his brother as cosigners?

"I want four signatures," Litt answers.

Four? Horwitz knows that Madoff's sons turned him in to the government the night before. Would they agree to stand bail for their father, after what he had done? He counters: "Why don't we put up another property?" There was Montauk, or Palm Beach.

"No, try to get four signers—at least try."

The negotiations over the bail arrangement—which would be disputed, criticized, and litigated for weeks—take less than five minutes.

Waiting for the paperwork, Horwitz is also watching for Ruth and watching the clock. He hopes to get Madoff out of the courthouse on bail before the press corps calls in reinforcements. As the hours slip by, their chance for an inconspicuous exit is evaporating. At midafternoon, Madoff's interviews are done and the marshals take him to a holding cell next to the large first-floor courtroom known as Part One, where federal defendants are arraigned before a magistrate judge. Horwitz and De Bello meet up with Ruth Madoff, take an elevator to the lobby, and head to Part One. Horwitz checks on Madoff in the holding cell and joins Ruth and Nicole in the crowded courtroom.

Federal magistrate judge Douglas Eaton, who will determine Madoff's bail, is not having a good day either. His entire morning was spent haggling over the fate of Marc S. Dreier, a corrupt Manhattan attorney who was arrested the previous Sunday and accused of peddling more than $500 million in bogus promissory notes to hedge funds. Prosecutors argued that releasing Dreier on bail posed "an enormous risk of flight." But Dreier's lawyer would not give up.

By the time Judge Eaton denies bail to Dreier, cases have piled up. One is a drug bust with numerous defendants, some of whom don't speak English. Translators are summoned. The hours tick by.

Horwitz finds a pay phone and calls a car service. He tries to craft an appropriate statement for the reporters already gathering in the courtroom. It is well past 5:00 PM before the legal paperwork is ready. Finally, Judge Eaton's clerk calls the case of *United States of America v. Bernard L. Madoff.*

Madoff, looking gray and poorly shaven, with a small cut on his left cheek, is brought in from the holding cell as Ruth watches from one of the crowded benches. Litt walks the judge through the agreement he has reached with Horwitz—a personal recognizance bond of $10 million, with four "financially responsible people" cosigning the bond. Travel will be limited to the New York area, Long Island, and Connecticut, and Madoff will surrender his passport.

After his turbulent session with the Dreier case, Judge Eaton is confident about releasing Madoff on bail. Here was a man who, after confessing to his sons, "took no extraordinary measures and sat there and waited to be arrested," he says later. With no objections from the prosecutors, he rules that Madoff is to be released immediately on Ruth's and his own signature, with the other conditions to be fulfilled later.

Horwitz and De Bello hurry Ruth over to the Clerk's Office on the same floor to sign the bail documents, and the Madoffs are free to go. Three reporters cluster around, throwing questions at them, but when Horwitz and De Bello hustle Ruth and Bernie out into the rainy night, the reporters don't follow.

As they hurry toward the waiting SUV, a photographer snaps a picture of Madoff, the raindrops on his gray raincoat sparkling like diamonds in the camera's flash. Horwitz gets Madoff into the front seat quickly and then squeezes into the back with De Bello and Ruth. Rain is pelting down by now, and the traffic is awful. It is almost 7:00 PM when the car delivers the Madoffs to their apartment.

By then, Ike Sorkin has landed at LaGuardia Airport and is recharging his phone from the ashtray outlet in his car as it idles in the middle of the huge puddle-filled parking lot. He calls his office and makes sure all the necessary legal chores have been done, then puts his car in gear and pulls out. When he reaches his Long Island home, he and Horwitz speak at length about the Madoff case. These two tenacious defenders are holding a nearly impossible hand. Madoff has confessed to an FBI agent in his own foyer. Absent proof that he is delusional or otherwise insane, there just isn't much they can do.

Before midnight, the news that stunned Wall Street in the late afternoon is spreading like wind-driven fire across the country. Bernie Madoff, a pioneer of the modern stock market and a man whom regulators trusted and consulted for decades, has been arrested after confessing to what he himself calls a $50 billion Ponzi scheme.

Even if you've never heard of Bernie Madoff, the sheer size of his fraud—*fifty billion dollars!*—guarantees that you will notice. Even in normal times, it would have been news, and these times are nowhere near normal. The financial system is already reeling with bankruptcies and bailouts. The year 2008 challenges 1929 as the most frightening and frenzied in the long history of Wall Street. The Bear Stearns brokerage house has failed. Fannie Mae and Freddie Mac, the two government-sponsored mortgage giants, have been bailed out; the venerable Lehman Brothers firm wasn't. Within a day of Lehman's bankruptcy, the nation's oldest money market fund was swept away by a tsunami of panicky withdrawals. Before that day ended, regulators were scrambling to rescue the insurance giant AIG, fearing that another titanic failure would shatter whatever trust continued to hold the fragile financial system together.

People are already furious, shaking their fists at the arrogant plutocrats who led them into this mess.

Then, in a camera flash, Bernie Madoff is transformed from someone whom no one but Wall Street insiders and friends would recognize into a man who is headline news around the world. Longtime clients, comfortable people who have lived carefully and who entrusted all their liquid assets to Madoff, will wake up tomorrow nearly destitute.

This is the day the music finally stops for history's first truly global Ponzi scheme—one that grew bigger, lasted longer, and reached into more corners of the globe than any Ponzi scheme that came before.

FRIDAY, DECEMBER 12, 2008

It's still the middle of the night in New York when lawyers in London arrive at the small Mayfair town house occupied by Madoff Securities International Ltd.

The European markets will open soon, and Madoff's London operation must be locked down and secured before that happens. As the shaken London staff watches, the lawyers take the necessary steps. They arrange for guards to monitor the office around the clock. They secure the bank accounts, locate important business records, take control of the computers, and change the door locks and security codes.

The lawyers are armed with a court order signed last night in New York at the SEC's request; they work for the receiver the judge appointed to take control of the Madoff firm, a securities lawyer in Manhattan named Lee S. Richards III.

A calm, rumpled man with both the look and the voice of the humorist Garrison Keillor, Lee Richards is considered one of the top white-collar lawyers in the country. He has handled almost a half-dozen prominent receiverships, and his firm, with offices in New York, Washington, and London, is trained for exactly this kind of emergency.

Yesterday, Richards was getting off his commuter train at Grand Central Terminal when he got a call from the SEC's Andrew Calamari alerting him to Madoff's arrest and asking if he could take on the receivership of the firm. Until it is clear that the firm is insolvent and should be put into bankruptcy, a receiver needs to be on site to protect its assets and secure its records, starting immediately.

Murmuring into his cell phone in the middle of the train station, Richards agreed to take the Madoff case. A few hours later, staff lawyers for the SEC asked U.S. District Court judge Louis L. Stanton to freeze the Madoff firm's assets and put Richards in charge. Judge Stanton signed the court order at 6:42 PM Thursday evening, and Richards went to work that night, hiring the forensic consultants he would need and mobilizing his London staff.

Around 8:00 AM today, as Madoff's offices are being secured in London but before the markets open in New York, Richards and several colleagues arrive at Madoff's Manhattan office. Lawyers and accountants from the SEC have been here most of the night, trying to find the border, if there is one, between the firm's legitimate business and the massive fraud Madoff says he conducted here.

The regulators are occupying the conference room on the eighteenth floor, where most of the administrative and financial staff and their records are located. Richards goes upstairs and sets up his command post in the large glass-walled conference room that stretches between Madoff's empty office and the slightly larger office still being used today by Peter Madoff.

Almost every Madoff employee shows up for work today, even Frank DiPascali—although he will leave sometime during the day and not return. By the afternoon, he will be sitting in the office of one of the city's top criminal defense lawyers, shaking and crying as he describes the work he has done for Madoff for so many years. Madoff, too, will spend this day with his lawyers, trying to understand what happens next.

At the Lipstick Building, Richards asks for the employees' cooperation and their patience; there is a great deal he simply does not know and cannot tell them.

The members of Richards's law firm have already curtailed access to the computer systems and confiscated employees' key cards. His forensic consultants start examining the customer account statements and the firm's financial records. As in London, security guards are put on twenty-four-hour duty. Richards's team soon learns that there also are two warehouses in Queens where records are stored and backup computer equipment is maintained; guards are put on duty there, too.

As the news of Madoff's arrest has spread, the firm's trading partners have threatened to back out on uncompleted trades. Richards's staff has to try to unwind or complete the deals with as little loss to the firm as possible. Other lawyers on his team are working to freeze the firm's bank accounts and its brokerage accounts at other firms.

At about 10:00 AM, two New York City police officers arrive at Richards's command center. He needs to come downstairs immediately, they tell him. About three dozen Madoff investors have poured into the lobby, the media is starting to arrive, and the crowd is becoming worrisome to the building's security staff. Richards quickly heads for the elevators.

The investors gathered in the lobby are anxious, but quiet and well-behaved—remarkably so, given the devastation so many of them are facing. Gathered here in the subdued glow of the holiday decorations, they are the first visible faces of the tens of thousands of people around the world who have been injured by Madoff's unthinkable fraud. They are proxies for all the trusting widows, all the second-generation investors, all the construction workers, dental office receptionists, retired teachers, restaurant owners, electricians, insurance agents, artists, writers, chefs, models, therapists, small business owners, modestly successful doctors and lawyers who all have suddenly been labeled as "Madoff victims."

Richards explains to them that it is far too early for him to have any information about their individual accounts—and he can't predict when he will have that information. There is nothing to be learned here in the lobby, he explains. The crowd gradually disperses as Richards returns upstairs.

2

BECOMING BERNIE

In the late spring of 1962, a twenty-four-year-old Wall Street trader named Bernard Lawrence Madoff was facing almost total ruin.

Madoff started his own brokerage business while he was still a senior at Hofstra University, in the winter of 1959/60, just as the stock market was about to embark on a wild decade that would be immortalized later as the "go-go years." The era was overheated, volatile, and peopled with characters who belonged in a Marx Brothers movie. And no corner of Wall Street was wilder or riskier in those days than the one where young Bernie Madoff had put out his shingle: the over-the-counter (OTC) stock market.

The enormous, decentralized, and weakly regulated OTC market of the 1960s may be hard for modern investors to imagine. The New York Stock Exchange, known as the Big Board, had long been dominated by Main Street—or, more accurately, by the people who owned and ran Main Street. Few pension funds or endowments owned common stocks, so a large majority of the Big Board's daily orders were from individual investors, people wealthy enough to feel comfortable in the market despite its turbulent history. They were cosseted by their family stockbrokers. Taking the long view for their children's trust funds, they bought shares in railroads, utilities, automakers, steel companies, the blue chips they knew and understood—and, in some cases, managed or had founded. Each day, they could check the prices of their shares in the evening newspapers.

In the years after World War II, however, new companies pursuing new technologies were cropping up everywhere, almost overnight. At the same time, family-dominated companies with few public shareholders needed to raise capital to grow. The shares of these unseasoned or thinly traded companies—some of them destined to become household names, such as Anheuser-Busch, Barnes-Hind, Cannon Mills, Tampax, Kaiser Steel, and H.B. Fuller—did not meet the requirements for listing on the prestigious New York Stock Exchange or its smaller sister exchanges around the country. But that didn't mean their shares didn't trade. They were the mainstays of the over-the-counter market, where Bernie Madoff planted his flag in the early 1960s—and where he first started to get rich.

Without doubt, there were plenty of people getting rich in those hyperventilating days. The year the Madoff firm opened its doors, 1960, was the next-to-last lap in the longest bull market the country had seen to that point—a spectacular climb that began in the summer of 1949 and would continue until New Year's Eve 1961. Over that time, the prices of blue chips in the Dow Jones Industrial Average would more than quadruple, with an average gain of nearly 13 percent a year. After the brief bear market in the first half of 1962—the long-forgotten lurch that would nearly destroy Bernie Madoff—the party rolled on into the late 1960s at roughly the same pace.

And those were the returns on conservative blue chips that traded on the Big Board. The gains in riskier OTC stocks during the bull markets of the 1960s were poorly documented, but one study put them perhaps as much as five times higher than the Dow Jones Industrial Average. These are stock price gains reminiscent of the technology stock bubble of the late twentieth century—or the Ponzi schemes of all ages. So Madoff investors who recall early annual returns of 20 percent may not be inflating their memories; such returns would not immediately have raised red flags in an era when the hottest mutual funds were sometimes doubling their value in a single year.

The possibilities of the young OTC market in the 1960s were recalled by Michael Steinhardt, who made a fortune on the Street and later invested a portion of his charitable foundation with a fund that passed it along to Bernie Madoff. "I thought, when we started up our company, I could compete effectively with older people in the business," Steinhardt said in one published interview. "Youth believed in such things, because we had grown up in the '40s, '50s and '60s and saw extraordinary technological innovation." He recalled buying stock in a company whose price increased ninefold in less than a year; he sold it, and within a year, it was bankrupt. "There were plenty of them like that," he said.

The first home of Bernie Madoff's one-man brokerage firm in 1960 was a spare desk at his father-in-law's accounting firm on Forty-second Street, near Bryant Park. Within a few months he had found two small rooms downtown at 40 Exchange Place—an anteroom for his wife, Ruth, who worked part-time as his office manager, and an inner office where he could work the telephones and try to make trades with other dealers.

Besides a license, running an OTC trading house in the 1960s required two indispensable tools: a telephone and access to the daily catalogs known as the Pink Sheets, published by the National Quotation Bureau. (The catalog pages devoted to stocks were printed on pink paper, while the pages listing bonds were printed on yellow paper.) A writer visiting the bureau in the late 1950s thought "the manufacture of The Sheets is perhaps the most amazing operation in the financial market."

Every weekday, in a stunning feat of manpower and logistics, bureau clerks manually collected price lists for nearly eight thousand stocks submitted by about two thousand over-the-counter dealers. The clerks collated the prices by stock name, entered the data on mimeograph stencils, printed the catalogs, and got them out the door to several thousand firms around the country in a matter of hours. Only dealers with full-service subscriptions, priced at about $460 a year, could submit price quotes.

That was a big expense for Madoff in his first few years in business, so he relied on day-old Pink Sheets collected from another brokerage firm's offices on the same floor at 40 Exchange Place. After all, Madoff realized, the prices were out of date before the sheets were even printed; all you really needed were the names and telephone numbers of the dealers making markets in the stocks you wanted to trade. And there is no question that Bernie Madoff was trading some stocks in these early days. The share certificates were delivered to Ruth's desk or picked up there by messengers, and the trades were manually entered into big ledgers maintained at the office. On a miniature level, she was his "back office," maintaining his trading records for at least the first year he was in business.

As hard as it is for wired-in and instantly connected twenty-first-century investors to accept, there was absolutely no way for the public to independently verify the prices of over-the-counter stocks in the 1960s. A retail customer interested in the price of an OTC stock would have to call a broker, who would likely have to make a half-dozen phone calls to people like Madoff to come up with a slightly reliable answer. The newspapers did not print daily prices for OTC stocks, as they did for exchange-listed stocks. It was an utterly opaque market, a black box for customers and barely more visible to regulators. But armed with broker names and price quotes from the Pink Sheets, an aggressive broker could work the phones looking for business. Madoff would have spent his days calling around to trusted counterparts at other firms to buy shares that he could resell at a higher price to another broker or maybe to a retail customer—at a price that the customer or broker took on faith or walked away from. The whole process was a vast tutorial in how to win and keep the trust of other people. Those who couldn't do that didn't survive; Bernie Madoff survived.

There is little documentary evidence of how Bernie Madoff made money in the 1960s, but this is so for most tiny firms of that era. His own version is that he made money primarily by trading, regularly buying OTC stocks at one price and selling them at a much higher price, and then using his profits to finance more trading. The only trace his early business left in the available records is an underwriting deal his firm handled in March 1962 for a little outfit called A.L.S. Steel, based in Corona, Queens. According to Madoff, his father was working as a finder for the company and arranged the deal. The underwriter's markup promised to the firm was handsome, but Madoff said he was not sure the transaction was ever completed.

Years later, the family legend was that he went from success to success in those early days, and this may have been true for the trading desk of his fledgling business. But as an investment manager, he began to bend the rules almost from the beginning, which led him to the brink of failure by mid-1962.

At the time Madoff was managing money for about twenty clients, many of them relatives and most of them small-scale investors who could not afford to take speculative risks. Nevertheless, by his own account, he invested their savings in the famously volatile "new-issues" market of the early 1960s, an early version of the hot stock offerings sold during the "tech stock" bubble of the late 1990s. Like the market for those flimsy Internet stocks, the new-issues market in those go-go years was filled with highly speculative stocks sold by young, unseasoned companies that occasionally flourished but more often failed. Caught up in the frenzied trend, Madoff violated long-standing market rules and common sense by selling such unsuitable investments to his risk-averse clients.

This lapse didn't fall into a regulatory gray area. Decades before he set up shop, market regulators had imposed and enforced what came to be known as "the suitability rule." Brokers were forbidden to sell their clients investments that were too risky for their individual financial circumstances, even if the clients were willing to buy them. Selling those hot new issues to his clients was wrong, and Madoff knew it.

If the new-issue market had continued to rack up the giddy gains of 1961, he might have gotten away with it. But after slumping steadily for weeks, the overall stock market fell sharply in the week of May 21, 1962—its worst weekly loss in more than a decade. Then, on May 28, the market stunned legions of young brokers like Bernie Madoff by plummeting to a daily loss second only to the shuddering one-day drop on October 28, 1929, on the eve of the Great Depression. Trading outpaced the stock ticker by several panicky hours. Although the market calmed down a few days later, the boom of the previous year was gone. Worst hit in the "little crash" of 1962, according to one account, were "the hot-issue boys, the penny-stock plungers, the bucket-shop two-week millionaires of 1961."

Those "hot-issue boys" included Bernie Madoff. When the market for new issues collapsed and the price of those stocks plummeted, his trusting customers faced substantial losses. "I realized I never should have sold them those shares," he later admitted.

Madoff didn't just break the cardinal rule of investor protection, the suitability rule, he lied about it, covering it up in ways that preserved his reputation and thus laid the foundation for all that came later in his life of crime. He simply erased those losses from his clients' accounts by buying the new-issue shares back from them at their original offering price, hiding the fact that his customers' profits had actually been wiped out by the market's turmoil. "I felt obligated to buy back my clients' positions," he later explained.

Doing so required him to spend all the $30,000 in capital he had built up in his first two years of business, he said. Unless he could raise fresh cash, he was essentially out of business. To recapitalize his firm, he turned to his father-in-law, Saul Alpern. Madoff said he borrowed some municipal bonds from Alpern and used them as collateral for a $30,000 loan—"a large amount to me in those days." The cash infusion allowed him to resume his firm's trading activities. It was a bitter taste of failure, "a humiliating experience," he said.

But if Madoff felt "obligated" to erase the losses his recklessness had created in his client accounts, he did not feel obligated to disclose what he had done to his small collection of customers, who continued to think of him as a brilliant money manager who could safely navigate even the rocky market of 1962. "My clients were unaware of my actions due to their lack of experience in the OTC market," he later acknowledged in a letter from prison. "If they were aware, they certainly didn't object."

Madoff insisted that this early trip across the line between right and wrong—illegally selling unsuitable stocks to his clients and then hiding their losses with phony prices—was not a Ponzi scheme, which is a form of fraud in which the profits promised to early investors are actually paid with cash raised from later investors, not from any legitimate investing activity. Madoff said that he simply used his firm's money to erase his clients' losses and burnish his own reputation as a trading star. That reputation would help him attract and hold the wealthy and influential investors who would become the first to testify to his genius.

Madoff initially suggested that he encouraged his father-in-law to think that repurchasing the shares was a legitimate business practice permitted by the original underwriting agreements. But, in a subsequent letter from prison, he said that Alpern "was aware of how this happened and understood why I felt obligated to do what I did. I was able to repay the loan within a year, which made both of us happy." Perhaps Alpern simply believed the young Madoff had learned a valuable lesson and would not violate the rules again. Or possibly—but far less plausibly, to those who knew Alpern—he knew that Madoff was playing fast and loose with investors' money and went along for the ride.

In any case, the incident did not visibly shake Alpern's trust in his ambitious son-in-law, and they remained on good terms for the rest of Alpern's life.

Beyond the indisputable facts that Madoff was an OTC trader and the market hit a jolting air pocket in the spring of 1962, one cannot know whether Madoff's version of his early misbehavior is even partially true, of course. As he told the tale to prosecutors in the emotional days after his arrest, he mixed in a garbled chronology of confusing details about doing high-risk "short sales" and other strategies for his biggest customers in later years, trades that he said left no clear paper trail. He created the indelible impression in the minds of the government lawyers that his Ponzi scheme began much earlier than he would later admit, possibly as early as this incident in 1962.

In Madoff's view, this early blot on his record was soon eclipsed by the increased business—and unbridled admiration—that his legitimate trading success brought him in the years that followed. But one must wonder how willingly new customers would have flocked to Madoff if they had known the truth about his disastrous losses in 1962.

∞

Bernie Madoff did not enter Wall Street through the burnished gates that were always open to the prep school graduates from Manhattan's silk-stocking neighborhoods. He came from a family of modest means and financial disappointments who lived in the farthest reaches of the city, in southeastern Queens.

His grandparents on both sides were immigrants who left Eastern Europe in the early 1900s. Bernie's paternal grandfather was Solomon David Madoff, who in 1930 settled his wife, Rose, and their family in the Bronx and worked as a tailor in New York's garment industry. Bernie's maternal grandfather was Harry Muntner, who owned and ran a neighborhood bathhouse on the Lower East Side, where few apartments had the luxury of private plumbing.

His parents, Ralph Madoff and Sylvia Muntner, married in 1932, when New York City was still in the vicious grip of the Depression. On the marriage license, Ralph Madoff described his employment as "credit," but he evidently worked his way up through a series of jobs in retailing and manufacturing. Madoff himself said his father attended college, but he was vague about the details. Clearly, Ralph Madoff was an ambitious scrambler, and at some point he landed a good white-collar job at the Everlast Sporting Goods Manufacturing Company in Manhattan, the nation's leading source for professional boxing equipment.

Ralph's economic position was solid enough that Sylvia and he felt they could start a family; in 1934 their daughter, Sondra, was born.

Sometime during these years, Ralph settled his family in Brooklyn. It was there, on April 29, 1938, that Bernie was born. Seven years later, in October 1945, his brother, Peter, arrived.

Dissatisfied at Everlast and encouraged by the robust economy, Ralph left sometime in the late 1940s to start his own sporting goods manufacturing business, Dodger Sporting Goods Corporation, which made the iconic Joe Palooka punching bag (still sought out by antique toy collectors) and other products tied to the popular "Joe Palooka" comic strip character. He was also able to buy a modest two-story redbrick home in Laurelton, one of the small communities clustered on the southern edge of Queens near what is now Kennedy Airport. In April 1946, he and Sylvia and their three children moved into what was then a close-knit, solidly middle-class Jewish community.

The young Bernie Madoff attended Public School 156 and became a Boy Scout, joining Troop 225. The beaches of Long Island's South Shore were nearby, and he became a strong swimmer, a skill that he used to get lifeguarding jobs in the summer. Behind this idyllic façade, however, the Madoffs faced serious financial anxieties. In early 1951, when Bernie was not yet thirteen years old, Dodger Sporting Goods filed for bankruptcy. The company had been struggling with rising raw material prices brought on by the onset of the Korean War, and it was nearly $90,000 in debt when it made its bankruptcy court filing. The failure was sufficiently public that some neighbors recalled Bernie's mother, Sylvia, having to get a clerical job at an area blood bank to help support the family. After a second business effort failed, Ralph's credit rating was badly damaged, and at one point a tax lien was imposed on the family home.

Giving up on sporting goods, Ralph Madoff went into the fringes of the financial industry as an independent "finder," helping fledgling companies find investors in exchange for a fee or a percentage of the money he raised. While finders were not automatically required to register as brokers, Ralph Madoff did register—but in a less than honest way. Late in the 1950s he formed a one-man brokerage firm called Gibraltar Securities and registered it with the Securities and Exchange Commission. Because of his bad credit and financial problems, though, he put the brokerage business in Sylvia's name, although it was the firm through which he conducted his sporadic work as a finder. It was an early lesson in deceit for a son determined to be more successful than his father.

Amid the prosperity of middle-class Laurelton, these serial business failures were traumatic for the Madoff family—Madoff himself later confirmed how upsetting they had been. But, at the time, he wrapped himself in a shell of quiet confidence and reassuring competence. He was a good-looking kid who seemed to fit smoothly into the social scene at P.S. 156 and, later, at Far Rockaway High School. He certainly was not a brooding loner; nor was he a passive follower. One former classmate recalled Bernie and a close friend starting their own junior high school fraternity, a social club called the Ravens, that met in the local synagogue but admitted both Jews and gentiles. It was a ready-made group of admirers, and Bernie was one of the smooth guys in charge.

In high school Bernie joined the swim team and was a decent competitor but not a show-off, his coach recalled. He was an adequate if indifferent student, earning Bs and Cs easily enough to keep himself out of academic trouble and get into college but never trying too hard to ingratiate himself with teachers or principals. A few classmates recounted some reckless pranks, but never anything that crossed the line. In short, Bernie Madoff seemed to be a normal, attractive teenager, using summer jobs and ingenuity to cope with the anxiety of his family's uncertain finances and making his way to a high school diploma in 1956 without much fanfare or attention.

With the Madoff family missing out on the widening prosperity of the 1950s, Ralph Madoff encouraged his sons to go to law school. For a survivor of the Great Depression unable to get a solid foothold in the postwar economy, this was an understandable wish—no doubt, he wanted his sons to earn degrees that would guarantee them the high-status jobs that eluded him.

Like everyone of their generation, the elder Madoffs would never have considered the stock market as a source of status or financial security. They had seen the market peak before the crash of 1929 and then fall 90 percent to its nadir in 1932. Fortunes evaporated. Posh homes were suddenly sold, and sleek roadsters were put up for sale at the curb, their gas tanks empty. Stock brokers wound up on bread lines. People with those memories found nothing glamorous about Wall Street—many of them saw it as a wicked gamble that promised easy wealth but delivered only anxiety and loss. If you had a little savings, you kept it in the bank, or maybe even in a coffee tin hidden at the top of the closet.

If investing on Wall Street seemed unwise, working there looked like a remote possibility at best for kids like Bernie Madoff in the 1950s—and not just because it was risky. Nobody made much money as a stock broker in the late 1940s and early 1950s, when government bonds were far more attractive to shell-shocked investors than corporate stocks. Besides, the executives at most of the top WASP firms on Wall Street would have looked right through a Jewish kid from a middle-class address in Queens. The long-established Jewish firms run by the Lehmans or the Loebs might have found room—on a trading desk or in the back office. But, even there, success would have meant climbing a long, unsteady ladder for a long, uncertain period of time.

Although he had absorbed his father's prickly preference for being his own boss, Bernie had no desire to become a lawyer. As a child, he expected to join his father's sporting goods business and eventually run it, but after the bankruptcy filing in 1951, he decided he'd like to sell sports equipment as a "manufacturer's rep," a sort of traveling salesman who wouldn't be tied down to the gray-flannel life of a law firm or corporate office. Most of the classmates who have offered their memories of Madoff's teenage and college years in the 1950s remembered the scrappy lawn-sprinkler installation business he got rolling in high school, after his father's businesses failed. They remembered thinking that he seemed like a young man on the make, who had felt the sting of doing without and dreamed of doing better.

And, of course, they remembered his romance with Ruthie Alpern.

Ruth Alpern's parents, Saul and Sara Alpern, were settled in Laurelton by the early 1950s, but, like Bernie, Ruth had been born in Brooklyn. On paper, their families shared some common history: both she and Bernie had immigrant grandparents who had worked hard to put their children on the road to Laurelton. Both were Jewish, although while Sylvia Madoff kept a kosher home, the Alperns were not particularly observant. And at least one or two rungs of the social ladder separated the newly middle-class Madoffs, beset by business failures, from the firmly professional Alperns.

Saul Alpern, who would emerge as one of the most puzzling figures in the early Madoff story, was the second son of Benjamin Alpern, a skilled watch repairman who settled in the United States in 1904. Saul was the first of the five Alpern children to go to college, graduating from City

College, well known for its accounting programs. By 1948, Saul Alpern and a partner had established a small accounting practice in Manhattan. People who knew him well recalled a quiet, reserved man with "a twinkle in his eye," but most dominant in their memory was his genial rectitude. If Saul said something was so, it was so, they said. He was man who dotted *i*'s and crossed *t*'s.

Ruth Alpern was born on May 18, 1941, four years after her older sister, Joan. A tiny blonde with enormous blue eyes, Ruth was both popular and pretty. One person who knew her in those years recalled her as a particularly sunny, optimistic person—perhaps a little naïve, but full of resilient humor. "You know the actress Goldie Hawn?" this person asked, recalling the original savvy *Laugh-In* comedienne typecast as a giggling blonde. "That was Ruth. She woke up every day without a care in the world. She was a lively, bubbly girl."

From the moment Ruth met Bernie, there was no one else in the world for her. They met the summer before Ruth started high school, when she was thirteen and he was sixteen. One of Ruth's friends held an informal party in a finished basement fitted out with a jukebox and some tables, like a little nightclub. Bernie came in, and Ruth seemed to be captivated immediately by the tanned, sun-bleached lifeguard. It was mutual; he walked her home from the party, the first steps in their lifelong journey together.

With Ruth still in high school—and with her parents wishing aloud that she would date more widely and not commit herself to one guy while she was so young—Bernie headed off to college in Alabama, a low-cost choice for his cash-strapped parents. But he missed Ruth and returned after a single semester to enroll at Hofstra University. As in high school, although scholarship was not his focus, he did well enough to appease his father by getting into law school. But before he'd gotten his acceptance letter from Brooklyn Law School, he had lost interest in his father's ambitions for him. He saw a different life for himself: a life married to Ruth and a career working for himself on Wall Street.

On November 25, 1959, with him still shy of his college diploma and her enrolled in nearby Queens College, Bernie Madoff and Ruth Alpern were married at the Laurelton Jewish Center. She was eighteen years old. A few days later, according to family lore, he filed the papers to open his own brokerage business, although the official birth date for Bernard L.

Madoff Investment Securities in regulatory ledgers is January 19, 1960. He was a college senior, just shy of twenty-two. He would later enroll in law school but would drop out after a single year, having spent almost every afternoon trying to drum up business for his newborn brokerage house.

By Bernie Madoff's own account, it was not until late in his college years that he seriously considered a life on Wall Street. But he certainly learned about Wall Street life in these early years—one of his close friends, Michael Lieberbaum, was the son of an early stock market success story. While Bernie was in high school, Michael's father—and thousands of other people—started selling shares in Jack Dreyfus's new mutual fund, one of the red-hot growth funds that revolutionized the postwar retail investment market. According to family accounts, the elder Lieberbaum got more than sales commissions from his association with the legendary Jack Dreyfus; he got the single best stock tip of his life: Buy Polaroid. He did, just as the company was about to go public, and it made him a millionaire.

Although Madoff said he rarely discussed the stock market with Michael Lieberbaum's father, it is certainly likely that get-rich-quick tales like this would have made Wall Street seem attractive to someone like him, hungry to make something of himself. But his high school and college years were also a turning point in America's cyclical love-hate relationship with Wall Street, as the fears from the Depression began to dissipate amid strong investment returns and prolonged prosperity. This new excitement about the stock market apparently caught Bernie Madoff's attention while he was in college. A few people who knew him in those years recall that he was touting stocks to his friends before he had his college degree—or a broker's license.

Madoff's entry into the world of Wall Street came at a time when federal and state regulators had barely begun to get their arms around the market. Fraud was chronic, like a low-grade fever. Thousands of poorly trained, unsupervised brokers were galloping into the boom to grab some of its extraordinary profits. In the early 1960s, regulators began a crackdown on the unruly proliferation of flimsy brokerage firms, many of them consisting of not much more than a self-taught broker and a phone.

One tiny firm caught in the regulatory crunch was Gibraltar Securities, the firm Ralph Madoff formed in his wife's name to conduct his work as a financial finder. He had never had much success with that work, and Gibraltar had been essentially dormant for several years, according to Madoff. On August 6, 1963, it was one of forty-eight firms cited for being delinquent in filing the required annual financial statements. In January 1964, the SEC dropped the proceedings after Gibraltar withdrew its registration and officially shut down. In post-2008 hindsight, there would be much speculation about this early run-in with regulators, but its primary significance within the family's life seems to have been that it was another tacit business failure for Ralph Madoff.

⟨∞⟩

Even after the hidden losses of 1962, Saul Alpern would continue to tell family members and close friends about how skillfully Bernie Madoff was playing the galloping market of the 1960s. He spoke about that prowess in quiet talks with his older brother, who used Alpern's firm as the accountant for his jewelry store; with his younger brother, an insurance executive; and with his youngest brother, a prospering lawyer. They would all invest with Madoff and would set up funds for their children with him. They would leave their money with him for decades, in fact, living on the profits he seemed to produce so effortlessly.

In a letter from prison, Madoff described for the first time how this business relationship with Saul Alpern supposedly worked. "In the 1970s, my father-in-law put together a limited partnership comprised of some family and clients of his accounting practice," he explained. Madoff set up an account at his firm for the partnership, and Alpern accepted checks from friends, relatives, and clients, passing the money along to Madoff to invest on their behalf—legitimately, Madoff insisted. The accounting firm received the trade confirmations and "would break up the trades into individual transactions at the identical prices and proportionate shares, according to each individual member of the partnership account," he said. "The individuals reported this information as capital gains on their respective tax returns. My father-in-law's firm would charge an accounting fee for providing this bookkeeping and tax service."

He added ingenuously, "I imagine it was similar to an investment club account."

Possibly Alpern thought he was merely introducing people to Madoff and mingling their money in his firm's accounts just to simplify things for them and for Madoff. Unsurprisingly, Madoff himself insisted there was nothing illegal in this arrangement. As he saw it, Alpern had too few investors to require him to file with securities regulators as an investment adviser or obtain a broker's license. But, in effect, this partnership was an informal, unlicensed mutual fund, taking in money from retail investors and handing it to Madoff to manage. Even so, nothing would ever shake the Alpern family's faith in their belief that Saul Alpern would never have knowingly led them into his son-in-law's fraud.

In 1958, Alpern had hired a young CPA named Frank Avellino, a graduate of City College in New York and a smart, slightly cocky young man, who was given a piece of the firm after the sudden death of Alpern's original partner in 1967. The next year, an experienced tax accountant named Michael Bienes arrived to work for Alpern, after several years at the Internal Revenue Service. Bienes immediately formed an intense bond with Avellino. The two men, born just months apart, would remain partners for almost a lifetime.

According to Bienes, Alpern kept simple records of the individual Madoff investors in a green plastic loose-leaf notebook. It seemed casual, but everyone who knew Alpern used the word *meticulous* at least once in describing him. Using forms he designed to fit into his notebook, he entered the amount each investor paid in and sent back a simple receipt for the money, perhaps with a personal thank-you note. In Bienes's version, Madoff initially accepted these individual accounts "from Saul's people," and Madoff's small back-office staff handled the paperwork. Later, Bienes claimed, Madoff told his father-in-law that things had to change.

In an interview taped for television, Bienes played Madoff's role in a scene that would have happened—if it happened at all—years before he even worked at the Alpern firm:

"No, I cannot handle small accounts like this. This is a pain in the neck and a pain in the butt."

Then he spoke Alpern's lines: "Look, open an account called A&A, and I will do the record keeping. I will handle the checks. I'll do it all."

"A&A" stood for "Alpern & Avellino," the name of Alpern's accounting practice. According to Bienes, Avellino also got "a piece" of the Madoff introduction business when he became a partner in 1970. Bienes did, too, when he became a partner a few years later. In 1974, Saul Alpern retired, and his old accounting firm was renamed Avellino & Bienes. The firm's accounts with Madoff were renamed the "A&B accounts."

According to Bienes, Saul Alpern insisted, "I'm taking the green book down to Florida. It'll give me something to do. And I'll mail the stuff up to [the firm's secretary] and she'll type it with the checks and send it out."

Madoff claimed that the account set up by Saul Alpern "grew to a maximum of 50 to 75 investors" under his father-in-law's stewardship. Bienes later estimated that this investment account was "only about 10 percent" of the accounting firm's business, even several years after Alpern retired, although he did not estimate how many investors were involved or how much money they had invested by the mid-1970s.

Along the way, Avellino and Bienes connected Madoff to another set of accountants with whom they shared office space. That pair of CPAs set up a separate fund to invest with Madoff through the A&B accounts. Their investors paid them a fee, and they paid a fee to Avellino & Bienes, but with a steady track record like Madoff's, nobody complained about the double-dipped expenses. Even if Madoff's returns were no better than those of the go-go mutual funds and red-hot stock market—and, typically, they weren't—they were a lot more predictable, a lot less volatile.

In his prison interviews and in subsequent letters, Madoff claimed that he was generating those solid, consistent profits for his father-in-law's partnership accounts through an investment strategy that he said was his small firm's specialty in the 1970s. It was called riskless arbitrage, and it was widely understood and accepted among the professionals on Wall Street in that era.

Riskless arbitrage is an age-old strategy for exploiting momentary price differences for the same product in different markets. It could be as simple as ordering cartons of cigarettes by telephone from a vendor in a low-cost state and simultaneously selling them over the phone at a higher price in states where they are more expensive, thereby locking in a profit. Or it could be as complex as using computer software to instantly detect a tiny price differential for a stock trading in two different currencies and execute the trades without human intervention—again, locking in the profit.

What distinguished riskless arbitrage from the more familiar "merger arbitrage" of the 1980s—which involved speculating in the securities of stocks involved in possible takeovers—was that a profit could be captured the moment it was perceived, if the trade could be executed quickly enough. A conventional trader would buy a security in hopes of selling it later at a profit; if he guessed wrong, he lost money. By contrast, an arbitrage trader would not buy a security at all unless he could almost instantly sell it, or its equivalent, at a profit; if he had to guess about whether he'd make a profit, he didn't do the trade.

In the 1970s, riskless stock arbitrage was as basic as exploiting brief price differences for a stock trading on several regional stock exchanges. It was not unusual for a company's shares to trade at $12 on the Pacific Stock Exchange in San Francisco at the same moment that the same shares were changing hands for $11.25 on, say, the Boston Stock Exchange. By simultaneously buying in Boston and selling in San Francisco, an alert investor could lock in that $0.75 difference as a riskless arbitrage profit.

At a more sophisticated level, a level Madoff was known to exploit, riskless arbitrage involved corporate bonds or preferred stock that could be converted into common stock. A bond that could be converted into ten shares of stock should usually trade for at least ten times the price of the stock—but it didn't always do so. If a bond that could be converted into ten shares of a $15 stock could be bought for less than $150—for $130 per bond, let's say—that was an opportunity for arbitrage. An investor could buy that bond for $130, simultaneously sell ten shares of the underlying common stock at $15 a share, and lock in a "riskless" arbitrage profit of $20—the difference between the $130 price he paid for the bond and the $150 he received for the ten shares he got when he converted the bond into stock.

Madoff also employed more complex strategies involving stocks that traded before they were even officially for sale, changing hands in the so-called "when issued" market at prices that sometimes offered arbitrage opportunities. Sometimes he took on more risk by not making simultaneous transactions, waiting to buy or sell in hopes that a move in the market would increase his profits. By one account, Madoff was especially active in arbitrage trades involving stocks sold in tandem with arcane securities called "warrants," which entitled buyers to purchase more stock at a specific price. Even as late as the 1980s, the Madoff firm was supposedly one of a handful of firms actively and visibly pursuing warrant arbitrage, which some traders at the time considered "easy pickings."

According to Madoff, arbitrage strategies like these were among the primary ways he made money for himself and his clients in the years before his Ponzi scheme began. "After the 1962 market collapse, I realized that just speculating in the market made little sense," he wrote in a letter from prison. "I realized the market was a stacked deck and was controlled by the large firms and institutions." The big trading firms handling orders from the giant retail houses would always have an advantage over tiny firms like his, he said, adding, "I searched for a niche for my firm and found it in market making of arbitrage securities."

Market makers were traders who consistently and publicly maintained a ready market in specific securities, buying from other traders who wanted to sell and selling to traders who wanted to buy. Continually offering to buy and sell the arcane securities involved in riskless arbitrage strategies—convertible bonds, preferred stock, common stock units with warrants—and trading those securities for his own account and those of his clients became Madoff's increasingly profitable market niche, he said.

According to Madoff, none of the big Wall Street firms were willing to do riskless arbitrage in small pieces for retail investors. But he was, and some of the biggest names on the Street would send him small arbitrage orders to execute for their customers, he said. "They liked to send me the business," he recalled. "They thought I was a nice Jewish boy."

Madoff was well positioned to earn honest arbitrage profits. Because transaction costs would wipe out most arbitrage profits, which tended to be paper-thin, arbitrage trading was usually pursued only by market insiders who could trade at far less cost than retail customers—market insiders such as Madoff.

Speed mattered in other ways, too. If it took too long to complete the paperwork involved in converting a bond into its equivalent shares of stock, the opportunity for a locked-in profit could vanish. Madoff's firm indisputably became adept at handling the conversions quickly and efficiently. Because profits could be assured only if a trader could buy and sell almost simultaneously, Madoff—with the help, in time, of his younger brother, Peter—began to build one of the fastest trading systems on the Street.

"This type of trading had limited risk exposure, which was what I was looking for," Madoff recalled in his letter. "I set about doing this trading for my firm's own account as well as my few clients. In the 1970s, I traded the strategies for the [Alpern] partnership accounts as well."

He concluded: "The combination of my market-making and arbitrage trading profits were substantial, and our capital grew nicely." His reputation grew right along with it.

How much of Madoff's version of his early success in riskless arbitrage trading is true? As noted, there are some indications that his firm gained a legitimate reputation on the Street for trading the warrants involved in arbitrage strategies—large-scale trading that other firms could see and participate in, not the backdated fictional trading that would become the hallmark of his Ponzi scheme. There were certainly opportunities for riskless arbitrage that could have produced sizable profits in those years. For example, between 1973 and 1992 the returns on convertible bonds were slightly higher and yet much less volatile than those on common stocks, and convertible bond arbitrage was another strategy Madoff claimed to employ.

But a subsequent lawsuit asserted that Madoff was falsifying convertible bond arbitrage profits in some customer accounts as early as August 1977. To someone familiar with riskless arbitrage, these 1977 trades do not provide unambiguous evidence of fraud. But an expert analysis filed in court in early 2012 cited many other instances of obviously fictitious arbitrage trades in customer accounts in the late 1970s.

The line between true and false is very hard to draw so long after the fact, especially given Madoff's masterful fluency in both truth and lies. There was money to be made in these exotic securities, and Madoff was known later as a big player in at least some corners of this relatively small marketplace. But he is also the man who covered up the losses he inflicted on his clients in the ruinous new-issue market in 1962.

So the possibility that Madoff was faking at least some of his clients' arbitrage profits in the 1970s certainly cannot be ruled out.

3

THE HUNGER FOR YIELD

As the 1970s began, Wall Street was changing as much on the inside as on the outside, and Bernie Madoff would ride those changes to a public leadership position that he would hold for almost forty years—a position that would reinforce his credibility with investors and regulators.

As so often happened, market regulation had grown lax during the intoxicating bull markets of the 1950s and '60s. The 1970s sobered things up quickly as the Securities and Exchange Commission, the principal regulator of the nation's financial markets, struggled to catch up with the extraordinary mess that the postwar market party had left behind.

By the end of the go-go years, the manual labor required to keep track of the paperwork generated by trading in those days of paper ledgers and scribbling clerks was beyond the capacity of many Wall Street firms. As the hot mutual funds stepped up their trading pace, the volume of trading grew and the paperwork fell further behind. When the rest of the public started to get excited about stocks, too, the volume picked up even more, and the paperwork lagged disastrously as paper stock certificates had to be physically moved from one brokerage house to another. Keeping track of all this moving paper soon overwhelmed the army of clerks hired to manage it, and the consequent delays and discrepancies made it increasingly difficult for federal regulators to ensure that all this activity was aboveboard and on the level. Old Wall Street hands called it "the paper crunch," and it bit down fiercely in 1968 and 1969, causing the ruin of a number of Big Board brokerage firms and impressing a young Bernie Madoff with the importance of automating the market's paperwork procedures.

By then, Ruth Madoff was no longer working at the firm—she had stopped a few months before their first son, Mark, was born in 1964.

Since 1961, Madoff had shared office space at 39 Broadway with a fellow entrepreneur named Martin J. Joel Jr., who was a client of Saul Alpern's accounting firm. In the same month in 1960 that Madoff launched his firm, Marty Joel and a partner had opened a brokerage firm called Joel, Zuchs & Company. The partnership soon broke up, and Joel invited Madoff to share his office space and split the rent.

Marty Joel would work with and around Madoff for decades. In 1961 he was an aggressive, ambitious young man in his late twenties who was running a small and slightly raucous brokerage business, haggling with regulators, and fielding lawsuits by customers. His repeated run-ins with industry regulators during the late 1960s suggested a certain carelessness about his compliance with the market's rule book. In 1970, the SEC suspended him from the brokerage business for seventy-five days because of repeated record-keeping and margin violations between 1966 and 1968.

While sharing the rent, Madoff also shared Joel's office manager, Carole Lipkin, who handled the administrative chores Ruth had once done. In a few years, Madoff hired Carole's husband, Irwin Lipkin, as his own "back-office" manager—the first outside employee of Bernard L. Madoff Investment Securities—perhaps to draw a sharper line between his firm and Joel's. There is no sign that Madoff's firm got tangled up in the regulatory brambles of those years, although he had been cited for minor technical violations in the early 1960s. Whatever their operational differences, Madoff and Joel socialized frequently, and their young families became friends.

Compared with the Big Board firms that served a growing army of retail investors, smaller OTC traders such as Madoff Investment Securities escaped the worst of the strangling paper crunch of the late 1960s, simply because they had fewer clients, traded largely on a wholesale basis with other traders, and were quicker to adopt labor-saving devices such as computers. Indeed, some of these firms not only survived but prospered by providing better service to the mutual funds and other institutional investors who had become frustrated by the logjam at the Big Board and were demanding faster execution of their trades. But this didn't mean it was easy; Ruth Madoff was briefly recalled from home in 1968 to help the tiny firm deal with the backlog of paperwork.

In response to the paperwork overload and the rising tide of brokerage firm failures in the late 1960s, Congress established the Securities Investor Protection Corporation, known as SIPC (pronounced "Sipik"), in 1970. Although its board was politically appointed, SIPC was not a government agency; it was a nonprofit organization financed through annual assessments levied on Wall Street firms. Its mission was to help ease the bankruptcy process for a failed firm's retail customers. The same law that created SIPC added elements to the federal bankruptcy code that applied exclusively to brokerage firms. Like the other firms on Wall Street, Bernard L. Madoff Investment Securities became a member and paid its annual assessments.

In the 1970s regulators also began to lean harder on Wall Street to automate and to enable trades to be completed in a reasonable amount of time and tracked for accuracy and legitimacy. Automation would also remove the need to physically transport share certificates; stock ownership would be documented electronically. Technology—in the form of faster, cheaper computers and more sophisticated communications equipment—gradually began to replace the nearly Dickensian recordkeeping process built around human clerks and paper ledgers that had failed so spectacularly in the "paper crunch" of the late 1960s.

But the same technology also started changing the very idea of what a stock market was—and this gave Bernie Madoff a legitimate opportunity to reach for greatness.

For traditionalists on the Street, a stock market was a centralized trading floor where men in loud-colored jackets stood face-to-face and shouted bids at one another for a few specified hours each day. That "auction" model—with stock traders bidding against one another like so many art collectors at Sotheby's or Christie's—seemed increasingly inadequate as mutual fund managers and other professional investors came to dominate the markets and as over-the-counter stocks became more attractive to them.

As an OTC trading house, Madoff's firm had never conducted business in the traditional auction-market way. The over-the-counter market, with tens of thousands of unlisted stocks, had no central trading floor where traders could shout out their bids. Instead, it was more like a vast telephonic flea market, whose map was the Pink Sheets. A dealer like Madoff could pick up some shares at one flea market on Monday and try to sell them at a higher price at another flea market being held that day, or at the same flea market on another day.

By the time someone in one flea market noticed a dealer's price tag on a stock, the stock could be selling for more or less somewhere else. So dealers such as Madoff put a comfortable cushion between the price at which they would buy a stock from another trader and the higher price at which they would sell it. That cushion was called "the spread." Another term for it would be "profit."

Spreads on over-the-counter stocks were enormous—sometimes as high as 50 percent—and those fat profits were almost completely hidden from the actual retail investor. Getting a piece of those profits was the hard part.

The market was dominated by a handful of big wholesale dealers with big inventory. Like hundreds of other small dealers, Madoff struggled to get attention. "Often as not, Madoff's firm did not get called when there was business to do," a reporter noted in Traders Magazine.

Along with a cadre of other farsighted brokers, Madoff quickly saw that if the Pink Sheets were computerized so that their prices could be constantly updated and made available to every dealer—as on the ticker on the Big Board—the dealer offering the best prices for a stock stood a better chance of getting noticed. "We felt, as a small market-making firm, that this would level the playing field for us," he told one writer. It would also give a much-needed boost to his stock-trading business.

He was not alone in his conviction that the Pink Sheets could be automated; there are at least a half-dozen people with a far better claim than his to having "invented" the automated market that became NASDAQ. But he backed the idea early and emphatically, even as some other market makers resisted it because "you had to show your hand, and they didn't want to do that," Madoff recalled. "If somebody just called you up from the Pink Sheets, you could say the price was stale and give different quotes to different people. The system we were proposing would give prices a level of transparency. It was quite controversial."

The federal regulators, however, were on his side. They quickly saw that computerizing the Pink Sheets would shed more light on price quotes and create more competition in the OTC market. That could narrow spreads and give investors a better deal.

In its push for more automation, the SEC demanded the help of its industry-run partner in the financial regulatory field, the National Association of Securities Dealers, or NASD. For three decades, the policing work of the SEC had theoretically been augmented by the NASD's own security measures. The organization was empowered to license brokers and to establish and enforce trading rules. Chronic scandals in these years, however, showed that the NASD's resources often fell short of its responsibilities. Its leadership was divided between small firms fretting about costs and giant firms worrying about investor backlash. And, like any watchdog that is fed and petted by the people it is supposed to be watching, its appetite for fierce enforcement was more of an ambition than a reality.

As divided and occasionally compromised as it was, the NASD's leadership saw that the status quo was not an option. The group's automation committee had struggled for years to automate price quotes in the OTC market, and in February 1971, to the muted alarm of the established traditional stock exchanges, an automated system built for the NASD by a computer company called Bunker Ramo made its debut, linking dealers across the country via an electronic network. It was called NASDAQ, an acronym for National Association of Securities Dealers Automated Quotations. Improvements to its primitive archetype—built on a software chassis similar to those already running airline and hotel reservation systems—would follow.

Madoff allied himself firmly with the forces of automation—and somehow his small firm found the money to invest in equipment and software. Did he get some of that money from the investors that Saul Alpern, Frank Avellino, and Michael Bienes were collecting? At least one former employee later thought so, according to allegations in subsequent litigation. But Madoff emphatically denied stealing from customer accounts during the 1970s and '80s and, nearly two years after his arrest, no evidence had been made public that contradicted him. In any case, the regulatory battles over automation would allow Madoff to add a few brushstrokes each year to his portrait as a committed market innovator, an ally in the crusade to drag the nation's tradition-bound markets into the modern age.

It is no coincidence that this transformation of the Madoff firm's repu-tation—from a struggling over-the-counter trading house to a cutting-edge market innovator—began with the arrival of Bernie's younger brother, Peter.

Peter Bennett Madoff was in kindergarten when his father's busi-ness failed, and he was a teenager when his brother Bernie married Ruth Alpern. His sister, Sondra, was more than a decade his senior. Like many last-born children, he made his own path—a more seamless transition to adult life than his older brother managed.

Instead of attending Far Rockaway High School, he applied and was admitted to Brooklyn Tech, one of the most prestigious competitive pub-lic high schools in the country. He graduated from Queens College in Flushing, New York, where he met his future wife, Marion, and earned his law degree from Fordham University in 1970, just after his daughter, Shana, was born.

By then, Bernie had a growing family. His first son, Mark, whose arrival in March 1964 prompted Ruth to end her brief tenure as Ber-nie's office manager, was followed by another son, Andrew, born in April 1966.

Despite the difficulties of breaking into the clubby over-the-counter market, the Madoff firm was apparently doing very well. Bernie moved his young family to Roslyn, on Long Island's increasingly affluent North Shore, and commuted each day to newer and larger offices at 110 Wall Street, about six blocks from the Fulton Fish Market on the East River. He and Ruth joined a country club; she enjoyed summer days there with the boys, and the family's golf games improved.

It appears that Peter worked at his brother's firm while he was still in school—industry records show that he got his broker's license and joined the firm in June 1969—and he came to stay after getting his law degree. He arrived amid some of the most revolutionary changes since the invention of the ticker tape and telegraph a century before. And he put the Madoff firm on the technological map, spending a lot of its money to do so.

There was little agreement, in hindsight, about whether the Peter Madoff of those days was a warm, engaging man or a sharp-tongued, demanding one. Some former employees, burned by their losses, recalled Peter in less than flattering ways. But even after Bernie Madoff's fall, the trade journals were full of comments from people who had known

Bernie and his brother for years and genuinely liked them. Peter Chapman, of *Traders Magazine*, found that Peter, like Bernie and his sons, "was almost universally liked" on the Street. The Madoff brothers "were just great, great people," said one of their institutional clients.

There were two vivid threads of agreement weaving through these differing recollections.

First, there was a common perception that Bernie subtly and humorously, but persistently, belittled his younger brother. There may have been nothing more to it than the age-old friction between a successful man and a promising kid brother trying to find his place at the table. Despite Peter's law degree—a credential that Bernie had decided wasn't worth his own time—he started out as a salaried employee of his brother's brokerage firm, albeit an increasingly well-paid one. Nearly forty years later, he would still be only a salaried employee, working for a brother who never made him a partner in the primary business to which he had devoted his entire working life. For decades, his only ownership stake in the primary Madoff firm was a sliver of equity in the firm's London subsidiary, formed in 1983, with his brother retaining an ownership stake of more than 88 percent of that unit.

It is possible that Bernie's treatment of Peter simply echoed the dynamics of their childhood. By 1970, their father, Ralph Madoff, had taken an interest in Bernie's firm, and he and Sylvia would sometimes help Bernie by riding out to inspect some company he was considering as an investment. Ralph's occasional presence at the firm could have reinforced Bernie's and Peter's childhood roles of Big Brother and Baby Brother. If so, the influence did not last long. In July 1972, Ralph Madoff died of a heart attack at age sixty-two. Two and half years later, in December 1974, Sylvia Madoff died suddenly as well, after suffering an asthma attack during a vacation cruise in the Caribbean. She was just weeks shy of her sixty-third birthday.

Even with the lower actuarial expectations of the early 1970s, it was a shock to the Madoff brothers to lose both parents so early and so young. Friends from that era would recall that Bernie became more fatherly toward his younger brother, stepping into Ralph's shoes as the family patriarch.

The second common perception from those who knew him well is that Peter Madoff was the essential force that propelled his brother's firm into the vanguard of marketplace computer technology, keeping it competitive and drawing favorable regulatory attention. In one account of Wall Street's automation, the authors introduced the Madoff brothers like this: "Bernard (who founded the firm) and Peter (the company's computer genius)." Even one of the lawsuits filed against him after his brother's fall credited Peter with developing the trading technology on which the firm's trading desk relied.

Bernie Madoff embraced the larger idea that technology was clearly going to reshape the stock market and had to reshape the Madoff firm, too. But his brother grasped all the nuts and bolts it would take to get there. As Peter's expertise grew, he took a larger role in overseeing the firm's trading operation, where the new technology hit the road every day.

If some insider accounts are right, Peter's contribution to his brother's firm was even more significant. These chronicles credit Peter as the one who saw the potential for making a market in stocks that normally traded on the New York Stock Exchange. "And it was that decision," one report noted, "that catapulted the firm into the big leagues of wholesaling."

The over-the-counter trading of exchange-listed stocks was called the "third market," a name that some scholars said was derived from Wall Street's view that the Big Board and other traditional stock exchanges were the "first market" and the OTC market was the "second market." The big Wall Street firms that were members of the New York Stock Exchange were obligated by its rules to trade the shares of NYSE-listed stocks only on the Big Board. So the third market—the trading of NYSE-listed stocks among dealers in the over-the-counter market—was a niche that smaller non-NYSE firms could exploit easily without being jostled by giants. As institutional investors flocked to the third market, where commissions were lower than on the Big Board, the increased trading volume generated new revenues for the smaller firms handling third-market trades. It was here that the Madoff firm first began to increase its share of Wall Street trading volume and build its reputation with other Wall Street leaders. And getting into the third market, according to many, was Peter Madoff's idea.

Peter's role during this turbulent decade of cascading technological change made him as influential in regulatory circles as his brother. He also became an increasingly important figure within the firm itself, taking on a host of important duties, including regulatory compliance.

It is beyond the world of trading technology that the mysteries arise. As chief compliance officer, how much did Peter know about what was going on in the private customer accounts opened at the firm? How much did Peter learn about what Bernie did with all the money that Ruth Madoff's relatives were sending to him through her father's old accounting firm? How much did Bernie share with him about the financial condition of those parts of the firm that Peter didn't see? In short, how much did Bernie tell Peter about his evolving fraud?

Absolutely nothing, according to Madoff himself and Peter's lawyer, commenting after Bernie's arrest and responding to questions in the years that followed—years in which Peter remained under investigation but was not arrested or charged with any crime.

Peter Madoff had his own investment accounts, managed by his brother, and those accounts would generate millions in profits for him and other members of his family over the years. Didn't he ever suspect that his returns were too good to be true? Records would later show a number of backdated trades in those accounts that had enriched him enormously. Didn't Peter ever sit down and check the paperwork on those accounts with Bernie to see how such remarkable profits were possible?

His answer, from the day of his brother's arrest, was "no." His legal defense in a string of lawsuits was that he, like thousands of other people, believed he could trust his spectacularly talented brother to manage the family's personal money—just as his brother trusted him to run the firm's core stock trading business and keep it ahead of the technology curve.

If Bernie entrusted Peter with anything beyond the firm's high-tech trading business, there was little on paper to publicly document it.

∽

By the late 1970s, Frank Avellino and Michael Bienes realized that they simply had to do something about their arrangement with Bernie Madoff.

The process that Saul Alpern had begun a decade earlier—receiving checks from investors, logging in the individual profits, mailing out checks for the withdrawals, noting when the money was reinvested—had gotten far too cumbersome, according to Bienes. The accountants were suffering under the same sort of paperwork crunch that had bedeviled Wall Street a decade earlier, but they did not have access to the mainframe computers that would have solved their problems, and personal computers were still a few years away. Besides, the partners still had an accounting firm to run.

Avellino & Bienes had inherited nearly all of Saul Alpern's accounting clients after the older man's retirement, but one important account did not make the trip: Bernard L. Madoff Investment Securities. The Madoff firm's books had been handled by Jerome Horowitz, another accountant in the Alpern firm who was sufficiently well-established that Bienes expected he would soon break off to set up his own practice—as he did. Despite the Alpern family connection, it actually was Horowitz who handled the annual tax accounting and audit chores for Madoff's brokerage firm. When Horowitz left the Alpern firm to strike out on his own in the late 1960s, he took Madoff's accounting business with him.

There were apparently no hard feelings about the move, as Bernie Madoff continued to invest money for the clients of Avellino & Bienes after his father-in-law retired. The number of accounts grew slightly "to accommodate IRA accounts and family members of their accounting clients," Madoff said in a letter from prison, but never exceeded a half-dozen accounts, all of which he said were involved in his hallmark arbitrage trading.

"It was my understanding that all of these Avellino & Bienes [accounts] would operate in the identical manner as the original account of my father-in-law," he said—in other words, money from many investors would be pooled in a few accounts at the Madoff firm, and the profits would be allocated appropriately by the accounting firm. He claimed to have warned the two accountants to keep the number of investors below the level that would require them to register as a public mutual fund—a claim Michael Bienes stoutly disputed in his public account of these years.

While the returns were attractive for Avellino, Bienes, and their clients—regulators would later say they ranged in the high teens, but there is no firm evidence of Madoff's track records in these years—the paperwork logjam was threatening to bury them. Bienes credits Avellino with the breakthrough idea: "Four words: Let's pay them interest. It's simple. You give them a stated rate. You pay it to them calendar-quarterly. They can roll it over if they want, or they can take a check if they want."

This step was noteworthy because it was the first big change in the way Avellino & Bienes handled the money invested with Madoff, a change that Madoff said was made without his knowledge or approval. It was also one that simplified the process enough so that the tiny accounting firm could handle an enormous number of customers and a stunning amount of money. There was no formal partnership structure or separate business unit created to mark this new approach by the two accounting partners. It was all very casual, but the accounting firm "always stood behind it," Michael Bienes said years later.

"That's how much we believed in Bernie," he stated.

It was an era when people desperately wanted something solid to believe in. The 1970s seemed like the decade that would ruin Wall Street. The contrast between Wall Street's dismal state and Madoff's apparent success with his arbitrage trading only enhanced his reputation.

"The stock market crashed in the 1970s, and no one noticed," the financial writer Jerry Goodman observed. Unlike the crash of 1929, the 1970s crash occurred in slow motion. As Goodman memorably summed up, "If the first crash was a dramatic leap from a sixty-story building, the second was like drowning in a bubble bath. The bubble-bath drowning sounds less scary, but you end up just as dead."

Inflation—fed by the government's pursuit of an expensive foreign war in Vietnam and an ambitious welfare program at home—was shredding the value of paper money. When Bernie Madoff opened for business in 1960, inflation was less than 2 percent a year. When President Richard Nixon took office in 1969, the annual inflation rate was 5 percent. In the first nine months of 1979, it would hit 10.75 percent. "Inflation this high during peace time was unprecedented in American history," one Federal Reserve scholar observed.

The dismal decade knocked the stock market to its knees; the previous decade's giddy go-go market was utterly gone. There seemed to be no safe place to stand in this storm. Stock prices gyrated wildly—no one could remember mood swings like this, month in and month out. Bonds didn't hold their value, especially late in the decade, as the Federal Reserve stepped up its effort to break the inflation fever by sharply increasing interest rates. American retail investors learned new words to worry about: *volatility* and *stagflation*.

Putting money in the bank, once the safest option, no longer seemed sensible. For years, Treasury rules had capped the rates that small savers could get; only the big institutions could earn interest rates high enough to keep ahead of inflation. When rates finally inched up for small savers, the nation's savings and loans went on a risky lending binge that promised to end badly. Even if you could find a bank or thrift institution that seemed stable, stability alone wasn't enough. The inflation of the 1970s was eroding the purchasing power of every dollar that careful savers had put into the bank or had used to buy bonds.

The hunger for yield became almost an obsession for an entire generation. You had to find something that would pay you more than the cost of living, or you were forever falling behind. Investors stampeded into the newly created money market mutual funds. Some even turned to complex partnerships investing in oil and gas reserves or silver and other precious metals, whose prices were soaring.

Prudent investors had once accepted the ironclad link between the level of risk and the rate of return: to get higher returns, you had to take greater risks. Corporate bonds paid a higher rate than Treasury bonds because corporate bonds were riskier; Uncle Sam wouldn't go out of business. Small OTC stocks climbed many times faster than the blue chips, but were also far more likely to wind up worthless. That was just the way it was. The price the brave paid for high yields included high risk and sleepless nights. Don't fool yourself, the wise men said: those who want sound sleep and more safety have to settle for lower yields.

Perversely, the greater risk now seemed to be to accept too low a yield on your investments. Apparently, the law that higher-paying investments were riskier than lower-paying ones had somehow been repealed. The 1970s had turned the traditional formula of risk and reward upside down. What you needed was safety *and* yield—the robust profits of speculation without all that nail-biting volatility, and the security of low-risk investments without the slow erosion of your savings.

That impossible dream was exactly what some lucky people said they got, year in and year out, from Frank Avellino and Michael Bienes: real, steady interest payments, zero volatility. Because Madoff's returns, like those of a lot of arbitrage traders of that era, were always within a narrow range, the payment of interest to their clients made sense to them. It meant that for some quarterly payments, they'd pay out a little more than they received from Madoff, and for others they'd pay out less than they received, but in the end it would all even out. And if most clients left the interest in their accounts to grow, the rough edges would become all but invisible over time. Avellino & Bienes seemed to have turned the speculative and risky practice of investing in the stock market into a smooth and predictable revenue stream—like interest on a high-grade corporate bond, without the erosion of capital. Bernie Madoff's steady returns made this possible.

In an inflation-obsessed environment, the change that Avellino and Bienes made in how they handled the investors first recruited by Saul Alpern—"let's pay them interest"—put Alpern's little business serving a cluster of "friends and family" into overdrive.

Madoff would later insist that he recovered from his missteps in 1962 and went on to make real money for these early clients—and given the hot market environment in the 1960s and the strategies he claimed to be using, he might have been telling the truth. In his first decade in business, the over-the-counter market was racking up annual gains many times greater than his investors were supposedly getting in those days. Even in the 1970s, Madoff could have been making more money as an institutional investor than Avellino and Bienes were paying out to their retail investors. Indeed, a few faint recollections among investors suggest he may actually have used the money from some early investors as working capital for his young firm, producing enough profits to easily cover the promised returns.

That still would have broken the rules, of course—had they known about it, regulators could have accused Madoff of misappropriating client funds. But it was at least statistically possible that he was successfully investing the limited amount of money that Saul Alpern was bringing in from family and friends.

Word spread, and the word was that the Avellino & Bienes firm was the only way to invest with the remarkable Bernie Madoff, who would not accept individual customer accounts.

That so many of the firm's accounting clients invested through the firm may simply reflect the role that accountants played in an era before "private bankers" and "investment advisers" were widely available to the moderately affluent people who ran small businesses. For them, their company's accounting firm was as close to a financial adviser as they could get—and who had time for anything more elaborate, even if you could find someone more qualified? They were running a business, after all.

So the number of Avellino & Bienes investors grew exponentially, and the amount of money involved grew right along with it. By the end of the 1970s the Madoff investment operation made up more than a third of the accounting firm's business. Four people in the firm's New York office handled calls and applications and mailed out the checks and statements: two data entry clerks, a receptionist, and an office manager who dealt with inquiries through the mail and over the phone.

And the firm always paid; no one ever complained or expressed doubts about their operation. No wonder the checks poured in and the referrals were incessant.

Bienes insisted later that he and Avellino "never advertised, we never promoted, we never sent out a Christmas card—and the money came in." When they had collected a substantial sum, they would send it to Madoff. At the end of each quarter, they would draw money from the firm's Madoff account and deposit it to cover the individual interest checks they mailed out.

Apart from the money, the amount of trust that customers invested in this back-of-the-envelope arrangement was remarkable. No one on Wall Street or in regulatory agencies in Washington had ever heard of Avellino or Bienes. There were no brochures, no fact sheets, no paperwork at all—and the two accountants made it emphatically clear that there never would be, so don't ask. All you could expect was a simple receipt stating the amount you'd invested and the promised interest rate. "That's all we'd say. We were very tough," Bienes recalled later. Those were the rules: put nothing in writing.

Meanwhile, they were also handling their firm's accounting work. "We had medium-sized, small clients, individual clients," Bienes later recalled. "A lot of them were oddballs, I gotta tell you. But then again, as Saul Alpern always said, the normal person does not go into business for himself—he goes and gets a job."

Bienes and Avellino were oddballs themselves, a pair of Damon Runyon characters set in real life. Frank Avellino had the curious habit of referring to himself in conversation in the third person, by his full name. Asked in subsequent testimony about any bank loans the partnership had obtained, Avellino said, "All I could say to you is, at one point in time, Michael Bienes and Frank Avellino borrowed millions of dollars from Chemical Bank, unsecured, period. . . . We voluntarily turned in our loan to the bank. They hated us for it."

Avellino did it, he explained, because "I don't like to give out financial statements, I don't like them to know—I'm a very private guy, by the way, as is Michael—it's none of their goddamn business, in plain English, and I think we could afford not to borrow."

Avellino and Bienes referred to the people who sent them money as "lenders," not investors. They repeatedly explained that their clients were lending them money to finance the accounting firm's investment activities. They were promising to pay those individual lenders a stated interest rate, which they paid with the profits they earned by investing with Madoff. Their persistence in this description suggests that they thought they could fit this lucrative business into a legal loophole for "demand notes," which did not have to be publicly filed with securities regulators.

Later, in response to a question about how the partnership made sure it could pay its promised interest rates to this expanding universe of "lenders," Avellino answered, "Michael Bienes and Frank Avellino . . . have their own assets, which we always know can be called upon because we are personally liable on those loans."

Despite these highly unorthodox arrangements, a host of investors came to believe that this, at last, was a legitimate solution to their gnawing investment dilemma. Traveling far beyond regulated Wall Street, they set up camp in a murky land with no written rules and no adult supervision. They nevertheless thought they had found a safe haven: they were getting the security of consistent returns without sacrificing the higher inflation-beating profits of more volatile, riskier investments. Wildly underestimating the risks they were taking, they felt lucky to have been allowed to invest money with—that is, to *lend* money to—Avellino & Bienes.

For so many smart but credulous investors, the road to Madoff led through a regulatory no-man's-land. And for many of them, that road was paved, wittingly or not, by their trusted business accountants. Frank Avellino and Michael Bienes were merely the first.

4

THE BIG FOUR

The computer technology that took root on Wall Street in the 1970s allowed the world to take a closer look at the stock-picking, market-timing wizards who seized the public's attention in the previous decade. Unfortunately for the wizard fraternity, analysts found that a portfolio carefully chosen by some lionized genius typically did no better than a portfolio of stocks chosen utterly at random.

The fatally seductive idea that there was a genius who could be relied upon to pick the right stocks at the right moment and beat the market by double or triple digits, year in and year out, without fail—well, that notion is a phoenix, a feather-headed concept that rises, more or less intact, from the ashes of every market meltdown.

Its indestructible appeal to a wealthy investor named Stanley Chais had enormous consequences for Bernie Madoff, who seemed to be exactly the kind of genius Chais and everyone else were looking for.

Chais was a courtly gentleman who, by the late 1960s, had sold and retired from his family's East Coast knitwear manufacturing business. Before moving to the Los Angeles area sometime around 1970, he lived in Sands Point, on Long Island, with his attractive wife, Pamela—one *New York Times* article from the era took note of her "peaches-and-cream complexion" and "tidily coiffed" blond hair—and their three children. Pamela Chais was the daughter of a Broadway playwright and was a promising playwright herself by the time the family moved west.

Before the family relocated, Chais met Bernie Madoff through Marty Joel, the freewheeling broker who had shared office space with Madoff at 39 Broadway and was a client of Saul Alpern's accounting firm. Chais and Joel had been classmates at Syracuse University and had remained friends. The Madoffs socialized with the Joels, so it was natural they would meet the Chaises. Chais was impressed by the money Madoff was making with arbitrage trading and decided to invest some of his own money in arbitrage. Soon he was making money, too.

Stan Chais and Bernie Madoff would remain connected for nearly forty years. The trust funds for the three Chais children and other family members were invested with Madoff. In time, Chais would have more than four dozen Madoff accounts, including those set up for his charitable foundation. Based on a few documentary traces, it seems possible that Chais also became acquainted with others in Madoff's immediate circle, including his father-in-law, Saul Alpern.

Chais was not just an individual Madoff investor; nor was he someone who simply set up a Madoff account and put other people's money into it, as Avellino & Bienes did. Starting in 1970, Chais set up three formal partnerships that raised money from other people and invested it with Madoff. This made Chais the forerunner of the hundreds of entrepreneurs who would create and peddle private funds designed solely to carry other people's money to Madoff's door.

Chais set up the first formal "feeder fund." A feeder fund is simply a fund that raises money from investors and puts it into one or more other funds. Feeder funds raising cash to invest with Madoff would proliferate like oversexed rabbits after 1990. But it all began here, with Chais's first partnership.

It was called the Lambeth Company, and it opened for business in 1970. The Brighton Company followed in 1973, and the Popham Company in 1975. Chais collected fees from his investors for running these three early funds, which looked very much like informal mutual funds, although he never registered them with the SEC. He did not believe he needed to because he had only a few dozen direct investors, according to people who knew him well. For similar reasons, he did not think he needed to be registered with the SEC to act as an informal investment adviser, they said.

Most of his clients found their way to him through word of mouth, either within the creative Hollywood circles frequented by his wife or through an accounting firm he used. And although he and his investment accounts were unregistered and unregulated, Chais and his many clients apparently felt confident that nothing would go wrong.

Each of Chais's three partnerships took in money from additional "sub-funds," other formal but unregistered partnerships that collected money and paid fees to their separate general partners. All the money, whether gathered directly through his own companies or indirectly through the sub-funds, was invested with Madoff.

The early paperwork for the three Chais feeder funds indicated that they were being formed to pursue arbitrage strategies—which matches the memories of a few early Madoff investors and other sources familiar with the accounts, and the version of events offered by Madoff himself.

A younger member of one family of very early investors—devastated by their later losses—said that his father was told by Madoff directly, at some point in the late 1970s, that he was using arbitrage as his money-making strategy. "He supposedly had come up with this computerized system for identifying opportunities to purchase preferred stock and short the common stock," he recalled.

So it seemed possible—perhaps Stanley Chais persuaded himself it was even plausible—that Bernie Madoff could have used legitimate arbitrage strategies to generate steady, reliable profits on the money Chais collected for the Lambeth, Brighton, and Popham accounts at Madoff's firm in the 1970s.

The strategy would begin to seem a little less plausible as the amount of money entrusted to Madoff grew with each passing year. Most arbitrage opportunities disappeared quickly if too much money was thrown at them too fast. And by the early 1980s, Madoff would be taking in a lot of money. Moreover, big institutional investors started to become more interested in convertible securities—the basic elements of these arbitrage strategies—in the late 1970s, and they would have been competing with Madoff for the best profit opportunities.

As far as Chais knew, however, Madoff had only a few clients and took in new ones only as a favor to a few close friends. Perhaps, in these early days, this was true. Madoff was already cultivating an air of quiet exclusivity. He expected his lucky clients to keep quiet about being in his elite club—talking about it would cause more people to pester him to get in and he didn't want that, he said.

This attitude not only lent cachet to his growing business, but it apparently also kept each cash source in the dark about the existence of the others. Over the years, it would be difficult for anyone to mark the point when Madoff's arbitrage-based investment business grew too large to be plausible.

Memories are fuzzy about exactly what kind of profits the Chais partnerships produced during the 1970s. Could Madoff have been producing steady arbitrage profits of 10 to 14 percent, year in and year out, as some people recall? Maybe. A lot of smart people allowed themselves to believe that's how he did it. And perhaps, in those early days of the first true feeder funds, they were right.

The accounts Chais set up with Madoff for his own family were not arbitrage accounts; those accounts allegedly bought stock in strong, promising companies and then held on to it for years, or even decades. When Madoff's account records were examined after his arrest, these Chais family "buy-and-hold" accounts were found to have performed far better than the formal arbitrage partnerships Chais set up for outside investors.

Lawsuits would later assert that by 2008 there were a number of odd errors in many Chais accounts. Stocks had been bought or sold on dates when the markets were closed, or at prices that were outside the stocks' range on those dates. There would also be accusations, denied by Chais, that he directed Madoff to backdate trades and guarantee there would be no losses in his accounts, or to fabricate trades to produce specific tax gains or losses.

The wealth that accumulated in Chais's own Madoff accounts, some of it fueled by the fees he collected from his outside investors, allowed Chais to become a devoted and consistent benefactor to economic and charitable institutions in Israel. He was also generous to Jewish charities in the United States and was widely respected and admired.

Family lawyers said later that Stanley Chais was utterly blindsided by Madoff's betrayal and had never suspected a thing. He believed that Madoff was one of those rare market geniuses—like Warren Buffett or George Soros or the Magellan fund's Peter Lynch—who have an instinct for consistently making a lot of money, no matter the market conditions. If he had had any idea Madoff was a crook, they said, surely he would not have left most of his family's wealth, his income from fees, and his illusory investment profits in Bernie's hands.

Stanley Chais was one of a quartet of very wealthy Jewish entrepreneurs who had set up accounts with Bernie Madoff by the end of the 1970s. The others in this elite club were Carl Shapiro, a legendary success in the garment industry; Norman F. Levy, a giant in the New York real estate business; and Jeffry M. Picower, the youngest of the four, who would start out peddling tax shelters and emerge by the end of the next decade as a man for whom the term *wheeler-dealer* might have been invented.

Unlike Chais, the other members of this core clientele did not form feeder funds or actively recruit streams of other investors for Madoff. But like Chais, they would stay with him for at least four decades, reaping astonishing profits and underwriting his credibility among other rich investors from Park Avenue to Palm Beach to Beverly Hills.

Their affinity for him seemed at least partly rooted in their status as self-made men who had great confidence in their own well-tuned bullshit detectors. Yet those detectors never seemed to buzz around Bernie Madoff. Young as he was—he would not turn forty until 1978—Madoff already had an air of calm mastery, free of any razzle-dazzle or phony showmanship. He didn't seem greedy for their patronage. He never tried to entertain them with jokes or personal stories; rather, he listened appreciatively to their jokes and their personal stories. He never seemed to be trying to impress them—and, perversely, that impressed them.

He first impressed Carl Shapiro in the early 1960s by delivering better service than Shapiro was getting from a bigger Wall Street firm. Shapiro, born in 1913, was raised in an affluent Boston suburb and graduated from Boston University. In 1939 he and his father formed Kay Windsor Inc., which colonized a low-class niche in the garment industry—cheap cotton dresses—and utterly transformed it.

"When Kay Windsor was formed, cotton dresses and inexpensive housedresses were synonymous," a reporter for the *New York Times* noted in 1957. "And retailers would quickly dispense with the services of any buyer foolish enough to suggest that cotton dresses be sold throughout the year."

Kay Windsor helped change that, producing stylish year-round cotton dresses that became a wardrobe staple for the "working girls" and suburban housewives of the early postwar boom. A gifted salesman and hard-driving manager, Shapiro had taken the reins himself in the early 1950s, when his father retired. By the end of that decade, Kay Windsor was one of the largest dressmakers in the business, and Carl Shapiro was a very wealthy man. He became even richer when he sold Kay Windsor to a larger clothing company in 1970.

By then, he was already doing at least a little business with Madoff. According to Madoff, the connection was made through Madoff's high school friend and fellow broker Michael Lieberbaum, whose family was woven into the small patch of Wall Street that Madoff occupied in those days. Mike Lieberbaum's brother, Sheldon, worked for a larger broker-age firm, and Carl Shapiro was one of its clients, Madoff said in his first prison interview.

Shapiro "was interested in doing arbitrage, and they had a difficult time doing it" at Sheldon Lieberbaum's firm, Madoff recalled. Plagued by the paperwork delays that would soon engulf all of Wall Street, that firm was taking too long to convert convertible bonds into common stock, a basic step in many arbitrage strategies, Madoff explained. "I did it faster," he said.

After Madoff's arrest, Shapiro told a roughly similar version of the story. "In those days, it took three weeks to complete a sale," Shapiro said. "This kid stood in front of me and said, 'I can do it in three days.' And he did." By some accounts, he gave the young broker $100,000 to conduct arbitrage trades for him and was pleased with the results. The bond between them grew stronger.

When Shapiro ultimately retired from the garment industry, he devoted himself to philanthropy in Boston and entrusted even more of his assets to Madoff. Many people would later say he trusted Madoff "like a son," but their initial bond was clearly all business—he staked Bernie Madoff at the arbitrage table, and Madoff used that money to make more money. For the hugely successful Shapiro, it apparently was a simple equation: he trusted Madoff because Madoff delivered.

Norman F. Levy came into Madoff's orbit later and through a more convoluted path, but he ultimately became one of Madoff's closest friends and most faithful admirers. A year older than Shapiro, Levy graduated from DeWitt Clinton High School in the Bronx in 1931, just in time to see the New York economy plunge into the Great Depression. By 1934, after working as a clerk and door-to-door salesman, he landed at Cross

& Brown, one of the largest real estate brokerage firms in the country. A close family friend said Levy joked that he was "the first Jew" ever hired by the venerable firm, whose roots went back to 1910. According to one account, he was hired on a two-week trial. If so, he clearly passed: within two years, he had scraped together enough to pay $700 for a Midtown building that he sold seven years later for a $15,000 profit. By 1967 he was president of the firm and well on his way to becoming an extremely wealthy man.

By the mid-1970s, New York City was on the brink of bankruptcy, and its real estate market was reeling. Levy owned a number of premier commercial office buildings but needed to generate more cash flow, Madoff recalled. They met through a daisy chain that began with Madoff's father-in-law, Saul Alpern. A prominent Jewish leader and retired chemical industry entrepreneur named Maurice Sage, who had been a client of Alpern's accounting firm, knew a country club friend of Levy's named Arthur Schlichter, who made the introduction. "We met and hit it off," Madoff said. Levy opened an account with Madoff in 1975 and maintained it until his death in 2005.

Like Madoff, Levy was a self-made man—but, unlike Madoff, he was gregarious, a little raucous, and utterly unpretentious. Tall and robust, he lit up a room with his personality, and Madoff seemed to bask in the warmth. Levy became a familiar figure to Madoff's staff, who welcomed his visits. Levy, in turn, welcomed Madoff's willingness to manage his financial life so that Levy could focus on what he knew best: gilt-edged real estate.

In time, Madoff became far more than Levy's broker. He orchestrated elaborate vacations for Levy's enjoyment and managed his family foundation's assets. His link to Levy gave him credibility in banking circles, where Levy was a coveted client. Madoff was known at JPMorgan Chase as Levy's "close friend and trader." Within a decade of meeting Madoff, Levy had at least $180 million in his Madoff account; in the next dozen years, his balance would grow to $1.5 billion. In 2001, a stunning $35 billion would pour into Levy's account and back out again in that one twelve-month period.

The fourth and most mysterious member of the early Madoff quartet was a tall, balding lawyer and tax accountant named Jeffry Picower. Like Levy, Picower met Madoff through Saul Alpern, although the connection was far more direct. Michael Bienes, who went to work for Alpern's accounting firm in 1968, was married to Emily Picower, Jeffry's sister. According to several sources, Picower—who was four years younger than Bernie Madoff and just out of law school—visited the Alpern firm's suite frequently in those early years. Madoff recalled that Alpern was Picower's personal accountant back then, but he confirmed that they met through Bienes.

Picower's father was a Polish immigrant who worked in the millinery industry in New York and settled his young family in Long Beach, a small beachfront town on the south shore of Long Island. As a young man, Jeffry was fiercely intelligent; he graduated from Penn State in 1963 and by 1967 had earned an MBA from Columbia and a law degree from Brooklyn Law School. He was certified as a public accountant in 1971 and wound up at Laventhol & Horwath, a nationally known accounting firm.

He had a genius for making money in the stock market, a passion for privacy, and a willingness to take big risks in pursuit of big rewards. Sometimes he lost—as in 1976, when he invested more than $600,000 with a brassy and persuasive Broadway producer who promised whopping returns of up to 50 percent but who turned out to be running a Ponzi scheme on the side. More often, he won, even if his clients didn't. He helped market tax shelters based on computer leases in the 1970s, and, by the time some of his clients' tax write-offs were being challenged by the IRS, he had made enough to establish himself as a significant investor in the mergers and takeover deals that were starting to proliferate on Wall Street by the early 1980s.

Picower's adversaries in later corporate battles would remember him as hard-edged, aggressive, and highly litigious, a man who skirted the edge of market rules and fair play time and again. Those takeover battles would put billions of dollars into his pockets—and, ultimately, into his Madoff accounts.

Among the quartet of early Madoff customers, Picower stood out as the only one with whom Madoff seemed to feel ill at ease. In a written response to questions posed after Madoff's arrest, Jeffry Picower and his wife, Barbara, wrote that Picower's ties to Madoff "started out as a professional relationship," adding that they "did not establish a personal friendship until years later."

By the early 1980s, Madoff had added another coterie of clients to the Big Four: a small group of wealthy French investors who liked to dabble in arbitrage in the U.S. market. In his first prison interview, he said he first connected with these French clients through Maurice Sage, the same notable Jewish leader who played a role in his introduction to Norman Levy.

One of these influential clients was Jacques Amsellem, a French citizen who invested in the American market throughout the 1970s, most prominently by building up a big stake in the Shopwell supermarket chain at the end of the decade. Amsellem opened accounts with Madoff that remained active until his death in 1994 and were then passed along to his widow and his grandchildren.

Through Amsellem, Madoff met another important French client, Albert Igoin, a French industrialist and Spinoza scholar. Madoff recalled making his first trip to Paris in the early 1980s to meet with Igoin, who he said "loved the stock market" and wanted to do small-scale arbitrage in U.S. dollars. Igoin and his American-born wife took Madoff out to dinner "at some terrible Chinese restaurant," he said. "It was my first dinner in Paris and it was awful."

The relationship was worth a little heartburn. Although Igoin was at least thirty years older than Madoff, they liked each other immediately and developed a close relationship. Igoin had a remarkable résumé, having served briefly in a leftist French cabinet before moving on to run a major navigation company. By the time he met Madoff, however, he was working largely as an elite financial adviser and, like Levy in New York, he helped open the doors of French banks to Madoff—and those introductions would generate billions of dollars of cash for him in the decades to come.

The 1970s, which brought so many new opportunities to Bernie Madoff, were not kind to most of the small brokerage firms that had sprung up in the early 1960s. After a spate of brokerage bankruptcies, regulators focused on the insulated environment that had let such fragile firms flourish: officially, a world without price competition.

Customers were supposed to pay the same fixed commission for every share they bought or sold, whether they got good service or bad. Brokers were supposed to receive the same fixed commission for every share they traded, whether the order was for one hundred thousand shares of one stock or one thousand shares of a hundred stocks. The biggest customers could demand backroom price breaks, of course, but small investors couldn't. Nobody thought this arrangement was a good idea except the small, uncompetitive brokers it protected.

During the 1970s the SEC pushed the industry to accept greater price competition, and fixed commissions were abolished on May 1, 1975—known thereafter on the Street as May Day. The change doomed legions of shaky brokerage firms with too much elegant, expensive overhead and too little computing power and back-office manpower.

Still, some small firms, especially in the regional financial centers around the country, remained a reliable source of financial advice for countless small business owners and moderately affluent investors. As such, they also unwittingly helped pave the path to Bernie Madoff.

One regional brokerage firm that became a trusted conduit for Madoff investors was Engler & Budd in Minneapolis. Mendel "Mike" Engler founded the firm in 1961, and the relationship between his firm and Bernard L. Madoff Investment Securities represented an important step forward in the evolution of Madoff's secret money management scheme: trust by association.

Saul Alpern's early recruiting efforts were clearly aimed at people who wanted to invest with his brilliant son-in-law, even if they were unfamiliar with the arbitrage strategies he pursued. Avellino & Bienes inherited that cadre of trusting investors, who spread Madoff's fame through whispered word of mouth. But Mike Engler recruited investors who might never have heard of Madoff, but knew and trusted Engler himself. It became a familiar pattern. Initially, people invested because they trusted Bernie Madoff; ultimately, people invested because they trusted the person or institution that was the last link in the long chain that led to Madoff.

Mike Engler met Bernie Madoff not long after Peter Madoff joined the firm in 1969. As part of his early chores for his brother, Peter Madoff traveled around the country selling the firm's wholesale brokerage services to smaller regional firms. Engler's business partner liked Peter and agreed to shift the firm's business to Madoff.

Engler & Budd was a successful regional over-the-counter dealer at a time when the OTC dealer club was still very small. Mike Engler became active on industry committees and attended industry conferences, as did the Madoff brothers. Both families vacationed during the ski season in Aspen, where the Englers owned a condominium, and both had ties to the retirement enclaves of south Florida. Mike Engler and his wife came to enjoy socializing with Bernie and Ruth. "They really thought the world" of the Madoffs, Engler's son recalled.

Although naturally reserved, Madoff seemed to enjoy talking with Mike Engler, who was an outgoing, exuberant entrepreneur from a family of successful businessmen. His father had developed an early chain of local movie theaters. With other relatives, Engler himself had founded a liquor store, a boat business, and a real estate development company.

When Engler later sold his brokerage firm in 1986, Madoff invited him to sign on with the Madoff firm as an "investment counselor," supposedly because Madoff was opening his purely institutional money management business for the first time to wealthy individuals. It was at about this time that Engler first entrusted some of his own wealth to Madoff—it was seen as a golden opportunity to have "the dean of Wall Street" manage his money, his son said. "It never would have occurred to any of us to be suspicious—nobody questioned Bernie Madoff," he said.

Engler also was a member of Temple Israel in Minneapolis and the Oak Ridge Country Club in nearby Hopkins, both fixtures of affluent Jewish life in the Twin Cities. As the years went by, more and more of Engler's country club friends, temple acquaintances, and brokerage firm clients would become Madoff investors, attracted by steady but not spectacular returns and by the sterling local reputation of Mike Engler.

"I called it my 'steady Eddie' investment," one Minneapolis widow recalled. Her late husband had decided to invest with Madoff after his old friend Mike Engler made a low-key sales pitch in the living room of their Florida vacation home in the early 1990s. "He didn't go into much detail," she recalled. "He said it was considered a hedge fund" and the minimum investment was perhaps $1 million.

Unlike her husband, she was a fairly experienced investor—before they married, she had invested with Fidelity's famous Magellan fund during its golden years and managed her own portfolio of blue chips and bonds. She had never heard of Madoff but did some homework, reading a few newspaper articles about him and calling a wealthy couple she knew in Boston. She learned that the couple, whom she considered sophisticated investors, had been investing with Madoff for thirty years and that other businessmen she trusted—"a very smart accountant" in town, a Minneapolis shoe company owner—had checked Madoff out, satisfied themselves that he was honest, and handed some of their money to him to manage. All those people she trusted had been trusting Madoff for years. That was the clincher. She sent in her money.

∽

By the late 1970s, although rich clients such as Stanley Chais, Norman Levy, and Jeffry Picower still got their old-fashioned account statements on paper, Bernie Madoff was enhancing his firm's reputation for market innovation in some pretty expensive ways. He had become a member of the Cincinnati Stock Exchange, a trailblazing exchange that was the first to eliminate its trading floor entirely and rely only on electronic trading. He invested a substantial amount of his firm's money to help finance that transformation, helping the exchange become a showcase for the virtual marketplace of the future. He and Peter rotated onto the new exchange's board. Those positions—they were, after all, directors of a recognized regional stock exchange—added to Madoff's visibility with regulators.

In 1979, Bernie Madoff also became a member of the NASD committee that helped create an electronic system linking all the regional stock exchanges (including Cincinnati) with the New York Stock Exchange, so that customer orders could be routed seamlessly among them for the best price. At his own firm and in the industry at large, Madoff was defying the conventional wisdom and betting big money on the automation of the stock market. Some had given up the market for dead in the 1970s, but it was about to experience one of the most robust growth periods in its history.

It would be a worldwide stock boom, and he would be ready for it.

Madoff opened a London office, called Madoff Securities International Ltd. The falling of regulatory barriers all across Europe made an office in London logical. The new affiliate opened for business in February 1983, in Mayfair. It existed mostly to trade foreign securities and maintain foreign currency accounts for the home office, but Madoff recruited people prominent in local stock exchange circles as his executive staff, and in time he would put his brother and sons on the board.

He opened the new affiliate with the help of an investor and friend, Paul Konigsberg, an increasingly prominent New York City accountant. Within a few years, Konigsberg had followed in Saul Alpern's footsteps, setting up an investment account that gave clients of his accounting firm, Konigsberg Wolf, their own path to Madoff. It was a pattern that would be repeated time and again at other accounting firms in the years to come.

As the money flowed in during the 1970s and early 1980s—from wealthy individual clients, from Avellino & Bienes, from trusted professionals such as Paul Konigsberg and Mike Engler, and from the Chais feeder funds in Beverly Hills—Bernie Madoff began to live a little larger.

Around 1979, while still living in suburban Roslyn, the Madoffs bought a handsome weekend house on the water in Montauk, at the far eastern tip of Long Island. Well beyond the already-trendy Hamptons, Montauk was a quiet and almost rustic beachfront community in the late 1970s. Still, the weekend house on the ocean, with its sheltered pool and broad, sunny deck overlooking the dunes, was an impressive acquisition for a young brokerage firm owner in his early forties who had two sons to put through college.

Bernie Madoff was not a conventional financial executive—far from it. Other dads might commute to work on the Long Island railroad with briefcases balanced on their knees. But on any given morning in the 1970s, Madoff would drive from his split-level in Roslyn to Port Washington, on Long Island Sound, where a Cessna seaplane would be waiting.

He was part of a group of adventurous Wall Street executives, all living near Port Washington, who used the plane for their daily trip to Manhattan, sparing themselves the frustrations of the train (dubbed "The Silver Snail") or the bumper-to-bumper highway traffic. It wasn't all that uncommon in those days—the seaplane base was fairly busy—but it was a slightly swashbuckling arrangement that was sure to forge friendships among the four or five passengers who squeezed into the narrow cabin for the scenic twenty-minute trip toward the sunlit towers of Manhattan.

Besides giving Madoff an easier commute, the seaplane was good business. Some of his traveling companions on that commute became his customers, or introduced other customers to him. One of those fellows was a genial American Stock Exchange trader and Roslyn neighbor named Maurice J. Cohn, known among his friends as "Sonny," who lived just a few doors away from the Madoffs.

Beginning in 1985, Bernie Madoff and Sonny Cohn would share far more than a seaplane.

5

THE CASH SPIGOT

The commuter friendship that began on the Cessna seaplane in the 1970s had ripened into a business partnership by 1985, when Sonny Cohn and Bernie Madoff formed Cohmad Securities, a name crafted from the first three letters of their last names.

An engaging wisecracker seven years older than Madoff, Cohn had been a fixture among the traders on the American Stock Exchange and the Big Board for nearly a quarter century. He began his career at Salomon Brothers but soon joined the proud and clubby fraternity of Amex floor traders, who were a little dismissive of the still-scruffy OTC market where Bernie Madoff was getting established. But as neighbors in Roslyn, the two men became close friends, indulging in goofy stunts—one friend recalled their putting a bright red phone in the rear window of the chauffeured Cadillac they briefly shared for their morning commute, to mimic the nuclear "hot line" in the White House.

Cohn used to observe that Madoff "never had a losing day"; he always talked like a winner, even when his stocks were down.

In 1982, a year before Madoff opened his London office, Cohn's floor trading firm, Cohn, Delaire & Kaufman, was bought by a big London Stock Exchange trading firm, Akroyd & Smithers. For a while, Cohn stayed on as chairman and CEO. But in 1984 a British investment bank purchased Akroyd & Smithers, and Cohn's position began to seem largely honorary. He grew increasingly restless and wanted something new and not too demanding to do.

Madoff was already planning a big move uptown. After years at 110

Wall Street, a boxy black building near the South Street Seaport, he leased the eighteenth floor of 885 Third Avenue, the cutting-edge tower at the corner of East Fifty-third Street that quickly became known to New Yorkers as the Lipstick Building for its tubular shape. There would be space for the fifty or so employees of the Madoff firm, with room to spare. (In time, Madoff's operation would expand to the seventeenth and nineteenth floors as well.)

Cohmad was clearly born to be Sonny Cohn's second act. In many ways, the new brokerage firm was a throwback to the small lone-cowboy firms that galloped onto Wall Street in the early 1960s, when Madoff and Cohn were just starting out.

By the late 1980s those firms were largely extinct and their brokers had scattered—outsold and outclassed by larger firms that built retail networks across the country and knitted them together with increasingly complicated technology. Cohn's new firm was a place where refugees from a forgotten Wall Street could roll back the clock, revel in the camaraderie of trading by telephone, and schmooze with their customers over a bountiful lunch at P. J. Clarke's saloon or drinks at the historic Harmonie Club.

There was nothing high-tech about Cohmad; it promised "old-fashioned service" to its clientele. Within a few years, it would become a haven for older brokers looking for a place to hang their shingle; one broker was seventy-seven years old when he joined the firm in 1991.

Marcia Beth Cohn was an exception, of course. She was Sonny Cohn's daughter and still in her late twenties when she joined Cohmad in 1988, after six years at Cowen & Company, a small brokerage firm. She owned 25 percent of Cohmad, her father owned 48 percent, and Sonny's brother and a longtime employee each owned 1 percent.

The remaining 25 percent was lopsidedly split: 24 percent was shared by the Madoff brothers—15 percent for Bernie and 9 percent for Peter—and the final 1 percent was held by a tall, well-dressed Bostonian named Robert Martin Jaffe.

Bob Jaffe was a sociable, attractive man with a dandy's flair for fashion. He began his Wall Street career in 1969 at E.F. Hutton & Company, and in 1980 he moved to Cowen & Company, where he worked for several years with Marcia Cohn. More significantly, he was married to Ellen Shapiro, a daughter of one of Madoff's first and wealthiest clients, the multimillionaire Carl Shapiro. The rumor in Boston was that Shapiro had introduced Jaffe to his first client. Perhaps Bernie Madoff gave Jaffe a sliver of Cohmad in the same spirit: as a helpful gesture for an old friend's son-in-law.

Bob Jaffe was forty-five years old in 1989, when he opened an office for Cohmad in Boston, where the Shapiro family was established in local social and philanthropic circles. Jaffe had a discerning eye, but not a perceptive one. "He is someone who identifies the best restaurants by looking at who goes there" rather than by making his own assessment of the menu, one professional acquaintance said.

Within a few months of the new office opening, state securities regulators rapped Cohmad's knuckles for doing business in Massachusetts without being licensed there. Sonny Cohn agreed to comply with the rules and supervise his agents more carefully.

As this suggests, Cohmad was a rather casual expression of the brokerage business, a reflection of the less rigorous regulatory climate in which Sonny Cohn came of age—a time when insider trading was not yet a crime, disclosure requirements were few, and regulators were less attentive to the OTC market.

Madoff's staff took care of most of Cohmad's paperwork. It is not clear who made sure it complied with complex state and federal securities laws—indeed, it's not clear that anyone did, although subsequent lawsuits would claim that the firm's compliance officer was Peter Madoff's daughter, Shana. The lines between Cohmad and Madoff's much larger firm became fuzzy, in places almost invisible. Cohmad handled a small number of stock exchange orders for Madoff's firm and had several hundred clients with traditional brokerage accounts. But most of its small corps of brokers spent their time introducing eager people to Bernie Madoff.

Cohmad offered them access to the investing genius already whispered about in affluent circles—the man Carl Shapiro and Norman Levy trusted with their own money, the man other wealthy country club members and charity dinner guests wanted to trust with their money, too. Soon the compensation that brokers got for introducing new investors to Madoff was Cohmad's primary source of revenue, a fact that went unreported by Cohmad and unnoticed by regulators.

The compensation arrangement seemed oddly structured. Each broker's commission was based on how much cash the investor handed over to Bernie Madoff, not how big the investor's account balances were in future months and years. Once an investor had withdrawn all the cash originally invested, the broker's commission stopped—even if the account still showed paper profits in the millions. Regulators would claim that this Ponzi-like accounting was evidence that Cohmad was complicit in Madoff's fraud. But the Cohns later argued successfully in court that this arrangement simply reflected the fact that they were not managing the money and therefore did not get any credit for the profits Madoff supposedly produced.

By the time Cohmad was formed, Bernie Madoff's reported strategy for producing those profits was changing—a shift that had begun in 1980, when his biggest clients pressed him (in his recounting) to "offer them another form of trading that would produce long-term capital gains rather than the short-term capital gains of arbitrage." The tax shelters of the 1970s were cracking, income tax rates seemed high, and his wealthiest clients wanted to reduce their tax bills. He claimed that he offered them a new strategy: "a diversified portfolio of equities hedged as necessary" with various kinds of short sales.

In a letter from prison, Madoff insisted that he cautioned his clients that the stocks in their portfolios would have to be held long enough to qualify for the capital gains tax break and, "more importantly, that the stock market would have to go up during the holding period, which was certainly difficult to predict." Still, he said, "a number of the wealthy clients chose to do this strategy—the Levy, Picower, Chais and Shapiro families most importantly."

By this point, he continued, he was "doing a hedged type of portfolio trading for a French bank." He decided that "the French institutional clients would be an excellent counterparty for this strategy as well. I was already trading with them as a counterparty for some of my arbitrage trades."

Was any of this true? It is certainly true that, by this point, Madoff had established a trading relationship with an elite French firm called Banque Privée de Gestion Financière, or BPGF. One of its officers, Jean-Michel Cédille, had met Madoff through their mutual friend Albert Igoin. Madoff claimed to have been offered an ownership stake in the bank and to have sold it later at a substantial profit when the bank was merged into a larger French institution. With its records long dispersed and both Igoin and Cédille deceased, it is almost impossible to verify this element of Madoff's story, but he clearly had ties to the bank; its old phone number was in his computer files at the time of his arrest. And he had French clients with long-standing accounts, who showed up as victims in bankruptcy court documents.

He also had clients who wanted to use those accounts in the 1980s to evade the higher French taxes and currency controls that were imposed after the election of François Mitterrand's Socialist government in 1981, he said. "Everyone in France was concerned about Mitterrand," he explained in one prison interview. "He was nationalizing banks, they were worried about outright communism. . . . You couldn't take French francs out of the country—the only way to hedge the currency was to buy U.S. securities." With the French currency losing value, Madoff's clients wanted to move their wealth into U.S. dollars—and he helped them do that.

Some of these French clients were later caught in tax disputes with authorities in the United States and in France. But, at the time, Madoff earned their gratitude—and acquired a set of clients who were less concerned about keeping up with the market than they were about staying invested in U.S. dollars. As Madoff saw it, that made them the ideal "counterparties" for the new strategy he devised for his profit-hungry, tax-averse American investors.

Soon after Cohmad was set up in 1985, Madoff began to tell many of his investors that he was changing his investment approach in their accounts from classic riskless arbitrage trades to the complex strategy that he would still be claiming to use until the moment before his Ponzi scheme collapsed twenty years later.

His approach made even his most complicated arbitrage trades look simple. Some options traders called his new strategy a "bull spread." Madoff came to call it his "split-strike conversion strategy."

In its honest form, the strategy was empowered by the innovations in options trading that were pioneered in the financial markets of Chicago in the 1970s. A stock option is simply a contract that gives its buyer the right (the "option") to buy or sell that stock at a specific price for a specific period of time. Much less expensive than the actual stocks, options gave speculators a cheaper way to bet on rising prices—an option that allowed them to buy a stock for $10 a share was a winning bet if the stock rose to $20 a share before the option expired. They could exercise the option, buying the stock for $10 and immediately selling it for twice as much. Options also provided cautious investors a hedge against declining prices—an option to sell a stock for $10 a share locked in some profits if the stock declined below that price.

Options on specific stocks began to trade freely on organized exchanges in the 1970s, but within a few years, novel option products were developed that covered entire portfolios of stocks, such as the stocks in the Standard & Poor's 500 index. But the concept was still the same: options provided a cheaper way to profit if the index went up and could cushion losses if the index went down.

So Madoff's new strategy was to buy a broad portfolio of stocks—one broad enough to perform roughly in step with the overall blue-chip market—and to use options to hedge against future price declines. The cost of the options would reduce his profits a bit, but the options would also reduce his losses. The strategy required a deep, liquid market for the options used to hedge the portfolio, but as options trading grew more popular in the 1980s, this did not seem to be a meaningful constraint.

Like his arbitrage strategies, this investment approach had some credibility on the Street. In December 1977 a public mutual fund called the Gateway fund was set up in Cincinnati to pursue roughly the same strategy. Its early track record was quite impressive but highly volatile. Between 1977 and the period during which Madoff supposedly adopted a similar strategy, its monthly returns bounced around from a loss of 7.7 percent in October 1978 to a gain of 7.5 percent in August 1982. Beginning in 1983, its twelve-month returns were formidable, if still unpredictable; in some twelve-month periods during the early 1980s, its gains exceeded 20 percent. This would no doubt explain why the strategy looked like a winner to Madoff, and if he achieved comparable returns he certainly would keep his investors happy.

Unfortunately, the Gateway fund remained too small and obscure to catch the attention of Madoff's later investors, who otherwise might have noticed that his pursuit of the same strategy was producing remarkably less erratic results.

Sonny Cohn explained the new strategy to a prospective customer a half-dozen years later, calling it "a simplistic and, most important, a very conservative strategy." After Madoff's arrest, Cohn's lawyers would insist that he had had complete faith in what he wrote—he was certain Madoff was pursuing a conservative strategy whose very consistency was proof that he was executing it superlatively well. After all, Cohn had bet his firm, much of his wealth, his daughter's future career, and his long Wall Street reputation on his trust in his old friend Bernie Madoff.

ഗ

Besides marking a change in Madoff's professed investment strategy, the mid-1980s also saw a shift in the operations of his old standby investors, Frank Avellino and Michael Bienes, who had inherited Saul Alpern's accounting practice and the little "friends and family" assortment of Madoff investors.

By 1983 their interest in their accounting business had dried up after a scorching courtroom battle over some audits they had done for a small leather importing company in Lower Manhattan back in the late 1970s. The appeals dragged on through 1984, and they consistently won. But Bienes later said the litigation was an enormous expense and distraction.

Moreover, Frank Avellino felt utterly burned out. He suffered from high blood pressure and heart problems. He couldn't endure the stress of juggling the litigation and the accounting work, so he and Bienes decided to shut down their accounting practice in 1983 and devote themselves exclusively to their Madoff business—which, as far as they knew, was the only way individual investors could tap into the money-making genius of Bernie Madoff, according to Bienes.

Soon they had expanded far beyond Saul Alpern's "friends and family," which had comprised fewer than a hundred relatively modest accounts, and now had more than a thousand customers with account balances nudging toward $100 million.

Those thousands of investors encompassed a hidden cottage industry of "subcontractors," longtime investors who exploited their blessed access to Avellino & Bienes to make a little extra on the side. They accepted money from their own "friends and families," pooled it, and invested it with Avellino & Bienes. These subcontractors would then divide the profits pro rata—perhaps minus a few dollars in fees. There is no way of knowing how many people privately became self-employed subcontractors for the accounting firm, but the numbers were certainly substantial. Some of them even set up their own financial advisory businesses on the strength of their link to Madoff.

Frank Avellino and Michael Bienes didn't worry about this. They had prospered beyond their wildest imagination from their own long association with Madoff. They'd purchased trophy homes, indulged in expensive hobbies such as art collecting, and become coveted patrons among the charities and cultural institutions in their communities.

But they were still remarkably casual about maintaining the paperwork for their enormous investment business. Their four-person staff in New York kept track of accounts—a customer's file typically consisted of no more than four sheets of paper—and handled queries from the public. The two partners assembled the checks coming in, sent the money to Madoff, and withdrew money from their account when investors requested disbursements. Every month they received account statements from Madoff's firm; every quarter they got a computer printout from a data processing company listing all the investors who had contributed to those accounts and how much each was owed.

That was all there was to it. No overhead, no complications, no red tape.

In that, at least, Frank Avellino and Michael Bienes were perfectly in step with the mood of the market and the agenda of regulators in the 1980s.

With the nation feeling bruised and cranky from a decade of plunging stock prices, rocketing gasoline prices, manipulated silver prices, rising inflation rates, and lagging employment, President Ronald Reagan came into office in January 1981 with a sunny determination to hack away at what he saw as generations of needless government regulation.

His deregulatory ambitions would firmly push back against a formidable enforcement appetite at the Securities and Exchange Commission. Indeed, the steady advance of that deregulatory philosophy would ultimately combine with weak management and inadequate budgets to leave the once-respected SEC too timid and unimaginative to cope with a widening brushfire of fraud over the next twenty-five years, including the near-fatal firestorm called Bernie Madoff.

After slouching through several decades, the commission had pulled up its socks in the 1970s and gotten serious about tackling the revolutionary changes on its turf, from options trading to insider trading. Congress, tacitly acknowledging that it had starved the commission for a decade, began providing an almost adequate budget. By the end of the 1970s the agency had stepped up its supervision of the nation's burgeoning mutual fund industry, pushed for tougher industry supervision of brokers, and developed new rules to govern hostile takeovers. Its work was challenging and interesting, and many bright, ambitious lawyers wanted to be part of it.

Some of the brightest and most ambitious wanted to work for the SEC's fabled Enforcement Division director, Stanley Sporkin, a fiercely committed public servant who had been at the commission for twenty years and had zero interest in using the job as a stepping-stone to a lucrative law firm partnership. Young staff lawyers prayed for a chance to work with him, and blessed their luck if they landed one of the tough, innovative cases that drew his attention.

In 1981, Sporkin was moved out of the SEC by President Reagan, who also tapped John Shad, a lifelong veteran of Wall Street, as the commission's new chairman. Shad was less hostile to the SEC's mission than the advocates of deregulation had hoped, balking at the deep budget cuts demanded by the new administration. But although he knew the Street had its black hats, he believed firmly that it "was essentially an honest place," fully capable of policing itself.

This was transparently not true. The industry-financed watchdogs at the NASD, the first-line regulators responsible for policing brokers such as Bernie Madoff, had an undistinguished record at best. Part of the impetus for the securities law amendments adopted in 1975 had been a general view in Congress that the NASD had fallen down on its part of the regulatory job. But Congress had no power to increase the NASD's resources or its appetite for regulation, and it continued to be a weak sister to the SEC.

On balance, Shad's tenure produced "a competent but cautious commission," one historian concluded. Those bright and ambitious staff lawyers looking for more than mere competence and caution gradually began to lower their expectations—or simply to leave. Within a decade,

Madoff would have his huge Ponzi scheme up and running and would be very grateful for their departure.

In the early Reagan years, Bernie Madoff seemed to be on a roll. The bull market born in August 1982 had sent stock prices soaring, and his firm's profits were sailing up with them. True, it was an increasingly rocky ride. Wall Street didn't mind the rising volatility, but many investors did—and more of them fled the volatile market and found their way to the steady returns Madoff offered. While there are no reliable records of those returns in the 1980s, a host of longtime Madoff investors fondly recalled the comforting consistency. They were not making as much money as other investors in that roaring bull market, but they were not riding on a roller coaster either.

As the decade neared its midpoint, Madoff's brokerage firm had a reported net worth of more than $18 million, up from $5.4 million just two years earlier; its capital reserves had more than doubled in the same period, to $7.5 million, which put it in the top-100 list of the Securities Industry Association in 1985. That same year, Madoff was elected to the first of four consecutive terms on the NASD's Board of Governors. This was a notable achievement as well. He also joined the board's international committee; he was one of the few small-firm representatives who had a foreign office. Clearly he relished the prestige; he served five terms on the panel. His opinions were sought on issues usually considered to be the exclusive domain of much larger brokerage houses.

By this time the bull market had cooled a little, but it soon got back on track as the country grew increasingly confident about the tax cuts and deregulatory agenda in Washington. Volume was skyrocketing on the electronic NASDAQ market, where the Madoff firm had become a significant market maker, standing ready to buy or sell hundreds of securities and thereby helping to maintain a liquid market for those shares. The NASDAQ, resisted by so many on the Street, had proved itself over the past decade by enlisting an increasing number of active traders and attracting a growing number of company listings and customer orders.

To mark all those achievements, Madoff awarded himself the time-honored Manhattan trophy: luxury real estate. In 1984 the Madoffs purchased a two-story penthouse in a classic prewar apartment building on East Sixty-fourth Street at Lexington Avenue. While not in some historically elite enclave like upper Fifth Avenue or Sutton Place, the Federal-style building had been built in the late 1920s and had a quiet prestige. The unit reportedly had been decorated by Angelo Donghia, a prominent Manhattan interior designer whose clients included newsmakers such as Donald Trump, Barbara Walters, and Ralph Lauren. Ruth Madoff made some minor renovations—chiefly customizing some closets and adding a greenhouse extension to link the spacious kitchen to the broad encircling terrace. It was a tastefully decorated and grandly comfortable apartment, and it marked a significant step up for the Madoffs, formerly of Laurelton, Queens, by way of Roslyn, Long Island.

In a few years, the Madoff firm acquired a ritzier address of its own, with its move in 1987 to the Lipstick Building. That relocation was partly organized by a young employee named Frank DiPascali. The move was the first of a series of ultimately devastating chores he would handle for his boss over the next two decades.

DiPascali had bounced around the Madoff firm for a decade. He had arrived straight out of high school in Queens in 1975, at the recommendation of Annette Bongiorno, a woman who was originally hired as a receptionist but who became a mainstay of Madoff's account administration staff, handling some of his most important client accounts. Bongiorno knew DiPascali from the neighborhood—like him, she started working for Madoff right out of high school—and she passed his name along to Daniel Bonventre, the firm's director of operations.

DiPascali initially worked as a research clerk for Peter Madoff. He claimed that he worked after that as an options trader, but he did not get his industry license to trade options until 1986. Mostly he did chores for Bernie Madoff, whom he increasingly considered his mentor and tutor. Madoff put him in charge of overseeing the installation of the technology platform at the new Lipstick Building offices, and DiPascali apparently handled the job splendidly.

To know exactly what else DiPascali did for Madoff in that transition, we would have to know exactly when the Ponzi scheme began—the middle to end of the 1980s seems like a distinct possibility. But clearly DiPascali forged a bond of unquestioned loyalty to Bernie Madoff and, by his own account, it was boosted by the excitement of being put in charge of the move uptown.

These years also saw Madoff develop connections at a number of large Wall Street houses, mutual fund companies, and other financial institutions. He was handling an increasing share of orders from professional investors, especially for stocks normally traded on the New York Stock Exchange—the so-called "third market" business that Peter had so presciently encouraged him to develop. His firm's net worth grew from about $18 million in 1985 to nearly $60 million at the end of the decade, and its capital reserves grew from just under $8 million to more than $43 million over the same period. Madoff's early entry into the London market was paying off, too. Many foreign stock prices were climbing at rates that made the domestic blue chips look anemic, and Bernie Madoff became a go-to figure for the industry press when international issues arose.

In 1986, Madoff got the sort of accolade everyone on Wall Street noticed: he was included in *Financial World* magazine's list of the one hundred highest-paid executives on the Street. According to the magazine, he had earned $6 million the previous year. "Madoff's sole proprietorship, founded 26 years ago, is involved in brokerage, venture capital and arbitrage," the magazine reported. "Obscure outside investment banking circles, the 48-year-old Madoff doesn't seek much publicity."

Even if the general public still considered Bernie Madoff obscure, his influence in industry circles was beginning to outstrip the relatively modest size of his family firm—even though it seemed to be growing exponentially. Its status as a "family firm" was reinforced when Mark Madoff, Bernie's older son, who had graduated in 1986 from the University of Michigan with a degree in economics, went to work for his father. By June 1987, Mark was a licensed broker at Bernard L. Madoff Investment Securities, a firm he could reasonably expect to inherit someday. Two years later, his younger brother, Andrew, fresh out of the University of Pennsylvania's Wharton School, would also get his license and come on board.

The year 1987 was quite a time to launch a career in the securities industry, as Mark Madoff soon discovered. When he got his license in the summer, market makers at the firm were trying to adjust to a jittery new normal. Waves of institutional buying and selling would suddenly hit scores of major Big Board stocks, the ones that Madoff's third-market traders handled. The orders were generated by computer programs automatically carrying out complex hedging strategies—even more complex than his own "split-strike conversion" strategy. Between January and July 1987, the market climbed almost straight up—the S&P 500 gained more than 30 percent in just seven months. It stumbled in the remaining months of the summer—an overdue correction, analysts said—but it still eked out a gain for the first nine months of the year.

Then came Black Monday, October 19, 1987, when the bottom simply fell out. A record-cracking 600 million shares were traded on the Big Board that day, as the Dow Jones Industrial Average plummeted 508 points—a 22.6 percent fall, more than twice the damage inflicted on the worst day of the historic 1929 crash. The S&P 500 dropped almost as far, just as fast.

The NASDAQ index fell only half as much—because the entire NASDAQ market fell apart instead. There were widespread complaints that OTC brokers were not answering their phones. The OTC market was "in shambles," according to one account, as countless customer sell orders simply were not being executed. "This added to the confusion and panic in the markets," the General Accounting Office later concluded.

Black Monday was the day investors learned that the NASD did not require its "market-making" dealers actually to maintain a continuous market in the over-the-counter stocks they traded, as the traditional stock exchanges did. Many of the smaller market makers were losing ruinous amounts of money and could not keep buying shares that they could sell only at a loss, if they could sell them at all. Instead, they limped to the sidelines. The NASD's rules allowed them to stop trading. For many, the alternative was bankruptcy.

More troubling, the trading technology that NASDAQ had touted as the face of the future had been utterly unequal to the pressures of this extraordinary day. Traders feared that the bids shown on computer trading screens were unreliable and out of date, and they were right. Even large firms refused to trade blind, and by the next day the over-the-counter market was blasted by the storm that hit the traditional exchanges on Black Monday. The damage prompted a senior NASDAQ staff member to tell the *Wall Street Journal*, "We're scared. Of course we're scared. We're looking at conditions in the marketplace that are indescribable; gigantic losses, it's staggering." It seemed that the much-ballyhooed market of the future—one in which Bernie Madoff had made his reputation—had utterly and unexpectedly failed.

The Madoff firm, dealing as a wholesaler for largely institutional clients, was buffered from the worst of the tsunami of panicky retail orders. With computer networks that could handle large volume at state-of-the-art speed, it made it through the storm. Mike Engler, Madoff's friend and associate in Minneapolis, would tell his son later that the Madoff firm actually made money for itself and its clients in these bleak days by using options to short the markets. And the Madoff firm was praised by regulators for its solid performance during Black Monday, when so many market makers were falling away.

The reality was different. The market crash had profoundly shaken the confidence of some of Madoff's largest clients. Men he thought he could count on to keep their portfolios intact and leave their wealth in his hands—men such as Carl Shapiro and Jeffry Picower—suddenly began to cash in their paper profits and withdraw their money. "They were worried all the gains they had would disappear in the years just after 1987," Madoff said in his first prison interview.

Madoff estimated that his investment accounts totaled about $5 billion at the time of the crash. But he claimed that much of this wealth was tied up in his complex hedging strategies—that he could not fully repay his big American clients without cashing out the French counterparties, who were expecting to stay invested in U.S. dollars. If he honored the withdrawal demands, he risked losing his French connections; if he didn't, he would lose his longtime American investors.

Those longtime investors grew even more nervous after the "minicrash" that hit almost exactly two years after the 1987 meltdown. Their withdrawal demands increased, and although Madoff acknowledged "there was nothing I could have sued them over," he was furious.

"Part of the agreement I had with them was that the profits would be reinvested, not withdrawn. And they were the only ones who didn't abide by that. They changed the deal on me," he said in the first prison interview. "I was hung out to dry."

Madoff's anger strongly suggests that the protracted cash crisis that began after the 1987 crash was real, even if his explanation for it raises more questions than it answers. His strategy involved big blue-chip stocks; even in the rocky post-crash markets he should have been able to liquidate a legitimate blue-chip portfolio, albeit for less than its pre-crash value. The Gateway fund had a losing year after the 1987 crash, too, but it went on to report only seven losing months between October 1988 and the end of 1992—why couldn't Madoff achieve the same results with the same strategy? Had he lied to his clients about hedging their accounts against losses? Or, as he suggested in a subsequent letter, had he negotiated another investment "deal" with these big clients, one that bore no resemblance to the "split-strike conversion" strategy he was supposedly using?

Madoff acknowledged that he spent much of the 1980s actively arranging a growing volume of complicated "synthetic" trades to help his biggest clients—including Norman Levy and Jeffry Picower—avoid income taxes on their short-term stock profits. He provided few clear details of these transactions, except to say that they were put in place with the expectation that they would be rolled over year after year. These tax-avoidance trades were not prohibited by law until 1997, but they fell close to the line, as Madoff would grudgingly acknowledge later. "I felt they weren't sham transactions . . . ," he said, "but they became more elaborate in their strategy. At worst, it was a gray area."

Were these complex tax-avoidance trades harder to unwind without enormous losses? Or did Madoff simply guarantee that these old stalwarts would not incur losses if they stuck with him, assuming he could eventually come out ahead if they maintained their positions and did not withdraw their profits on demand? Madoff may never give a straight answer to these questions, but he is clear about the consequences of this crisis.

"Before I realized it, I was in the hole for a few billion dollars," he acknowledged in his first prison interview. This didn't happen overnight—it started happening at least by 1988, and it must have involved enormous sums to have reached that level by 1992.

Clearly the complex portfolios and cash pressures that would mark his Ponzi scheme were starting to take shape, even though Madoff insisted his Ponzi scheme had not yet begun and there is evidence that at least a few trades took place in the accounts of some favored long-term clients during these years.

Of course, this is the story "according to Madoff," possibly the least reliable source in history. So it might be true that, years before the 1987 crash, he was already robbing Peter to pay Paul—robbing the Avellino & Bienes accounts, perhaps, to pay Chais and Picower, Levy and Shapiro. He has consistently denied this, and so far there has been no evidence to the contrary in the public record. But he did not deny that the roots of his Ponzi scheme were planted in the cash demands he faced following the 1987 crash—and, after all, even if his Ponzi scheme was already up and running, those unexpected withdrawals after the crash would have pushed him to the wall.

Bernie Madoff may have been squirming behind closed doors, but to the outside world, he emerged from the crash as a star of the OTC world. He was still a member of the NASD Board of Governors, and he now became an influential voice in putting NASDAQ back together over the next three years.

Apart from the damage from the crash, the NASDAQ market was also struggling with the consequences of the NASD's flabby discipline—shortcomings that the less adventurous SEC under John Shad repeatedly failed to address. Discipline for infractions was limp and late, to the frustration of regulators and irate customers. For all its technological glitter, the young market was still an adolescent, unruly and resistant to increased supervision. Indeed, one must wonder if Madoff's firsthand awareness of the NASD's failings as a regulator encouraged him to think he could get away with his Ponzi scheme long enough to work his way out of the losses he was incurring.

Around this time, Madoff was plowing capital into his firm's equipment and software so that it could handle automated orders faster, pressing his competition to keep up. In 1983, Peter had led the firm's adoption of new customized software to run an in-house automated order system. When it was completed after the 1987 crash, it would set a new standard for speed in handling customer orders.

After the crash, Madoff continued to invest in the Cincinnati Stock Exchange—again, a surprisingly big expense for the firm—which helped that venerable regional exchange conduct all its business electronically.

When the NASD introduced predawn trading at the end of the decade, the Madoff firm and a handful of others were already there—they had invested in the staff necessary to do after-hours trading in the evenings and through the night.

In 1990, further enhancing his growing reputation with the industry and its regulators, Bernie Madoff became the chairman of the NASDAQ market. His back-office work on the trading committees and his own firm's initiatives on the technology frontier were more significant in shaping NASDAQ than his three one-year terms as its chairman, but the position was a pretty good soapbox. He would need it in the battle that would define Bernie Madoff for many veterans of Wall Street's trading community—the battle over his practice, introduced in 1988, of paying retail brokerage firms a few pennies per share to steer their customers' orders to him.

He called those pennies "payments for order flow" and "rebates." The exchanges that had traditionally gotten those orders, chiefly the New York Stock Exchange, called the payments "bribery, pure and simple" and "kickbacks." They fought fiercely to have the practice declared illegal, but they ultimately lost the battle with regulators after the firms taking Bernie's pennies were found to be getting faster and cheaper execution of their orders than on the Big Board. Indeed, by the early 1990s, more than 5 percent of all the trades in stocks listed on the Big Board would actually occur inside Bernie Madoff's computers, untouched by human hands. One scholarly market study observed that "although the Madoff firm isn't technically a stock exchange, it functions as a de facto surrogate for the New York Stock Exchange."

Madoff's practice of paying for order flow put him on the wrong side of a lot of powerful people on Wall Street, many of whom had access to back-office sources of information about him and his firm. Apparently, none of his hostile and prominent critics found any trace of a hidden Ponzi scheme—if they had, they certainly would have used it to discredit and destroy him in this bitter battle over his rebate practices.

Their failure to find it, however, may not mean that the scheme had not yet begun; it may simply mean that Madoff had planted the first seeds of his Ponzi scheme in one of the least visible and least regulated fields in the financial landscape: offshore hedge funds.

By the late 1980s, Madoff was playing on a much bigger social stage, one that would enhance his reputation among a host of generous donors and charitable institutions—many of which would later become his clients and, ultimately, his victims.

On paper, all of his big clients seemed to be getting rich—only Madoff knew how precarious his finances were. By one popular measure, the stock market had climbed more than 17 percent a year between the birth of the bull market in August 1982 and the end of 1989. And in the circles he now frequented, rich people were supposed to be generous people. So, inevitably, Madoff became an increasingly active donor, giving to the pet charities of favored or coveted clients, buying tickets to the right benefit dinners, meeting the right people.

In 1980s Manhattan, the "right people" included Howard Squadron, a prominent New York lawyer with a finger in countless political and cultural pies—and a man who would unwittingly be one of the first to steer important Jewish charities into Madoff's orbit. His relationship with Madoff would become an increasingly familiar pattern within New York legal and accounting circles.

Squadron had once been the boy wonder of the New York legal world. In 1947, barely twenty years old, he collected both a bachelor's degree in history and a law degree from Columbia University. Besides being a very smart man, he became a very well-connected one. He spent two years as a staff counsel at the American Jewish Congress and would later become the organization's president. The American Jewish Congress was a melting pot for wealthy donors to Jewish causes and institutions, and it was there that Squadron first met Bernie Madoff.

A tireless recruit on numerous educational and cultural boards, Squadron was instrumental in the rescue of the New York City Center, an important cultural institution. He chaired the City Center board for nearly a quarter century and, along the way, enlisted Madoff's support. In time, important people at the American Jewish Congress and City Center would become clients of Squadron's good friend Bernie Madoff, and Madoff himself would join the City Center board—where his fellow board members would include Squadron's wife and a member of the Wilpon family, which owned the New York Mets.

When Squadron's firm landed Rupert Murdoch's News Corporation as a client, Howard Squadron became very rich. He would invest a good deal of his wealth with Bernie Madoff and would introduce clients and friends to him as well.

Lawyers at several New York City firms set up formal partnerships so their clients could invest with Madoff. The same pattern developed at prominent accounting firms, such as Konigsberg Wolf and Stanley Chais's accountants, Halpern & Mantovani in Los Angeles, both of which formed conduit accounts through which their clients could invest indirectly with Madoff. Even Friehling & Horowitz, the small accounting firm that handled Madoff's brokerage firm audits, became a portal for others to invest with him.

It was in these bull market days of the 1980s that a former SEC lawyer named Jeffrey Tucker decided to leave the law firm he'd formed and set up an options trading fund with one of his clients. That client shared Midtown office space with a handsome former banker named Walter Noel Jr., who was trying to build his own money management business by relying on his affluent connections and those of his Brazilian wife. Noel thought Tucker's new fund might have promise for his foreign investors. "Walter was very impressed with their trading—not just the strategies but the returns," a contemporary recalled.

Sometime in 1989, Tucker parted company with his former client and began working exclusively with Noel to put the finishing touches on a new fund to be called Fairfield Greenwich. At about this time, Tucker's father-in-law, a retired knitwear manufacturer, suggested that Tucker and Noel check out a brilliant money manager he knew: Bernie Madoff.

What was it about Madoff that made all these smart, analytical people trust him so much, so easily, for so long? Impressions gathered from personal experience with Madoff and from interviews with dozens of people who knew him provide a few clues. Unlike so many successful con artists, Madoff was never showy or brash, never overtly "charismatic." Instead, without saying a word, he seemed to create a quiet but intense magnetic field that drew people to him, as if he were true north, or the calm eye of the storm. One associate called it "an aura." Like a gifted actor, he drew one's attention simply by stepping onstage, by entering a room.

He wore his expertise casually—"he had the decoder ring," one former regulator recalled—and he seemed seductively unflappable in times that felt messy, chaotic, and scary to everyone else. He inspired confidence and made people feel safe. Another close associate recalled Madoff's cool smile during the almost weekly bomb scares at the Lipstick Building that followed the terrorist attacks in 2001; he was always the last one out of the office, ushering his nervous charges down the stairways. Like the calm-voiced pilot in the cockpit or the nightmare-soothing father at the bedside, he simply made it seem as if everything were under control, that everything would be fine. Those close to him knew he could be angry, pushy, controlling, cutting, and rude, but even then he conveyed the reassuring toughness of a no-nonsense drill sergeant who never panicked or lost his grip, who drove his men hard but brought them all back alive.

Whatever the formula for Madoff's fatal charm, his meeting with Tucker and Noel must have been encouraging. In the middle of the summer of 1989, they invested $1.5 million with him, money they'd raised through a vehicle they later called the Fairfield International fund. Six months later, they put another $1 million into Madoff's hands. By November 1990, they were ready to market their new $4 million Fairfield Sentry fund and let the world in on their success with Madoff—almost literally "the world," as it turned out.

This is the period that generates the sharpest questions about the origins of Madoff's crime. Clearly his financial circumstances underwent a sharp change in the aftermath of the 1987 crash, pressuring him in ways that may have pushed him from the gray areas of tax games and currency flight into a full-scale Ponzi scheme. Absolute certainty is impossible—unless and until he and his accomplices come clean or new documentary evidence can be dug out of the rubble of his business records or those of the people who dealt with him. But reasonable conjecture is possible, and it ultimately focuses on these pivotal years in the last half of the gilded 1980s.

The conditions for a Ponzi scheme were all in place. Besides his new connection with Tucker and Noel, Madoff had caught the attention of a few other young offshore hedge funds. Riding the first wave of widening interest in hedge funds, these funds all started sending him large and increasing amounts of cash. The business taken over by Avellino & Bienes—which probably had only a few dozen customers in the 1960s and which Madoff said was still "not much of a business" by the late

1970s—hit an enormous growth spurt after 1983, driving more cash into his hands. At the same time, the cash demands from some of his biggest clients after the 1987 market crash put a great strain on his liquidity.

Those big clients "were very instrumental in creating my problems" because they "failed to honor their agreements," he wrote in an e-mail from prison. He continued, "I'm sure you wonder how I could be so gullible. I guess I couldn't face the fact that as close friends, I couldn't trust them."

He obviously saw how ironic it was for him, of all people, to complain about being betrayed by close friends. "I'm sure some of my other friends wonder how I did what I did to them," he went on. "There was no justification for this. The difference I guess is that I thought I would get out of my problem and I had made so much money for them in the past with legitimate trading."

He added, "None of this changes the timing I claim the bogus trading started."

By his own admission, however, Madoff was facing big and unwelcome cash demands at just the moment when the cash spigot was turning on in force. It was a tempting bit of timing, and one that supports the conclusion that, at the latest, his Ponzi scheme started in the years right after the 1987 crash, using the money from his new investors to finance the withdrawals by his older ones.

He insisted later that this was not true, that these rivers of new cash did not tempt him to cheat—at least, not until a few years later.

6

WHAT THEY WANTED
TO BELIEVE

As the 1990s began, Bernie Madoff was running a legitimate and apparently successful brokerage firm, with 120 employees and profits approaching $100 million a year. His firm was responsible for a remarkable 10 percent of the total daily trading volume in Big Board stocks and was handling 350,000 trades a day for larger Wall Street retail brokerage firms and giant mutual funds. As much as his rivals at the stock exchanges hated his practice of paying firms a small rebate for sending him their customer orders, academic studies showed that he still executed those orders at least as fast as anyone, and at prices that were as good as or better than customers could have found elsewhere. His "order execution" prowess impressed regulators and enhanced his firm's reputation. His sons were developing a small propriety trading operation that made investments for his firm's own account, and his firm's software systems were considered among the best on the Street.

Behind closed doors, however, he was also running an immensely larger money management business, one that regulators knew nothing about. This hidden investment advisory operation was supposedly generating commission income for his firm and steady returns for investors whose accounts now totaled at least $8 billion. These included private investors such as Norman Levy, Jeffry Picower, and Carl Shapiro; feeder funds such as those run by Stanley Chais and Walter Noel; "introducers" such as Mike Engler and the brokers at Cohmad; and, of course, the legions of small investors whose money resided in a few large accounts labeled "Avellino & Bienes."

Madoff grew increasingly careful about concealing how wide and deep the river of cash flowing into his investment advisory business had become. He admonished his feeder fund sponsors to keep quiet about who actually managed their money; he cautioned private clients not to talk about how much business they did with him—or even that they did business with him at all. His caution reflected the fact that his "split-strike conversion" strategy, like the arbitrage strategy it replaced, faced inflexible size constraints. Only so many shares of the blue-chip stocks supposedly in his portfolio were traded at one time, and the number of shares traded was reported every day. Only so many options were traded on the public exchanges in Chicago, and the volume of those trades was reported daily, too.

So a legitimate "split-strike conversion" strategy could not grow endlessly large. The bigger Madoff got, the harder it would be for savvy investors to believe that he was producing an honest profit. At some point, there simply wouldn't be enough options trading in the public or private markets to hedge the amount of stock he would have been buying, and there would have been little chance he could really buy and sell stocks on the scale required without shoving the markets up and down in very visible ways.

Still, his whole aura of success as an investment manager was that he never failed to deliver the returns his investors expected. He had brought them profitably through all the bad times—the market's tumble in 1962, the doldrums of the 1970s, even the 1987 crash and its rocky aftermath. No one knew that he had borrowed money from Saul Alpern to replenish his customers' accounts in his early years, and no one knew that he had been squeezed by a rash of withdrawals in the late 1980s. All his clients knew was that he offered steady returns even in volatile times—and they all wanted to invest more money with him.

It was in this setting, he says, that his Ponzi scheme began. As long as most of his clients left their balances intact, "rolling over" their reported profits and making few if any withdrawals, he could pay out the occasional disbursement from the flood of new money coming in.

It is the classic genesis of a Ponzi scheme on Wall Street. A money manager falls short of cash to cover some expense or placate some customer or deliver on some promise, and he steals a little money from client accounts. The rationale is always that he will be able to pay off his theft before it is detected. Perhaps this occasionally happens—those are the Ponzi schemes we never learn about. More typically, the sum of stolen money grows much faster than the honest profits do, and the Ponzi scheme rolls on toward certain destruction.

According to Madoff, this is what happened to him, although he disputes the timing. He got into a hole—possibly before 1980, more likely by the mid-1980s, but certainly by 1992—and he just couldn't get out again. His investment advisory business became a vast game of musical chairs. The only way he could hide the fact that there weren't enough chairs left for all his clients was to keep the music going for as long as he could.

∞

The music almost stopped in the summer of 1992. In early June, a pair of skeptical investors had sent two documents to the New York office of the Securities and Exchange Commission describing an attractive investment scheme that made them uneasy. One was a fact sheet about the "King Arthur Account." The two-page document certainly made the investment sound appealing. "This is a safe fund with no risk of capital paying high income," it said. The account yielded 13.5 percent a year, paid quarterly—14 percent for investments of $2 million or more.

It's no wonder the two prospective investors were skeptical: those rates were more than three times the interest rates available in safe "no-risk" certificates of deposit at their banks. And they were notably higher than the gains produced by the much riskier S&P 500 stock index over the previous year—which were about 8 percent without counting reinvested dividends, about 11 percent with dividends included. According to the fact sheet, these remarkable returns were generated through "riskless trading" in arbitrage accounts that the sponsors, Avellino & Bienes, maintained with a "wholesale dealer" in New York who traded in high-volume Big Board stocks. (The reference to arbitrage is curious; Madoff was already telling other investors he was using the "split-strike conversion" strategy—and, indeed, the small Gateway fund had been producing legitimate gains from that strategy in recent years that matched or exceeded the King Arthur fund's promises. But no one could honestly have called it a "no risk" investment.) The fact sheet was on the letterhead of a financial adviser in San Francisco and was probably written around 1989.

The second item supplied to the SEC was a brief no-nonsense letter that Lola Kurland, the office manager at Avellino & Bienes, had sent out in response to an investor's query in August 1991. It stated that the firm provided financial services only to "relatives, friends and former clients. . . a very private group." The letter's arch style was pure Avellino. "We do not encourage new accounts and therefore we do not solicit same," it said. "Summarily, this is a very private group and no financial statements, prospectuses or brochures have been printed or are available."

Both documents made it clear that the participants' money would be treated as a loan to the firm, which would use it to invest in its own accounts with the unidentified New York broker.

The documents also made it clear—at least to the lawyers in the SEC's New York office—that there was something very fishy about the King Arthur Account.

One of those lawyers got in touch with Frank Avellino.

Avellino could not have been shocked to hear from the SEC. A short time earlier, he had received a call from his friend Richard Glantz, an attorney in California. Glantz's father had been an officemate at the old Alpern firm and was one of the earliest subcontractors to raise money for the Madoff accounts. The younger Glantz had shared in that business and steered others to it.

Avellino bantered a bit and then listened in growing horror as Glantz explained why he had called. He said that an investment adviser he introduced to Avellino in 1989 had just gotten a letter from the SEC with a warning about the King Arthur fact sheet that the adviser had been distributing. Avellino might hear from the regulators himself, Glantz said.

Then the predicted call from the SEC came in. Avellino promptly phoned Michael Bienes, who recalled the conversation years later: "I gotta tell you something. We got a call from the SEC, and they're asking questions," Avellino said.

The questions were about "some guy out in California" who was funneling money to Avellino & Bienes through Glantz. This California guy "was printing up brochures with our name on it," Avellino continued. Of course, this violated the pair's long-standing prohibition on providing any written sales material to customers.

"Oh my God, no. What is he, insane? He knows the rule," Bienes responded. "Anyone who deals with us knows the rules. What happened?"

"Well, they're coming over to see us."

Avellino clearly took the lead in dealing with the SEC's interest in the firm. So, most likely, he was the one who called and broke the news to Bernie Madoff.

Madoff did two things. First, he called his friend and longtime investor Howard Squadron and asked if his law firm would take on the case. Squadron steered the call to his partner Ira Lee "Ike" Sorkin, a stocky man with an expressive face and thick graying hair who had joined the firm in 1976 after three years as a staff attorney in the SEC's New York office and a busy five-year stint as a federal prosecutor.

In 1992, Ike Sorkin knew Bernie Madoff only slightly—a few quick chats at benefit dinners for the Jewish philanthropies they both supported, nothing more. But he knew almost every A-list securities defense lawyer in Manhattan and had worked with or tried cases against many of them. He spoke the SEC's language fluently. In 1984 he had briefly left the Squadron firm to return to the SEC, whose New York office was in disarray as the agency wrestled with the changes John Shad was implementing. For the next two years, he ran the New York office as its administrator; then he happily returned to the Squadron firm.

After lining up an effective lawyer for the two accountants, Madoff also began a frantic effort to create phony records that would back up their claims about how much money was in their Madoff accounts. The effort left a paper trail that would be reconstructed by the bankruptcy trustee more than fifteen years later—a trail that provides some of the most persuasive evidence available that Madoff's fraud was up and running well before this encounter with the SEC.

When the SEC staffers first contacted Frank Avellino in June 1992, the conversation only increased their suspicions. One of them noted in a subsequent memo: "When asked what he does with the money borrowed, Avellino stated that he invests money in real estate and 'some securities.'"

But Kurland's August 1991 letter had been emphatic: "We do not deal in real estate or anything other than securities." And the fact sheet from the California investment adviser did not mention real estate.

Avellino's credibility was already crumbling.

Shortly thereafter, someone from the SEC team got a call from Ike Sorkin saying he represented the partners at Avellino & Bienes. He assured the investigators that "nothing inappropriate" was going on and offered to bring in the two men to talk voluntarily, without a subpoena. His clients' story was that they borrowed money through a word-of-mouth network and made interest payments to the lenders from the profits they made by investing the borrowed money. Whatever profits were left over, they kept.

At 1:30 PM on July 7, 1992, Frank Avellino and Michael Bienes arrived at the SEC's downtown offices at 75 Park Place, an undistinguished building two blocks west of the famous Woolworth Building. With them were Sorkin, one of his partners, and a summer intern from the firm. Flushed from the July heat, they were shown to a fourteenth-floor conference room, where three SEC lawyers and another summer intern were seated across the table. For the next four hours, Sorkin would do his job, sparring repeatedly with the SEC lawyers. They listened patiently and directed more questions at Frank Avellino, who responded alternately with windy lectures or terse roadblocks.

"Mr. Avellino," one of the SEC lawyers asked, "what type of business is Avellino & Bienes in?"

"Private investing," Avellino responded.

"Could you elaborate on that?"

"Yes. Michael Bienes and Frank Avellino have private investments," Avellino answered, falling into his habit of avoiding the pronoun "I."

Eventually, he explained how the "very private group" served by his partnership had grown by word of mouth, without the partners soliciting any business.

"If Lola Kurland gets a call—it's usually my Uncle Lou who would call up Lola, because he's been there since Day One with me—he would say that Joe, John, Tom, 'will be calling you and he is somebody related to me, so if they call, you can accept the call,'" Avellino said.

And just how many people had loaned money to Avellino & Bienes through this folksy tag-team process?

"Approximate guess?" Avellino asked.

"Yes," the government lawyer answered.

"About a thousand."

It's not clear if the SEC staff already knew how big this case was. If not, this must have been a heavy moment.

And how much did Avellino & Bienes owe to those one thousand lenders?

Sorkin broke in to quibble about how much money had flowed in and when it had come, but Avellino's answer made it into the transcript: "$400 million."

Roughly a thousand people had about $400 million tied up in this little firm that operated out of the Wall Street equivalent of a broom closet. According to Avellino, all that cash—plus a "cushion" of cash that brought the total to roughly $440 million—was invested in securities held in various partnership accounts with a Wall Street broker named Bernard L. Madoff.

The SEC lawyer did not seem to recognize the name.

When the accounts were finally analyzed, it turned out that a "very private group" of more than 3,200 people were listed as lenders to Avellino & Bienes, receiving interest payments ranging from 13.5 to 20 percent.

Two days later, a team from the SEC showed up at the Avellino & Bienes offices on the eighth floor of the soaring new Heron Tower on East Fifty-fifth Street. (Apparently concerned about rumors, Sorkin asked the investigators not to "badge" the building's reception desk in the lobby— just to give their names, without showing their government credentials or disclosing their employer.) They gathered records and started piecing together the universe of creditors.

One of those creditors was Telfran Associates, whose founding partners included the father of Avellino's friend Richard Glantz. Regulators told Avellino & Bienes and Telfran to stop accepting fresh "loans" and began to frame a civil lawsuit accusing them of selling unregistered securities through what amounted to an illicit mutual fund. Regulators anxiously sought assurances that the money was all still there, safely invested with Bernie Madoff.

Was it?

Madoff would insist later that he had not yet begun his Ponzi scheme when the SEC came after Avellino & Bienes—that the money was all there, all invested in arbitrage trading—but that simply is not credible. Even his faithful lieutenant Frank DiPascali acknowledged as much in an off-the-cuff remark to a federal judge years later, saying that he first realized he was engaged in a fraud "in the late '80s or early '90s."

A civil lawsuit in the Madoff bankruptcy case would later assert that Avellino and Bienes had lied to the SEC about how much money was supposed to be in their Madoff accounts. According to that lawsuit, the balance actually shown on their account statements did not include the promised "cushion" of cash; rather, it was almost $30 million short of the total the two accountants owed their investors.

The lawsuit claimed that this shortfall was a result of the fraudulent use of the investors' money for the accountants' own benefit—an allegation their lawyers denied—and that Madoff covered for them. He did this, the lawsuit contended, by creating a phony account on June 23, 1992, and falsifying enough backdated trading profits in the new account to magically close the gap and forestall regulatory suspicion.

The entire episode was a grueling test for Madoff. A subsequent lawsuit would claim that the ordeal wound up costing him nearly $60 million in elaborately concealed hush money in the years to come. It also bore down on Frank DiPascali, the high school graduate who had made himself useful in so many ways since he was hired in 1975. He had been generating the account statements that were sent out regularly to customers, assisted by other close associates on the small staff devoted to Madoff's investment clients. Even after Madoff launched his fraud, these statements continued to look sufficiently convincing to deflect any skeptical inquiry from investors, largely thanks to DiPascali.

But constructing those records was kindergarten fraud compared with the task posed by the SEC investigation in the summer of 1992. If the Ponzi scheme was already up and running, as seems likely, Madoff had to produce trading records for seven Avellino & Bienes accounts that would show the necessary volume of consistently profitable trades, going back at least several years. These records had to be convincing enough for federal regulators, not just for customers and private accountants. And they were needed immediately—before the SEC showed up to look at the documents on file at the accounting firm.

DiPascali, a small terrier-like man with the unpolished speech of his native Queens, came through for Madoff. Using self-taught computer skills and the historical stock and options prices available to any brokerage firm, he created a convincing paper trail covering several years of complex trading activity that almost certainly had never occurred. Based on those phony records, an SEC lawyer later reported that his staff had "analyzed" the Avellino & Bienes trading accounts at the Madoff firm, "verifying the equity value in these accounts." A footnote showed that Madoff had fluently explained it all to them, as he would for years to come, with calm confidence and trading terminology that was most likely over their heads.

Still, DiPascali's fabricated records and Madoff's deft conversations with regulators unschooled in current trading jargon were just delaying tactics—necessary but nowhere near sufficient to keep the trap from snapping shut. Within months, the SEC would get a court order requiring Madoff to return the $400 million to Avellino & Bienes's customers by the end of November 1992.

Madoff later acknowledged that this cash demand posed difficulties for him, although he denied it was because he was already running a Ponzi scheme. Rather, he claimed it was because the "bona fide arbitrage" positions in the Avellino & Bienes accounts, like the arcane "synthetic" trades in the accounts of his other big clients, could not be easily or rapidly liquidated. "I was actually doing the trades," he insisted. But almost certainly this was not true; most likely, there were no convertible bonds or preferred stocks in the Avellino & Bienes accounts at all.

Still, even Madoff conceded that he urgently needed about $400 million, and there were a limited number of ways he could get it. According to him, he raised the cash from three of his biggest clients: Carl Shapiro, Jeffry Picower, and Norman Levy. The three men simply agreed to "take over the positions" in the Avellino & Bienes accounts and put in fresh cash to do so, Madoff claimed. "Shapiro, Picower, and Levy all sent in actual money, new money," he said.

Records unearthed in subsequent investigations confirm that Madoff got a lot of the cash he needed from the accounts of Norman Levy. They do not show if he did so with Levy's permission, or even his knowledge.

It is possible that Levy really did think he was "taking over" the investments that supposedly had been in the Avellino & Bienes accounts, without knowing they were fictional. Or it is possible that Madoff, who had discretion over Levy's accounts, simply moved the fake positions into his account to explain where the money had gone. After all, DiPascali could doctor the account statements as necessary.

What seems hugely unlikely to everyone who knew Norman Levy is that he knowingly helped Bernie Madoff preserve his Ponzi scheme. After all, Levy later named Madoff as an executor of his estate and let his two children entrust their foundation endowments and some of their personal wealth to him, an inexplicable expression of faith if he knew Madoff to be a crook.

Whatever stratagem Madoff used to get cash from Levy would have worked just as well with Picower and Shapiro. By late November, Madoff had scraped together the money he needed to placate the SEC regulators, who did not inquire where he got it or pursue any of the intriguing loose ends that dangled around the case.

In the meantime, Frank Avellino, a millionaire many times over, haggled for months over the $429,000 in fees charged by the auditor the SEC had forced him to hire. "I am not a cash cow and I will not be milked," he said in a memorable affidavit filed in that dispute. "I personally oversaw Avellino & Bienes' books and records," he told the court. "In all the years that we ran our business prior to the intervention of the Securities and Exchange Commission, we did not receive any unresolved complaints from our lenders. We were never sued by a lender. We did not miss our interest payments."

The problem, he said, was that the accountants were demanding all sorts of sophisticated records that simply did not exist, that had never existed. All the firm had was a few sheets of paper for each lender, so that was all it could turn over to the accountants.

By the time the dispute dragged to a close in the spring of 1993, not even the federal judge handling the case had much faith in Frank Avellino. "I don't believe your client," the judge bluntly told Ike Sorkin in court. "I heard his testimony, I saw his demeanor, I heard his inconsistencies. . . . I don't believe him. So to the extent there are credibility issues to resolve, I resolve them against your client."

The case, which began and ended with doubts about Frank Avellino's honesty, was a parade of red flags. And the *Wall Street Journal* hung some of those flags out in the open with a modest article on December 17, 1992, detailing the SEC's investigation of a money trail that ended at Madoff's door. But the warnings were not pursued, to Madoff's intense relief; paradoxically, some investors were actually reassured by the *Journal* article about Madoff. It accused him of nothing, after all.

The SEC lawyers breathed a sigh of relief, too, thinking they had returned $400 million to thousands of investors who had innocently wandered into a flimsy, unregistered, and unregulated mutual fund. On top of the disputed audit expenses, the $350,000 fine imposed on Avellino &

Bienes was large by the standards of the day. The unregistered investment operation and its Telfran subsidiary were shut down.

The SEC was satisfied and moved on to other issues. One of the sad quirks of the Madoff case is that, of his thousands of investors, the only ones who could have recovered all the fictional wealth shown on their account statements and kept any money they had withdrawn in the past were those clients of Avellino & Bienes who took the money the SEC returned to them in 1992 and walked away.

Most of them didn't do that. They didn't realize that they had been rescued. They thought instead that they had been banished from Eden, shut out of a wonderful low-risk investment that still paid good interest rates. So they were delighted when Madoff invited them all to open new accounts directly with him, even if the rates were lower than they had been getting from Avellino & Bienes. Most of the money Madoff had paid out was put right back into his hands.

What role did Avellino and Bienes play in restoring that cash to Madoff's Ponzi scheme? They denied that they were involved at all, with Bienes publicly insisting they were both just glad to get out of their inadvertent SEC difficulties and walk away from their Madoff business relatively unscathed.

The litigation filed later against the two accountants in bankruptcy court, however, laid out a very different scenario, one in which the two men allegedly kept silent about Madoff's obviously fraudulent activity, helped recruit new players to step into their shoes as introducers, and encouraged their former clients to invest directly with Madoff. In return, the lawsuit claimed, the two men demanded that Madoff pay them guaranteed profits of 17 percent a year on their own new Madoff accounts, along with secret commissions of 2 percent a year on the money their former investors handed back to him.

In Frank DiPascali's world, these payments allegedly came to be known as the "schupt" payments—the bankruptcy trustee would later theorize that the term was a phonetic garble of the word *schtup*, a crude Yiddish verb whose rough Anglo-Saxon equivalent is *screw*.

The SEC investigation in 1992, incomplete though it was, had significant consequences for Bernie Madoff's expanding fraud.

First, it forced Madoff to apply to his Ponzi scheme some of the computer technology he was already using in his legitimate business. It was simply impossible for Frank DiPascali to concoct manually the trading records and monthly statements for the thousands of new accounts Madoff had suddenly inherited from Avellino & Bienes. Madoff needed to automate the Ponzi process somehow, and he turned to DiPascali for help.

DiPascali, in turn, allegedly relied on two computer programmers who had joined the firm a few years earlier and who were later accused of designing software for one of the firm's new IBM AS/400 computers that simplified the process of generating the fictional account statements. DiPascali and some of his staff allegedly researched the necessary trades from the historic record, and then the customized Ponzi software would allocate those trades, in perfect proportions, among the various customer accounts using a simple "mail merge" computer function.

Besides reducing the manual labor involved, this automation provided new opportunities for deception. It was around this time that Madoff leased separate space on the seventeenth floor of the Lipstick Building—ostensibly for his new IBM computers but actually to create a more secure environment for his increasingly elaborate fraud. As he later recalled, he set up the separate suite because "I could not have operated in view of the other people on the 18th floor." The nondescript warren of offices and cubicles on the seventeenth floor became Frank DiPascali's domain, a private laboratory for his creative deceptions.

As DiPascali perfected his craft, he branched out. He devised fake clearinghouse forms that showed up on computer screens—perfect replicas, regularly updated. On Madoff's orders, he kept a supply of old letterhead stationery and used it when backdated paperwork was needed for files that regulators wanted to see. In time, he even ordered the creation of a software program that made it look to an observer as if a trader at one computer terminal were buying or selling for an investor's account, when in fact the "trader" was merely exchanging keystrokes with another staff member at a computer hidden in a room down the hall.

This Potemkin village paper trail became so convincing that Madoff was able to fool dozens of insufficiently skeptical regulators and inadequately observant lawyers and accountants for years.

∽

Another consequence of the SEC's breakup of the casual "friends and family" network run by Avellino & Bienes was that Madoff came to rely far more on those larger, more professionally marketed sources of cash known as hedge funds.

Hedge funds had been around since 1949, but until the late 1960s they were largely invisible; they just quietly produced remarkable profits for their wealthy and intensely private investors while avoiding regulatory and, for the most part, media attention. The theory behind hedge funds was that inherently risky strategies—buying stocks with borrowed money or selling stocks short—could be combined in a single fund in ways that would actually reduce overall risk and produce profits in good markets and bad. The goal was never to have a losing year, whether the market was up or down—the Holy Grail for investors throughout time, the siren song that would bring so many of them to Madoff's door.

The hedge fund was pioneered by a sociologist and financial journalist named Alfred W. Jones, who, by the early 1960s, was providing his investors with stunning annual average returns of 65 percent. But the 1969 bear market brought a lot of these new funds down to earth; even the fabled Jones fund incurred losses of up to 40 percent in the first nine months of the year.

Many hedge funds failed in the rough market of the 1970s, but the mystique proved to be utterly resistant to bad news. The idea took hold in the 1980s that hedge funds were superior to the regulated mutual funds used by middle-income investors, and wealthy, sophisticated investors flocked to them.

What persisted in every incarnation of hedge funds was the remarkable fee structure: the manager received 20 percent of the profits he made with his investors' money. As years passed, an annual management fee of 1 percent of a fund's assets was added to the typical hedge fund manager's paycheck. The fees dwarfed those charged by regulated mutual funds, but men of wealth and wisdom were willing to pay them—that's just what it cost to have a wizard handling your portfolio. One scholar referred to the performance fees as the "rent" investors paid to get a genius to manage their money.

There seemed to be little brilliance behind the Fairfield Greenwich Group, the family of funds run by Jeffrey Tucker and Walter Noel Jr. that sponsored the largest of all the giant funds caught in the Madoff scandal. Madoff himself would later observe that its partners "aren't rocket scientists." And "genius" was not a term usually applied to the firm's amiable chairman and cofounder Walter Noel, although he was much smarter than he was given credit for.

It is hard to imagine two men less likely to forge a durable, multibillion-dollar relationship. If Bernie Madoff was a villain created by Horatio Alger from a draft by Anthony Trollope, then Walter Noel was a minor character dashed off by F. Scott Fitzgerald: a study in prep school style and social striving.

Born in Nashville and educated at Vanderbilt University, Noel was handsome—tall and lean with chiseled features, thick dark hair, and exuberantly bushy eyebrows—and genial enough to win office in some modest campus organizations. Despite later impressions, he was smart enough to make Phi Beta Kappa at Vanderbilt and earn both a master's degree in economics and a law degree from Harvard, in 1953 and 1959 respectively. Between his two stints at Harvard, he served in the U.S. Army. His engagement announcement in 1962 said he had worked as "a Russian linguist for three years." At the time, he was working as a consultant for Arthur D. Little Inc. in Lagos, Nigeria. He later helped develop an international private banking operation for Chemical Bank and in 1983 set off on his own to advise private international clients.

While Madoff married the pretty teenager he courted on the bus to Far Rockaway High School, Walter Noel's bride was the lovely Monica Haegler, whose wealthy and cosmopolitan parents split their time between Zurich and Rio de Janeiro and sent her to elite private schools in Brazil and Switzerland.

While Madoff's two handsome sons would graduate in the 1980s from good colleges, Michigan and Penn, Walter Noel's five beautiful daughters would graduate from *very* good colleges—Harvard, Yale, Brown, and Georgetown—and four of them would marry into influential European and Latin American families. Monica Noel had her own wealthy family connections. A cousin was a rich Brazilian financier and industrialist, and a brother, at one point, was the Brazilian representative for Credit Suisse. Portuguese, Spanish, Italian, and English were interchangeably used around the Noel family table.

By the time Avellino & Bienes was forced to close its doors, Walter Noel had been in business with the former SEC lawyer Jeffrey Tucker for a half-dozen years and had been investing with Madoff most of that time. From the beginning, Noel left the legal scrutiny and structural details of the funds to Tucker, whose father-in-law first made the introduction to Madoff in 1989. With his grounding in securities law, Tucker was the one who went out and supposedly kicked the tires in the due-diligence examinations that Fairfield Greenwich Group conducted. By contrast, Noel was the easygoing salesman, explaining the new funds to existing clients, courting new clients at the private banks and foreign institutions he knew from his earlier career, and spreading the word among the wealthy families with whom he and Monica socialized on their home turf in Greenwich, Connecticut, or at privileged enclaves such as the Hamptons and Palm Beach.

It was during these early days of cultivating Fairfield Greenwich—which almost certainly coincided with the early days of the Ponzi scheme—that Madoff and DiPascali perfected the talking points for their "split-strike conversion" investment strategy and tried them out on Tucker and Noel. It worked like a charm.

Of course, there was nothing illicit about the strategy itself; it was familiar to any equity options trader at the time. In 1989, Tucker and Noel could not have known that Madoff's alleged execution of that strategy over the years would produce profits more consistent and substantial than the strategy itself ought to have produced. They could not know that the amount of money Madoff would ultimately claim to be deploying would have moved through the stock and options markets like a battleship in a bathtub if he'd actually been making trades. At the beginning, it made sense—and it made money, especially for them. After all, as the fund managers, they pocketed 20 percent of the net profits Madoff produced for their private investors.

By 1990 they had invested about $4 million with Madoff through their Fairfield Sentry fund, incorporated in the British Virgin Islands to serve foreign investors. In 1993 they created a version of the fund for domestic clients and called it the Greenwich Sentry fund.

Fairfield Sentry's steady profits made it attractive, but its returns were unspectacular compared with other hedge funds being hawked in this very elite bazaar. From 1990 until 1994, the fund merely kept pace with the overall market, as measured by the S&P 500 index. Even some public mutual funds, such as Fidelity's popular Contrafund and its legendary Magellan fund, were producing better returns and charging fees that were microscopic compared with those Fairfield Sentry's investors had to pay. And it got worse: from late 1996 until the end of the decade, Fairfield Sentry actually lagged behind the S&P 500.

Clearly, the Fairfield Sentry fund and its offshoots would not sell themselves. They likely would not sell at all unless their demerits were burnished into virtues. Walter Noel was good at that; an innately conservative investor himself, he made the Sentry fund sound like a carefully crafted, rigorously monitored investment for cautious people who were willing to trade some upside profits for stability and safety in the long run.

The pitch worked, and the firm grew. Its marketing materials soon began to take on the sheen of polished professionalism. Young accountants and MBA graduates were hired. They set up elaborate charts that assessed fund performance against various benchmarks. They developed a formal checklist of questions to ask about a money manager's operations—questions they put to Bernie Madoff when they tagged along on Tucker's visits. Madoff or DiPascali would answer some of the questions, show them the fake records, perhaps even do a little phony computerized trading in their account as they watched, and then show them the bogus clearinghouse statements that backed up what they had been told.

Some questions Madoff simply refused to answer. In hindsight, his intransigence may seem like a blatant red flag, but at the time, given Madoff's status in the financial industry and apparent success on Wall Street, it was all too convincing. The young due-diligence staffers apparently did not raise any concerns with the partners. Or, if they did, they were ignored.

The faith that the Fairfield Greenwich Group partners had in Bernie Madoff's integrity may have been affirmed in the mid-1990s, when more than two dozen market-making firms were accused of fixing prices on the NASDAQ stocks they traded. The scam had been going on for years, undetected or at least uncorrected. Some of the biggest firms on the Street had acquiesced in the bullying cartel, and their industry-financed regulators at the NASD had failed for years to catch them.

It was the worst scandal the over-the-counter market had faced in Madoff's tenure on the board—but his hands were squeaky clean. The private lawyer who led the earliest investigations confirmed that his team never saw any indication that Madoff's firm was involved in the bid-rigging. In a letter from prison, Madoff said his firm was "not a party" to the scandal because "it was our belief that [the] NASDAQ market's credibility depended on creating a more competitive transparent efficient market-place." And by that point his firm was more focused on the profits to be made trading Big Board stocks in the "third market" and was indifferent to the games others were playing with the over-the-counter stocks. It is also possible that Madoff had warned his traders against participating in the scheme because he was trying to avoid any actions that might bring his Ponzi scheme under scrutiny.

Given his firm's size and prominence in the NASDAQ market, how-ever, Madoff was conspicuous by his absence from that scandal. For Walter Noel, Jeffrey Tucker, and their due-diligence teams, the notion that they were dealing with one of the few exonerated market makers on NASDAQ may have been comforting, especially if they were growing a little frustrated at his eccentric way of doing business and his unwavering refusal to tell them everything they wanted to know.

As Fairfield Greenwich expanded and raised money to invest else-where besides with Madoff, its people reviewed audits and asked care-ful questions of those other money managers. Like Madoff, the other managers were successful, and the other small funds prospered. Unlike Madoff, those other managers actually answered questions fully and pro-vided the documentation requested. In time, Fairfield Greenwich began to take pride in the quality of its due-diligence work and describe it in glowing terms in its marketing materials, to distinguish itself from the other hedge funds popping up and offering oddly similar returns.

By the mid-1990s a growing share of the Sentry-selling work was being done by a team assembled by Andrés Piedrahita, the Colombian-born husband of Walter Noel's eldest daughter, Corina. Piedrahita's prior career on Wall Street had been routine: a half-dozen years as a "finan-cial consultant" at Prudential Bache, followed by three years as a vice president at Shearson Lehman Hutton. In 1991, less than two years after his marriage, Piedrahita set out on his own, forming a hedge fund mar-keting business called Littlestone Associates. (His surname means "little stone" in Spanish.) In 1997, Piedrahita's company and its international sales staff merged with his father-in-law's partnership, and he became a "founding partner" of the new Fairfield Greenwich. One of his first chores in the new regime was to open a London office for the firm.

The same year, Walter Noel's daughter Alix married Philip J. Toub, a trader at another hedge fund, in a romantic ceremony that was held at the open-air Bamboo Church on the exclusive island of Mustique, in the Grenadines. (Monica and Walter Noel had purchased a sugar-white hillside home there in 1995, while the Madoffs were settling into a $3.8 million resort home in Palm Beach. "Mustique is the antithesis of Palm Beach," Monica told a writer from *Town & Country* a few years later. "It's still rustic, you see. It's also very international. And there are no Hermès bags.") After his marriage, Toub also joined the Fairfield Greenwich sales force and became one of its most successful members, drawing on his business connections in Brazil and the Middle East.

In 1999 another of Noel's sons-in-law, Yanko Della Schiava, came aboard, marketing the firm's funds in southern Europe from his home in Lugano, Switzerland. In 2005, a fourth son-in-law, Matthew C. Brown, a Californian, would also join the Noel family firm.

Madoff could not have had a more polished and cosmopolitan sales force—nor, it seemed, a more effective one. By the end of 1999 the little hedge fund that had entrusted $4 million to him in 1990 had an almost staggering $3 billion in its Madoff accounts, and its assets were growing more than 30 percent a year, through new deposits and putative earnings. Hundreds of millions of dollars had come into Fairfield Greenwich's Madoff-related funds from other hedge funds in Europe and the Caribbean. As its assets grew, so did the firm's management fees—and, consequently, the size of the fortunes financing the lifestyles of its lucky partners.

The Noels, with their island luxuries, and the Tuckers, who took up thoroughbred breeding in upstate New York's tony Saratoga region, lived very well. It is not clear exactly how much Tucker and the extended Noel clan collected in fees in the 1990s, but it probably totaled more than $45 million in 1998, a year when there were only a handful of partners sharing in the tiny firm's revenues. (Records filed in later lawsuits would show that the firm would collect nearly $920 million between 2002 and 2008.)

And, while the Noels and Tuckers may have lived no better than their extravagant peers in the hedge fund world, they did live more publicly, with splashy magazine photo spreads of their exotic homes and society page appearances by the Noels' glamorous daughters. The proud old money of Greenwich, Saratoga, and the Hamptons might have sneered, but the socially ambitious new money of the hedge fund world probably thought the beautiful Noel family and the sporty Tuckers had hit the jackpot of life.

And they owed it all to Bernie Madoff.

༺༒༻

The cash from offshore hedge funds, rich European families, and private boutique banks—all the sources of wealth familiar to the partners at Fairfield Greenwich—were critical in allowing Madoff to expand the pool of money available to his Ponzi scheme in the 1990s. Another increasingly important spigot was connected to the nonprofit world, whose endowments, educational institutions, foundations, and investment committees came to trust Madoff with more and more of their wealth.

What Walter Noel was to the jet-setting, sophisticated world of international wealth, J. Ezra Merkin was to the intimate, fraternal world of Jewish philanthropy. Unlike Noel, though, who had climbed his way into cosmopolitan society, Merkin was born into the financially generous and deeply religious community that became the core clientele of his hedge fund career—and a significant target of Madoff's devastating fraud.

Ezra Merkin grew up in the shadow of his wealthy and fiercely intelligent father, Hermann Merkin, a firmly observant Orthodox Jew who fled Nazi Germany and later did intelligence work for the U.S. Army. After the war, Hermann Merkin built his fortune in New York, the bulk of which came from his stake in a fleet of oil tankers. He also started a small investment banking company; his constant pursuit of new ideas and stock tips led him to cultivate a number of talented young traders on Wall Street. One of them recalled the ritual of lunching with Hermann Merkin in those postwar years. The elderly gentleman was always accompanied by a silent, well-dressed lieutenant who kept a small notebook tucked into his suit pocket. If the trader mentioned a stock he liked— perhaps a promising new technology company such as IBM—Merkin would flip a heavily accented question to his companion. "Do I have any IBM?" The companion would quickly consult his notebook. If the answer was no, Merkin would tell the trader: "I'll take a thousand shares." Then they'd turn back to their lunch. This former trader thought it likely that the young Bernie Madoff was among those whom the elder Merkin cultivated over lunch.

But Wall Street wasn't the only thread that tied Bernie Madoff to the

Merkin family. In 1955, Hermann Merkin left his home synagogue and helped to establish the new Fifth Avenue Synagogue. During the years that he served as its president and then its chairman, the synagogue became the spiritual home of a number of wealthy congregants who, in turn, became generous supporters of important Jewish causes and institutions—and, ultimately, important investors with Madoff.

As his wealth grew, Hermann Merkin became an increasingly generous donor himself, especially to Yeshiva University. He served on Yeshiva's board of trustees for nearly forty years, and he was vice chairman in 1996, when Madoff was invited to join the board.

Jacob Ezra Merkin, one of six children, was a worthy successor to the family's scholarly Orthodox traditions. He attended prep school at Ramaz, one of the premier private Jewish academies on Manhattan's Upper East Side. He majored in English at Columbia University, graduating Phi Beta Kappa and magna cum laude in 1976. He received his law degree with honors from Harvard in 1979 and spent time studying in Israel. One friend recalled him as "a voracious reader," and another described him as "pious, prayerful and profound." Close friends saw his self-deprecating sense of humor but also his sometimes harsh dismissal of those he considered his intellectual inferiors.

After briefly practicing law at an elite New York firm, he followed his father to Wall Street. He worked for a well-established hedge fund, and then set out on his own, forming what became Gabriel Capital Corporation. In 1988 he created a pair of hedge funds that came to be known as the Gabriel fund and the Ariel fund. He was a deft salesman for his funds but was far less involved in actually managing the money in them; he quietly outsourced that task.

From the beginning, the investment decisions for the Ariel and Gabriel funds were being made almost exclusively by a young man named Victor Teicher, an intuitive investor with an irrepressible personality who had been sharing office space with Ezra Merkin for several years. That fact was not disclosed to the investors, so there was no public embarrassment when Teicher was convicted in 1990 on insider trading charges unrelated to his work on Merkin's funds. (According to Teicher, he continued to advise the two Merkin funds after his conviction and, by phone, during a thirteen-month incarceration that began in 1993, a claim disputed by Merkin.)

In 1989, beset by poor performance following the 1987 crash, Merkin started thinking about putting a portion of the Ariel and Gabriel money into the hands of another hot money manager: Bernie Madoff. At some point around 1990, Merkin paid a visit to the exclusive, intensely private market wizard in the Lipstick Building.

Anyone glancing into Madoff's fishbowl office or listening at the door that day would have been struck by the contrast between the man behind the desk and his visitor, settled ponderously into one of the office chairs. Merkin was a grizzled, bespectacled man in his mid-thirties, already a little jowly on his way to becoming portly. Madoff, just past fifty, had not slipped far from his lifeguard's physique and wore his tailored clothes with grace. Merkin was erudite, prone to showing off with literary allusions and philosophical musings. He seemed to be an essentially honest man who was inclined to embroider the facts a little to enhance a story or avoid an awkward truth. Madoff spoke like a down-to-earth guy with no intellectual pretensions, but he actually was a consummate con artist who was certainly on the brink of running a Ponzi scheme, if not already doing so.

Despite their differences in age and temperament, the two men hit it off. Merkin seemed to enjoy their initial conversation—his sister later speculated that he saw Madoff as "a kind, *haimish* sort of guy compared to my father."

Merkin listened as Madoff described the investment strategy he credited with producing his steady, utterly reliable returns—the same "split-strike conversion" talking points that had been so successful with the Fairfield Greenwich founders. One of Merkin's associates would later theorize that Merkin thought of Madoff as a skilled mechanic, not a gifted theorist—as if Merkin were an architect condescending to discuss design with the general contractor. But this contractor seemed to be getting the job done, and Merkin ultimately decided to place some of the money in his two hedge funds with Madoff.

As with Teicher, Madoff's role as one of the managers of those funds was not officially disclosed, although Merkin would later argue in court that many investors were aware of the Madoff relationship and, indeed, eagerly sought it out.

According to Merkin, his father first introduced him to Madoff in the late 1980s. Hermann Merkin was known for being exceedingly stingy with his praise, so it apparently carried great weight with his eldest son that he spoke well of Madoff.

It must have, because other people on Wall Street whom Merkin knew and respected did not share his father's good opinion of Madoff. Victor Teicher was instinctively dubious about the lack of volatility in Madoff's returns, even in rocky markets. Merkin had "described Madoff in terms of what he was doing, in the consistency of the returns, and I felt that that was just not possible," Teicher said later. "I've never seen anyone, I mean, have such consistent returns . . . it just didn't seem like it was possible." He would remain suspicious of Madoff for years.

Merkin got similar warnings from John Nash, a legendary investor and cofounder of the Odyssey Partners hedge fund. Nash and his son had made a small personal investment with Madoff and did not trust his results. They withdrew their money and shared their doubts privately with Merkin.

But Merkin's faith in Madoff—or, perhaps, his faith in his father's opinion of Madoff—carried the day. In 1992, the year of the Avellino & Bienes investigation and the year Madoff later identified as the launch date for his Ponzi scheme, Merkin formed a new hedge fund called Ascot Partners to invest exclusively with Madoff.

Because Madoff was paid only through commissions on the trades he was supposedly making for Ascot, the plump management fees generated by the new hedge fund flowed entirely to Merkin. Later lawsuits would calculate that Merkin collected nearly $170 million in management fees from the Ascot fund alone between 1995 and 2007, and more than $500 million in fees from the two other funds that were partly invested with Madoff. Like Walter Noel and Jeffrey Tucker, Ezra Merkin was on the road to enormous wealth, thanks to Bernie Madoff.

Ezra Merkin would be as generous with his wealth as his father had been, but he would also be more willing to spend it on comforts and luxuries for himself and his family. Around 1994 he paid $11 million to move his family into an eighteen-room apartment in one of Manhattan's fabled buildings, 740 Park Avenue. He purchased tens of millions of dollars of museum-quality art, specializing in works by the twentieth-century artist Mark Rothko, whose enormous color-washed canvases would come to dominate the apartment's decor.

Throughout the 1990s Merkin balanced such conspicuous consumption with sizable gifts to his synagogue and to institutions such as Yeshiva University and his prep school alma mater, Ramaz. Philanthropies embraced him. He chaired the investment committee at the UJA-Federation of New York for ten years and ultimately served on the boards of Yeshiva University, Carnegie Hall, and several other nonprofit organizations. His reputation opened doors for him at other nonprofit endowments—at Bard College, Tufts University, New York University, and New York Law School. In time, nearly three dozen nonprofit groups would entrust their money to Merkin—and thus to Madoff.

In a letter from prison, Madoff expressed great regard for Merkin: "Ezra Merkin is one of the brightest and [most] wonderful people I have ever known. He is an honorable man." Bernie and Ruth would occasionally have dinner with Merkin and his wife at their luxurious apartment and mingle with their prominent friends from Jewish charities and educational institutions at other private dinners and charity events.

The Nobel laureate and Holocaust survivor Elie Wiesel later recalled one such dinner with the Madoffs. "We did not speak about markets," he said. "We spoke about ethics. . . . He presented himself as a philanthropist." He remembered Madoff trying to lure him to Queens College, Ruth's alma mater, by offering to endow a chair for him there.

However heady such encounters were for Ruth and Bernie Madoff, his relationship with Merkin helped to cement Madoff's reputation among Jewish philanthropists. The allure was poignantly simple: his investment skill would amplify their generous impulses. As Wiesel put it, in explaining why he decided to invest his entire endowment with this modest, magnetic man from Queens: "Everybody we knew told us we could do so much more if we could make more money with Madoff."

In these circles, Madoff's reputation for generosity was enhanced after he and Ruth purchased a handsome home in Palm Beach in 1994 and, in 1996, were accepted as members of the Palm Beach Country Club, a haven of predominantly Jewish wealth since its founding in the 1950s. It was widely known that prospective members had to demonstrate that they regularly made annual charitable donations that were at least equal to the club's hefty initiation fee, which likely was between $150,000 and $200,000 at the time.

The Ascot Partners paperwork gave Merkin latitude to place his investors' money with other managers. But, given what he was actually doing, it is difficult to read the documents as anything but misleading. They gave the impression that Merkin was the primary manager of the fund, and they indicated clearly that, if he chose other managers, he would diversify the assets among them. In fact, from the beginning he had intended to invest the Ascot fund exclusively with Madoff, and that is what he did—a fact he never disclosed in the formal documents that were provided to new investors.

Instead, he told them that the fund "will engage primarily in risk arbitrage investments in private debt claims and publicly traded securities of bankrupt and distressed companies." It might also make indirect investments in "mutual funds, private investment partnerships, closed-end funds, and other pooled investment vehicles which engaged in similar investment strategies," the documents said.

Even if Madoff had honestly been pursuing his "split-strike conversion" investment strategy on Merkin's behalf—and he was doing no such thing—it would not have remotely matched those parameters.

7

WARNING SIGNS

As the world celebrated the advent of a new century, Bernie Madoff was riding high. The 1990s had seen an extraordinary surge on Wall Street, including a red-hot rally in Internet technology stocks trading on NASDAQ. The automated OTC system Madoff had helped establish was now the hottest market on the planet. The electronic trading of stocks, which Madoff pioneered in the 1970s, had emerged as a powerful tool for individual investors, who increasingly relied on the financial markets for their retirement security. Legions of "day traders" began playing the market from their home computers, buying and selling stocks and learning that fortunes could be made through puts, calls, shorts, and other gambits once available only to established traders such as Madoff himself.

The democratization of the markets did not lessen the appeal of Bernie Madoff's investing genius. Yes, fortunes could be made, but they could also be lost, and investors persisted in believing there was a way to lock in high returns without exposing themselves to high risk. When the tech-stock bubble burst in the opening months of 2000, it served to affirm Madoff's reputation as a safe haven in turbulent times. By now he had established himself as one of the most exclusive, most successful money managers in the business. For some time he had cultivated the impression that new investors simply couldn't get in—he had all the money he wanted; he wouldn't even discuss the business with would-be clients. It was akin to winning the lottery if he agreed to add your hedge fund to his coterie of institutional clients. This approach was masterful, of course. It proved that Groucho Marx's famous rule also worked in reverse: everyone wanted to join the club that wouldn't let them in.

And the lucky ones who had already gotten in—Avellino & Bienes, Fairfield Greenwich, Cohmad Securities, Stanley Chais, Ezra Merkin, a host of charities and private foundations, an army of offshore hedge funds—did not want to annoy the fussy goose laying all those golden eggs. They had staked their reputations, their money, and their clients' money on the premise that they could trust Bernie Madoff. They simply ignored or dismissed the quiet cautions and caveats that were starting to seep through the hedge fund community that Madoff's returns were too consistently good to be credible.

Then, those whispered suspicions became public.

The May 2001 issue of a widely followed hedge fund industry publication called *MARHedge* carried a lengthy article by writer Michael Ocrant disclosing the stunning scale of Madoff's extremely private money-managing business. Ocrant estimated that Madoff managed more than $6 billion. This actually was far less than he was pretending to manage, but even that sum would have made Madoff one of the largest individual investment advisers in the world, even though the money was ostensibly flowing in through hundreds of other investment advisers.

Ocrant wrote that more than a dozen credible people in the hedge fund world—none identified by name—were mystified by Madoff's performance. They didn't doubt the annual returns, but Ocrant observed that such results were "considered somewhat high for the strategy" Madoff claimed to be using. Ocrant reminded readers about Gateway, the small public mutual fund that had pursued a similar "split-strike" strategy since 1978 but "experienced far greater volatility and lower returns during the same period."

The experts Ocrant consulted "asked why no one has been able to duplicate similar returns using the strategy and why other firms on Wall Street haven't become aware of the fund and its strategy and traded against it, as has happened so often in other cases." The article also questioned why Madoff agreed to take only the trading commissions the funds generated, allowing the fund managers to keep the lion's share of the very hefty fees. His role, his fee structure, his secrecy—it all ran counter to the rules of the hedge fund game as they knew it.

Ocrant acknowledged that "four or five professionals" he interviewed understood the strategy and did not dispute its reported returns—further evidence that Madoff had at least selected a plausible cover story for his fraud, which had likely been in operation for at least a decade by now. But even those professionals doubted that Madoff could be pursuing the strategy the way he claimed, using S&P 100 stocks and options, especially with $6 billion under his management.

In a spontaneous, apparently relaxed after-hours interview with Ocrant at the Lipstick Building offices, Madoff dismissed those doubts, saying that the private funds were a little more volatile than they looked in the monthly and annual returns and that his deep experience and his firm's trading strength and sophistication fully explained the results.

His trading strength had been affirmed barely a year earlier by some of the biggest names on Wall Street. As computer-driven trading networks multiplied across Wall Street, regulators pushed to eliminate the Big Board's restrictions on where its members could trade its listed stocks. In anticipation of that liberated future, five brokerage houses banded together in 2000 to invest in a new trading system called Primex. The five were Goldman Sachs, Merrill Lynch, Morgan Stanley, Salomon Smith Barney, and Bernard L. Madoff Investment Securities, which was actually developing the new network. "Never in my wildest dreams did I think I would have partners like these," Madoff told reporters when the consortium was announced.

Madoff was not arrogant or dismissive with Ocrant. Rather, he was charming and bemused. He took his time, showing Ocrant around the trading floor, easily and confidently discussing his disputed investment strategy, and casually offering plausible-sounding explanations for his success.

"Market timing and stock picking are both important for the strategy to work," Ocrant wrote, "and to those who express astonishment at the firm's ability in those areas, Madoff points to long experience, excellent technology that provides superb and low-cost execution capabilities, good proprietary stock and options pricing models, well-established infrastructure, market-making ability and market intelligence derived from the massive amount of order flow it handles every day." All of this was certainly true—it was what gave Madoff such credibility on the Street; it just had nothing to do with his investment returns.

Madoff explained that he hadn't set up his own hedge fund or demanded hedge fund fees because he believed his firm should stick to its "core strengths." This explanation did not satisfy the "expert skeptics" Ocrant consulted. "Most continued to express bewilderment," he wrote, "and indicated they were still grappling to understand how such results have been achieved for so long."

The following week, a similarly skeptical view about Bernie Madoff's money management operation was expressed by another writer, Erin Arvedlund, in *Barron's* magazine, a mainstream financial publication likely to reach far more investors than Ocrant's story.

After the two articles appeared, Madoff put aside his usual "take it or leave it" attitude toward his big investors and reached out immediately to reassure his largest feeder funds.

Jeffrey Tucker of Fairfield Greenwich had paid little attention to the Ocrant article and wasn't rattled at all by the "somewhat critical" article in *Barron's*. "Much of it I thought was, frankly, just irresponsible journalism," he said later. But then he got a call from Madoff.

"Are you getting feedback from your clients?" he asked.

"We have some who are concerned," Tucker answered, adding, "the principal concern I have is that the assets are there."

"Come up this afternoon," Madoff said.

When Tucker arrived for this impromptu due-diligence visit, Madoff was ready, thanks to Frank DiPascali's creative efforts. Besides the phony trade confirmations and account statements that had been generated for more than a decade, he had set up the bogus "trading platform" that made it appear as if actual trades were being conducted with European counterparties, although the reciprocal trader was actually an employee on another computer terminal hidden in a different room. And he had the clincher: apparent proof that all the stocks he claimed to have purchased were safely held in Madoff's account at Wall Street's central clearinghouse, the Depository Trust & Clearing Corporation, officially called the DTCC but known informally among veteran traders as "the DTC."

This was the acid test for DiPascali's masterpiece, a computer simulation of a live feed from the DTCC. He had taken care to duplicate exactly the clearinghouse's logo, the page format, the printer font and type sizes, and the paper quality of actual DTCC reports. Of course, these counterfeit DTCC records would always verify that the required number of shares were there in Madoff's account, safe and sound. Only an authorized call to the DTCC itself would have proven otherwise, and the clearinghouse was careful to keep customer information confidential.

Tucker later told regulators about this pivotal visit with Madoff at the Lipstick Building. The executive office suite, now established on the nineteenth floor, was familiar to him. The computer screen behind Bernie's sleek desk was accessible, and DiPascali was there with stacks of ledgers and journals.

Far from resenting any implied suspicions, Madoff encouraged Tucker on this occasion to be skeptical, to verify the trading being conducted for the Fairfield Sentry fund. Tucker was shown an official-looking "purchase and sale blotter" showing a record of each trade for his funds. Then he was shown a journal that supposedly contained stock records for the Madoff firm.

"Pick any two stocks," Madoff said.

Any two? Tucker first picked AOL Time Warner, which he knew was among the Sentry fund's holdings. Meanwhile, either Frank or Bernie had activated the computer screen, explaining that it would provide a live feed to Madoff's account at the DTCC.

"They continued to move pages of the screen until they got to the AOL page," Tucker recalled. In the stock journal, he could see the number of AOL shares that Madoff should have owned for his hedge fund clients; on the screen, he could see the number of shares credited to Madoff by the clearinghouse. The two numbers tallied.

Tucker had never actually seen a live feed from a broker's DTCC account, as subsequent lawsuits would point out. Even if he had, it is unlikely he could have detected that this one was fake. After all, DiPascali had access to a real DTCC account screen every day—there was one available to the legitimate brokerage firm—and he had taken great pains to ensure that his imitation exactly matched the original.

Madoff encouraged Tucker to pick another stock, but Tucker was satisfied. The shares were there; there was no possibility of fraud. He left reassured that there was nothing to the *Barron's* article, no reason at all to be concerned.

Even without the tour-de-force demonstration provided to Tucker, most of Madoff's burgeoning collection of hedge fund clients apparently shrugged off the skeptical articles in May 2001, certain that their trust was justified by Madoff's character and reputation. One of them, Ezra

Merkin, kept a copy of the *Barron's* article in his files for years but continued to invest hundreds of millions of dollars with Madoff.

∞

Another copy of the *Barron's* article would also rest for years in the files of the SEC's Office of Compliance Inspections and Examinations in Washington, D.C. This was the branch of the federal agency responsible for inspecting brokerage firms like Bernie Madoff's.

The office's director had sent the clipping to her associate director, with a note on the top saying that Arvedlund was "very good" and that "This is a great exam for us!" But no examination of Madoff's firm was ordered; apparently, the only action the associate took in response to the article was to file it.

Lack of action had become almost reflexive at the understaffed agency, uncertain of its mandate and unsure of itself. The 1990s had seen morale plummet at the SEC, as Congress passed laws that weakened the regulatory environment for financial firms. One disheartening piece of legislation was the Private Securities Litigation Reform Act of 1995, which made it more difficult for private lawyers to take companies to court over their accounting or management practices. Another came a year later, when Congress broadened the loophole that allowed hedge funds to avoid registration with the SEC. This naturally made it easier and more lucrative to launch a new hedge fund without much regulatory oversight. Thousands of money managers took advantage of this increased leeway.

For years, the quality of the SEC staff had been under relentless pressure, primarily because of tightfisted budgets. The staff turnover rate had climbed so high that it attracted the concerned attention of the General Accounting Office. The turnover rates for SEC lawyers, accountants, and investigators, which averaged 15 percent in 2000, were twice the average rate for comparable government positions. In a 2001 report, the GAO found that a third of the agency's staff—more than a thousand employees, at least half of them attorneys—left the agency between 1998 and 2000. At the salaries available, it seemed unlikely that those spots would be claimed by anyone but raw recruits. In the years ahead, increasingly creative Wall Street criminals like Bernie Madoff would be policed by increasingly inexperienced and ill-trained SEC investigators. The dishonestly bullish reports that Wall Street analysts had turned out on flimsy technology stocks and the fraudulent accounting used by technology giants such as Enron and WorldCom in the 1990s would ultimately be exposed—but not through the SEC's efforts or initiatives, and not in time to avoid massive damage to employees and investors. At a congressional hearing in the wake of those scandals, Senator Paul Sarbanes of Maryland would quote an unidentified observer's assessment of the SEC: "Morale is at its lowest point. This place is a shambles of what it was 10 or 12 years ago."

Just a month before the *Barron's* article was published, an assistant enforcement director in the SEC's New York office had received a referral about Madoff that had come from the agency's Boston office. It was a complex, somewhat arcane complaint from a quantitative analyst who said he had analyzed Madoff's returns mathematically and was convinced that Madoff was a fraud.

The accusation came from Harry Markopolos, a portfolio manager at Rampart Investment Management in Boston. Markopolos had become interested in Madoff's returns a few years earlier, when a Rampart executive asked him to investigate why Rampart's options hedging strategies could not achieve the kind of returns routinely posted by Bernie Madoff. The son of immigrant Greek restaurant owners in Erie, Pennsylvania, Markopolos had earned a bachelor's degree in business administration from Loyola University of Maryland and a master's degree in finance from Boston College. Along the way, he worked for his family's restaurant chain, served in the U.S. Army Reserve, joined a family-affiliated brokerage firm, and worked at a small investment partnership before arriving at Rampart in 1991. By 1996 he had met the rigorous requirements for the chartered financial analyst credential and was active in the Boston Security Analysts Society.

Markopolos was an intelligent, slightly naïve man with a pronounced weakness for hyperbole and crude sexist humor. In his memoir, he reported teasing his future wife by offering to pay for her to get breast implants instead of the two-carat diamond engagement ring she wanted. "That way it's something we both can enjoy," he supposedly told her. In the memoir, he wrote, "We settled for a carat and a half."

Even his friends agreed that he was a little odd. The man who would become his firmest ally in the SEC's Boston office, the veteran investigator Ed Manion, observed that few people who met Markopolos were indifferent to him. "Either you like him or you don't like him," Manion said, adding that he thought Markopolos's personality "fostered" that reaction. "Sometimes Harry is not too smooth" at handling the "people-to-people stuff," he observed. Indeed, Markopolos would unashamedly joke that the difference between a male and female SEC staffer was that the female could count to 20 and the male "could count to 21—but only if he takes off his pants." He added, "That usually irritates the women, until I add, 'But that assumes that he can find it, and unfortunately at the SEC none of them can actually find it. That's how clueless they are.'" As this anecdote suggests, he made no secret of his contempt for the market's senior regulators.

When Markopolos analyzed Madoff's returns, he found that they did not remotely track the performance of the blue-chip securities Madoff was supposedly buying. He saw no honest reason why Madoff would let his feeder funds reap the huge management fees while he got only the trading commissions. He doubted there were enough index options in the world to hedge a portfolio as big as Madoff's. And he noticed that Madoff had lost money in only three of the eighty-seven months between January 1993 and March 2000, while the S&P 500 had been down in twenty-eight of those months. "That would be equivalent to a major league baseball player batting .966," Markopolos noted later. (This analogy would have been less convincing to professional investors than it sounded to laymen. For one thing, the Gateway mutual fund, which pursued a similar strategy, had only fourteen losing months in the same period, so it had a batting average of .839—and even with twenty-eight losing months, the S&P 500 had been batting .678 during those years. These, too, would be implausible-sounding achievements for a baseball player, but both were indisputably the result of legitimate market activity, not fraud.)

Still, Markopolos immediately and accurately concluded that Madoff was cheating somehow—either running a Ponzi scheme or using his knowledge of incoming orders to trade ahead of his customers and thereby benefit from the price changes caused by their transactions, an illegal practice known as front-running. Excited by these findings, he brought them to Manion's attention. In May 2000, Manion arranged for Markopolos to sit down with Grant Ward, the senior enforcement lawyer in the Boston office.

The meeting did not go well. "Harry tends to lose people," Manion acknowledged later. Markopolos was a proud quantitative analyst—a "quant" in Wall Street lingo—who unfortunately overestimated his ability to explain things clearly to non-quants. Explaining a complex idea at a whiteboard, Markopolos would draw a circle here, then an arrow pointing to another circle there, then a third arrow pointing to yet another circle somewhere else. Manion described the experience as one of expanding mystification, adding: "And Harry would say: See, there it is, you know. And you look at the stuff and say, well, I don't see it."

At the meeting with Ward, Markopolos and Manion could tell that Ward's eyes had glazed over before Markopolos had gotten past the first "exhibit" point in his analysis of Madoff's returns. It probably did not help that Ward was just months away from leaving the agency for a job in private practice, but, to be fair, the opening point was an eye-crossing tangle of market jargon and mathematical terms that began like this:

> Returns can't be coming from net long exposure to the market:
> Part A, a split-strike conversion is long 30–35 stocks that track
> the 100 stock OEX index, short out-of-the-money (Delta < .5)
> OEX index call options, and long out-of-the-money (delta, -.5)
> OEX index put options. . . .

For a non-quant like Grant Ward—indeed, for most regulatory attorneys—this might as well have been ancient Sanskrit.

Ward later assured a frustrated Ed Manion that he had sent the Madoff tip to the SEC's office in New York for follow-up. But there is no public evidence that he ever did—and an official investigation would later conclude that he had not. When asked about it, Ward said he had no recollection of the meeting with Markopolos at all, although the official report concluded that this, too, was untrue.

For the next year, Markopolos continued to track Madoff's statistically impossible success. In a note to Manion, he said, "These numbers really are too good to be true. And every time I've thought a company's or a manager's numbers were 'too good to be true,' there has been fraud involved."

With Manion's encouragement, Markopolos prepared an updated report on Madoff for a new Boston enforcement chief. This time, on

April 3, 2001, Markopolos's analysis was actually sent to the New York office, where it was referred to an assistant regional enforcement director, who was a competent and well-respected lawyer. A day later, she sent her supervisor an e-mail saying that she had reviewed the Madoff complaint but didn't think it warranted further investigation. "I don't think we should pursue this matter further," she wrote dismissively.

Reading the Markopolos document years later, she was mystified by her decision, which she said she did not even remember making. "My impressions are that this is a document that I probably would have needed to consult somebody about," she said. "I hope I consulted somebody. I honestly don't remember." She added, "I also would have thought that the author of this document was odd, to say the least. But I hope that would not have led me to dismiss this—but I just don't recall."

∽

The terrorist attacks of September 11, 2001, shoved the nation's attention away from the stock market and any possible SEC investigations and diverted the media's attention away from the obvious follow-up stories suggested by the Ocrant and *Barron's* articles and the persistent Wall Street whispers about Bernie Madoff. In fact, the New York staff of FINRA, the Financial Industry Regulatory Authority, was forced to evacuate its Wall Street offices after the attacks on the World Trade Center, and its legal staff took refuge in Madoff's Midtown offices. When the stock market reopened on September 17, Bernard L. Madoff Investment Securities was standing ready with the rest of Wall Street, posting bids, taking orders, fighting back.

As the stock market gradually recovered and Americans tried to adjust to a new perception of world affairs, the hedge fund party that was helping to fuel Madoff's fraud resumed in full force. The dollars entrusted to largely unregulated hedge fund managers increased by more than a third between 2001 and 2003. Institutional investors were adding hedge funds to their portfolios, drawn by profits that far outstripped those available in the public mutual fund world and sustained by the faith that they could accurately assess the increased risks that invariably accompanied these higher returns.

While hedge funds ostensibly remained off-limits to all but the rich and sophisticated, the perception that middle-income Americans "deserved" the right to share in their high returns, already given credence in some corners of academia, was gaining traction among policymakers and regulators. Little was said about whether middle-income investors had the same risk-assessment skills as their institutional counterparts—or, indeed, if the institutional investors were as good at weighing risks as they thought they were. It would not be long before ordinary working Americans would catch the hedge fund bug and seize the opportunity to send their money, directly or indirectly, to a hedge fund doing business with Bernie Madoff.

One way for middle-class investors to get into the hedge fund world was through something called a "fund of hedge funds," a financial instrument that made its debut in the U.S. market in the summer of 2002. It was a concept borrowed from the mutual fund industry of the 1960s. Back then, investors could buy shares in a "fund of mutual funds," paying a double dose of fees for the privilege of having someone else assemble a portfolio of top-performing funds. A fund of hedge funds was the same idea, dressed in Armani. Smaller investors could put as little as $25,000 into the publicly offered fund, whose managers would pass it along to a stable of promising private hedge funds. (Even that modest minimum was self-imposed; legally, these were mutual funds, which were not required by law to set a minimum investment.)

"Funds of hedge funds raise special concerns because they permit investors to invest indirectly in the very hedge funds in which they likely may not invest directly due to the legal restrictions," SEC chairman William H. Donaldson said in congressional testimony in April 2003. They may not have been able to invest directly because the law allowed hedge funds to accept only "accredited investors," those who had at least $1 million in net worth. By 2003, however, an increasing number of middle-income American families were meeting that requirement. Housing values were high and still climbing, giving many families substantial amounts of equity in their homes, and their IRAs and 401(k) retirement plans had been around long enough to have accumulated substantial assets. As a result, millions of Americans became potential hedge fund customers.

Indeed, a growing number of them had already moved their "self-directed" IRAs into the hands of Bernie Madoff. A self-directed IRA was typically one that contained investments other than the traditional (and traditionally regulated) stocks, bonds, and mutual funds. These alternatives ranged from commodities to real estate but prominently included hedge funds. Once the savers made their own investment choices, the tax code required them to use a support firm, called an IRA custodian, to follow the account holders' directions, make the investment purchases, and do the administrative work. An early Madoff investor in Florida found a small firm called Retirement Accounts Inc. that would administer the IRA he had invested with Avellino & Bienes, despite the fact that the accountants' loose operation was not registered, provided no prospectus, and maintained minimal records.

Word spread, and in time Retirement Accounts Inc. was the administrator for hundreds of self-directed IRAs invested with Madoff. After several takeovers and mergers, it became a unit of Fiserv Inc., a giant financial services company. By 2008 it would be handling roughly eight hundred self-directed IRAs invested with Madoff, the value of which was said to exceed $1 billion.

Another way for middle-income Americans to gain a stake in hedge funds and other private, lightly regulated investments—and, therefore, get a chance to fall into Bernie Madoff's trap—was through their workplace pension funds.

For some years, giant public and corporate pension funds had been putting tiny fractions of their assets into "alternative investments," including hedge funds. By 2003 countless smaller pension plans also were investing in these higher-risk "alternatives"—indeed, dozens of them were already investing in Bernie Madoff.

As early as 1989, six small labor unions in upstate New York had started investing pension assets with Madoff through an investment advisory firm on Long Island called Ivy Asset Management. The founders of Ivy had been introduced to Madoff in 1987 by one of their own clients, and they maintained a relationship with him for more than a decade. Other fledgling financial advisers were soon investing their pension fund clients' money with Madoff through Ivy, which collected substantial fees in exchange for its advice and due-diligence examinations. Some new limited partnerships were formed solely to invest with Madoff via the Ivy firm, and a number of pension funds were attracted to their steady, reliable returns.

By 1991 some Ivy executives had heard disquieting rumors about

Madoff, according to e-mails obtained through subsequent litigation. By 1997 they had noticed that the volume of publicly traded index options was too small to cover the implementation of Madoff's investment strategy just for their own clients—and they believed him to be handling several billion dollars for other clients as well.

Flying back to New York City with Bernie Madoff after a meeting with one of the upstate union pension funds, a senior Ivy executive allegedly asked him about this mismatch between options volume and the assets he managed. Madoff brushed off the question, saying he might trade a few options with banks or foreign exchanges, but that it was rare.

The Ivy executive apparently did not argue with Madoff—although he knew that the mismatch actually happened quite frequently—but he must have looked unconvinced. A few months later, perhaps to head off any lingering doubts, Madoff mentioned to this executive that he occasionally traded options on other exchanges. But the options that Madoff supposedly used were traded exclusively on the Chicago Board Options Exchange. His story still didn't add up.

In the face of these lame explanations, the Ivy executive theorized that Madoff was lying. Coming close (but not close enough) to the reality of the Ponzi scheme, the executive suspected that Madoff was really using investors' money to finance his legitimate stock-trading business. The "investment earnings" credited to their accounts might actually just be "compensation for the use of their money," he suggested in a note to Ivy's founders in May 1997. In short, Madoff might be lying about how he was making money for his investors—paying them a share of his firm's legitimate proprietary trading profits, rather than investing in his arcane hedged strategy—but at least he was actually making money for them, the Ivy executive evidently surmised.

This thesis—that Madoff's investors were actually lenders who were unwittingly financing his own trading activity and getting paid for it with some of his firm's profits—gained substance two years later when the Ivy executive talked with a prominent hedge fund manager, who was not identified in court records. The Ivy executive described the conversation in an internal memo:

> [The manager] met last night with someone he has known for a long time who works for Bernie. [He] said, "lets talk reality here."

[He] advanced the subordinated lending theory about what the strategy really is. His contact gave it a nod—"you can think of it that way."

One of Ivy's founders grew even more pointedly doubtful about Madoff over the next few years, although he later denied he suspected a Ponzi scheme. In an internal memo in 2001, he observed that "Madoff can personally bankrupt the Jewish community if he's not 'real.'" Responding in 2002 to a staffer's attempt to analyze and explain Madoff's remarkably consistent returns, he wrote, "Ah, Madoff. You omitted one other possibility—he's a fraud."

Based on their growing uneasiness, the Ivy executives had eased their own wealth and that of their private clients out of Madoff's hands by roughly 2000. But they did not remove their pension clients' money from their Madoff accounts, according to a subsequent lawsuit against them. Apparently the unions were happy with the steady returns. Moreover, Ivy benefited from the continuing fees and from having the pension money counted as part of its "assets under management," a key benchmark in the investment advisory business. So the small pension plans for a host of union workers, totaling more than $220 million, stayed with Madoff.

These local unions truly were small fry among the legions of pension funds marching into the world of hedge funds. When the giant state public pension funds, such as California's and New York's, collectively increased the percentage of their assets invested in hedge funds by just a point or two, the result was a flood of billions of dollars looking for hot new funds run by brilliant new managers.

And one of the people who helped find those managers was a smart, ambitious woman in suburban New York named Sandra Manzke, one of the few women to rise to the top of the hedge fund industry—and one of the earliest hedge fund managers to introduce mainstream pension plans and middle-income investors to Bernie Madoff.

Manzke was an articulate, opinionated, and very astute woman who had risen through the analytical side of Wall Street in an era when the nice executive offices were a very long way from the ladies' room. In the early 1970s she developed methods for measuring fund performance for a small but prestigious mutual fund firm. After collecting a fine arts degree from the Pratt Institute and dabbling briefly in the movie business, she returned to Wall Street with a mane of blond hair and a theatrical style. By 1976 she had landed a spot at Rogers, Casey & Barksdale, one of the most prominent pension fund advisory firms in the country.

At that time the financially dismal stock market of the 1970s was unfamiliar ground for most pension plans, which had long restricted themselves to bonds and other less risky investments. But bonds were not even keeping up with inflation, much less with the growth in promised benefits to retirees. By the mid-1970s even the proverbial "prudent men" of the fiduciary world were recognizing that prudence required them to add equities to their portfolios.

Manzke's specialty was to search out promising new mutual fund managers and steer her pension fund clients' money into their hands. She was one of the first to introduce pension fund clients to soon-to-be legendary fund managers such as Peter Lynch, Fred Alger, and Mario Gabelli.

In 1984 she left Rogers Casey and struck out on her own, forming what became Tremont Partners. It was a struggle at first, but she found her footing, and her little firm soon had a great track record with its clients. Some of her earliest clients were the public pension funds for the town of Fairfield, Connecticut, which signed on with her in early 1985.

But her real fortune was in her Rolodex, and not just because she had Bernie Madoff's number. She seemed to know almost everybody in the increasingly busy intersection between pension funds and hedge funds, and she had elaborately interwoven partnerships with many of them. By 1990 she had become a director of a new family of offshore hedge funds called the Kingate funds, managed by a London-based pair of Italian businessman, Carlo Grosso and Federico Ceretti. A pioneering Kingate fund was incorporated as early as 1991 and was probably investing with Madoff from the beginning—Madoff himself identified Kingate as one of the first hedge funds to invest with him. By March 1994 a second Kingate fund had opened a Madoff account; less than two years later, there was a third.

Besides these offshore funds, Manzke put Tremont Partners at the forefront of developing accessible hedge funds for domestic American investors. In 1994, Tremont launched what became the Rye funds, a popular choice among advisers to pension plans and individual retirement accounts. Ultimately, more than $1 billion would find its way through the Rye funds into Madoff's hands.

The Rye funds were born in the same year that Manzke acquired a partner at Tremont: Robert I. Schulman, who had previously run Smith Barney's $60 billion Consulting Services Division and its "Retail New Product Development Group." With his round, open face and curly hair, Bob Schulman was a popular and respected figure on Wall Street. According to one lawsuit, he was vocal in his praise for Madoff and his performance over the years, but later testimony showed that Manzke already had access to Madoff before Schulman arrived at Tremont.

In the spring of 2001, as Michael Ocrant and *Barron's* were publishing skeptical articles about Madoff's secret money-managing business, the giant OppenheimerFunds group was doing its due diligence on a deal to purchase Tremont Partners. There is no public evidence that the articles caused any consternation among the lawyers and analysts putting the deal together. The deal was done and, by July, Sandra Manzke and Bob Schulman had swept a big pile of chips off the table.

Beyond its Oppenheimer connection, Tremont formed complex and prestigious alliances across the international hedge fund map. In a joint venture with Credit Suisse, it popularized a hedge fund performance index, tempting creative bankers to devise new ways to bet on the hedge fund sweepstakes by designing exotic derivatives pegged to the index.

Manzke and Schulman became sought-after sages as regulators struggled to understand "the implications of hedge fund growth," the topic of a public forum in 2003. They exuded confidence in the hedge fund industry, although Manzke was fiercely outspoken in her belief that regulators ought to require hedge fund managers to be more cooperative with "fund of funds" advisers like her.

At one forum, she told regulators, "It's very difficult to get answers out of managers, and they hold all the keys right now. If you want to get into a good fund, and you ask some difficult questions, you may not get that answer." Indeed, you may not get into that fund. She may have had Madoff in mind when she expressed this frustration—he famously challenged those who questioned him closely to take their money out and leave him alone. Being banished by Bernie would have been a death sentence to any fund whose entire existence, including its lucrative management fees, was based on access to him.

In 2002, Sandra Manzke's professional past and profitable present collided when analysts from her old launchpad, now called Rogerscasey Inc., took the measure of the Tremont line of hedge funds—and warned its clients away.

The basis for this warning was that Tremont simply could not see inside Madoff's black box—it "receives limited independent third-party transparency," the firm said, translating its simple message into the jargon of the financial consultant. Rogerscasey's analysts did not like Madoff's habit of moving entirely into Treasury bills at the end of each year, clearing his own trades and sending out his own trade confirmations—which, they noted, he "could be making up." Rogerscasey's rating for the Madoff-related Tremont funds was "sell."

Notes in the Rogerscasey files for the Tremont funds, dated February 26, 2004, actually included some clear, unequivocal English: "The Madoff exposure is a potential disaster. Even though some products would not be directly affected. . . . Tremont's products will still see their reputations vaporized when Madoff rolls over like a big ship."

By 2002, Madoff's hidden Ponzi scheme was booming. Fairfield Greenwich Group had more than $4 billion invested with him by then, and additional billions were pouring in from the Kingate funds, the various Tremont products, and the three Merkin funds. Hundreds of millions had come in from all the loyal investors originally collected by Avellino & Bienes and plucked from the SEC's lifeboats by Bernie himself, making calls and having meetings. If anyone running such a gigantic fraud could ever feel secure, Madoff should have.

But beneath the surface, his Ponzi scheme was being plagued by one of his oldest clients, Jeffry Picower. Picower was the aggressive tax lawyer who drifted into Madoff's orbit in the 1960s, when Saul Alpern's accounting partner Michael Bienes married Picower's sister. By now Bienes was married to someone else, but Picower had become one of Madoff's biggest investors—and one of his growing headaches.

The core job for any Ponzi scheme, of course, is to keep enough money flowing into it so that current investors are comforted and reassured by the ease and speed with which great sums can be withdrawn. By now, Madoff's earliest investors were elderly, some of them were fabulously rich, and most of those were unflaggingly generous. They were pulling tens of millions of dollars from their Madoff accounts each year to educate grandchildren, support schools, build hospitals, renovate art museums, sponsor medical research, and support a host of worthy charities and endowed chairs.

But no one dipped more deeply or steadily into his Madoff wealth than Jeffry Picower and his wife, Barbara. They were a quiet couple, rarely popping up in the boldface society columns of Palm Beach or on the *Forbes* list of the wealthiest Americans. But they surely belonged on that list. Indeed, Picower was far wealthier than even Madoff realized.

Picower had won spectacular high-stakes bets on promising medical and technology companies and corporate mergers, reaping just over $1 billion on a single deal and circulating his profits regularly through his Madoff accounts. Over time, he invested about $620 million in actual cash and securities with Madoff. With Madoff's steady rates of return, Picower's account balances ultimately ran up into the billions of dollars. As early as 1986 he was wealthy enough to invest $28 million in an arbitrage fund run by Ivan Boesky, the notorious trader who boosted his fund's profits illegally by buying tips from Wall Street insiders and who was the model for the Gordon Gekko character in Oliver Stone's 1987 movie *Wall Street*. By the late 1990s, Picower's trading account at Goldman Sachs—almost certainly just one of his many Wall Street brokerage accounts—was reportedly worth $10 billion. At one point, he arranged a $5 billion margin loan in that account, which indicates he was so rich that Goldman knew that he could easily cover the loan if the market turned against him.

Picower's name showed up frequently in Frank DiPascali's in-box, with requests for withdrawals that escalated sharply between 1995 and 2003 but which had begun in earnest after the 1987 crash, according to Madoff. Available records show that Picower and his wife withdrew $390 million from their Madoff accounts in 1996, more than seven times the amount they withdrew in 1995.

The Picowers took out more than $400 million in 1997, more than $500 million in 1998, and nearly $600 million in 1999. And that was just the warm-up. In the four years between 2000 and 2003, they took out a total of $3.4 billion—in 2002 alone, they made fifty-two withdrawals totaling just over $1 billion.

To put this into perspective, it is as if every penny that Fairfield Greenwich Group's investors had given to Madoff by 2000 had been handed over to Jeffry Picower by 2003.

After their $1 billion withdrawal in 2002, the Picowers broke into the philanthropic headlines by endowing the eighty-thousand-square-foot Picower Institute for Learning and Memory at the Massachusetts Institute of Technology, which sought to become the world's premier center for research into the brain and its agonizing ailments, from autism to Alzheimer's.

From the day these withdrawals became public after Madoff's arrest, one of the deepest mysteries of the case was why Picower—who did not introduce other clients to Madoff, did not run a feeder fund for him, did not even make big gifts to Madoff's pet charities—was allowed to remain an investor despite his enormous and rapidly escalating withdrawals.

By this time, Madoff and Picower seemed to have a close relationship—the Madoffs frequently shared private jet flights with the Picowers from Palm Beach to New York, and the two couples dined out together fairly often—but as far as Madoff was concerned, the apparent friendship was a sham. "Picower had no friends," he snapped during his first prison interview. "He was a very strange person. It was always a very tense relationship."

There was ample evidence that Madoff occasionally "fired" difficult clients. Why didn't he politely tell Picower to take his money and go elsewhere?

According to Madoff, Picower had simply become the Ponzi equivalent of a bank too big to fail: an investor too big to fire. Covering Picower's annual withdrawals was difficult enough; coming up with the money to completely redeem his multibillion-dollar account would have been impossible. "I had to keep him attached to me," Madoff admitted, offering a glimpse into the expediency that so often masqueraded for friendship in his life.

Picower had been victimized by a Ponzi scheme in the 1970s. Was he now astute enough to realize what Madoff was doing and devious enough to exploit the leverage that knowledge gave him? Madoff often suspected that the answer was yes. In September 2003, for the first but not the last time, Madoff did not fully honor one of Picower's withdrawal requests, paying only a fraction of the amount Picower wanted—with no apparent complaints or repercussions. By then, Picower had withdrawn far more than the money he had originally deposited into his Madoff accounts. Perhaps he simply figured that he'd continue to milk Madoff's fraud-fed accounts until the money finally ran out, knowing that Madoff had no choice but to let him do so.

Certainly at one point Picower believed that Madoff was legitimate—more than a decade earlier, he had put hundreds of millions of dollars' worth of cash and securities into his Madoff accounts, and he left money in those accounts through several market storms that might well have toppled a Ponzi scheme. His lawyers and family insisted later that these actions proved that he did not know Madoff was a crook.

As with everyone who stayed at this party until the bitter end, it comes down to separating the villains from the victims, the knaves from the fools. If Picower was numbered among the fools, he became one of the richest fools in the crowd—richer, by far, than the people who were certainly villains, including Madoff himself.

෴

Besides the hidden pain that Picower's cash demands were inflicting on Madoff's Ponzi scheme, the new century also brought unexpected pain to the Madoff family and the legitimate family business, Bernard L. Madoff Investment Securities.

In September 2002, Madoff's nephew and employee, Charlie Wiener, learned that his young daughter had cancer. As she was being treated, Peter Madoff, who had already been treated for bladder cancer, learned in November that his son, Roger, had a vicious form of leukemia. In the early spring of 2003, after Roger had begun the debilitating treatments he would record in a posthumous memoir called *Leukemia for Chickens*, Bernie's son Andrew went in for tests. He, too, had cancer—a tentative diagnosis was mantle cell lymphoma, another very nasty adversary.

As the new decade advanced, Peter Madoff's focus of attention telescoped down to a single hospital bed. One hospital staff member would poignantly recall Peter gently rubbing ointment into his son's feet to comfort him just a few days before his death. Ruth and Bernie used their family foundation to support research into the disease and other cancers of the circulatory system; Roger's sister, Shana, was active in various fund-raising efforts but was deeply bruised by her grief. It was a difficult time that strained family ties in every direction.

He would later deny it, but Madoff's prized market-making business was sick, too. The computerization and competition he had long championed with regulators had indeed reduced the cost of trading stocks—but they had also reduced the trading profits of firms like his. Reconstructed records suggested that the visible Wall Street business run by Bernie Madoff and his family lost almost $160 million between 2001 and 2003, losses that Madoff insisted were offset by the capital he had retained over the years. But those losses added greatly to the complexity of the Ponzi scheme.

Madoff's growing roster of hedge fund clients—most likely unwitting but doubtlessly gullible—were raking in enough money from an ever-broader field of investors to allow Madoff to accommodate Jeffry Picower's unwelcome withdrawals. And Frank DiPascali was finding ways to launder the stolen proceeds into streams of revenue that would look legitimate on the faltering brokerage firm's books, revenues that would raise no eyebrows inside or outside the firm.

To do so, DiPascali painstakingly calculated what the commissions would have been if Madoff actually had been doing the stated volume of trading for his clients. He then swept the appropriate sum of money out of the Ponzi scheme's bank account and into the London affiliate's bank accounts, and then moved it back to New York, to show up on the New York firm's ledgers as legitimate commission income supposedly generated from trading in European markets—which meshed with Madoff's cover story about why his brother and sons didn't see his hedge fund trades going through their own trading desk in New York.

Despite the personal heartaches of those years, Madoff and DiPascali had both grown pretty smug about keeping their secrets—and pulling in the cash.

There always seemed to be enough fresh money to cover the intra-office bailouts, the fat paychecks for DiPascali and some of his busy staff members on the seventeenth floor, the executive suite salaries and bonuses, and the loans for the Madoff family on the nineteenth floor. There was always money for the first-class travel, first-class shopping, first-class living, and, of course, the first-class philanthropy. It was a style of living that mirrored the lives of Madoff's largest investors, the trusting people who had accompanied him on his journey to the land of almost unimaginable wealth.

Carl Shapiro was still one of Boston's most respected philanthropists, and he was also a prominent but less active figure in the glittery country club life of Palm Beach, where he and his wife, Ruth, lived in a full-service suite at the luxurious Breakers Hotel. Their elegantly gowned daughters and his dapper son-in-law Robert Jaffe showed up at a host of expensive charity events every year, and their names and faces popped up frequently in the local society pages.

Sonny Cohn, the cofounder of Cohmad Securities, still lived comfortably on Long Island, where he and his brother had become notable donors to the North Shore Long Island Jewish hospital system. But he was spending more time with a group of congenial fellow multimillionaires in the Miami area and entrusting Cohmad's operations to his daughter Marcia Beth, who had known Madoff since she was a child and trusted him completely.

Stanley Chais and his wife, a successful screenwriter, lived with almost ostentatious simplicity in Beverly Hills—his car was an aging Japanese import, and their home was far from elaborate by neighborhood standards. Life was becoming harder for Chais, who was beginning to suffer from the rare blood disorder that ultimately would claim his life in 2010. But his family and clients seemed to be prospering from the Madoff accounts he managed, and his philanthropic gifts earned him praise and attention in Los Angeles and Israel.

Madoff's old friend and representative in Minneapolis, Mike Engler, had died in 1994, but his widow and adult children remained in Madoff's orbit, joining his family for ski trips and golf outings for years and entrusting their wealth to his genius. Their close ties to Madoff were reassuring to the many other Madoff investors among their circle of friends.

Ezra Merkin had become a lion of Wall Street, admired for his eloquent quarterly letters to his investors and surrounded by the obvious trappings of success: museum-quality art, a trophy apartment in one of Park Avenue's legendary buildings, and a seat on the board at a host of prestigious schools, universities, and charities. The president of the Fifth Avenue Synagogue his father had helped establish, he was widely seen as a pious, generous man of great wealth and wisdom.

To the outside world, Madoff's brokerage firm seemed to be prospering, too. By 2004 it had nearly two hundred employees and a reported net worth of $440 million—a fivefold increase over the previous decade, and twice the value reported just five years earlier. This put it firmly in the ranks of the fifty largest firms on Wall Street.

Nobody seemed to ever poke too seriously into what was going on there. There had been a few bumbling queries from the SEC in the past few years, but Madoff had easily deflected them. A few smart consultants and a few private banking teams had come across the same inconsistencies that worried the Ivy Asset Management team in the late 1990s and had quietly blacklisted Madoff. Even some very influential people— prominent hedge fund managers, some senior people at Credit Suisse, all of whom would have carried weight with regulators—had written him off and warned their clients to get out. Fortunately for Madoff, none of these influential people seem to have picked up the phone and shared a few forceful warnings with Madoff's regulators or with any law enforcement agency.

It was as if these skeptics had seen that his operation was a firetrap that could ignite at any moment. But their response was simply to usher their own clients to the exits and quietly walk away. If the crowded building ultimately went up in flames, it wouldn't be their fault that the fire marshals and building inspectors hadn't been smart enough to figure it out on their own, would it?

So, amid the anxiety and personal anguish in the Madoff family and his billion-dollar headache over the Picower accounts, at least something was going right for Bernie: his Wall Street reputation was brighter than ever, his secret fraud was safe from regulators, and boatloads of new cash were arriving almost daily.

8

A NEAR-DEATH EXPERIENCE

"What are you looking for?"

On April 20, 2005, Bernie Madoff confronted the two SEC examiners who had been occupying a glass-walled office on the nineteenth floor for three weeks. He was no longer the charming host who had entertained them recently with tales about the old days on Wall Street. He was an angry, streetwise bouncer who was itching to kick them out. "Tell me what you're looking for," he insisted.

The SEC staffers, William David Ostrow and Peter Lamore, were surprised at this outburst of temper—but not as surprised as they had been when Madoff, the chairman of the firm, insisted on being their only contact in the office. They'd both been around long enough to know how odd that was, especially at a firm this size. They should have been dealing with someone lower in the food chain.

But Madoff was handling this examination personally; he always dealt with regulatory examiners personally. He had too much to hide, and there were only a few people he trusted to help him do that. Frank DiPascali on the seventeenth floor had been busy ever since the call came in about this exam. DiPascali had been checking the fake paper and computer records they had created to obscure the Ponzi scheme. The elaborate records backed up Madoff's lies and supported his cover story: that he was just a hired hand who executed hedge fund trades for less than a nickel a pop.

It had worked with the SEC before.

On December 18, 2003, Madoff was walking through the Lipstick

Building lobby when his cell phone rang. He recognized the caller as Lori Richards, a high-level SEC staffer in Washington. It was Richards who had flagged the *Barron's* magazine article about Madoff in 2001 as "a great exam for us." Nothing had been done back then, but in 2003 someone on her staff got a detailed tip from a hedge fund manager questioning Madoff's returns, and she was following up.

"Bernie, it's Lori," she said.

"Hi, Lori."

"I need you to help me out. Can you tell me about your hedge funds?"

Madoff stood still. "I don't have a hedge fund," he answered.

"I didn't think so," she replied.

Madoff quickly added, "I execute trades for hedge funds."

The distinction he made seemed to satisfy the SEC official, although she indicated that there would be a follow-up examination. When her staff came up with more questions, Madoff easily deflected them. The inquiry then just rolled to a halt without even a final report closing the file. The records from that exam were piled into a pair of boxes and forgotten.

Although Madoff was ready for the visit from Ostrow and Lamore in 2005, this exam had been particularly annoying. Lamore was okay, a smart kid, but Madoff thought Ostrow was obnoxious. He had gritted his teeth as Ostrow paged through e-mail records, expense account records, telephone bills—an aimless fishing expedition, as far as he could see. He'd kept his temper when Lamore asked for yet another computer run, in a different format this time.

So far, the examiners hadn't asked about the hedge funds—or about custody accounts, or trading records, or third-party confirmations for all the options and blue chips that Madoff was supposedly buying and selling. What on earth *were* they looking for, if not for that?

Ostrow and Lamore tried to calm Madoff. It was just a routine examination of the brokerage firm's books and records, they said, the kind of thing that happens all the time.

This was not entirely true; the examination was not routine. It was a belated response to a set of e-mails that an alert SEC staffer had found in the files of a prominent hedge fund firm during a truly routine examination nearly a year earlier. The fund manager, Renaissance Technologies, had an indirect stake in Madoff through its Meritor hedge fund. The Renaissance e-mails, written in late 2003, expressed the same mystification about Madoff's performance and practices as the *Barron's* and Ocrant articles had in the spring of 2001.

In one of the e-mails, a senior executive shared his doubts with his investment committee. "First of all, we spoke to an ex-Madoff trader," the executive said. "He said Madoff is pretty tight-lipped and therefore he didn't know much about it, but he didn't really know how they made money." Then, a respected hedge fund consultant "told us in confidence that he believes Madoff will have a serious problem within a year. We are going to be speaking to [the consultant] in 11 days to see if we can get more specifics."

But this executive already had pretty much made up his mind. "The point is that as we don't know why he does what he does we have no idea if there are conflicts in his business that could come to some regulator's attention." It just didn't make sense to risk a scandal for the relatively modest return they expected. "The risk-reward on this bet is not in our favor," he concluded, adding, "please keep this confidential."

The SEC examiner showed the intriguing e-mails to his supervisor, who took them seriously and asked him to learn more from the hedge fund. But when the SEC staffer returned, the Renaissance executive was dismissive. The author of the e-mail had been at a conference "where there was some chatter about Madoff," the executive said, but it was all unsubstantiated, as far as he knew. True, the hedge fund had cut its stake in the Madoff deal, but that was simply because of mediocre returns.

It was an odd explanation. The doubts expressed in the extensive e-mail chain were cogent, well researched, and unequivocal. As early as 2003, these men had stopped trusting Madoff's game and started cashing in their chips. And they knew other smart people on Wall Street who had done the same. They surely could have helped the young SEC examiner who was trying to figure out what Madoff was doing.

But apparently the people at Renaissance—like those at Credit Suisse and Rogerscasey, who had quietly blacklisted Madoff by early 2004—didn't want to get involved. A top Renaissance executive, Nat Simons, later explained that he felt that all the information Renaissance had was readily available to the SEC. "Despite the fact that we are kind of smart people, we were just looking at matters of public record. . . . It's not like we needed a Ph.D. in mathematics," Simons said.

Besides, he said, the information they relied on wasn't that hard to get. Indeed, although Simons didn't know it, the SEC had already gotten this information without any help from elite players such as Renaissance. Although it dismissed Harry Markopolos's accusations in 2000 and 2001, it received similar warnings in May 2003, the very tip that prompted Lori Richards to call Madoff on his cell phone that December and ask about his hedge fund business.

The tip came in to the SEC's Washington office as a result of a 2002 survey of the hedge fund industry by the SEC's Investment Management Office. At that time, the agency encouraged executives to report any suspicious activity—and on May 20, 2003, a hedge fund managing director actually did. He told the SEC, in confidence, that his firm had considered investing in two different Madoff feeder funds but backed off both times. There were all kinds of red flags, he said, but the most worrisome was the fact that nobody he talked with in the options trading community confirmed doing any business with Madoff. Of course, that community of traders was supposed to keep customer information confidential, but it still seemed strange not to confirm even a general business relationship with someone who should have been one of their biggest customers.

The tip was sent along to the SEC office that handled brokerage firms, where it sat unexamined for months. When it was finally dusted off, the inquiry that followed did not focus on the mysterious lack of options trading—but it still came agonizingly close to uncovering Madoff's fraud. Someone on the exam team had the idea of getting two years' worth of Madoff trading records from the industry regulators at the NASD— which would immediately have shown that he was not trading billions of dollars' worth of blue-chip stocks and options.

But the request was never sent, for reasons no one involved could later recall.

An official study would later conclude that the staffers decided it was easier to request the trading records from Madoff himself, not from the NASD—and with Frank DiPascali's help, Madoff came up with fake records, of course. Questions were left hanging, but in early 2004 the shorthanded SEC staff members were told to shift their attention to a wide-ranging investigation of the mutual funds industry, which seemed more important because mutual funds were mainstream America's primary investment vehicle.

No one logged the tip from Harry Markopolos in 2001, or the nearly identical one from the hedge fund manager in 2003, into the agency's internal data base of investigative information. So there were no records of those earlier, unexamined warnings when the e-mails from Renaissance Technologies were found in 2004.

At least the Renaissance e-mails were taken seriously at the SEC—albeit at a glacial pace. In fact, they were the reason William David Ostrow and Peter Lamore were sitting in an office in the Lipstick Building in April 2005 watching Bernie Madoff lose his temper.

Almost shouting, Madoff repeated his original question: "What are you looking for?"

Lamore shot back, "Well, what do you want us to look for? What do you think we're looking for?"

Madoff answered immediately: "Front-running—aren't you looking for front-running?"

Front-running was a form of insider trading. Any trader who could see his firm's incoming orders could anticipate which ones were big or numerous enough to move a stock's price up or down. By inserting his own trades in front of those large, market-changing orders, he could profit on his insider's knowledge.

For the SEC, and for many skeptics on Wall Street, front-running would always be the default explanation for the chronic doubts about Bernie Madoff. His firm's trading desk handled hundreds of thousands of transactions a day from the nation's biggest mutual fund companies, online brokers, and Wall Street trading desks. It seemed perfectly plausible that Madoff could step into that order flow, trading for his private clients ahead of market-moving orders to lock in foolproof profits. The SEC did not seem to realize that the split-second computerized trading networks Madoff had helped to create had made the illicit practice much harder to carry off. And since front-running was a crime that Madoff's sons and brother were absolutely certain he was not committing, at least not on their trading desk, the regulators' fixation was actually reassuring to those who thought they knew Bernie best.

To the SEC staffer supervising Ostrow and Lamore in this 2005 exam, however, front-running was the major focus of this exercise. He had instructed them to investigate "the possibility that Madoff is using his vast amounts of customer order flow to benefit the $6 billion in hedge fund money that we believe he manages."

In the SEC's defense, some of Madoff's own sophisticated investors also seemed to think that Madoff's access to his firm's order flow was somehow behind the profits he produced for them, although they would later vehemently deny this allegation when it was made against them in private lawsuits. Some experts quoted in Michael Ocrant's examination of Madoff in 2001 also put forward this theory. Years later, one Italian money manager said *market intelligence* was the code word that popped up in the investment conference chatter in Europe and, occasionally, in some hedge fund prospectuses.

Another possibility whispered about in the hedge fund community was that Madoff was secretly allocating his firm's most profitable stock and options trades to his hedge fund clients, an illegal practice known as "cherry-picking." Considering the volume of trading he conducted for his giant wholesale customers, perhaps he was boosting his hedge fund clients' profits—or smoothing out their volatility—by creaming off the best of the day's trades for them and filling his wholesale orders with second-best, good-enough prices.

In either case, the assumption was clear and simple: Madoff was benefiting his investment advisory clients by cheating his firm's big institutional trading customers. But as long as the hedge funds were the beneficiaries of this somewhat technical violation of the rules, why should they worry? At worst, the regulators would catch Madoff and shut down the game. At best, his hedge fund clients would keep getting those slightly soiled profits for years.

For almost another month, Ostrow and Lamore scoured unhelpful records and gathered more details about Madoff's trading operation. Their supervisor even went so far as to request trading information for the month of March from Barclays, one of the banks whose name showed up on transactions in London, on the theory that Madoff might have been trading for his hedge funds through the bank there. On May 16, 2005, the supervisor received a curious response from Barclays: the bank said that Madoff's firm had recently opened an account but that "no relevant transaction activity" had taken place during March. The supervisor did not share the response with Lamore or Ostrow, apparently thinking it was unhelpful.

A week later, on May 25, the two examiners and their supervisor met to interview Madoff and confront the issue head-on. Did Madoff manage money for hedge funds?

Initially Madoff stuck to his basic hired-hand story: "We do a few trades on behalf of brokerage firms and institutions, which include a number of hedge funds." How many? Maybe four.

Ostrow flipped a copy of the four-year-old article by Michael Ocrant onto the table in front of Madoff and then leaned back. "So tell me about this article."

Madoff glanced at it. "What about it? Lori Richards has a whole file I sent her with this information. They have it." He explained that a team from the SEC's Washington office had come to see him back in 2003 looking at the same issue.

The news was a shock to the men from the New York office, although Madoff thought their surprise was an act. He had assumed they knew about the earlier exam and, in fact, were following up on it.

Recovering, Ostrow said something about the SEC being a large organization where things could slip between the cracks. He drew Madoff's attention back to the article on the table. He and Lamore had already found more than four funds that claimed to pursue his strategy.

Madoff conceded that perhaps there were as many as fifteen entities using a trading algorithm he had developed. But they were all foreign investors, and he did not keep custody of the securities for any of them. Sure, he'd give the examiners a list of the entities, no problem. Account statements, too? Sure.

Initially, he said, the model involved trading baskets of blue-chip stocks and hedging them with options. But the model stopped using options about a year ago, Madoff added—no doubt to discourage the examiners from asking for the nonexistent counterparties for these fictional option trades. Frank DiPascali had the faked account statements ready, but not even he could fake options trading records. And, of course, the first phone call to an alleged options counterparty would have blown the whole fraud sky-high. The guy would have said, "I've never done OTC options with Madoff," and it would have been over.

So Madoff acknowledged the hedge fund business but shrugged off its significance, assuring the embarrassed examiners with a trace of conde-scension that it was all old news to the SEC anyway. They'd cleared up the whole thing back in 2003.

The next day, at about 4:30 PM, the supervisor in New York sent an e-mail up the chain to Lori Richards's associate director in Washing-ton, reporting Madoff's claim that he had already told the SEC about his hedge fund business. "We are hoping that if what he is saying has any truth at all to it that you might have some info related to his hedge fund related activities you could send us," the e-mail read.

It took some time to find the boxes marked "Madoff"; they were stacked in a hallway, heading for the archives. It took a while longer for Ostrow and Lamore in New York to get access to the computer system in Washington where some data files were stored. In telephone conferences, they were told that the earlier exam hadn't found anything helpful any-way—the staff had never even drafted a closing report on their findings.

Meanwhile, their supervisor was watching the clock. He was satis-fied that his team had disproved the front-running allegation. So, at a meeting on June 16, 2005, he told the two examiners that they needed to wrap things up and move on to the next exam. Over the summer, they compiled their report, which would conclude that Madoff was telling the truth when he denied front-running his trading customers to benefit his hedge fund clients.

This was perhaps the only thing he was telling the truth about.

৩

Everybody else in the hedge fund business in the summer of 2005 seemed to be doing fine, but the level of cash in Madoff's bank account—the JPMorgan Chase account that served as the slush fund for his Ponzi scheme—was starting to drop.

What on earth was happening to the money?

At first there seemed to be a number of possible explanations.

One of Madoff's biggest feeder funds, Tremont Partners, was in tur-moil. Its founder, Sandra Manzke, had announced in April that she was setting off on her own, starting her own fund family called Maxam Capi-tal. She expected some of her clients would leave Tremont and follow her. But there could be some slippage in the process.

Meanwhile, the team at Fairfield Greenwich Group was hit with $175 million in redemptions in April, another $85 million in July, and $30 million in early September. Fairfield Greenwich had hiked its management fees, and some of its clients balked and walked. And the fund's performance was slipping: Sentry's returns had been below 7 percent since the previous October. Fairfield Greenwich was discovering that many of Sentry's investors were simply not willing to accept profits of less than 7 percent a year.

Of course, Madoff was arbitrarily deciding what kind of returns Fairfield Sentry and all the other feeder funds would produce. The only variations were caused by the fees the funds charged their investors. If Fairfield Sentry's gross returns (before fees) dropped, it was because Madoff had dropped them. Perhaps he was trying to conserve his cash by reducing the profits he was paying. If so, the strategy backfired: he was consuming more of his existing cash to pay redemptions, and since the lower rates made the feeder funds less attractive, less new cash was pouring in.

Even then he might have avoided a real crisis if it hadn't been for the scandal in the late summer of 2005 that engulfed a collection of hedge funds called the Bayou Group.

The Bayou Group was founded in the mid-1990s by Samuel Israel III, a well-connected trader who worked the hedge fund boom for all it was worth. By 2005, he was living large on the fees from his hugely successful funds, which had assets totaling $411 million—assets that were verified in the independent audits done annually by the small accounting firm of Richmond Fairfield Associates.

On July 27, 2005, not long after one large investor started asking pointed questions about Bayou's auditor and assets, Sam Israel announced that he was closing the funds. In mid-August the skeptical investor arrived at Bayou's offices in Connecticut to collect a promised redemption check from the fund's chief financial officer. The check bounced. When the investor returned to demand an explanation, he found an empty office and what looked like a suicide note in which the CFO confessed that the Bayou Group was a fraud.

The police were called, the CFO was found alive, and on September 1, he and Israel were accused of running a $400 million Ponzi scheme. The fraud had gone on since at least 1998, sustained by the convincing annual audits from Richmond Fairfield Associates, a fictional accounting firm cooked up by the CFO. He and Israel would subsequently plead guilty to federal fraud and conspiracy charges and be sentenced to twenty-year prison terms.

At first, Bernie Madoff may not have paid much attention to the unfolding scandal. His old friend Norman Levy was gravely ill when the crime made headlines. Levy and Madoff had been close for decades, ever since Levy began investing with him in the mid-1970s. Over the years, they had traveled together. Bernie and Ruth toasted Levy's hospitality and laughed at his garrulous jokes, marveling at the way he continued to squeeze joy out of his steadily diminishing physical strength. By the summer of 2005 his larger-than-life energy had dwindled to almost nothing, but his mind was still sharp. One of his last calls from his deathbed was to say good-bye to his dear friend Bernie. His son would recall that Levy's last words to his children were: "Bernie Madoff, trust Bernie Madoff."

Levy died on September 9, 2005, at the age of ninety-three. He had named Madoff as the executor for his financial assets, which included at least $250 million invested with Madoff himself. It was a lot to sort out. And giving him his due, Madoff may have been genuinely grieved by the loss of his old friend, despite the lingering resentment he felt about the withdrawals Levy and his other big clients had made in the late 1980s. For whatever reason, the Bayou collapse did not immediately seem to register with him.

Still, the case triggered a brief spasm of skepticism among hedge fund investors, who started to look more closely at the annual audits and ask more questions about the safety of assets. Moreover, some of the people defrauded in the Bayou scam also had money with Madoff, either directly or through a feeder fund. The skeptical investor who had found the Bayou CFO's confession had a small stake in one of Ezra Merkin's funds. The Wilpon family, which owned the New York Mets and had invested with Madoff for years, had had a stake in Bayou through the family's Sterling Stamos hedge fund. More than a dozen other Madoff investors lost money in the Bayou fraud. If they started looking more closely at their other investments, Madoff was right in their line of sight.

There is clear evidence that the Bayou case sent tremors through parts of the foundation of trust that Madoff had relied on for decades. Some of Fairfield Greenwich's institutional clients e-mailed the firm after the Bayou scandal to ask explicit questions about Madoff's auditor and about where their assets were being held for safekeeping. It is likely other feeder funds were getting similar inquiries. In any case, within weeks of the Bayou headlines, Madoff's cash levels began to drop, despite the healthy growth elsewhere in the business.

Given that Bayou's tiny auditing firm turned out to be fictional, the fraud focused investor attention on Madoff's tiny accounting firm, Friehling & Horowitz. When several Fairfield Greenwich partners checked the firm out, they eventually learned it was a one-man operation based in a tiny office park in an almost-rural corner of Rockland County, New York. Its only active CPA was David Friehling, a pleasant middle-aged man who coached his children's sports teams and served in the local CPA society. Friehling's partner, Jerry Horowitz, his father-in-law and Saul Alpern's former colleague, had retired to Florida years ago. Friehling's only brokerage industry clients were Madoff and Cohmad Securities, the tiny firm that was co-owned by Madoff and shared his suite in the Lipstick Building.

The problem with Madoff's audit firm, real as it was, was not its size. The problem was that it wasn't actually auditing Madoff's firm. David Friehling simply took the information he got from Madoff and turned it into something that looked like an independent annual audit. He knew it was wrong, but he later claimed he never suspected that Madoff was operating a Ponzi scheme. Even though Madoff asked him to cut corners on the audits, Friehling still trusted him. Friehling and his family and many of their friends had most, if not all, of their money with Bernie.

The partners at Fairfield Greenwich never considered Friehling a necessary line of defense against fraud. Their funds were separately audited by one of the world's largest firms, PricewaterhouseCoopers, not Friehling & Horowitz. Any audits done for the Madoff brokerage firm were Bernie Madoff's business, not theirs.

They didn't share what they had learned about the Friehling firm with their concerned investors. Instead, they put out sales material detailing how their firm's due diligence would have protected investors against a "Bayou-type" fraud. For example, they wrote, "We would question Bayou's obscure auditing firm."

What had been a slow drip from Madoff's slush fund account during the summer of 2005 became a steady leak through the autumn. Between October and the following April, more than $900 million would be withdrawn just from Fairfield Greenwich's various Madoff accounts—on top of almost $300 million pulled out before the Bayou crisis.

During that period, representatives of various European banks and hedge fund clients insisted on visiting Madoff to review his financial controls—and, although he was running low on cash, he was fully stocked with persuasive documentation and impressive testimonials.

David Friehling was summoned to Madoff's offices on November 18 for a meeting with the due-diligence team from the Optimal fund family, a Swiss-based hedge fund unit of Banco Santander, the Spanish financial giant, and a popular Madoff feeder fund among Latin American investors. A memo about that meeting reported that Friehling claimed his audits took "250 hours in a year-long process" and that "assets, liabilities, and income are 100% verified." The team was also told that the audit included "verifying balances with the DTC and other brokers and checking internal statements against customer statements."

Later such claims would seem preposterous; no one could have actually tried to verify Madoff's customer accounts with the DTCC clearinghouse without discovering the Ponzi scheme. But the affable Friehling apparently gave some comfort to the Optimal team. "David seemed surprised to hear Madoff Securities described as a secretive organization—he seemed unaware of that reputation and does not encounter any hurdles in his work there," the memo noted.

At one due-diligence meeting, Frank DiPascali posed as the head of institutional operations and, somehow, got away with it. Federal prosecutors would later assert that Dan Bonventre, Madoff's longtime director of operations and one of his highest-paid executives, coached DiPascali in the role.

DiPascali's primary contribution to keeping the fraud alive and concealed during the approaching storm, however, was hidden in the motherboard and circuits of the IBM computer serving his domain on the seventeenth floor. With the right keystroke commands, DiPascali was apparently convinced he could generate computer records elaborate and realistic enough to fool anyone.

The care that DiPascali took to create a convincing computerized environment for Madoff's fraud was remarkable—the result was worthy of all the high-tech accolades publicly awarded to Madoff's legitimate brokerage firm. The basic program to generate the mountainous volume of bogus account statements for the Ponzi scheme had been in place since at least 1994. But starting in late 2003, the amount of custom-designed software serving the Ponzi scheme proliferated dramatically. Six separate programs, and the huge data files they manipulated, already were being used to manage, modify, and generate the records that visiting regulators and accountants might require. Four more software programs were in the works in 2005 and would be finished before the end of the year.

There were programs that generated random numbers of share purchases to make the fictional trading records look more plausible. With a few function keys, the fictional trades could be sliced into bits and assigned, pro rata, to customer accounts—after automatically adjusting the prices for the four-cent commission Madoff was supposedly charging. One program changed the identities on a host of account statements in one sweep to make it look as if the securities supposedly in those accounts were being held by a variety of banks and other institutions, not by Madoff. Another program hijacked the monthly DTCC clearinghouse records from the legitimate brokerage firm upstairs and added the Ponzi scheme's bogus trades to it, producing a scrupulously accurate-looking DTCC report that Madoff could use to verify his fictional stock positions.

The computer-generated records had already gotten Madoff through the impromptu due-diligence session with Fairfield Greenwich's Jeffrey Tucker in 2001 and through earlier SEC examinations. He was sure they would quell any suspicion from the visiting skeptics now.

But all the convincing computer charades in the world wouldn't save him if his fraud ran out of real, hard cash. And by November 2, the balance in Madoff's slush fund account at JPMorgan Chase was down to just $13 million—nowhere near enough to cover the $105 million in redemption checks that had to be mailed in the next three days.

Any hesitancy, any delay in payment, would surely trigger a panic. Everything now hung in the balance: the luxurious life, the nearly worshipful gratitude from his "investors," the status and respect in the industry, the entire edifice of his life—a lie he had lived so long it probably seemed like reality by now.

Since 1992, Madoff had survived each SEC examination and due-diligence visit unscathed. He had fooled regulators, hedge fund administrators, and auditors for years, conjuring up counterfeit records and bogus computer data that seemed to satisfy them. But you cannot conjure up a counterfeit bank balance and write checks on it. The money is there or it isn't—and it wasn't.

His Ponzi scheme was $92 million in the red. Madoff had just three days to find more money or his checks would bounce, just as Bayou's had.

∽

The cash crisis of November 2005 pushed Madoff's fraud right to the brink. Only some timely cash transfers from his legitimate business accounts and an eleventh-hour bank loan to his firm forestalled immediate disaster. But the price of that bailout was that the border between Madoff's fraud and his legitimate Wall Street business—his greatest pride, the lifelong occupation of his brother and sons—was blurred beyond repair.

While the Ponzi scheme was nearly out of money, the Madoff brokerage firm wasn't. Its bank accounts were healthy, its credit was good, and its business looked strong, at least from the outside. Indeed, under the direction of Madoff's sons, the firm's proprietary trading desk was generating profits for the firm and consistently outperforming the overall market. And it still handled an impressive share of the market's trading volume. So, as a stopgap measure, Madoff moved some of his legitimate firm's money into his Ponzi scheme's bank account on November 3, 2005, to cover its outstanding checks. The next day, as a longer-term lifeline, he appropriated some bonds that belonged to Carl Shapiro, one of his oldest customers, and used them as collateral to get a bank loan for $95 million. The proceeds, received ten days later, were supposedly for his legitimate business, but were promptly shifted into his Ponzi scheme's dwindling account to cover continued withdrawal demands.

A subsequent criminal indictment asserted that it was Dan Bonventre, who had worked at Madoff's side for more than three decades, who actually carried out these rescue measures and hid them from regulators and from others at the firm. Bonventre denied that he knew anything about the fraud; the criminal case against him was still pending in February 2012. Bonventre had joined the Madoff firm in 1968, when he was still in his early twenties, after having worked briefly as a bank auditor, and he was mostly self-taught when it came to running the operational side of a midsize Wall Street brokerage business. He was a senior executive at the firm by 1975, when Frank DiPascali came on board, and by 1978 he was director of operations.

Prosecutors and regulators at the SEC later claimed that Bonventre had been falsifying records for years to prevent any trace of the Ponzi scheme from showing up on the ledgers of the legitimate Madoff business, a charge Bonventre also denied. As that legitimate business faltered in the late 1990s, Madoff arranged to move as much as $750 million in stolen money into the brokerage firm's accounts over the years by making the cash look like legal profits from his investment advisory business, according to federal prosecutors. When the cash crisis hit, prosecutors said, phony ledger entries were created to explain why money was now moving in the opposite direction. Bonventre's lawyers insisted he was "absolutely innocent" of any knowing role in Madoff's fraud.

Whether Bonventre acted knowingly or was hoodwinked by Madoff, hundreds of millions of dollars were in fact moved from the brokerage firm's account to the Ponzi scheme during the cash crisis that struck in the fall of 2005. The cash, much of it borrowed from the brokerage firm's banks, would help keep the Ponzi scheme alive into the spring of 2006.

It was a long and precarious season for Madoff—one that got much worse when he learned in mid-November 2005 that the SEC had opened yet another investigation of his hedge fund operation, just months after closing the last one. And this time, acting belatedly on yet another poorly understood tip, it was knocking on the door of his biggest feeder fund, Fairfield Greenwich.

The source of the inquiry was once again an accusation from Harry Markopolos, the skeptical "quant" in Boston. In October 2005 he made his third attempt to persuade the SEC to open an investigation of Bernie Madoff. Deliberately looking to shock the regulators, he entitled his report "The World's Largest Hedge Fund Is a Fraud." Like his earlier efforts, the submission discussed all the red flags that Markopolos saw flying from Madoff's operation: a consistency of return that was humanly impossible, stealth trading that left no trace in the stock or options markets, absurdly generous or inept counterparties who were always willing to be on the losing side of their Madoff trades. Like his earlier efforts, the report was complicated, arrogant, and dismissive of the SEC's own quantitative abilities. "Very few people in the world have the mathematical background needed to manage these types of products but I am one of them," Markopolos wrote. It was so clear to him that Madoff was running a Ponzi scheme; why didn't everyone else see it?

What happened to Markopolos's third submission to the SEC is a textbook lesson in bureaucratic bungling. Animosity, arrogance, defensiveness, ignorance, stubbornness, inattention, simple laziness—all that "people-to-people stuff" of office life—were part of the equation. You didn't need to be a quant to see how it would add up.

But it started well enough.

Members of the Boston enforcement staff read Markopolos's latest memo and met with him in person for several hours on October 25, 2005. They were impressed—indeed, alarmed. While the memo acknowledged that front-running was a remotely possible explanation for Madoff's success, it emphasized that a Ponzi scheme was far more likely. If Harry was right, the investor losses would be in the *billions* of dollars.

But once again the Boston office was stuck with the bureaucratic reality: Madoff was in New York, so the SEC office in New York would have to investigate him. The Boston team tried hard to impress the New York office with the credibility of this informant and the urgency of his warning. In an uncommon move, the head of the Boston office personally made the referral to his counterpart in New York, to underscore how important he thought the tip was.

The e-mail went out the day after the meeting with Markopolos and included an attachment summarizing Markopolos's concerns: "The informant believes that Madoff may be running one giant Ponzi scheme, and there are signs that it may be close to crashing down on him. According to the informant, if that happens, it would have widespread ramifications, as a lot of people have placed a lot of money with Madoff."

A branch chief in Boston followed up the next day, October 27, with an e-mail to all three assistant enforcement directors in the New York office, offering to hook Markopolos up directly with the appropriate staffers in New York.

The warning from Boston could not have been clearer: the SEC needed to find out if Madoff was running a Ponzi scheme.

The team assigned to the task in New York had virtually no experience investigating Ponzi schemes. A key investigator there had very little experience at all, having been at the SEC for just nineteen months. The leader of the team would later say she had been "hamstrung by a lack of resources and personnel" and by the unresponsiveness of others within the agency who could have been helpful but weren't. The culture of the agency discouraged staff members from reaching outside their own "silo" for help, so staffers knowledgeable about Ponzi schemes were not consulted. And even those who thought they knew something about Ponzi schemes clearly didn't. Despite the clarity of the warning, people on the team would later recall that they never truly thought it was credible that a man like Bernie Madoff could be a criminal—he simply didn't fit their ill-informed image of the "typical" Ponzi scheme artist.

Finally, Ed Manion's prediction about people either instantly liking or disliking Harry Markopolos proved true. It seemed to Markopolos that the New York branch chief, Meaghan Cheung, the hands-on leader of the new investigation, had instantly taken a dislike to him. Even after Boston had vouched for Markopolos, Cheung seemed to remain distant and unreceptive—and her opinion spread to the other two women on the team. "I remember hearing that she thought he was kind of condescending to the SEC, in terms of SEC expertise and knowledge," one of her subordinates recalled later.

While some might say a little condescension was justified, given how the agency had handled his previous tips about Madoff, Markopolos didn't help his cause with his approach to the women in New York. He later recalled that, in his first telephone conversation with Cheung, he questioned her inadequate knowledge of derivatives and dismissed some of her earlier successful accounting fraud cases. He said later that she seemed "offended" by this. In fact, his questions were totally irrelevant: No knowledge of derivatives is required to investigate a Ponzi scheme. If it's truly a Ponzi scheme, there *are* no derivatives; there's just a liar with a bank account. In fact, Cheung's previous experience might have been more relevant, since accounting fraud investigations sometimes involve verifying whether the assets shown on the balance sheet actually exist, the precise question a Ponzi scheme investigation must answer.

If Cheung had known more about Ponzi schemes, she would have known how to deal with Markopolos's arrogant and misguided questions. But she didn't. And if Markopolos had known more about dealing with people, he never would have asked those offensive questions in the first place. But he didn't. For a quant, the human equation is often the most difficult to solve.

In late 2005, Harry Markopolos made one last effort to expose Madoff by going, at last, to the media. On the advice of a friend at a Washington-based taxpayer advocacy group, he approached John Wilke in the Washington bureau of the *Wall Street Journal*. Wilke had spent most of his distinguished career in Washington, where he wrote about corrupt congressmen and the companies that corrupted them. When Markopolos first contacted him, Wilke was already at work on another significant project. While he listened to the tipster, he may have been unwilling to pursue a story that intruded on the turf of the *Journal*'s securities industry reporters in New York. Some of Markopolos's allies urged him to approach other reporters—at the *Journal* or at other news organizations in New York—when Wilke did not pick up on the story, but Markopolos wanted to work only with Wilke. By February 2007, Markopolos was discouraged and chose to interpret Wilke's reluctance to pursue the story as evidence of a conspiracy. "I was convinced," he later wrote, "that someone high up at the *Journal* had decided it was too dangerous to go after Bernie Madoff." Senior editors at the *Wall Street Journal*, which had tackled some of the most powerful figures on Wall Street and in Washington over the years, flatly denied that anything was behind Wilke's decision not to investigate Madoff in 2006 except his own professional priorities.

In the New York SEC team's defense, they also were misled by their colleagues about the earlier Madoff investigations, none of which had actually addressed the question of whether he was running a Ponzi scheme. One man who supervised the 2005 examination claimed that Lamore and Ostrow had investigated "basically some of the same issues" and found nothing. Lamore agreed to meet with the new team, but his response was dismissive. "In short, these are basically the same allegations we have heard before. The author's motives are to make money by uncovering the alleged fraud," he said. Lamore was referring to a bounty that the SEC offered for tips about insider trading cases, a category of crimes that included front-running. "I think he is on a fishing expedition and doesn't have the detailed understanding of Madoff's operations that we do which refutes most of his allegations," Lamore continued. Another supervisor agreed: "There is still a little mystery as to what Madoff does," he said, but a Ponzi scheme or front-running didn't seem likely "from what we've seen."

The impression the new team got was that the previous examiners hadn't thought there was anything to Markopolos's analysis suggesting a Ponzi scheme. No one bothered to go through the older case files carefully, so no one noticed the nearly identical complaint the hedge fund manager made in 2003 or the Renaissance e-mails found in 2004. And no one noticed that the earlier investigators never actually looked for a Ponzi scheme at all.

Lamore did note that his team had not approached any of Madoff's hedge fund clients, so the new team decided to cover that base at least. It sent a letter to the Fairfield Greenwich Group, asking for crates of documents relating to its dealings with Madoff. The plan apparently was to check whether Fairfield's account statements (which DiPascali had fabricated) matched up with the account statements Madoff had given Lamore's team (which DiPascali had also fabricated). If Madoff was operating a Ponzi scheme, this was a useless exercise.

But it got Madoff's attention. There he was with his cash balance hovering close to zero and suddenly his biggest, most reliable source of cash was receiving letters about him from the SEC.

The danger to his fraud increased on December 13, when the junior member of the New York SEC team discovered an "odd discrepancy" between Fairfield's documents and the previous team's notes on its interview with Madoff in May. In the spring, Madoff had claimed that he hadn't used options as part of his strategy for about a year. But the current Fairfield account statements still showed options trades. There did not seem to be any explanation, other than that Madoff was lying to someone. Since Madoff's feeder funds all believed he was still buying options for them, it would be devastating if the SEC started suggesting that he wasn't.

Still, even the discrepancy over his use of options did not suggest to the SEC team that relying on Madoff as a source of truthful information was a bad idea. He remained an extremely reputable figure on Wall Street, as far as they knew. Reflecting on the case later, one investigator wrote a colleague that there wasn't "any *real* reason to suspect some kind of wrongdoing."

In December 2005 the chief risk officer at Fairfield Greenwich confirmed in an SEC interview—conducted after the SEC gave him permission to consult with Madoff before testifying—that options remained part of the Madoff strategy. The investigative team decided it would be a good idea to track down some of the counterparties to these mysterious options trades before questioning Madoff about it. It would have been an excellent idea—indeed, if it had been diligently pursued, it would certainly have exposed Madoff's crime. But this didn't happen.

Bernie Madoff and Frank DiPascali spent January 2006 producing documents in response to the SEC's new demands—although the huge stacks of paper did not include any OTC options contracts. On January 26, DiPascali went downtown to the SEC's offices to answer questions about the counterparties supposedly on the other side of Madoff's trades, and his lies were sufficiently convincing to keep the investigators offtrack for a while longer.

Regulators and prosecutors later accused Dan Bonventre of spending this perilous January dealing with the Ponzi scheme's worsening cash crisis, using another $54 million in government bonds from Carl Shapiro's account as collateral for a $50 million bank loan in mid-January. The loan proceeds were put into the Ponzi scheme account to cover continuing withdrawals. On at least four occasions, money from the legitimate firm's bank accounts had to be tapped to cover giant withdrawals from the Ponzi scheme. It was not clear how long this could go on before the legitimate firm started suffering a cash squeeze as well—or someone working there picked up gossip about the curious transfers and loans.

Meanwhile, SEC investigators continued to poke around at the feeder funds that Madoff relied on for the fresh cash he desperately needed. On January 30, 2006, they interviewed Jeffrey Tucker from Fairfield Greenwich. Two days later they sent a letter to Tremont Partners demanding the same list of documents they had sought from Fairfield in December.

Then, in mid-February, the team asked Madoff for a piece of paper that he knew could send him to prison. They wanted a list of all the accounts through which he executed, cleared, or settled any trades, including the disputed options trades—trades they still believed he was making, despite his earlier testimony. Of course, he was not executing, clearing, or settling any trades at all, but he could not refuse the request without setting off all kinds of tripwires at the SEC. So, on February 23, Madoff gambled big and produced a six-page list of the financial entities through which he was allegedly conducting trades for his hedge fund clients, along with his account number at the DTCC clearinghouse.

Then he waited for the sky to fall.

9

MADOFF'S WORLD

It is hard to fathom how Bernie Madoff managed to handle the protracted liquidity crisis and SEC investigation of late 2005 and early 2006. Even on paper, the magnitude of the cash drain was shocking. Between April 2005 and June 2006, investors withdrew roughly $975 million from the Fairfield Sentry fund alone, nearly 20 percent of its assets. The situation looked so dire that it is hardly surprising that Dan Bonventre and two computer programmers who worked with Frank DiPascali on the seventeenth floor emptied their Madoff accounts in the spring of 2006 and moved the assets elsewhere—although all three have denied that they knew anything about the fraud or its teetering finances. Madoff could scarcely refuse to let them pull the money out. Even if they were not helping his Ponzi scheme stay afloat, and they flatly denied that they were, it would have raised alarms if they had not been able to make the withdrawals. On April 13, Madoff arranged to tap his brokerage firm's operating account once again to cover another $120 million redemption request from the Sentry fund, which had withdrawn $150 million just a month earlier.

Despite the peril facing his Ponzi scheme, Bernie Madoff apparently did not put any restrictions on his family's access to cash. The overall stock markets were strong; the global hedge fund business seemed to be healthy. Anyone who believed that Madoff was running an extremely successful hedge fund business would necessarily have believed that he had money to burn. Every other successful hedge fund manager did.

If his family members knew that his secret Ponzi scheme was in the grip of a potentially fatal cash crunch, they certainly were doing nothing to make it easier for him, and their redemptions were certainly ones he could have refused without question if they had been his accomplices. In December 2005, Madoff loaned each of his sons $5 million. Between September and April, he allowed his brother to withdraw $3.2 million from the accounts Bernie managed for him. No one in his family hurried to close out their accounts during this crisis and move their assets to safer havens. They left the great bulk of their wealth—their pensions, their deferred compensation, their children's trust funds—in Bernie's hands.

In retrospect, the fact that the family continued to withdraw cash but did not empty their accounts suggests that they were unaware of both the fraud and its imminent peril in the fall of 2005. They simply continued to tap Bernie's piggybank, as they had always done, as if everything at the firm were running as smoothly as it always had.

Madoff's unstinting largess may also have reflected the reality that life beyond the business was far from smooth for the Madoff family. Peter's son, Roger, was losing his long battle with leukemia and had been slipping toward death all through the winter, attended by his young wife and his heartbroken family. On April 15, 2006, he died at age thirty-two. Bernie's secretary, Eleanor Squillari, would later say that the Peter she had known for so many years died that day, too.

It was during these months of private anguish, in this secretly precarious season of SEC scrutiny and frantic loans and cash transfers, that Madoff nearly lost his battle to keep his Ponzi scheme alive. By April 2006, he had transferred more than $260 million from the brokerage firm's accounts into the Ponzi scheme's slush fund to cover withdrawals and keep the fraud afloat—and it still wasn't enough.

The tide began to turn on April 18, when Madoff's problematic investor Jeffry Picower deposited $125 million into one of his Madoff accounts—no doubt a very welcome infusion of cash, since it was made just five days after Fairfield Greenwich pulled out $120 million. It is one of the bits of evidence that suggests that Picower was better informed about Madoff's continuing crime than even Madoff suspected—or at least than either man ever admitted.

After its timely arrival in his Madoff account, Picower's fortuitous deposit underwent a remarkable transformation. Within two weeks, it had grown on paper to $164 million, thanks to big gains on some stocks supposedly purchased with the money. According to Picower's account statements, however, the lucrative stock purchase was made three months earlier, ten weeks before the $125 million check actually arrived in his account to pay for the stock. And in September 2006, after Madoff's cash crisis had eased and new money was pouring in daily, Picower withdrew his $125 million, leaving paper profits of $80 million in the account after just five months. It is possible that Picower thought he had bought the shares months before on margin and paid for them after the fact. But the bankruptcy trustee would later interpret the transaction as circumstantial evidence that Picower helped bail out Madoff and was rewarded with fabricated profits generated through backdated trades. It is almost inconceivable that Madoff could have cooked up such blatantly fictional trades in the account of an investor as sophisticated as Picower without him noticing.

The welcome and mutually rewarding Picower check and, at last, an ebb in withdrawals weren't enough, though, to save the corrupt scheme in that season of crisis. Madoff still had to get the SEC off his back. Fortunately for him, the agency's investigators were hampered by their refusal to trust Harry Markopolos and his analysis. They failed to do the tough homework of studying the files of previously bungled investigations. They knew little about Ponzi schemes and the people who built them. But with all their shortcomings, Madoff's regulators got tantalizingly close to exposing him in the spring of 2006.

Sometime in May, the SEC investigative team drafted letters to send to Barclays Bank and the Bank of New York, asking them to confirm Madoff's trading activity. Responses to those letters would have put him at risk because they would have revealed that there simply wasn't any trading activity going on. For some reason, however, Meaghan Cheung and her colleague Simona Suh decided to delay sending the letters until Madoff himself was interviewed later that month. Ultimately, the letters were never sent—later, no one could recall why.

Then, in mid-May, the SEC team asked a staff member at FINRA, the Financial Industry Regulatory Authority, to check on Madoff's options trading on a particular date. The FINRA staffer reported that Madoff had done no options trading at all on that date. Still, the team simply chewed over the bizarre report and dismissed it, persuading themselves that Madoff either was failing to disclose his trades or was making them overseas. Despite all his obvious lies, they never suspected he was not making any trades at all. By then, after so many years of caution and bureaucratic inertia at the SEC, that lie apparently was simply too large to fit into the agency's limited imagination.

The entire investigation, eventually, came down to Madoff himself.

A little before 10:00 AM on Friday, May 19, 2006, Bernie Madoff arrived at the SEC's New York office in the American Express tower, adjacent to the huge empty footprint of the World Trade Center. He came alone, without a lawyer. Across the table were five SEC staff members, including Meaghan Cheung, Simona Suh, and Peter Lamore.

Madoff seemed relaxed and cordial. He grew expansive when he talked about the art of trading stocks and the science of computers, which he conceded was not his strong suit. "If I was talking to a brain surgeon and they started talking about the terminology—*that* I wouldn't know. But if they said, 'see this scalpel, stick it in there,' now I understand," he said.

Everybody had different computer algorithms to guide their trading, he went on. "People design their systems to say 'I don't care about this, I care about that.'" But he didn't attach much importance to the widely available information that flows into the marketplace. "People are always trying to ask me 'what makes a good trade?' Or 'why can you trade better than other people,' and so on. It's the same thing—we are proprietary traders and market-makers. Some guys have more guts than others. Some of them are just stupid—they don't get frightened when they should be getting frightened. Some people just feel the market. Some people just understand how to analyze the numbers that they are looking at."

The explanation for his success was that simple, he suggested without quite saying so: he was one of those people who "just feel the market."

He was asked why he didn't do his options trading on one of the public exchanges instead of in the opaque over-the-counter market. "Everybody goes to the over-the-counter market on options. That's the way the market is," he said. Listed options could be traded only "during the U.S. hours, which you don't want to do." Besides, he added, "there's really not the liquidity in the options market. It's improving, but it's not where you would want to go."

He seemed confident, knowledgeable, relaxed—there was no sign that he had almost run out of cash. There was no indication that, after handing over that list of fictional counterparties in February, he feared he had already run out of time. Every day for the last three months he had expected to hear that the SEC had called some of the names on the list and found out he was lying. So far they hadn't—indeed, they never would—but suddenly that potentially fatal list was there in front of Madoff, on the table in the SEC's conference room.

"I'd like to go over this list and have you explain in a little more detail the function of each account," Simona Suh said. "The account, Depository Trust Clearing Corporation, what is the function of this account?"

Madoff answered truthfully, "That's the general clearance account for the firm, that handles all the settlements of transactions for the firm."

Did the clearinghouse set up separate accounts for the different institutional customers?

Yes, Madoff said. Well, there was one big account, but different codes for whether the securities belonged to the brokerage firm or to an institutional customer.

"You know what those codes are?"

"No," Madoff said.

"But DTC would know?"

"Yes," he said.

Well, that was probably the final, fatal step—the moment when his time ran out. "I thought it was the end, game over. Monday morning, they'll call the DTC and this will be over," he recalled later. "And it never happened."

That "astonished" him, he said, because "if you're looking at a Ponzi scheme, it's the first thing you do."

If the investigative team had checked Madoff's clearinghouse account that day or on the following Monday, they would have found that it held less than $24 million in blue-chip stocks, at a time when it should have held either billions of dollars' worth of stock or an equal amount in Treasury bonds, based on the account statements they had seen.

But the investigators misunderstood how the clearinghouse worked and wrongly assumed that it would be hugely laborious to sift out the hedge fund transactions from the firm's normal high-volume trading business. So they didn't follow up on the DTCC account.

By this point in the Madoff interview, Peter Lamore was beside himself. Madoff had been sitting there for hours, bold as brass, describing his options trades—almost exactly a year after telling Lamore he wasn't using options as part of his investment strategy anymore. Simona Suh confronted Madoff with the discrepancy.

"Do you recall telling Peter that, as of January 1, 2004, you no longer incorporated options into the strategy for the institutional trading business?"

"I said they're not part of the model," Madoff lied smoothly. "The options are not deemed to be part of the model. I did not say—my recollection certainly is not that I said that the accounts don't use options anymore to trade. I said the options—that the options were taken out of the model, and they're not part of the model any longer."

Suh followed up: "So what change were you referring to in that statement?"

"Well, they used to be part of the model," Madoff explained. They had been taken out, he continued, because they weakened his intellectual property claims to the software that guided his investment strategy. "We consider the model our intellectual property. It states so, I believe, in the trading authorization directive," he said. But there simply wasn't "enough meat" on the options portion of the model. "So we took it, basically, out of the model and treated them separately," he said.

Hadn't he told Lamore that, as of January 1, 2004, the clients could hedge the strategy by buying their own options?

"No," Madoff answered.

"You do not recall making that statement?"

"I recall saying what I just said, that they were [originally] part of the model, that they were no longer part of the model, but that—I remember specifically saying that the options are still used to hedge the transactions."

Lamore was furious. "I just remember sitting there in the testimony saying, he's lying," he recalled years later. "It was just remarkable to me."

Like so many others, Lamore did not contemplate that a man who would tell such a brazen lie might also commit a brazen fraud. "I mean, 'lying or misleading' to 'fraud, Ponzi scheme' to me was a huge step—a huge leap."

It was a leap Bernie Madoff took every day, but the SEC failed to understand this. When its team officially closed this flawed investigation on January 3, 2008, after a long period of inactivity, it would conclude that, despite all the lies they had discovered, there was no evidence of fraud.

Nine months after Madoff's nearly ruinous 2005 liquidity crisis erupted, his Ponzi scheme was finally back in the black.

It had been a big-budget battle. By the time Madoff was sitting down to spin the SEC at the end of May 2006, he had borrowed $342 million under his brokerage firm's letter of credit to keep his Ponzi scheme alive. But by the end of August 2006, when the SEC finally dropped its thoroughly fumbled investigation—it merely required him to register as an investment adviser—the borrowed money had all been paid back to the brokerage firm's banks. Even by the end of June, Madoff had been able to start whittling down the debt, arranging to transfer $262 million back into the firm's operating account by reversing the accounting gimmicks that were used to hide the payments made earlier in the year.

How did Madoff's imperiled Ponzi scheme get back on its feet so quickly? With a lot of help from his friends—specifically, some new hedge fund friends.

It helped enormously that the global appetite for hedge fund investments had quickly shaken off any queasiness left over from the Bayou fund collapse. The turnaround in Europe was nothing short of spectacular. A money manager there who in 2001 had purchased shares in a Kingate fund invested with Madoff decided to cash out in 2005. "I said, 'I want to sell,'" he recalled, "and people were saying, 'me,' 'me,' 'me.' In fifteen minutes I could have my money." He made 40 percent on that stake but kept watching for an opportunity to invest in Madoff through other funds. He shrugged: "We all thought he was front-running. But so what?"

Thanks to the continuing sales effort led by Walter Noel's handsome sons-in-law at Fairfield Greenwich, Madoff was well situated to benefit eventually from this rebound, although Fairfield Greenwich did not start to recover from its 2005 decline until late in the year and saw its biggest gains in 2007.

The real powerhouse behind Madoff's fraud-saving success in Europe in 2005 and 2006 was Sonja Kohn, the energetic founder of a boutique bank in Vienna called Bank Medici. Born in 1948 in Vienna, Sonja Blau married Erwin Kohn, a career banker, in 1970 and raised five children. Early in their marriage, they operated an importing business in Milan and Zurich, but in 1983 they moved to New York, and by 1985 she had obtained her broker's license. An exuberant and somewhat flamboyant woman who was fluent in at least four languages, she worked briefly in the late 1980s for Merrill Lynch and Oppenheimer. Although some remembered her generating big commissions for the firm in those days, two of her Merrill Lynch customers complained that she had steered them into unsuitable investments, and records show the firm paid more than $125,000 to settle the disputes.

Publicly, Sonja Kohn recalled that she had been introduced to Madoff in the 1990s, when his "hedge fund" had the endorsement of "people and companies who were the gold standard of the financial community." In fact, Kohn was introduced to Madoff in the mid-1980s by Madoff's cheerful Roslyn neighbor and business partner Sonny Cohn.

When Cohn was mulling over ideas for life after retirement, his accountant at the well-known firm of Oppenheim, Appel, Dixon & Company suggested he talk with a dynamic Austrian woman who supposedly was one of the "biggest producers" at Merrill Lynch. There was a meeting—but apparently no meeting of the minds about any kind of joint venture. Sonja Kohn was very tough-minded and had big ambitions and expansive ideas, while Sonny Cohn was probably looking for a quiet sort of semiretirement. Still, Cohn did introduce Sonja Kohn to Madoff, who was more than a match for her in toughness and ambition.

In April 1987, Sonja Kohn formed a small company in New York called Erko. A few months later, she formed Windsor IBC, a brokerage firm wholly owned by Erko. Within a few years, she would stand at the center of a dizzying international complex of corporate shells, holding companies, offshore trusts, and private partnerships, the most prominent of which was her flagship institution, Bank Medici, founded in 1994.

The first to become publicly known was a small investment firm she established in 1990 called Eurovaleur, a hedge fund collective based in New York that worked with some of the top money managers in Europe. When she showed up in Madoff's appointment book, even two decades later, she was most commonly identified as being from Eurovaleur, not Bank Medici.

In 1996, a decade after her fruitful association with Madoff began, Kohn set up another small New York company called Infovaleur, later described as a financial research service. One of its most lucrative clients was Bernie Madoff, whose legitimate firm had easy access to any Wall Street research it wished to see. The trustee liquidating Madoff's firm years later would assert that Infovaleur was "a sham," one of many shell companies designed simply to receive tens of millions of dollars from Madoff and send the money along to other shell companies controlled by the Kohn family and its associates in Gibraltar, elsewhere in Europe, and Israel. The cash—which allegedly was always handed over face-to-face, never mailed—was Kohn's compensation for the billions of dollars she helped steer into Madoff's Ponzi scheme over the years, the trustee claimed.

Another lawsuit by the trustee would contend that Madoff's small affiliate in London, Madoff Securities International Ltd., had been a link in this chain of compensation since 1987. That case described meetings at which one of Madoff's longtime senior executives in London personally delivered Kohn's quarterly check "over tea at the Ritz or Claridge's in London." These fees were identified in Madoff's records as being for research, but the intermediary was "well aware that whatever research Kohn did provide to Madoff was worthless," the trustee alleged. The London executive did not comment but took steps to dispute the trustee's allegations in court. Through her lawyers, Kohn insisted that she never had any knowledge of Madoff's fraud.

After meeting Bernie Madoff in the mid-1980s, Kohn made no secret of her admiration for him—although she abided by his wishes and obscured his role in the sales literature for her funds. According to his employees, she visited his offices frequently and was always greeted by Madoff with great warmth.

Like Ezra Merkin in Jewish charity circles and Walter Noel in the hedge fund world, Sonja Kohn was a linchpin for Madoff since the early 1990s, linking him to new sources of cash in Europe and beyond. She introduced him to Mario Benbassat, the founder of a Swiss firm called Genevalor, Benbassat & Cie, and his two sons. Their firm would set up five early feeder funds in Europe, including the hefty Thema funds, and ultimately would put almost $2 billion into Madoff's hands. Benbassat was a director of another prominent Swiss investment firm called Union Bancaire Privée, and in 2003 UBP set up its own collection of Madoff feeder funds, one that would ultimately gather $1 billion in fresh cash for him. Subsequent litigation also identified Sonja Kohn as the person who introduced Madoff to Carlo Grosso and Federico Ceretti, the two Italian money managers based in London who set up the Kingate funds to invest with Madoff in the early 1990s and ultimately steered $1.7 billion his way. She also reportedly introduced Madoff to Charles Fix, a scion of a Greek brewing empire who had established himself as a money manager in London—and who, ultimately, invested hundreds of millions with Madoff through the Harley and Santa Clara hedge funds.

To these investors, Kohn's credentials were impeccable. In her distinctive bouffant auburn-red wig and expensive but slightly frumpy outfits, she became known as "Austria's woman on Wall Street," dividing her time between Europe and New York. When Bank Medici was granted a full-service banking license from the Austrian government in 2003, she and her husband established themselves again in Vienna, where she already had been honored for her contributions to the Austrian economy.

Then the established bank that had been her minority partner when she formed Bank Medici was acquired by Creditanstalt, one of Austria's largest financial institutions, and she was catapulted into the aristocracy of European banking. After more mergers, her minority partner, now called Bank Austria, was acquired by the giant Unicredit bank holding company of Italy. It wasn't long before Unicredit had its own family of Madoff feeder funds called the Primeo funds.

From her gilded and baroquely furnished offices overlooking the Vienna opera house, Sonja Kohn would help steer nearly $9 billion into Madoff's hands in the decades after their initial meeting in 1985, according to the trustee's litigation against her. Her hedge fund empire would expand across Europe and beyond, into the former Soviet Union and the offshore fund world of the Caribbean.

From Madoff's standpoint, one of the most significant things Sonja Kohn did was to help create the Herald fund, which opened for business in April 2004. Of the half-dozen giant feeder funds serving Madoff in those years, none sent more fresh money to him during his 2005 cash crisis than the Herald fund, according to a subsequent academic study. From its inception, the Herald fund would pump more than $1.5 billion into Madoff's hands, but much of that flowed in during its early years of operation, when he needed the cash so desperately.

Still, the Herald fund was only the pace car for other newborn European feeder funds that helped rescue Madoff. Another promising source of cash in 2005 was Access International, a private money management firm run by two elegant Frenchmen. Access was the sponsor of the Lux-Alpha funds, formed in 2004, which brought in a steady stream of fresh cash in Madoff's hour of need. The chief executive of Access was the warm but aristocratic René-Thierry Magon de la Villehuchet, but his longtime friend and banking partner, the more prosaically named Patrick Littaye, was the one who provided the link to Bernie Madoff.

Subsequent lawsuits against Access would assert that Littaye insisted that no one at Access deal with Madoff except through him. It isn't quite clear how the two men met. Madoff recalled that the connection was through a French bank executive whom he knew through his old friend Albert Igoin in Paris, whose ties to Madoff dated to the 1970s. Littaye later recalled that he first met Madoff in 1985, when he phoned Madoff's office to confirm a transaction for one of his private banking clients. In any case, the two men seemed to enjoy each other's company, and Madoff was impressed by Littaye's European connections.

In 1995, Littaye and de la Villehuchet, a gifted salesman, formed Access International, quietly investing its private clients' money with Madoff. With the formation of the new LuxAlpha funds in February 2004, Access became an even more formidable source of money for Madoff. With the imprimatur of UBS, a prestigious international bank based in Switzerland, the fund attracted investments from such historic names as Rothschild et Cie and brought in a number of aristocratic family fortunes—including de la Villehuchet's own money, the wealth that enabled him to preserve the beautiful provincial estate near St. Malo, on the north coast of France, that had been in his family since 1685.

It seemed that nothing could shake the trust that Littaye and de la Villehuchet placed in Madoff. In early 2006 an Access executive confirmed an odd fact noticed by people on his staff: the options supposedly traded by Madoff were not reflected in the records of Wall Street's central options clearinghouse. When this executive raised the issue with the Access founders, they insisted on hiring an experienced independent hedge fund analyst to provide a second opinion about Madoff—and this analyst's opinion was also firmly negative. In early May the analyst joined Littaye and de la Villehuchet for lunch in the soaring wood-paneled dining room of the University Club in Midtown Manhattan. "I did my best to inject doubt in a courteous yet effective manner," the analyst recalled later. But Littaye, appearing "highly sensitive and defensive," allegedly stood up for Madoff, questioned the analyst's "business judgment," and dismissed his concerns.

By 2006, Madoff had planted his flag on virtually every continent. His presence in Europe had expanded dramatically, with Bank Medici in Vienna and Union Bancaire Privée in Geneva not only running feeder funds directly but also providing advisory services to some of Madoff's other feeder funds—including Fairfield Greenwich Group, based in New York and Bermuda. The Italian-based Unicredit's Primeo funds attracted a small investment from a multinational development bank in Central Africa and, in turn, added the money to the $1.5 billion that flowed into the Herald fund. An offshore company called Euro-Dutch Management, run by Dutch bankers, raised more than $2.3 billion for its Madoff feeder funds based in the Cayman Islands. In the course of raising a total of $4.5 billion in fresh cash for Madoff, Fairfield Greenwich would draw money from Singapore, Qatar, Abu Dhabi, Dubai, Korea, and Tokyo. The Optimal funds sponsored by the prestigious Banco Santander in Spain would ultimately raise at least $1.5 billion from investors in the wealthy enclaves of Central and South America.

Even these big feeder funds had feeder funds of their own, which in turn had feeder funds, creating a vast worldwide irrigation system that sustained Madoff's fraud with steady high-pressure streams of cash. Many of the feeder funds paid "retrocession fees"—the trustee would later call them "kickbacks," but they also could be called sales commissions—that provided a tangible reward and a powerful incentive for those who brought in new investors.

As hedge funds were gaining strength in Europe, Asia, and the Middle East, they were also multiplying in America. One illuminating example of the proliferation of hedge funds after 2006—a trend Madoff milked to the maximum—was a one-man hedge fund in Florida called Anchor Holdings LLC.

Many of Anchor's clients were small family or individual "hedge funds," with names such as the "John Doe Hedge Fund" and the "Jane Doe IRA Hedge Fund." A few were union or professional pension plans. At its peak, when Anchor Holdings supposedly had more than

$12 million in assets, its largest individual account was under $750,000, and its smallest was a Roth IRA account worth just $3,224.43. Anchor Holdings invested these modest nest eggs in another hedge fund, which invested all its assets in an apparently diversified portfolio of international hedge funds. That portfolio consisted of the Primeo fund, the Santa Clara fund, and four other hedge funds—every single one of which was invested exclusively with Madoff. Believing they had avoided the risk of putting all their eggs in one basket, these small investors had actually handed their savings over to one man: Bernie Madoff.

It is no wonder that some members of Congress were demanding that the SEC increase its attention to the hedge fund industry's incursions into the middle class. Anchor Holdings could have been Exhibit A in the argument that hedge funds had "gone retail." But since hedge funds were not required to register with the SEC—a badly drafted rule requiring registration was struck down by an appellate court in 2006 and never redrafted—the SEC had no way of knowing about Anchor Holdings or the countless other funds just like it.

In December 2006 the SEC tried to stem the stampede of middle-class savers into barely regulated hedge funds by raising the net worth requirements for "accredited investors"— those who were wealthy enough to buy hedge funds legally—to $2.5 million, from $1 million. By doing so, however, it walked into a buzz saw of opposition from people who were already invested in hedge funds but would not qualify under the new standard. As one Congressional Research Service report observed, "These investors did not wish to be protected from risks that the SEC might view as excessive." The effort was shelved.

Some critics of hedge fund registration noted that when Europe introduced a registration regime, it simply made hedge funds seem safer and therefore more attractive to middle-income investors. And some high-profile academics on both sides of the Atlantic were producing learned and widely touted papers supporting the concept of "hedge funds for everyone." Why, they asked, should the profits of hedge fund investing be limited only to the wealthy and sophisticated?

More than social cachet was involved, although one wry observer noted that mutual funds had become "so yesterday" on the summer patio circuit. The low interest rates established by the Federal Reserve to sustain the economy in the aftermath of the technology stock collapse in

2000 had sharply reduced the amount of money a generation of aging Baby Boomers could safely earn on their retirement savings. At the same time, the growing housing bubble was increasing the value of their primary asset, their homes. With mortgage rates so low and home values so high, many people could, and did, borrow against their home equity, invest with Madoff, and earn far more income for retirement than they could have earned with a bank CD or low-risk mutual fund.

So, both at home and abroad, directly and through their pension funds, more investors were putting their retirement nest eggs into hedge funds—and enough of that money wound up in Madoff's basket to more than cure the cash crisis that had looked so deadly for him in November 2005.

∾

Another important factor in Madoff's remarkable rebound was the boom in derivatives tied to hedge fund performance, a subset of the derivatives mania that was intensifying on Wall Street and in other financial centers around the world.

At this point in the Madoff tale, Harry Markopolos would be drawing circles and arrows on his whiteboard. But it's helpful to think of derivatives simply as private contracts between a seller and a buyer; each contract is designed to achieve a particular purpose. The purpose of these particular contracts was to allow the buyer, for a fee, to share in the future gains of a specific hedge fund without having to invest in the hedge fund directly.

Why would anyone have wanted to do that? Well, there were a number of reasons. Perhaps an attractive hedge fund was not accepting new investors; a derivative contract designed to track that closed fund would give investors the benefit of being in it even though the door was shut.

More significantly for Madoff, some of these derivative contracts allowed the buyer to invest with borrowed money, which meant that the investor could earn two, three, or even four times the gains produced by a particular hedge fund—leveraged profits that the hedge fund itself could not have provided. Eventually, derivative contracts would be designed to track a number of Madoff feeder funds, but initially the primary "tracking fund" was the giant Fairfield Sentry fund, whose assets totaled nearly $5 billion at the end of 2005.

In August 2006, as the global appetite for all kinds of exotic derivatives grew, a prominent Spanish banking group called Banco Bilbao Vizcaya Argentaria (BBVA) sold $20 million worth of these derivative contracts designed to pay investors five times the future profits of the Fairfield Sentry fund. A month later, it sold another $5 million of the notes. The bank had a substantial presence in Latin America, in addition to its Spanish business, and its gleaming reputation stood behind the unfamiliar new product.

Soon, Nomura Bank International, a worldwide institution with special strength in the Asian markets, would issue $50 million in derivative contracts offering to pay three times the future gains in the Sentry fund. Compared with some of the derivatives being sold on Wall Street at the time, the deal looked conservative.

In December 2006, another $25 million in Sentry-tracking contracts, derivative notes offering five times the fund's profits, was issued by Madoff's own bank, JPMorgan Chase, an institution born in 2000 from the merger of two of the most fabled names in American banking history. J.P. Morgan & Co., of course, was founded by the legendary financier who almost single-handedly reversed the financial panic of 1907. The Chase Manhattan Bank, which traced its ancestry to 1799, had been led for more than two decades by David Rockefeller, a grandson of America's first oil baron, John D. Rockefeller. The JPMorgan Chase notes attracted the attention of an Italian money manager who had been searching for a way to invest in Madoff. The notes produced better returns but were still tied to the conservatively managed Fairfield Sigma funds, the Sentry fund's euro-based affiliate. "It's like they were giving you a parachute with a more exciting trip," he said. "And it was J.P. Morgan!"

Fairfield Greenwich founders Walter Noel and Jeffrey Tucker had come a long, long way from sharing office space with an options trader back in 1989. Now they were sharing their life-size gamble on Bernie Madoff with one of the most historically successful banks in the world.

The development of these derivatives was important for Madoff because the banks selling them had to hedge the risks they were taking on—and they did this by investing directly in the hedge funds whose performance the derivatives were supposed to track. The funds, in turn, invested that money with Madoff. He let it be known that he disapproved of these leveraged derivatives, but they were a new source of cash for him in the summer of 2006, when he needed it desperately.

But these and other Madoff-linked derivatives—which would soon be offered by HSBC, Citibank, Fortis, Merrill Lynch, and several other global institutions—were also a significant milepost in the evolution of Madoff's Ponzi scheme. Initially, people had invested with Madoff because they trusted him. In time, they invested because they trusted whichever prominent accountant, lawyer, or pension fund adviser opened the door to Madoff. Then they invested with prominent individual investors who knew Madoff, such as J. Ezra Merkin and Sonja Kohn, or in feeder funds such as Fairfield Greenwich and Tremont Partners, whose founders knew him. Now people who had never heard of Bernie Madoff were tying their fate to his because they trusted the giant banks that were selling these complicated contracts, banks whose chief executives probably had never heard of Madoff either.

Looking at the fine print for these derivatives with skeptical hindsight makes the investors' trust seem quite remarkable. Bank lawyers had worked a long time on these complicated agreements to protect the banks' interests and insulate them from liability. Investors were warned repeatedly that they should be prepared to lose *all the money* they invested in these contracts.

In the final terms for the contracts sold by JPMorgan Chase in December 2006, some variation of the word *risk* is used 139 times. One of those citations went like this:

> Possibility of Fraud and Other Misconduct: There is a risk that the manager of the fund or a hedge fund could divert or abscond with the assets, fail to follow agreed-upon investment strategies, provide false reports of operations or engage in other misconduct.

In other words, caveat emptor: buyer, beware.

Of course, similar warnings were scattered through the paperwork for almost every hedge fund in the marketplace. Apparently, people who had invested far more than they could afford to lose did not seriously believe they actually could lose everything. Besides, all those smart, well-compensated managers running these funds were doing the due diligence that would detect a fraud, right?

The notion inherent in these warnings—that you paid for the higher profits the hedge funds produced by taking on much higher risks—was apparently dismissed as just so much legalese. Nothing to lose sleep over.

The final maneuver Bernie Madoff used to pull his Ponzi scheme out of the nosedive of November 2005 was to substantially increase the rates of return his feeder funds could offer, making the funds more attractive to investors. For example, the return on the Fairfield Sentry fund in 2006 was nearly a third higher than its 2005 results. It was a gutsy gamble. If Madoff had guessed wrong about where investors were in their perpetual journey between fear and greed, the move could have been disastrous—if withdrawals had continued, a higher rate would instantly have accelerated the evaporation of his cash.

But the financial landscape in early 2007 made the risk look less worrisome. Home values had been climbing for years, and it seemed they always would. The S&P 500 index had almost regained the ground it lost after the tech-stock collapse in 2000. Even the battered NASDAQ composite index was back where it had been in January 1999, before the last puff of air went into the Internet bubble. Financial deregulation still looked like an excellent idea. So did all the creative financial engineering that produced the Fairfield Sentry derivative notes and the countless other complicated derivatives that were being embraced by institutional investors everywhere.

So it appeared that Madoff had guessed correctly when he raised his rates, and his gamble paid off. Investors were still more interested in high profits than in safety. And, of course, his investors—whether hedge fund managers or heartland retirees, leading economists or lagging industrial unions—all privately convinced themselves that, with Bernie Madoff, they were somehow getting both.

∞

Beneath the surface of public attention, things were already crumbling by late summer of 2007—for Madoff and the nation.

In Madoff's own realm, bankers and hedge fund administrators were quietly growing more leery of his secrecy and consistent results. The proliferation of his hedge fund investors and the construction of all those complex derivatives had increased the amount of attention he was getting in banking circles. A number of bank due-diligence teams were growing increasingly worried by what they were learning—and not learning—on their visits with the managers of various Madoff feeder funds. By 2007, executives at one giant bank serving his hedge fund clients were looking for ways to immunize themselves legally from any responsibility if whatever Madoff was doing ended badly.

Even Madoff's own longtime banker, JPMorgan Chase, was growing suspicious—or, at least, some of its high-level executives were. On June 15, 2007, the top risk-management officer at Chase's investment bank sent a lunchtime e-mail to some colleagues. "For whatever its worth," he wrote, "I am sitting at lunch with [another senior Chase executive] who just told me there is a well-known cloud over the head of Madoff and that his returns are speculated to be part of a ponzi scheme." Luckily for the Ponzi scheme, Chase's retail bankers had not increased either their scrutiny or their skepticism, so Madoff could still move billions of dollars in and out of his Chase accounts, no questions asked. But the whispered doubts about him were getting louder every day.

On the larger stage, the foundation under Wall Street's house of cards was beginning to shudder. Mortgage defaults were rising, mortgage derivatives were weakening, and Wall Street banks and analysts were worrying about the debts of a host of insurance companies and hedge funds that were heavily invested in those crumbling mortgage-based derivatives.

Even if most civilian stock market investors still saw no cause for alarm, did Bernie Madoff, with his "feel for the market," sense how fragile the situation had become? Did he catch wind of the increasingly skeptical whispers and suspect that his time was running out?

Perhaps. For whatever reason, 2007 was his year of living extravagantly, his year of living like the feeder fund kings whose lavish lifestyles and big-ticket shopping he had helped make possible. In March he took delivery of a custom Brazilian-made jet, decorated, like his office, in tones of black and gray. The plan was to put the jet up for charter to defray the cost—it had cost him and his co-owner at least $24 million—but it still made family travel luxurious. In June a new $7 million yacht was delivered to a mooring near his town house outside Cap d'Antibes, in the south of France. This gleaming white addition to the Madoff armada was a streamlined eighty-eight-foot Leopard "Superyacht" with three guest staterooms, each with a private bath, and three berths for the crew. In the spring, Madoff attended a series of expensive charity events—at a

$50,000 table here and a $25,000 table there, he sat in his English-tailored tuxedo smiling a little and sipping Diet Coke.

He entertained a cosmopolitan parade of visitors at the Lipstick Building: Manuel Echevarria from Banco Santander's Optimal funds; Patrick Littaye, from Access International; and Carlo Grosso, the Italian based in London who ran the Kingate funds, one of his earliest feeders. Things were still looking good; sales were strong.

In the spring, Madoff attended a Hofstra University benefit honoring Frank G. Zarb, a Wall Street veteran who had been recruited to pull the NASD out of its 1994 price-fixing scandal and who had crossed swords with Madoff a few times in regulatory battles.

Sponsors weren't sure Madoff would even show up; although he was a Hofstra graduate, he had given very little to the school, focusing his philanthropy elsewhere. But he did attend the benefit and, at some point during the evening, approached Hofstra's president and chatted about pledging $1 million to the school.

Madoff's family also enjoyed the surging wealth, of course; why wouldn't they expect to share in Bernie's obvious success? Peter Madoff and Madoff's sons may have known that the market-making business was down to tissue-thin profit margins. The proprietary trading desk's profits were good but fluctuated with the markets. But, increasingly, those sources of revenue were dwarfed by the money supposedly being generated by Madoff's hedge fund business. As they all knew, this was true at many Wall Street firms these days.

For years, as Madoff's hedge fund business had grown, the firm had supported the family's lifestyle in an ever-grander fashion. In the still-cloudless days of early 2007, it may have looked like it always would.

In 2007, Madoff doubled Frank DiPascali's annual salary from more than $2 million to just over $4 million, a handsome payday for the helpful high school graduate from Queens. It wasn't his sole source of income. Since 2002, DiPascali had taken about $5 million directly from the bank account Madoff maintained for the Ponzi scheme, falsifying the paperwork to make it look legitimate. He used some of the money to buy a new sixty-one-foot fishing boat and to fill his suburban New Jersey home with toys, ranging from a pool table to a bright red popcorn cart. DiPascali neglected to share all his good news with the Internal Revenue Service. He did not file his personal income tax returns for 2002 and

2006, perhaps because he was simply too busy with the paperwork for the Ponzi scheme. He wouldn't file in 2007 either.

DiPascali's colleague Annette Bongiorno, who had been working largely from Florida for the past decade and had handled administrative chores for Madoff for nearly thirty years, saw her salary and bonus triple in 2007, from $200,200 to $624,000. Prosecutors would later accuse her of playing a longtime role in the fraud, asserting that she handled the creation of phony account statements for Madoff's largest individual investors. She emphatically denied the charge and was scheduled for trial in 2012.

In mid-May, Bernie and Ruth left for southern France, where they would relax in their small villa for nearly two months. They played golf at various clubs and courses near the Mediterranean, enjoyed exhilarating excursions on the new yacht, and settled into the gracious rhythm of a French summer.

In the fall, Madoff attended his niece Shana's wedding to Eric Swanson, a former lawyer for the SEC. While Swanson was at the SEC—but before he started dating Madoff's niece—he supervised one of the bungled Madoff examinations. An investigation later by the SEC's inspector general concluded that, while the relationship looked like a conflict of interest, there is no evidence it had any impact on the unwise decisions that derailed that exam. For what it's worth, Madoff would say later that he hadn't even known Shana was dating an SEC lawyer until shortly before the wedding—Peter had not wanted to tell him, he said.

As always, Madoff was the "bank" for family and staff. He made loans to Shana to invest in an energy company that she and Andrew were putting together. He made loans to his sons and several employees. He agreed to loan his still-grieving brother $9 million and started planning a special gift for him: a vintage Aston-Martin automobile, like the one featured in the early James Bond films, to be delivered in the spring of 2008.

And on October 20, 2007, Madoff did a favor for Frank Levy, the son of the late Norman Levy, by appearing on a panel at the Philoctetes Center, which the younger Levy cofounded in 2003. The topic was "The Future of the Stock Market," and Madoff gave a bravura performance.

"You have to understand, Wall Street is one big turf war," Madoff said. ". . . By benefiting one person you're disadvantaging another person."

And don't forget that it's a for-profit business—a fact "which sometimes the regulators lose sight of, as do the academics," he continued. "In every aspect of it, the person that is buying the share of stock is convinced he knows something that the other person, who's selling it to him, does not know."

Madoff cogently explained the forces that automation had unleashed on the Street. "Wall Street—just so you understand the scale of it—is one of the few industries where the cost of doing business for the consumer has gone down dramatically, from a commission standpoint. Yet the expense of doing business, from the industry's perspective, has dramatically increased. The cost of regulation has dramatically increased."

He laughed and shrugged. "Now, no one is going to run a benefit for Wall Street," he continued. "So whenever I go down to Washington and meet with the SEC and complain to them that the industry is either over-regulated or the burdens are too great, they all start to roll their eyes—just like all of our children do whenever we talk about the good old days."

Responding to a question about how firms were surviving, he said, "Today, basically the big money on Wall Street is made by taking risks. Firms were driven into that business, including us, because you couldn't make money charging commissions." Trading for their own accounts—"that's where the money is made."

He also discussed the question of criminality on Wall Street. "By and large, in today's regulatory environment, it's virtually impossible to violate rules," he said. "This is something that the public really doesn't understand. If you read things in the newspaper and you see somebody violate a rule, you say, 'Well, they're always doing this.' But it's impossible for a violation to go undetected, certainly not for a considerable period of time."

As he spoke, almost exactly two years after his Ponzi scheme had been on the brink of exposure, he was at the apex of one of the most staggering crimes in financial history. By one estimate, more than $12 billion from all over the world had poured into his Ponzi scheme in just the previous twenty-four months—and in the next twelve months, almost all of it would pour out again, finally shattering the façade he had maintained so successfully for so long.

10

THE YEAR OF LIVING
DANGEROUSLY

Today is the first day of the last year of Bernie Madoff's epic fraud.

The paperwork has been completed for a $9 million unsecured loan from the company to Peter Madoff, whose titles at the firm now include senior managing director, chief compliance officer, head of the options department, and (since a few years ago) chief compliance officer for the private money management business Bernie runs on the seventeenth floor.

Still, the Madoff firm is casual about titles—Bernie almost seems to make them up as he goes along. Peter's primary title has always been "Bernie's brother." And this latest loan, to finance a real estate investment, reflects this reality. Due in five years, it carries an annual interest rate of 4.13 percent, a very low rate given the uneasiness currently gripping the credit markets.

At most big firms these days, an executive's request for a $9 million insider loan with a gentle interest rate would be coldly and firmly denied as "inappropriate." While the stock market seems healthy, the credit markets have been deteriorating since late summer. The housing market is starting to turn sour. Risks ignored just a year ago are starting to loom larger in the market's mind. Even so, longtime employees of Bernie Madoff's firm have no trouble borrowing cash when they need it. Bernie rarely says no.

But this loan to Peter—like all the insider loans that have come before and will follow in the months ahead—is sucking out cash that Bernie Madoff will need when the unprecedented turmoil bearing down on Wall Street finally hits.

Tonight is the firm's office holiday party, and employees are enjoying the margaritas and Mexican beer at Rosa Mexicano, a popular bistro on First Avenue, a few blocks from the office. This is the first time the firm has held its party here. Last year's site was a trendy young-crowd nightclub called Au Bar, with loud music and dancing. This spot seems more compatible with the firm's comfortable family-party style.

Ruth Madoff applauds the change in venue. "Book it for next year right now," she says to one employee with a happy laugh.

The party might almost be a family reunion. Beyond his own family ties, Madoff's employees work with their fathers, their cousins, their nephews, their stepsons, even their neighbors. Some of them—notably the staff on the seventeenth floor—were hired right out of high school and have never worked anywhere else.

The traders may joke about Madoff's nearly obsessive demand that they keep their desks clear and tidy, and they may roll their eyes at his crude humor, but the firm still seems like a great place to work. Besides being generous with insider loans, Madoff also manages much of the money his relatives and other senior employees have saved: their deferred compensation and retirement savings. Although he is prickly and secretive about it, everyone knows that giant hedge funds and wealthy individuals are constantly jockeying to get Madoff to manage their money. Employees feel lucky that he is looking out for them, too.

There may be a hint of edginess in the air tonight. Madoff's traders exchange jokes with the other traders at big Wall Street outfits, and lately, behind the laughter, they all are hearing faint rumbles from the approaching storm.

Perhaps it comforts them to reflect that Bernie Madoff has seen rough weather before—from the shaky markets right after the terrorist attacks in 2001 all the way back to the glut of unfinished paperwork that nearly choked Wall Street in the late 1960s. He's seen it all and survived it all.

WEDNESDAY, JANUARY 23, 2008

On Madoff's calendar, this evening belongs to New York City Center, the innovative cultural institution he and Ruth have supported for years and on whose board he has sat for more than a decade. The center is holding one of its crowd-pleasing performances, a tango tour de force perfectly suited to its distinctive Moorish-style auditorium on West Fifty-fifth Street. The faded facility, built as a Shriners temple in 1923, needs an enormous amount of renovation work, and a major fund-raising campaign is already being planned.

As Ruth and Bernie slip into their seats, Wall Street's growing anxiety about an approaching recession probably seems like a faint distraction. Madoff has at least $5 billion in the bank to sustain his Ponzi scheme, small bits of it contributed by people seated around him in this auditorium and giant slabs of it deposited by his global collection of hedge fund clients.

In theory, that cushion should see him through even a bad recession. But hedge funds hurtle into a trend, stampede out again, and swerve at unexpected moments like a herd of wild beasts. If they all panic at some clap of economic thunder, Madoff will be lucky to avoid getting trampled.

And if he goes down, many of the rich donors that City Center relies on will go down with him.

THURSDAY, FEBRUARY 14, 2008

Bernie Madoff catches a night flight to Palm Beach, where hundreds of his investors live. Among them is Carl Shapiro, the retired garment industry entrepreneur who has been a client since the 1960s. Shapiro is celebrating his ninety-fifth birthday with a gala organized by his daughters. The Madoffs are invited.

The party the next evening is a head-turning event, even for Palm Beach. There are armloads of orchids, towers of roses, and caviar and champagne in stunning abundance. The columnist Shannon Donnelly, the leading Palm Beach celebrity watcher, is on duty to collect the details, like the touching moment when Shapiro takes the microphone to serenade his wife of nearly seventy years.

Donnelly notices forty notable society names among the guests, including the owner of the New England Patriots football team and a well-known Chicago financier. She doesn't mention Bernie and Ruth Madoff—their names are almost entirely absent from the local society archives in Palm Beach, even though they have owned a home on this thin, rich island for almost fifteen years.

Many of the guests who will be mentioned in Donnelly's column are Madoff's customers. It isn't so much that they trust Madoff—if they know him at all, they probably sense the almost obsessive reserve that keeps most people at a distance. But they believe in Carl Shapiro, and Shapiro clearly believes in Madoff. How could you doubt Carl Shapiro's judgment?

The birthday party is a great success. After some quiet conversation with the Shapiros, Bernie and Ruth Madoff say their farewells and slip into the soft Palm Beach night for the short drive through the Breakers Hotel golf course and along palm-lined Royal Poinciana Way to their home on North Lake Way.

An intricate banyan tree almost obscures the front of the house, throwing night shadows on the drive and scattering leaves on the narrow second-floor balcony. The home is deceptively large, stretching deep behind its modest façade. By local standards, it is not lavish—it certainly is less grand than Peter Madoff's château-style home nearby, and it can't hold a candle to the $33 million mansion owned by Bernie's longtime client Jeffry Picower, on the ocean near the island's southern tip.

As Palm Beach reckons such things, Bernie and Peter Madoff are newcomers. But Shapiro and his family have vouched for Madoff—Bernie listed Shapiro's son-in-law Robert Jaffe as a reference on his successful application to the Palm Beach Country Club. Before long, dozens of multimillionaire club members would be fishing for a chance to meet Bernie, to invest with Bernie.

What they don't know is that Madoff has grown larger than any of them can imagine. If his hedge fund clients stick with him, he doesn't need the genial guests who gathered tonight for Carl Shapiro's celebration. And if the hedge funds desert him, there is little that even Shapiro can do to save him, no matter how willing and trusting he may be.

THURSDAY, FEBRUARY 21, 2008

Bernie Madoff welcomes a British bank executive into his office on the nineteenth floor. The banker works in London for HSBC, which handles the administrative paperwork for a growing roster of global hedge funds, including several that do business with Madoff.

This is not a social call. Some HSBC units have been recommending various Madoff feeder funds to their clients for years, starting with the Fairfield Sentry fund in 1999. A number of the bank's offshore hedge fund clients are invested with Madoff and are trusting his firm to hold their assets for safekeeping. Legally, that makes Madoff the "sub-custodian" of the funds, since HSBC is accepting fees to serve as their official custodian. As much as everyone trusts Madoff's reputation, this is an unusual arrangement, especially with the world in such a skittish mood.

The banker needs to answer a simple question: Are the securities that the hedge funds have left in Madoff's custody actually there?

They aren't, of course. Madoff knows this—and by now there is enough quiet gossip about him in the hedge fund community to suggest that what he already knows others are starting to suspect.

Even within HSBC there have been skeptics. As early as 2001 a few bank executives were expressing doubt about Madoff. In September 2005 the bank asked a major accounting firm, KPMG, to review the "operational risks" of Madoff's business. When the report came back in early 2006, it included a chilling list of what could go wrong, from misdirected trades to outright fraud. But despite warnings and some internal doubts, the bank apparently felt that Madoff's stainless reputation and his standing with market regulators made such nightmare possibilities sound outlandish.

Still, next month, the bank will ask KPMG to do yet another assessment of the risks of doing business with Madoff. Perhaps this is what the banker has come to say. Or perhaps that examination will be ordered as a result of his visit today.

Despite that renewed scrutiny, HSBC will continue to provide administrative and custodial services to the funds that deal with Madoff for almost ten more months.

After the stock market lurches to its sweaty close today, coworkers see Marcia Beth Cohn climb the oval staircase to the nineteenth floor and slump into the secretary's chair near Bernie Madoff's glass-walled office. She is a wiry, athletic woman with very short dark auburn hair. She swivels toward Madoff, standing nearby, and asks with a shaky smile:

"O, wise man, what is going to happen to us?"

Earlier today, the Federal Reserve extended an emergency line of credit to the Bear Stearns brokerage house, which was caught in an old-fashioned "run on the bank." It is the first time in history that the Fed, a bank regulator, had stepped in to rescue a brokerage firm. Rumors of unrecognized mortgage losses are shaking people's faith in other giant Wall Street firms, too—the shares of Morgan Stanley and Lehman Brothers were swept into the downdraft that cut Bear's stock price in half today. The Dow closed down nearly two hundred points.

There is probably no brokerage house on Wall Street with closer ties to Madoff's firm than Bear Stearns. It has been a client of Madoff's trading desk for years. Bernie and Ruth Madoff have good friends among senior Bear Stearns executives. When the Wall Street division of the American Jewish Committee honored Madoff at a fund-raising event at the Harmonie Club in 1999, the reception was hosted by Bear Stearns chairman Alan C. Greenberg.

For Marcia Beth Cohn, though, the threat is more than academic. She is president of Cohmad Securities, the tiny brokerage firm that shares office space with Madoff's firm but clears its small volume of stock trades through Bear Stearns. Despite her wry tone, she seems genuinely frightened. What if some of her customer orders get caught in Bear Stearns's collapse?

It is a day to frighten anyone, but Madoff is characteristically calm. He gives the small group around her a quiet but reassuring lecture on the safety net that protects customer accounts on Wall Street. He is confident that Bear Stearns will find its footings once today's panic ebbs.

But federal regulators are already scrambling to find a buyer for Bear Stearns before the Asian markets open on Sunday evening. At the last moment, JPMorgan Chase will agree to buy the firm, after being promised substantial loan guarantees from the Fed. But it will offer only $2 a share—for Bear Stearns stock that closed today at $30 a share.

The bank will ultimately raise its bid, but the damage will have been done. Investors will bail out of the financial sector, fearing that failures once considered unthinkable no longer are. From this weekend on, pension funds and other institutional investors will demand more information about the banks and brokers they deal with. There will be more questions put to Madoff, more answers demanded, and more nervous withdrawals.

It is an anxious, faintly terrifying day, but this is nowhere near as bad as it will get. Indeed, this is all just prologue.

FRIDAY, APRIL 25, 2008

A partner at the Fairfield Greenwich Group, one of Madoff's earliest and biggest hedge fund investors, is studying the rate at which cash is pouring out of its flagship product, the Fairfield Sentry fund, whose $7 billion in assets are entirely invested with Madoff. The Fairfield Greenwich firm has quietly put itself up for sale, and the partner knows that any well-heeled buyer will scrutinize these numbers to calculate the firm's potential value.

An explanation will definitely be required, based on the numbers the partner shares today in an e-mail to some of his colleagues. Redemption rates are high—twice the hedge fund industry average. The partner can explain this: "With monthly [redemptions allowed] on 15 days notice many investors use Sentry like a checking account," he notes. This contributes to the Sentry fund's appeal—and to its vulnerability.

On the plus side, Madoff has capped how much money he will take from Fairfield Greenwich, so redemptions allow them to satisfy investors who were shut out in the past. On the negative side, the redemption rate could dash the firm's hopes of finding a buyer.

In a more private e-mail a few minutes earlier, the partner had been more candid. The downside risk of not replacing the withdrawn cash "is very significant," he wrote. It would reduce the firm's revenue from management fees and, thus, its value to a prospective buyer.

"And unfortunately," he continued, "the upside is capped by capacity at

Madoff so the risk/reward is disproportionate—a less obvious risk with Madoff than the risk that he 'blows up' but a real one nevertheless."

Other hedge funds, private bankers, and wealthy individuals scattered around the world have invested billions of dollars in the Fairfield Sentry fund. If one of the risks these investors are taking is that Madoff will blow up, it clearly is not obvious to them.

WEDNESDAY, MAY 14, 2008

Bernie Madoff looks quizzically at the two men who have been waiting in his nineteenth-floor conference room since 11:00 AM, and gestures them into his adjacent office.

"I don't know why I agreed to see you," he says. He doesn't sound rude, just a little confused.

Madoff moves to his seat behind the desk as the visitors, a retired New Jersey businessman and his accountant, settle into the chairs across from him.

The businessman mentions the name of the wealthy Madoff investor who had made the introduction. Madoff looks blank, as if he does not recognize the name. He has thousands of investors—but his visitors do not know that. They still think Bernie Madoff is an exclusive, highly selective investment adviser. After all, the businessman made at least a half-dozen calls before finally getting this spot on Madoff's calendar.

"All right, as long as you're here . . . ," Madoff says, as he seems to relax slightly, his cherubic face taking on a kindly smile. He does not have a lot of time to spare, he adds—he will be leaving the next day for the south of France. They trade some pleasantries about his vacation plans. He seems in no hurry to make a sales pitch; he shows no sign of wanting the businessman's money.

Suddenly the businessman asks, "You didn't grow up wealthy, did you?"

Madoff smiles. He begins to recount his humble beginnings, the classic biography of the self-made man, something he has in common with his visitor.

Finally they get down to the details.

What is his fee? There is no fee.

What is the minimum investment? Five million dollars.

"I'm not really prepared to put in that much at first," the businessman says. Typically he starts small with a new money manager, waiting for good results before committing as much as Madoff requires.

Madoff shrugs. "Well, you can put in two million now, but by the end of the year you have to put in the rest."

At that, the businessman's accountant knows this discussion is going nowhere and he turns his attention to his surroundings. There is not a single item on Madoff's desk—not even a pencil. He notices the array of costly Roy Lichtenstein prints on the wall, all variations on the figure of a bull, Madoff's icon. He takes in Madoff's expensively cut dress shirt and handsome tie, his silver hair curling stylishly over his collar. Madoff truly seems indifferent to the outcome of the meeting.

The businessman continues to quiz him—that's his style, as his accountant can attest. He pokes and prods until he gets answers.

Abruptly, Madoff becomes firmer. "Listen," he says, "you ask a lot of questions. I just want to make one thing clear: With all due respect, once you invest, you can't call me. You'll deal with someone else."

The businessman smiles—his accountant knows the comment has shut the door on any possibility of a deal. Perhaps that's what Madoff intended. As much as he needs this man's cash, he cannot afford this relentless curiosity. After a few more pleasantries, they rise, exchange handshakes, and walk toward the double glass doors leading to the elevators.

FRIDAY, JUNE 6, 2008

Today the Madoff firm sends a check for just over $6 million to lawyers handling Mark and Stephanie Madoff's purchase of a new gray-shingled house on the beach in Nantucket.

It is a beautiful property, larger and better situated than their former vacation home there, which they've just sold for $2.3 million. Located on the exclusive island's south shore, it has five bedrooms and baths, a gracious guest cottage, a pool and hot tub, and a 180-degree view of salt grass, sand, and ocean from its deep wraparound porch.

There is room for their two-year-old daughter to play and for Mark's two older children, from his previous marriage, to come for summer visits full of bike rides, fishing trips, and games.

Perhaps it isn't wise for Madoff to let Mark borrow so much cash right now. The trends are getting more worrisome. Some of Madoff's important feeder funds are withdrawing more than they're bringing in. Even the vast Fairfield Sentry hedge fund, that $7 billion behemoth, is losing cash.

But to refuse Mark would be almost impossible. How would he explain it, after all these years of being the family's bank? His two sons live the way the heirs of any successful hedge fund manager would expect to live. Operating at the level Madoff pretends he has reached—with many billions in assets supposedly invested with him, with a net worth in the hundreds of millions, with three vacation homes of his own—how could he explain that it simply wasn't a good time for him to part with a mere $6 million?

The younger Madoffs will close on the home on Monday, just in time for the sweet summer months on Nantucket.

FRIDAY, JUNE 13, 2008

It's not really his job, but the financial consultant in Boulder, Colorado, feels he must warn the Fairfield Greenwich Group about the options trading Madoff did for the Fairfield Sentry fund last month. For one thing, it violated the rules that Madoff is supposed to be following when he does trades for the fund. Stock options are to be used only to hedge existing stock positions, not to generate profits independently. But this is exactly what Madoff reported doing last month: he bought twice as many options contracts as his stock positions required. In fact, his excessive options trading accounted for $95 million of the fund's monthly earnings.

Something just doesn't add up. This isn't the first time the consultant has noticed that Madoff was "over-hedging," but it is the most extreme example.

In an e-mail this morning to the fund's chief risk officer, the consultant concedes that he may be a bit out of bounds, since he was hired merely to summarize the trading activity "without providing editorial commentary." However, he continues, "I must mention to you that I find the May options trading activity to be unusual and difficult to explain, and would encourage you to investigate it further."

The risk officer replies a bit later that he, too, "found the activity somewhat abnormal." But he has two weeks of travel ahead, so they agree to discuss the trades in a phone call later in the month.

During that call, the consultant will share his fundamental fear. Even as skillful a trader as Madoff cannot wind up on the winning side of every single options trade, so there is the risk that he is backdating his trades to fake his profits. Someone needs to find out who is trading with him. More urgently, someone needs to verify that Madoff actually is holding all the assets he supposedly has purchased for the Fairfield Greenwich funds.

There probably is a simple explanation for these options trades; most likely they were the only fictional trades Madoff could concoct that would explain how he made money when the entire market was down. But it was clumsy—and too obvious. Perhaps he wonders why nobody at Fairfield Greenwich has called him on it, but no one ever has.

And, despite the consultant's urgent warnings today, no one ever will.

TUESDAY, JULY 15, 2008

Bernie Madoff is meeting with four visitors from Florida—and he knows this meeting could cost him as much as $33 million.

Three of the visitors are associated with the MorseLife Foundation in West Palm Beach, which operates one of the premier senior care facilities on Florida's golden East Coast. The fourth is a financial planner in Merrill Lynch's West Palm Beach office, who has recently expressed a few mild doubts to the foundation's board about its Madoff investment. His specific concern is that the foundation is putting too many of its eggs in Bernie's basket. In the spring, he recommended pulling out some of the Madoff money and investing it elsewhere.

The MorseLife Foundation, whose board is dominated by the same sort of wealthy Jewish philanthropists Madoff has cultivated everywhere, opened an account with him in 1995. Since then, the foundation has invested more than $11 million and has never made a withdrawal. On this hot summer day, these visitors believe that MorseLife has about $33 million in that account, representing almost 60 percent of its total endowment.

There is nothing in the account, of course. It is just another small pipeline into Madoff's huge criminal enterprise. But if MorseLife asks for some of that money back, Madoff will have to write a check—further reducing the pool of cash that is keeping his fraud alive.

He is caught in an increasingly dangerous market environment. This week, the stock of the once-impregnable mortgage giant Fannie Mae is in freefall. Madoff knows some of his big, nervous hedge fund clients could soon demand their billions back. But steady long-term endowments such as that of MorseLife have been his bread and butter for years. It will greatly magnify his worries if they start pulling money out, too.

No doubt he is determined to charm the man from Merrill Lynch.

Madoff is relaxed and calm, as always, and he clearly succeeds in reassuring his visitors about his hedged, conservative "split-strike conversion" strategy. Shortly after this meeting, the Merrill executive will reverse his position and accept the foundation's continuing investment with Madoff.

Still, it is an ominous victory. Not long ago, the question of whether the foundation should stay would never have come up at all, much less have made its way into Bernie Madoff's appointment book.

WEDNESDAY, AUGUST 20, 2008

There is a strong whiff of worry in the e-mail traffic today at Fairfield Greenwich Group. Nervous investors and prospective clients are pressing for answers about Madoff—indeed, one client is pulling $74.5 million out of the Sentry fund specifically because of its concerns about Madoff. And staffers at HSBC are asking questions as part of an operational due-diligence analysis of the Sentry fund.

Even after years of due diligence, Fairfield Greenwich's chief risk officer, Amit Vijayvergiya, conceded in an e-mail yesterday that "there are certain aspects of BLM's operations that remain unclear" to him and his colleagues. They are trying to respond to the questions from HSBC, which is still focused laser-like on Madoff.

The root of all these worries is counterparty risk. Even institutions confident about their own health know they can be brought down by the failure of an institution on the other side of a trade or on the receiving end of a loan. There are frightened whispers all over the Street about Lehman Brothers and Morgan Stanley. Those worries could become self-fulfilling prophecies—if counterparties are afraid that Lehman or Morgan won't survive, they may refuse to trade with them or lend to them, thereby ensuring the very failure they fear.

Trust—it all comes down to trust.

In one of his shorthand messages today, Vijayvergiya reminds the firm's Risk Assessment Committee that "the biggest single counterparty exposure risk we have at FGG" is Bernard L. Madoff. "I think the larger question is if the Risk Group is comfortable with BLM counterparty risk."

It used to be. Is it still?

SUNDAY, SEPTEMBER 7, 2008

The weather is hot and humid, but a soft west wind is making the Long Island shore a little more comfortable. Bernie Madoff's calendar shows that his son Andrew and Andrew's children are to spend this weekend with him and Ruth at the beachfront home in Montauk.

Anyone who leaves the beach and switches on the television today will find the news almost unthinkable: the federal government is seizing control of Fannie Mae and Freddie Mac, the two largest mortgage finance companies in the country. The bailout is the brainchild of Secretary of the Treasury Henry Paulson, and its price tag is rumored to be in excess of $25 billion.

The alternative could be far more costly. Fannie Mae and Freddie Mac have issued billions of dollars in publicly traded debt backed by home mortgages. Fears about the quality of those loans is driving investors out of the credit markets; money to finance new mortgages is drying up.

Andrew Madoff surely knows this news will roil the markets tomorrow, and he and the other traders at his father's firm will probably have a grueling day.

Privately, Bernie Madoff knows this news will further alarm his institutional investors, especially the overseas hedge funds he is fleecing through his Ponzi scheme.

But no one without a crystal ball could know that this epic bailout—detailed under outsize headlines in all the next day's newspapers and debated on television talk shows as an unwarranted and dangerous intrusion of the federal government into the private sector—will soon look like a mere footnote to the calamity bearing down on Wall Street.

MONDAY, SEPTEMBER 15, 2008

September is the perfect time to visit the south of France. The air is sweet and fresh, the vineyards are glowing, the sea is vivid and clear. Bernie and Ruth Madoff and some friends had come over on the company jet before the weekend. They plan to fly on to Italy after a few days here at the Madoffs' small stucco town house, tucked into the rear corner of a modest complex called Château des Pins.

But the news from New York is so alarming that the Madoffs and their guests probably just hover inside around the television, ignoring the sunshine on the hills above Cap d'Antibes.

Lehman Brothers, one of the most fabled names on Wall Street, filed for bankruptcy this morning, after a frantic weekend of failed negotiations with bank regulators and government officials. Treasury officials refused to throw the firm a lifeline; the Fed did not offer financial backing to attract a willing buyer. This time—after Bear Stearns, Fannie Mae, and Freddie Mac—there was no bailout. It is the largest bankruptcy in American history.

Within hours there are dire predictions that another Wall Street giant, the insurance firm American International Group, is sinking under the weight of its derivative losses. Beset by fear and seeking capital, executives at Merrill Lynch are rushing into a shotgun wedding with Bank of America. The stock market seems to be in a death spiral, and even seasoned Wall Street veterans are shaken by the faint trace of panic they hear in the voices of customers, regulators, and television commentators.

"Let's go home."

It is the group's decision, really, not just Bernie's. Something deep in the bedrock of Wall Street is cracking, and the tremors can be felt even here. There are calls to the airport to ready the jet. Bags are quickly packed. As the aircraft streaks up to its cruising altitude, perhaps Madoff takes one last look at the charming landscape dropping away beneath him.

He is flying into the financial storm of the century; he will not fly out again.

TUESDAY, SEPTEMBER 16, 2008

The financial world is reeling.

Lehman Brothers is in bankruptcy. The sale of Merrill Lynch to Bank of America is seen as a fire sale, and the stock prices of all the brokerage houses and banks are tumbling. The overall market was down a stunning 5 percent yesterday as regulators grappled with whether, and how, to rescue AIG, which was on the brink of defaulting on its derivative-based obligations to other giant institutional investors around the world.

The Treasury announced a rescue package for AIG this morning, but unexpected cracks from the impact of Lehman Brothers' collapse are showing up elsewhere. Today, The Reserve fund, the nation's oldest money market fund, "breaks the buck" by reporting a net asset value of less than a dollar a share. The news feeds the growing panic. If this financial meltdown can infect even supposedly secure money funds, for decades the middle-class substitute for a bank account, there is no safe haven.

At Fairfield Greenwich Group, whose wealthy investors have long thought of Madoff as a sort of plutocratic money market fund, clients are seeking clarity and comfort.

Today the group sends out a reassuring "Dear Investor" letter from Amit Vijayvergiya, the chief risk officer. He quickly mentions that the Sentry fund has no exposure to Lehman, Bank of America, or Merrill Lynch. "Currently," he continues, the Sentry portfolio "is fully invested in short dated U.S. Treasury bills."

In this storm, you can't get any safer than that. So this is great news for Fairfield Sentry investors and further proof of Madoff's mastery of the markets.

Or it would be, if it were true. But it's not; it is a half-truth based on a lie wrapped in a mistake.

The previous day, in an e-mail to colleagues at 10:55 AM, Vijayvergiya reported on a conversation he'd had with Frank DiPascali, who was manning the phones on Madoff's mysterious seventeenth floor. DiPascali told him that almost 20 percent of the Sentry fund was still invested in stocks and options, the scene of the worst market carnage. And this wasn't likely to change for a day or so because Madoff and DiPascali "do not want to sell into weakness today and are looking for an exit opportunity tomorrow morning or Wednesday."

In a follow-up call later that Monday, DiPascali said he was "looking to do an orderly exit tomorrow," Vijayvergiya told his partners. Tomorrow is here and the reassuring letter has been sent out, although it is not accurate: DiPascali has not confirmed his "orderly exit" from the highly disorderly market.

The entire notion of an "orderly exit" is a fantasy, of course. There is nothing to exit. There are no stocks to sell, no Treasury bills to buy, no strategies to unwind. It's all a charade.

It is a lie that will not match the next set of lies from Madoff and DiPascali. A few days from now, Fairfield Greenwich will get the account statements for these harrowing days. They will show that Madoff will not reach the safe harbor of Treasury bills until Friday, three days from today. The account statements are all lies, too, but an increasingly frantic DiPascali apparently is losing track of which lie he's telling to whom.

MONDAY, SEPTEMBER 22, 2008

Washington is one big war room, as regulators at the Federal Reserve, the FDIC, the Treasury Department, and the SEC all try to fight the panic that is breaking out on a half-dozen fronts. Trying to stem the stock market sell-off, the SEC is reviving an emergency measure it temporarily imposed in July. It is a rule that would have impeded Madoff's ability to carry out his complex split-strike conversion strategy—if he had actually been trying to do so. The rule bars short sales on financial stocks, some of which have long been included in the portfolios of Madoff's feeder funds.

In an exchange of e-mails today at Fairfield Greenwich, a partner frets about the impact of the rule on Madoff and his counterparties, the big banks supposedly handling his options trades. Another partner asks a more fundamental question: Why are the banks willing to deal with Madoff at all right now, given how close to paralysis the markets are? His understanding is that banks are "not providing risk capital to anyone," he adds.

Frank DiPascali will try to reassure the nervous partners that the financial stocks have been pruned from the strategy, so the short-sale ban isn't a problem.

But the key question remains. In the midst of this spreading panic, why would any bank still be willing to trade billions of dollars' worth of increasingly risky options with Madoff?

The most obvious answer is the most unthinkable one: they aren't.

TUESDAY, SEPTEMBER 23, 2008

Bernie Madoff's calendar shows a visit today from Sonja Kohn, the founder and controlling shareholder of Bank Medici, her boutique bank and investment firm in Vienna. The vibrant Austrian usually sails into Bernie's private realm like a grand duchess, beaming and delighted to see everyone—there's almost a celebratory air to her visits. Kohn has known Madoff personally for more than twenty years, and the relationship has made her rich and respected all across Europe, a far cry from her pre-Madoff status as a simple Wall Street stockbroker.

So much has changed since Kohn's last visit, in November 2007. Back then, the Bank Medici network of Madoff feeder funds was still reporting investment gains. By and large, the funds were still solid sources of cash for Madoff's hidden Ponzi scheme. But the anxiety that has gripped the market since "the Lehman weekend" is undermining even his most unshakable investors.

Neither knows it, but today is Sonja Kohn's last visit with Bernie Madoff. There is no independent account of what is being said inside his glass-walled office—indeed, according to the trustee, Madoff routinely directed that all records of his dealings with Kohn be destroyed—but the checkbook he uses for his Ponzi scheme suggests that the news is bad.

Nine days from now, Madoff will write a check for $113 million to cover redemptions from the Herald fund, a mainstay of the Bank Medici network. A month later, he will write the fund another check for a staggering $423 million. More than a half-billion dollars in cash is about to pour out of his bank account, at the worst possible time.

If this is the news that Sonja Kohn is delivering to her friend Bernie Madoff today, there is absolutely nothing for him to celebrate.

WEDNESDAY, SEPTEMBER 24, 2008

The check is for $10 million.

For a change, it is written to Bernie Madoff, not by him. It represents the assets of thirty-five labor union pension plans managed by a single trustee. These small pension plans have been ideal victims for his Ponzi scheme. The money flows in on a regular schedule, the claims for withdrawals are typically small and predictable. These funds are not as large as the ones he once coveted, but their money adds up.

It is extremely welcome today.

Next week, Cohmad Securities will expect its monthly check representing its commissions for introducing investors to Madoff—a precise payment of $214,722.03. Also, in his role as the family banker, he's promised to help Andrew purchase a new Upper East Side apartment, one of just a dozen units in a modern seven-story boutique building on East Seventy-fourth Street. The unit has a price tag of more than $4 million.

Of course, it would be safer for Bernie if he ignored Andrew's loan request and simply added the entire $10 million to the Ponzi scheme's bank account, which is being rapidly drained by jittery hedge fund withdrawals.

Perhaps Madoff is worried that it would create too much suspicion if he were suddenly to refuse his younger son after so many years of largess—and after he loaned an even larger sum to Mark for the Nantucket home he and his wife purchased in June. Or perhaps Madoff just wants Andrew, the son who battled cancer and was spared, to have this sleekly beautiful apartment.

The one thing he has no intention of doing, however, is investing the $10 million check so that it can generate money to cover hardworking union members' pensions in the years to come. He pours it into the river of cash that nourishes his fraud and benefits his family, as he has done so many times before.

But surely he can see that the river's flood stage is long since past.

THURSDAY, OCTOBER 2, 2008

The Fairfield Greenwich offices, high in a forty-story tower on East Fifty-second Street, are just a few blocks from Bernie Madoff's suite in the Lipstick Building. It would be an easy walk on this cool, overcast day.

The three men making the journey—Jeffrey Tucker, Walter Noel, and their younger colleague, chief counsel Mark McKeefry—need to get some answers about an investment strategy that seems to be defying gravity. All the tools that Madoff relies on, from blue-chip stocks to privately negotiated options, are encased in the icy fear now gripping the markets. In this climate, who on earth is willing to trade with Madoff? The question has tortured some Fairfield Greenwich partners for weeks.

Tucker, Noel, and McKeefry file into Madoff's offices. Frank DiPascali joins them from the seventeenth floor; Amit Vijayvergiya is hooked in by telephone, perhaps from his office in Hamilton, Bermuda.

Madoff starts applying his magic formula: exclusivity, confidence, masterful knowledge. He reminds them once again that he shouldn't even have to submit to these due-diligence quizzes, given how much in demand he is among global investors. He mentions that a friend at JPMorgan Chase asked him to meet with some of that formidable bank's due-diligence people from London and he simply refused. "Same thing one week later," he says, sounding disgusted. He refused again. He doesn't need to shake a few hands and show a bunch of people around his office.

He tells them confidently that his market-making business is getting more profitable than it's been in several years. He still has "access to liquidity," he says casually, as if the entire world were not frozen by panic. There's a lot of liquidity out there for his "split-strike conversion" customers and his market-making business, too. He's doing just great, despite all the turmoil.

Tapping his deep knowledge of the market's history, he explains exactly how other Wall Street firms got into trouble: With the shift away from partnerships to publicly traded brokerage houses, managers had no incentive to stay on top of their business. All they cared about was hitting the next quarter's earnings estimate. To do this, they dabbled in exotic products they never understood and took on too much debt. He knows to avoid those pitfalls, he says, because he's built his business from the ground up.

It is vintage Bernie. But it doesn't address the questions posed by the men from Fairfield Greenwich.

Madoff simply refuses to name the employees at the firm involved in executing the Sentry fund's strategy. He won't discuss the firm's succession plan. He won't identify the people whose signatures are required to move money out of client accounts. Most disappointingly, he will not identify even one of the "large institutions" who are the counterparties to his options trades—"for obvious reasons," he says.

No one presses him or challenges him to explain why he can trade when no one else can. No one asks him about the improper options trades their consultant in Colorado discovered last spring. No one presses him on anything, really—even though e-mails were flying around their offices just a week ago fretting over how Madoff was managing to function when even the foreign currency market, one of the deepest and most active in the world, was almost at a standstill.

Nevertheless, Madoff and DiPascali both emphasize calmly that everything discussed today must be kept confidential.

In letters and e-mails to clients next week, the men from Fairfield Greenwich will put the best possible spin on this visit. But as they file out into the October chill, they still do not have the answers they need to stem the rising tide of anxiety among their investors—or the rising tide of cash flowing out of Fairfield Sentry.

WEDNESDAY, OCTOBER 8, 2008

Bernie Madoff's client Stanley Chais is in town from Los Angeles, staying at his Fifth Avenue apartment overlooking the first splashes of autumn color in Central Park.

In his early eighties, Chais is still an attractive man, tall and rugged with a deep tan, tidy white hair, and a dashing film-star moustache. But he is increasingly frail, battling a rare blood disorder, and in June he wrote investors in his partnerships that his son Mark is going to take over the administration of those accounts.

The Chais accounts have been draining cash from Madoff's bank account all year, and Chais made another small withdrawal yesterday. They've had a long and apparently warm relationship, but Madoff privately wonders if Chais suspects his fraud. Is he toying with Madoff, figuring he'll have to comply with any withdrawal request rather than risk exposure?

Madoff isn't sure, and he can hardly ask. Later, Stan Chais will deny vehemently that he knew anything about Madoff's fraud when he made these withdrawals or, indeed, at any time during their long relationship.

To be sure, the check Madoff wrote for Chais yesterday is tiny compared with the hundreds of millions in assets that Chais's accounts supposedly hold, wealth that will vanish when Madoff's fraud collapses.

From Madoff's perspective, the cash draining from Chais's accounts is trivial compared with the amounts he has wired recently to the Kingate Euro fund, one of his oldest offshore feeder funds.

No, a client like Chais—whose phone number is the first one programmed into Madoff's speed dial—can never do the kind of damage to his teetering Ponzi scheme that can be inflicted by a few skittish international hedge fund clients.

As a crisply clear day ebbs into a cloudy night, Bernie Madoff and Stanley Chais meet at Fred's, the warmly lit restaurant on the ninth floor of the upscale Barney's department store on Madison Avenue—just two old friends having dinner.

THURSDAY, OCTOBER 16, 2008

The day gets off to a bad start for Amit Vijayvergiya. It starts with a call from the derivatives desk at JPMorgan Chase, one of the global banks that have structured and sold complex derivatives designed to track the performance of the Fairfield Sentry fund.

Vijayvergiya listens as the bank staffer poses a series of questions about—what else?—Bernie Madoff. The bank's questions have become more frequent and insistent, and nothing Fairfield Greenwich says about Madoff seems satisfactory.

Then the bank sends in its upcoming redemption requests, and they are a shock. An executive in Fairfield's London office had been trading e-mails with a contact at the bank within the past week, but the redemption amounts discussed, a few million euros, were almost routine. Today's request is much larger than its original estimate.

With the sudden spike in the bank's redemption requests and these questions about Madoff, something is obviously wrong. What's happened?

Yanko Della Schiava, Walter Noel's Italian son-in-law and one of the primary sales agents for the funds in Europe, tries to find out. He makes calls to some of his contacts at the bank, without success.

JPMorgan Chase is revving up to pull $250 million out of the Fairfield Sentry fund, virtually its entire investment. It is also pulling cash from a few other Madoff-managed funds involved in its derivatives deals, including the Herald fund. It clearly is worried about more than just counterparty risk.

THURSDAY, OCTOBER 23, 2008

Maurice E. Maertens, the chief investment officer for New York University's endowment, and his assistant are ushered into J. Ezra Merkin's office in the black granite tower at 450 Park Avenue. The thirty-three-story building caters to hedge funds, and Merkin's thirty-second-floor suite is prime real estate in that community.

Maertens, the longtime head of Ford Motor Company's pension fund, was wooed out of early retirement in 1997 by the NYU investment committee. By then, NYU was already an investor in Merkin's Ariel fund, having bought its first $20 million stake in January 1994. Now its investment—which the committee assumes is being managed by Merkin—has supposedly grown to more than $85 million.

At today's routine meeting, Merkin recommends that NYU invest directly in a fund run by Bernie Madoff. True, Madoff clears his own trades—there is no third-party custodian holding the assets—but he has offered a good steady return year after year, Merkin says.

Maertens and his assistant are instantly dismissive. As an institutional investor, NYU would never invest with any fund that "self-clears." Without equivocation, Maertens tells Merkin that an investment with Madoff would not be suitable.

For some reason, Ezra Merkin does not say, "But you are already invested with Bernie Madoff through the Ariel fund." Merkin has invested about a third of the Ariel fund's assets, more than $300 million, with Madoff. It is part of roughly $2 billion that Merkin thinks his three hedge funds have in their accounts with Bernie. Indeed, Merkin's trust is so solid that he has added another $10 million to his Madoff accounts this month.

Maertens will later recall that they simply moved on to other topics. When their routine business is done, the NYU executives exchange handshakes with Merkin and leave.

TUESDAY, OCTOBER 28, 2008

A senior JPMorgan Chase executive in London signs and dates a startling confidential report to the Serious Organised Crime Agency, a national law enforcement body in Britain. In the section of the form entitled "Reason for Suspicion," the report describes the bank's complex derivatives deals involving three funds that all invest with Bernard L. Madoff Investment Securities.

The bank is concerned about Madoff's performance, "which is so consistently and significantly ahead of its peers, year-on-year, even in the prevailing market conditions, as to appear too good to be true—meaning that it probably is," the banker writes. On top of that, Madoff refuses to shed any light on how he achieves those results. So the bank has sent out a redemption notice to one of the funds and is preparing to pull its money out of the other two.

After that first notice went out, a bank executive talked with a fund manager in Geneva whose firm sold its clients the Madoff-linked derivatives affected by the redemptions. In the taped conversation, conducted in French, the Swiss fund manager made references to "Colombian interests who will not be happy" with JPMorgan Chase's actions, "statements that the value of the funds in question must not fall and thinly veiled threats to the security of bank staff," the banker reports.

A transcript of that telephone call, disclosed later in the French press, picks up with the London banker insisting that he's always been clear about how risky the complex derivatives were.

"I can see the price you want," the banker says, "but in reality this is not the price you can get. . . ."

The man in Geneva asks, "You hear that the price would be lower?"

"Right now, yes," the banker replies.

Still protesting, the man in Geneva sputters a bit: "If we really had to get there—and we wanted to be friends, I also insist on the second point—you know we have friends in Colombia that can cause damage when they are getting in—when they get angry, and it almost seems that someone is trying to upset [them] just now."

The banker seems taken aback. "Is that a threat or—?"

Laughter from Geneva interrupts his question. "No, it's just information," the man says. "You know, we are simple people from Switzerland."

On the same day that the JPMorgan Chase executive in London is reporting these suspicions about Madoff, a worried businessman in Dubai arrives for a meeting with his private banker. Meetings like this are occurring all around the globe, as everyone seeks safety from the turbulence sweeping the financial markets. No place is immune, not even this booming city on the Persian Gulf.

Since 2004 the wealthy businessman and four partners have been invested in the Fairfield Sentry fund. He recalls his banker recommending the fund as a "cash substitute," a hedge fund with a long track record of small but safe and steady returns. Indeed, he remembers being impressed when the banker said the fund had achieved "mythical status" for its consistency. He was impressed and flattered that, although the Sentry fund was supposedly closed to new investors, the bank could get him in. The investment that he and his partners made in the account has supposedly grown to more than $5.3 million.

However, now the businessman wants out. He directs his banker to redeem all the Sentry shares he and his partners hold. He takes the formal paperwork required for a redemption request with him and returns it to the bank the next day, expecting the money to be returned to him and his partners by the end of November.

TUESDAY, NOVEMBER 4, 2008

Today America goes to the polls to decide whether Senator Barack Obama or Senator John McCain will be the next president of the United States, and the stock market stages a roaring Election Day rally that pushes the S&P 500 index up more than 4 percent and adds more than three hundred points to the Dow.

Today is also when Bernie Madoff almost certainly begins to wonder if he will survive the panic of 2008—or if he even wants to.

On the seventeenth floor, Frank DiPascali gets the news first: the Fairfield Sentry fund has filed two redemption requests for next month totaling a staggering $850 million. This brings the Fairfield Sentry withdrawals since September to $1.25 billion, not counting millions withdrawn from some of the smaller Fairfield Greenwich funds.

The other big hedge funds are pulling money out, too. But for more than a decade, the Sentry fund has been Madoff's biggest source of cash. Perhaps it's only fitting that it is now his biggest source of worry.

For days, he has been on the phone to Palm Beach, gently imploring his old friend Carl Shapiro to hurry and make a $250 million investment in his Madoff account. The money is on its way, Shapiro tells him, and it is. When it arrives, it will make a splash in the increasingly shallow pool of cash in Madoff's bank account.

That may be all he needs—just enough money to build a bridge between today and that future day when Wall Street will finally calm down and the cash will start to flow into the Ponzi scheme again.

Of course, any realist can see that, this time, Shapiro's money is far too little and far too late. But that realist would not be Bernie Madoff. Even now, Madoff is sure he can forestall disaster. Prospective clients still want to meet with him. He can push Jeffry Picower to put some fresh cash into his accounts—he's got the dollars, billions of them. Maybe some other faithful clients will add to their accounts, too.

He can get enough money to stay afloat, he tells himself. He will not acknowledge failure or defeat—only fatigue. He has been doing this tap dance for so long, juggling the bank accounts, whispering the reassuring lies, dazzling everyone with his fancy footwork. But now he asks himself: Do I really want to keep dancing any longer, even if I can?

Increasingly, he is inclined to say no.

THURSDAY, NOVEMBER 27, 2008

It is Thanksgiving Day, and on the West Side of Manhattan the Macy's parade is producing happy squeals, snare drum flourishes, and traffic snarls. On the East Side, Third Avenue is quiet, its stores and businesses mostly closed for the holiday. In the lobby of the Lipstick Building, the newsstand is shuttered and a few building security staffers are at the reception desk when the men from Banco Santander arrive. They are directed to the south bank of elevators and ride up through the silent building to the nineteenth floor.

The most important person in the elevator is Rodrigo Echenique Gordillo, a distinguished-looking man in his early sixties who has been on the board of the giant Spanish banking company for twenty years. Echenique Gordillo has flown in from Madrid solely to keep this appointment with Bernie Madoff. He is surprised that Madoff scheduled it on the holiday, but Madoff said it was the only day available, and the meeting is important.

A lawyer by training, Echenique Gordillo is here at the request of the CEO of the holding company that owns Banco Santander. The bank's Optimal hedge fund unit has more than $3 billion invested with Madoff—or thinks it has.

At least twice in the past six years, Optimal's analysts have written memos citing weaknesses in Madoff's financial and audit controls. Nevertheless, the unit's due-diligence team and senior executives always managed to persuade themselves that Madoff was still safe—after all, he'd been managing money for years, he was regulated by the SEC, he owned a well-established and respected wholesale brokerage business, and he was a senior statesman on Wall Street with an excellent reputation.

But that was before the death of Bear Stearns, the bankruptcy of Lehman Brothers, and the bailouts of Fannie Mae, Freddie Mac, and AIG. Times are different. Risk weighs more on the scale than it once did, and reputation weighs less.

Echenique Gordillo and his colleagues step out of the stone-paneled elevator. Madoff himself is standing at the glass doors leading into his executive office suite. The floor seems otherwise deserted; not even Madoff's private secretary is there. Madoff settles into his chair and, after some pleasantries, Echenique Gordillo unpacks his questions.

To his surprise, Madoff is not conciliatory; he does not try to cajole or persuade. When the issue of redemptions comes up, the mood becomes tense, maybe even threatening.

Later there will be conflicting whispers back in Madrid about what happened next. According to one account, Madoff warned the Spaniards: Take your money out now and you will never be allowed back in. The door to Madoff—the door to the $77 million in annual management fees the bank has been booking in its hedge fund unit in recent years—will be closed to Santander forever. It is certainly a threat that Madoff has made to others before.

If there are threats made today, they are ineffective. The meeting is quickly concluded, and the bankers ride the elevator back down to the silent lobby. There definitely will be redemptions from Santander's accounts with Madoff.

WEDNESDAY, DECEMBER 3, 2008

Sometime today, Bernie Madoff sits down for a talk with Frank DiPascali, to make sure his faithful lieutenant knows where they stand. The Ponzi scheme's bank account at JPMorgan Chase, which held more than $5.5 billion just six months ago, is down to a few hundred million dollars, nowhere near enough to cover the billions in pending and threatened redemptions.

And when the money in the bank is gone, Madoff tells DiPascali, there will be nothing left for investors. He's tired of trying to scrape new money together. It's over.

DiPascali has long known that Madoff was conducting a massive fraud—how could he not have? He created the counterfeit paper trail and bogus computer verification that sustained the scheme through a half-dozen investigations over the years. He has lied to regulators, accountants, and clients for at least fifteen years, if not longer.

He will later claim that he lied to himself, too, comforting himself with the outlandish belief that Bernie had "other assets," oceans of wealth hidden beyond DiPascali's limited horizon, enough to make good on all the promises reflected in those account statements.

If that comforting delusion ever existed in Frank DiPascali's mind, it dies today. If there were a hidden pool of wealth stashed away somewhere, Madoff would surely tap into it now to keep them afloat. The markets cannot stay this terrified forever. If he had just a few billion more, maybe it would be enough to see them through.

But there is only the money left in that nearly depleted bank account, and Madoff is tired of the relentless struggle to replenish it. He wants to use this money to cash out the accounts of favored friends and family members, not to cover the checks he's supposed to write to a bunch of hedge funds. He asks DiPascali to start preparing a list of those favored accounts and their current balances, so he can divvy up the remaining money among them.

Sometime after this conversation, DiPascali allegedly slips down in the elevator to meet with one of his staff members, JoAnn "Jodi" Crupi, on a windy street corner near the Lipstick Building. Prosecutors will later claim that this is when he breaks the news to Crupi that Madoff is out of money, that there are no assets available to cover the billions he owes to his customers.

Did DiPascali ever really believe that delusion? If so, he copes with its destruction well enough. He does not grab whatever assets he can and flee the country. He does not report his mentor to the FBI to seek leniency for his own crimes. He returns from his street corner meeting and starts following orders. The checks will be ready for Madoff's signature by the middle of next week.

THURSDAY, DECEMBER 4, 2008

Jodi Crupi, an angular woman with olive skin and thick dark hair, has worked for Bernie Madoff since 1983, and allegedly has been handling the account statements for at least one of his big individual investors since about 2000. Prosecutors, relying on DiPascali's confidential testimony, will later assert that her duties also include providing Madoff with "the daily report," a running tabulation of the amount of cash flowing in and out of the bank accounts for his investment advisory business, along with redemption requests that have been received but not yet honored.

If so, disaster is written on the page in front of her today. There is less than $300 million in the bank account, and the pending requests for redemptions now total just under $1.5 billion—the withdrawal requests have doubled in just the last ten days.

SUNDAY, DECEMBER 7, 2008

According to federal prosecutors, Frank DiPascali leaves his spacious hilltop home in suburban New Jersey on this bitter and blustery day and drives to a nearby Panera Bread cafe to meet with Jodi Crupi, who lives in Westfield, New Jersey, but purchased a deluxe beachfront home on the Jersey Shore last month.

DiPascali will claim that, in recent days, he and Crupi have repeatedly discussed how they will explain their work at the Madoff firm to law enforcement authorities when the fraud finally unravels. This is allegedly the topic they tackle today. According to DiPascali's account, reflected in a subsequent federal indictment, Crupi tells him she plans on "sticking to my story," that she always thought Madoff was conducting legitimate trading abroad.

Crupi will subsequently deny that she ever knowingly assisted DiPascali in sustaining Madoff's epic fraud. She will plead not guilty to a federal indictment and insist that she was duped by her so-plausible boss, like everyone else.

Nothing that happens later can change what happens next. Before the coming week is over, the world that DiPascali and Crupi live in will shatter into a thousand pieces. The firm they have served for decades will be under federal control; their unflappable leader, Bernie Madoff, will be under arrest; and they will both be under suspicion for allegedly helping him maintain the largest Ponzi scheme in history.

11

WAKING UP IN THE RUBBLE

The day after the music stopped for Bernie Madoff, the long march began for his victims. Like a major earthquake or a devastating cyclone, the collapse of the Ponzi scheme left his victims bereft, betrayed, and emotionally homeless. The world they knew had been destroyed; they could not stay in that world, and yet they could only guess at the path that would carry them into a less precarious future.

The humiliated regulators and the harried lawyers who had to sift through the debris faced journeys of their own—toward redemption, out of chaos.

Everyone in this ruined landscape had been forced to set out on an expedition of discovery, grueling and uncertain but just possibly heroic. The men and women of the SEC would seek to restore their honor. The lawyers hired to unravel Madoff's fraud in bankruptcy court would try to find any hidden treasure and bring it back to those he ruined. But the individual fraud victims, who had believed for too long in this wizard of lies, were on a quest to find the most elusive prize of all: justice.

Most of them began their trek with only the vaguest idea of the terrain ahead. They did not know that some bridges had already been washed out. Most tragically, they could not see the crossroads around the bend where at least half of them would be detoured into a labyrinth of bitter fury and frustration.

At first, there was no way to know even how many victims there were, much less where they were going and what they would find when they got there. The only clue was that staggering number from Madoff himself: $50 billion.

Within hours of Madoff's arrest, self-proclaimed financial experts on the Internet had dismissed the figure as grandiose and implausible. Others accepted it as possibly true but argued that it probably represented only paper profits, not cash losses—as if a paper loss that wiped out everything you owned was somehow less damaging than a cash loss. In fact, Madoff's estimate was low. It would soon be established that $64.8 billion in paper wealth vanished when Madoff was arrested, including cash losses of about $20 billion.

A few institutional victims surfaced quickly. The Picower Foundation, the Chais family foundation, and Norman Levy's family foundations closed their doors almost immediately, stunning their employees and grant beneficiaries.

By Friday, December 12, a few elite hedge funds had sheepishly disclosed to investors that, for all their preening claims about careful due diligence, they had been ripped off.

Those "Dear Investor" letters started to flutter out of fax machines and arrive as e-mail attachments and urgent FedEx deliveries around the world: "As we are sure you are aware, Bernard L. Madoff was arrested yesterday . . ." (But as you may *not* be aware, your fund invested substantially all of its assets in another fund that invested in three other funds, all of them entirely invested with Madoff.) "We are shocked . . . are consulting counsel . . . are collecting all pertinent information . . . will keep you informed." The recipients of these letters were calling lawyers of their own, and those lawyers were getting calls from the media.

The shock and horrified embarrassment was especially keen for the giant Madoff feeder funds whose managers had taken such pride in their due diligence and yet sustained such enormous losses: Fairfield Greenwich Group, Ezra Merkin, Bank Medici, the Tremont funds. Bloggers immediately branded them as likely accomplices, refusing to accept that such smart, sophisticated people could have been fooled for so long by a crime as elementary as a Ponzi scheme.

Major banks across Europe began issuing press releases: Banco Santander's Optimal funds were invested with Bernard L. Madoff . . . Funds affiliated with UBS may have been invested . . . HSBC may be exposed through its hedge fund administration unit . . . BNP Paribas has about $500 million at risk through trades and loans to hedge funds.

Tipsters who had listened for years to their country club companions brag or whisper about their Madoff accounts sent anonymous notes or left voice-mail messages for reporters, naming names.

Lists were built, expanded, corrected. Naturally, the glittery names surfaced first: Fred Wilpon, an owner of the New York Mets; Norman Braman, the former owner of the Philadelphia Eagles; Baseball Hall-of-Famer Sandy Koufax; Mort Zuckerman, the real estate tycoon and owner of the New York *Daily News*; the actors Kyra Sedgwick, Kevin Bacon, and John Malkovich; the noted screenwriter Eric Roth; the ex-wife of the actor Michael Douglas; the heirs of the singer-songwriter John Denver; a foundation set up by Jeffrey Katzenberg, a cofounder of the DreamWorks studio in Hollywood, where his partners were the star record producer David Geffen and the Oscar-winning director Steven Spielberg, whose foundations were also affected.

What immediately became apparent was the astonishing geographical reach of Madoff's crime, a perverse monument to two decades of financial globalization. The lists soon included Swiss private bankers, a Singapore insurance company, a Korean teachers pension fund, an Italian bank holding company, major Japanese banks and insurance companies, trust funds in Hong Kong, Dutch money managers, a sovereign wealth fund in Abu Dhabi, a French cosmetics heiress, minor royalty in England and Monaco, two Catholic schools on St. Croix, hedge funds in Luxembourg, and wealthy families in Mexico, Brazil, Argentina, and Dubai. One legal consortium in Europe would later estimate that as many as three million people were touched by the scandal.

In the United States, the visible victims included trustees of cultural institutions in New York, retired Wall Street executives, wealthy real estate developers in Chicago, respected academic figures in Boston, a foundation in Seattle, a state legislator in New Jersey, and a cluster of retirees in Aspen, Colorado. Even the International Olympic Committee had a sliver of its assets invested with Madoff.

Against that cosmopolitan tapestry, a more primitive response began to surface. News sites on the Internet had to regularly scrub away anti-Semitic slurs from the comments posted in response to stories about Madoff and his fraud. When the Nobel laureate and Holocaust memoirist Elie Wiesel, revered for his courage and humanity, confirmed that Madoff had stolen his small foundation's entire endowment—for some, the ultimate betrayal—many in the Jewish community became alarmed about the backlash that Madoff might inspire in such ugly times.

At one breakfast panel, held at the "21" Club in Manhattan, Wiesel offered his own explanation for how the scandal could have happened. "It's almost simplistic," he said. "The imagination of the criminal exceeds that of the innocent." His meaning was clear: a criminal can imagine committing his own crimes, while his victims cannot imagine *anyone* committing such crimes.

When Wiesel was asked if he could ever forgive Bernie Madoff, there was a long, almost painful silence. Then this man who seemed to have forgiven so many for so much quietly answered, "No."

The Institute for Jewish Research in Manhattan organized an evening panel discussion to contemplate "the Madoff enormity," as the moderator, Martin Peretz, described it. The auditorium was packed to capacity; the panelists were distinguished, thoughtful, and worried. Some feared that Madoff's betrayal struck at the cords of trust that had allowed the Jews of the Diaspora to survive and succeed in financial centers for centuries. But the historian Simon Schama reminded the audience that an increasingly tolerant America had just elected its first black president, Barack Obama; perhaps such ancient bigotry was no longer in fashion. Besides, he asserted, there was no evident surge in anti-Semitic vitriol in these post-Madoff days.

Journalists in the audience knew better; they had only to look in their e-mail in-boxes.

Within a week of Madoff's arrest, the Anti-Defamation League reported a sharp increase in vicious slurs against Jews on the Internet, most related to Madoff. The fact that Madoff and many of his victims were Jewish created a "perfect storm for the anti-Semites," warned Abraham Foxman, the longtime head of the organization. The list assembled by the ADL included comments such as these posted on mainstream magazine and newspaper Web sites: "One Jew thief robs another bunch of Jew thieves—I suppose that's what you'd call a victimless crime"; "Ho hum, another Crooked Wall Street Jew. Find a Jew who isn't Crooked. Now that would be a story"; and "Just another jew money changer thief. It's been happening for 3,000 years."

In reality, Madoff's crime had far outstripped its original Jewish connections. Almost all of the hard cash wiped out by the fraud had poured in since Madoff's cash crisis in late 2005, and it had come from hedge funds around the world, from aristocratic Europeans and shadowy Russians and sovereign wealth funds in the Persian Gulf. If those investors had heard of Bernie Madoff at all, they associated him with the rise of NASDAQ and the automation of Wall Street, not with the Jewish country clubs on Long Island and in Palm Beach or the board of trustees at Yeshiva University.

But he *had* been a member of those Jewish country clubs, and hundreds of their members had lost decades of accumulated paper profits. And he *had* served on Yeshiva's board, and the university was scrambling to calculate the funds that had been so suddenly erased from its endowment. His earliest sales networks relied on word of mouth, and they had their roots where his Jewish friends and relatives had originally gathered: in the synagogues, at the Jewish clubs and resorts, on the boards of Jewish charities, hospitals, and schools.

So his crime certainly began as an "affinity fraud," the pleasant-sounding term criminologists use when one member of a close-knit, trusting community exploits that trust to steal from others in the group. It has happened everywhere, wherever members of a cohesive group have enough faith in one another to blind them to the lies piling up around them. A pastor steals from his devoted congregation. A retired military man exploits the troops. An immigrant from Haiti, or Russia, or China, or Cuba—anywhere, really—steals from countrymen who have settled into new homes in America.

At the beginning, Madoff exploited the trust and respect he had earned in a close-knit Jewish community. His reputation in those circles was his original passport to financial credibility in the wider world. He enhanced his reputation with ties to other trusted members of the group such as Ezra Merkin and Stanley Chais; his own nonprofit investors included giants such as the American Jewish Congress, the Jewish Community Foundation of Los Angeles, and Hadassah. By the end, he was pulling in cash from every corner of the globe, but it was a harvest that had grown from his own Jewish roots.

So, inevitably, this became a Jewish scandal among Jews themselves. Rabbis reflected on its lessons; a Jewish country club invited speakers to talk about it; a professor at Yeshiva University added it to the syllabus of his religious ethics class. Jewish charities, foundations, and endowments vowed to be less trusting and more rigorous in their investment practices. Some investors wept or raged over what Madoff would mean for the Jews, but many others were sustained by courage and mordant humor. The *Jewish Journal*'s online news site featured a new blog about the unfolding Madoff case and called it "Swindler's List."

The crucial puzzle of those early days—the one that would shape public reaction for months—was this: Who were Madoff's victims? Aside from some worthy charitable and cultural institutions, were they just a few movie stars, plutocrats, and hedge funds, each mourning a $100 million loss? Or had tens of thousands of ordinary middle-class families also lost hundreds of thousands of dollars in retirement savings?

Unfortunately, the second scenario was closer to the truth. For every boldface name like Steven Spielberg or Larry King, there were a host of dentists and small-time lawyers and retired teachers and plumbers and small business owners. Roughly a thousand Madoff accounts had fictional balances of less than $500,000. But there was simply no way to know this, not at first.

There were e-mails and calls to the media from ordinary people such as a housewife in Brooklyn; a zoning lawyer in Coral Gables, Florida; and a part-time museum curator in Connecticut—all explaining that they or their elderly relatives had been living off the modest nest eggs entrusted to Madoff generations before. Some had nothing left now but Social Security. Soon there were reports that the pension plans for some small medical practices and construction-trade union locals had been wiped out. Yet some of those victims were reluctant to be identified, or had been warned by their lawyers to remain silent. Unfortunately, their star power was feeble compared with that of the founders of DreamWorks and the owners of the New York Mets.

The public and the media were slow to understand that the key question to ask was not "How much did you lose?" but "How much do you have left?" Many, if not most, of the notable names had lost tens of millions but had plenty left, by any reasonable standard of human comfort. Some of the obscure victims had lost only thousands but had nothing left except their cars, their mortgaged houses, and the cash in their wallets.

It was perhaps understandable that it took so long for that fundamental question to surface. The first commandment of investing is "Don't put all your eggs in one basket." It didn't seem possible for this rule to have been so widely and so catastrophically ignored, even by nonprofit trustees and pension plans with fiduciary obligations. Typically, the failure of a legitimate midsize brokerage firm like Madoff's would not wipe out every single penny its customers had. Plenty—or, at least, something— would be left in a company pension plan or a bank account or a money market fund. As for the hedge funds, they supposedly catered only to wealthy, sophisticated people who were, by definition, too smart to hazard their entire fortune on one investment. Indeed, this had been one of the reasons for not regulating hedge funds more tightly over the years.

Fires, earthquakes, and hurricanes were readily recognized as events that required an emergency response to alleviate human suffering; the Madoff fraud was not. Few people even wondered at first if there were victims who had been totally wiped out overnight by this crime, victims in need of immediate help who could not turn to their relatives because they, too, were suddenly destitute.

So the public imagination focused on the sequined names of the wealthiest victims, people who would suffer no more than embarrassment from their Madoff losses. Madoff's crime thus came across as just another overdue comeuppance for the rich and greedy people who had helped drive the nation into a ditch in 2008. Politicians were wary of leaping to the defense of beleaguered victims they suspected were just hapless hedge fund managers and Madoff's country club cronies.

Instead of focusing on how to help the neediest victims, they focused on where to put the blame.

༄

On the day of Bernie Madoff's arrest, the veteran bankruptcy lawyer Irving H. Picard was in his Manhattan office, located in a gray-trimmed Midtown tower above Madison Square Garden, when he got a call from a senior attorney at the Securities Investor Protection Corporation in Washington, the safety net organization for brokerage customers.

"Could you be the Madoff trustee if we needed you?" the attorney asked.

Picard was the obvious choice: he had handled more SIPC bankruptcy liquidations than any lawyer in the country. He promised to check immediately to see if his law firm had any conflicts that would prevent him from taking the assignment.

The timing was not ideal. At sixty-seven, Picard had one foot out the door of his old law firm, based in Newark, New Jersey, with a branch office in Manhattan. He was seriously considering a move to the Rockefeller Center offices of Baker & Hostetler, a giant Cleveland law firm expanding its New York presence. His friend and former law partner David J. Sheehan, also in his mid-sixties, was already at Baker and wanted him to come aboard. But nothing had been formalized, and the two men planned to discuss the matter further after the first of the year.

Soon after Picard hung up from the SIPC call, he found a snag: his firm had long represented U.S. senator Frank Lautenberg of New Jersey, and the senator's children and family foundation were Madoff investors—now Madoff victims. He discussed the potential conflict with his partners in Newark and thought they had agreed the firm would not handle the Lautenbergs' claims so that Picard would be free to take on the SIPC case.

That evening, as Picard and his wife were leaving a diner on West Fifty-seventh Street to attend a Boston Symphony concert at Carnegie Hall, he noticed a phone message from a partner saying that reporters were asking about Lautenberg. Ducking out of the rain, he called back, reminding the partner about the conflict this would pose for the SIPC case.

In the next morning's papers, his partner was quoted speaking on the Lautenbergs' behalf. Picard clearly had to choose: his current law firm, which was growing less congenial, or the Madoff case. Sheehan, who had already been asked by SIPC to be counsel to whoever became the trustee, discussed the move with Picard that night over dinner with their wives at a sleek Belgian bistro near Central Park.

By Sunday afternoon Sheehan had gathered a team of Baker & Hostetler partners to interview Picard. He was offered a job and was assured that the offer stood regardless of whether he landed the SIPC assignment. Early Monday morning, December 15, he called his law firm to tender his immediate resignation and called Sheehan to accept the Baker & Hostetler offer.

When SIPC's lawyers went into federal court that afternoon to seek Picard's appointment as the Madoff trustee, he was in a short stretch of no-man's-land between his former job and his future job. More than a year later, his new ninth-floor office in Rockefeller Center—with its astonishing close-up view of the rose window of Saint Patrick's Cathedral, just across the street—looked as if he had just arrived and had yet to unpack.

Picard and Sheehan had teamed up on nearly a dozen brokerage firm liquidations over the years, but their personal styles were dramatically different.

A trim six-footer with thinning hair and a wide smile, Picard was methodical and even-tempered, carefully (perhaps overly) legalistic in his conversations and quietly corporate in his conservative wardrobe. He'd been raised in Fall River, Massachusetts, the son of a well-to-do dermatologist and the grandson of affluent German-Jewish immigrants. He had gone into the law after changing his mind about an accounting career.

After several years as an in-house lawyer on Wall Street and five years at the SEC, he was appointed in 1979 as the first U.S. trustee for the federal bankruptcy courts in New York, a new position Congress had created in the Justice Department to address rising concern about bankruptcy fraud. He then went into private practice and, in 1984, was hired to handle his first SIPC liquidation. Over the years, this became one of his specialties.

The other half of this odd couple was David J. Sheehan—small and shaggy, a mercurial, combative litigator with a biting wit, a grizzled beard, a messenger bag to throw over his parka, and impishly chic black-framed glasses.

Sheehan was the son of a janitor in the urban New Jersey town of Kearny. He worked his way through college and law school. In the face of the Vietnam draft, he enlisted as a lieutenant in the Navy Judge Advocate General's Corps and spent his tour of duty handling legal matters at the Brooklyn Navy Yard.

His civilian law practice was eclectic—everything from product liability cases to trademark battles to pro bono work on death penalty cases.

The unifying theme was courtroom work. While Picard seemed more at ease in conference rooms, negotiating the out-of-court settlements and litigation strategies that were a staple of his work, Sheehan relished courtroom combat and enjoyed the intellectual and administrative challenges of a complicated trial. He was regularly recognized as one of the top litigators in the city.

On the other hand, SIPC, the agency Picard and Sheehan would work for during the contentious years of the Madoff liquidation, was a frail and poorly equipped vessel to trust in the rough seas they were sailing into.

SIPC's job, defined by the federal statute that created the agency in 1970, had been to make sure customer claims came first in bankruptcy court—ahead of general creditors such as the landlord and the cleaning service—and to maintain a fund to pay cash advances to customers waiting for the court to process their claims. Although SIPC's procedures were better than the old approach (which treated all claims alike and provided no cash advances), they essentially just moved investors to the front of the line in bankruptcy court. SIPC did little, however, to speed up the tempo at which that line moved through the court system—and this was going to become an enormous problem for the Madoff victims, some of whom did not even have a cushion of cash for daily expenses.

The Madoff case also would drive home the fact that SIPC provided a far less extensive safety net than the deposit insurance programs created for banks and savings and loans after the Great Depression. (It would have been strange if Congress, in 1970, had intended to make investing in stocks as safe as putting money in the bank. Stocks paid higher returns than banks precisely because they involved greater risk.) Despite the comments of a few legislators at the time, few people in Washington considered SIPC as "insurance" against wall-to-wall fraud inside a brokerage house—until Madoff's victims came along.

By 2008, SIPC had been shaped by its own courtroom history in ways that would compound its difficulties in handling the Madoff mess. If a brokerage firm failed for financial reasons, everyone agreed that SIPC's role was to oversee the transfer of customer accounts to a healthier brokerage firm. If assets were stolen from customers by some rogue broker, clearly the customer's first line of defense was always the broker's employer.

But what if the brokerage firm failed because of a systemic fraud—for example, a Ponzi scheme such as Madoff's? Unfortunately, SIPC's court battles in fraud cases over the years had left a trail of limited and occasionally inconsistent decisions that would become a churned-up battlefield before the Madoff case was over. Most, if not all, of those court challenges arose from the liquidation of two-bit brokerage firms selling penny stocks—firms whose customers either had relatively small claims or, in some cases, were not entirely innocent bystanders. That experience, too, was going to be singularly unhelpful in preparing SIPC to deal with the Madoff liquidation.

Then there was SIPC's reputation for customer service, which was spotty, to say the least. As early as 1992, the General Accounting Office urged the agency to explain more clearly to investors what it did and did not cover. A dozen years later, the GAO was still critical of how SIPC handled its public relations duties. SIPC did not even have an office of public affairs to ensure that the public got accurate, timely information about what was going on in high-profile cases. Instead, it left most of the public relations chores to whichever lawyer it hired to handle each case—a witless approach, since lawyers were typically trained not to talk at all about their cases outside the courtroom or the judge's chambers.

Fundamentally, SIPC—like so many people in Washington, on Wall Street, and along all the Main Streets across America—had simply scaled back its vision of what could go wrong in the financial markets. As firms became more professional and better capitalized, the risk of a huge failure began to seem remote. By 1996, SIPC's emergency fund to cover cash advances to defrauded customers had grown to more than $1 billion—far more than the organization ever expected to need, given that it was handling only a few small cases a year. So that year, it cut its member assessment from a percentage of each firm's revenues to a flat fee of $150 a year.

As early as 1992, the GAO warned that SIPC was not really prepared for a titanic failure. But the warning was not taken seriously by Congress, Wall Street, the SEC, the investing public, or SIPC itself.

Despite its flaws, SIPC attracted little public or congressional attention after the 1970s simply because it became increasingly marginal to the world of Wall Street. Strong markets and targeted regulations sharply reduced the number of brokerage firm failures. In its first four years of existence in the early 1970s, SIPC liquidated 109 firms, some of them well known. Since then, its busiest year had been 1992, when it had thirteen open cases. In the four years before 2008, there were just five; there were none at all in 2007. Three small firms failed early in 2008, but they certainly did not put SIPC on the public's radar.

This changed a bit on September 15, when Lehman Brothers filed for bankruptcy, the largest brokerage firm failure in history. But with Lehman's customer service and accounting infrastructure still in place, things went smoothly. More than 135,000 customer accounts with more than $140 billion in assets were seamlessly moved into the hands of two other brokerage firms within weeks. While the legal battles among Lehman's giant Wall Street counterparties would continue for years, Lehman's retail customers were barely inconvenienced by the massive bankruptcy.

Then came the Madoff case. Bernard L. Madoff Investment Securities had been a charter member of SIPC, but this did not automatically mean that the Madoff fraud was a SIPC case or that its victims would be eligible for the limited cash advances the organization offered.

The victims clearly were not the kind of customers served by Madoff's legitimate wholesale brokerage business. The customers of that business were the likes of Fidelity and Merrill Lynch, whose traders made their own decisions about what and when to buy and sell.

Moreover, Madoff had been registered with the SEC as an investment adviser since 2006. Although his customers opened their accounts with standard brokerage firm paperwork, they clearly had relied entirely on Madoff to pursue his own investment strategy on their behalf. This was one reason the SEC had forced him to register as an investment adviser in the first place.

And if one thing was crystal clear in the murky law governing brokerage bankruptcies, it was that SIPC did not cover a member's investment advisory business.

In the days since Madoff's arrest, the small SIPC staff in Washington had been wrestling with its responsibilities. Before anyone knew what had actually happened, a decision had to be made. The SIPC board and staff apparently concluded quickly that refusing to take responsibility for the Madoff fraud claims, while possibly defensible in a court of law, would be politically suicidal.

The only formal business Madoff had was his SIPC-protected

brokerage firm. Even after he registered as an investment adviser, he did not incorporate a separate unit for his advisory clients. All the customer account statements were on the brokerage firm's letterhead. And there on that letterhead, tiny as a ladybug, was the logo announcing that Madoff's firm was a member of SIPC.

With the firestorm brewing in the weeks after Madoff's arrest, it was simply impossible for this Wall Street–financed organization to walk away from this gigantic Wall Street swindle. So the SIPC board and staff stretched their definitions a little and took on the Madoff fraud claims.

They then stretched a little further and decided to make every valid claim eligible for the largest cash advance SIPC offered. By law, victims with claims for cash were limited to a $100,000 advance; those with claims for securities could get up to $500,000. Although SIPC did not know what was supposed to have been in those Madoff accounts or what might still be there, the agency decided that every Madoff claim would be treated as a claim for securities, not for cash.

So before most of Madoff's devastated victims had even heard of SIPC, the agency made two decisions that would benefit many of them greatly at its own expense. Those steps would not earn it any high ground in the battles to come; SIPC would be confronting the most formidable legal challenges in its history, and angry Madoff investors would be demanding that it be completely overhauled.

But those battles were still in the future on the afternoon of Monday, December 15, when Picard and Sheehan bundled up for the subway ride downtown for a hearing before Judge Louis L. Stanton on the twenty-first floor of the federal courthouse just off Foley Square. They were accompanied on the trip by a senior lawyer for SIPC and were joined by SEC attorneys just before the hearing. Judge Stanton knew the issues; he had signed an emergency after-hours court order the evening of Madoff's arrest authorizing Lee Richards to take immediate control of the Madoff operations in New York and London.

At the hearing, the SEC proposed that SIPC be allowed to put the domestic brokerage firm into bankruptcy, with Picard as the SIPC trustee and Baker & Hostetler—in reality, an army of lawyers led by David J. Sheehan—as the trustee's counsel.

A little after 4:00 PM, Judge Stanton signed the order granting the SEC's request, after directing Picard to post a $250,000 bond.

Richards would remain in control of the London operation for a few more days, until it was put into bankruptcy in the British courts. He was still operating out of the Lipstick Building on Monday evening when Picard and Sheehan arrived, after a briefing by federal prosecutors at the U.S. Attorney's Office.

Leaving his "war room" in the nineteenth-floor conference room, Richards gave the two lawyers a tour—through the impressive black-and-gray trading room at the opposite end of that floor, then down the oval staircase to the more congested administrative offices on the eighteenth floor, and finally to the heart of the mystery: the seventeenth floor. The office suite on that floor was nondescript and strangely banal, considering the financial damage and emotional pain that had rippled out from those rooms over the previous five days. Just some cheap-looking desks, some computers, and some file cabinets—but no people. As they returned upstairs, Richards recalled with a laugh that Frank DiPascali had been there last week but "went out for a cup of coffee and didn't come back." Richards then headed to the airport and his flight to London, as Sheehan and Picard got to work.

For that pair of old friends, the Madoff liquidation would be the opportunity of a lifetime, the capstone to their long careers—and the most difficult case they had ever handled.

They had encountered fraud cases, even Ponzi schemes, before. But they had never faced anything on this scale. The tally of customer losses was staggering, and the victims were spread around the globe. The firm itself was a crime scene, with FBI agents and federal prosecutors in charge. Employees on whom they would typically have relied for information were hiring lawyers and clamming up. They couldn't find the kind of records they expected to find; instead, they found millions of pages of puzzling documentation stuffed into thousands of boxes at three locations around the city, much of it on old-fashioned microfiche.

There were more than a hundred employees, heaven knew how many general creditors, and at least four thousand active customer accounts, each one representing a person, a family, a partnership, the beneficiaries of a pension plan, a gigantic hedge fund with thousands of clients of its own, or a government agency investing money for an entire nation. Some of the firm's customers were clearly innocent and almost destitute, but others were fabulously wealthy and possibly accomplices—and on the day Picard and Sheehan were appointed, they had no idea how to tell them apart.

On paper, the job assigned to them was simple: gather as much of the dissipated money as possible and divide it among the eligible claimants under the supervision of the bankruptcy court. But the journey Picard and Sheehan would have to take to reach that goal put them on a collision course with more than half of the Madoff victims.

∞

The next day, Tuesday, December 16, a different legal drama was playing out. A crowded room in the offices of the U.S. attorney in Manhattan was the setting chosen by the harried prosecutors for their first confidential meeting with Bernie Madoff and his lawyers. To some former prosecutors in the room, it was a curious setting for the delicate ritual known as "the proffer."

The proffer is the occasion when a defense lawyer brings his client in to answer questions and provide information under a limited grant of immunity covering the day's conversation. If the defendant's information is good and his desire to cooperate is persuasive, the proffer can give him a shot at a plea bargain—a deal of some kind—and give prosecutors a road map for future cases against others who may be implicated in the crime.

As in any emotionally charged interview, ambience matters. A smart prosecutor will want the defendant to feel at ease, relaxed, almost intimate with the people questioning him. But there was no hope for that at this proffer. There were nearly a dozen people in the room, some at the long central table and others in chairs against the walls, and Madoff hadn't even shown up yet.

The prosecutor, Marc Litt, and his boss, Bill Johnson, sat at the center of one side of the table. Around them were two FBI agents, several lawyers from the SEC, and a few people from SIPC.

Then, at around 11:00 AM, Madoff walked in, accompanied by his lawyers Ike Sorkin, Dan Horwitz, and Nicole De Bello. They took their seats at the table, directly across from Litt and Johnson.

After the formalities—chiefly, the clarification of the limited immunity agreement—Litt and Johnson began questioning Madoff, drawing him out.

Madoff recounted how he got started in his business, how he wanted to establish himself with the well-to-do Jewish businessmen he cultivated; he wanted to impress them. He got in some trouble back in 1962, had to borrow money from his father-in-law to cover some customer losses. He was doing all sorts of complicated trading, which he struggled to explain. He got in trouble again, started to cheat a little. Then he slipped into the full-scale Ponzi scheme. He expected to get out again quickly, but he never could. It got too big.

He insisted that he had run the elaborate Ponzi scheme himself. No one helped.

What about when you took vacations? Would you communicate through Frank DiPascali?

Madoff shrugged. No, he said, he was just careful; no one else was involved.

No one in the room believed him.

After several hours, the group broke for lunch. Madoff and his lawyers brought paper-wrapped delicatessen sandwiches back to the table.

The proffer session resumed. By now questions started popping from around the room, and some of them misfired, interrupting Madoff's answers and derailing another questioner's train of thought.

Somewhere in all this intellectual disorder, Madoff was asked how and when his crime began—and no one would agree later about what they heard, perhaps because no one specified "which crime?" Some people heard him date his Ponzi scheme to the 1960s, when he lost money for his clients and had to borrow from Saul Alpern to make them whole. When he lost more money later on—no one later recalled if he said when this was—he said he couldn't go back to Alpern to be bailed out again. So he started to steal from one client to pay another.

Others would later insist that the early fraud that Madoff described was not the Ponzi scheme, which he would claim began in the early 1990s, but rather, the faked investment returns he reported to his clients back in the 1960s.

Which was it? As always with Bernie Madoff, the truth was a slippery creature. It wriggled out of this crowded room before anyone could catch it and lock it up.

But if the truth could not be locked up, this didn't mean Madoff himself could roam free. At his initial hearing before Judge Douglas Eaton the previous Thursday, Madoff's lawyers had agreed with prosecutors on a recognizance bond of $10 million, to be cosigned by four "financially responsible people." Now, nearly a week later, Madoff could not get four people to sign a surety bond to secure his bail; only his wife and brother were willing.

His sons would not consider it. Even if they had not been silenced by their fury and grief, their lawyer would not let them speak to their parents, determined to protect them from any suspicion that they might be colluding with their father after the fact.

Madoff could not turn to his closest friends, either; they were also his victims. Even if their lawyers would let them take the call, it would be fatal to their credibility in the courtroom battles ahead to be seen helping the man who had stolen so much from so many.

So, on Wednesday, December 17, Litt agreed to accept a compromise. In lieu of more signatures, Madoff would have to submit to home detention with electronic monitoring and would pledge the homes in Montauk and Palm Beach, which were in Ruth's name. In addition, Ruth would surrender her own passport, as Madoff had. Magistrate judge Gabriel W. Gorenstein approved the new arrangement without a hearing.

That afternoon, casually dressed in a navy canvas baseball cap and a black quilted Barbour jacket, Madoff returned to his apartment on East Sixty-fourth Street after being fitted with his electronic monitoring device. There had not been time for his lawyers to arrange security for the trip home, so Madoff was alone when he approached the gauntlet of cameras and microphones on the sidewalk outside his apartment.

The media crowd scurried to keep him on camera as he moved steadily toward the door, his face a mask, his mouth a thin, tight line. Someone blocked his way as questions were shouted at him. Someone else shoved him on the left shoulder; he tried to ward off the shove, pushing back and moving forward. Shaken, he finally reached the lobby and disappeared into the building. The recorded scene would be played repeatedly on television over the coming days.

If prosecutors, blindsided by the furious public reaction to Madoff's release on bail, were looking for an opportunity to reopen the issue, the shoving match provided one. By Thursday morning, they started questioning Madoff's lawyers about whether it would be safe for him to remain free.

His lawyers scrambled in an effort to preserve his freedom without burning up assets the government would need to claim for his victims. They managed to arrange a twenty-four-hour security detail headed by a former New York City police detective, Nick Casale, and staffed largely by retired NYPD officers.

With that in place, the prosecutors agreed that Madoff would be confined to his apartment around the clock, leaving only for court dates or medical emergencies.

The talk show comics immediately called it "penthouse arrest."

For the people at the SEC, especially in the New York office, Madoff's arrest was a stomach-sinking moment.

It took just a few hours to find traces of the previous investigations in the files. Some staff members had worked on the most recent ones and had signed off on the memorandum that read, "The staff found no evidence of fraud." For a short time, they could still hope that Madoff had launched his vast Ponzi scheme *after* they closed their 2006 investigation of the tips from Harry Markopolos. This implausible hope lasted less than a day.

"When I first heard the news that Madoff had been arrested, I didn't think it was in relation to this," recalled the 2006 team's senior supervisor. "I thought he'd done something different, and it wasn't until the next day that I realized it was this."

Harry Markopolos's reaction to news of the arrest was characteristic. By his own account, he armed himself with a shotgun to prepare for the possibility that the civilian regulators at the SEC would acquire weapons, raid his house, seize his computer and documents, and destroy them, all to save themselves from public humiliation. At a more practical level, he provided copies of his extensive documentation to reporters at the *Wall Street Journal*. On Tuesday, December 16, a *Journal* reporter called the SEC's Washington office with questions about its dealings with Markopolos.

Late that evening, SEC chairman Christopher Cox emerged from a daylong meeting of the commission and issued a statement about the Madoff affair. He said that SEC investigators were working with law enforcement to review "vast amounts" of information that showed "the complicated steps that Mr. Madoff took to deceive investors, the public and regulators."

This face-saving reminder about Madoff's criminal ingenuity was eclipsed by Cox's next revelation: "The Commission has learned that credible and specific allegations regarding Mr. Madoff's financial wrong-doing, going back to at least 1999, were repeatedly brought to the attention of SEC staff, but were never recommended to the Commission for action. . . . I am gravely concerned by the apparent multiple failures over at least a decade to thoroughly investigate these allegations."

Cox had reached out personally to the agency's aggressive inspector general, H. David Kotz, directing him to open an independent investigation of what went wrong. He also ordered all SEC staff members who had "more than insubstantial personal contacts with Mr. Madoff or his family" to remove themselves from the ongoing investigation.

Cox's announcement landed with a thud—the sound of a once-proud agency hitting bottom. The SEC, which had been coasting for years on an outworn reputation for excellence, slammed into the rock-hard consequences of more than a decade of neglect and denial. Cox himself had endorsed many of the deregulatory policies and budget priorities—and had overlooked the management deficiencies and dwindling skills—that contributed to the disaster. But there was more than enough blame to go around.

The agency's reputation had already been bruised earlier in the year by its clumsy supervision of the giant investment banks and other regulated institutions that had fallen into failure or folly—including Bear Stearns and Lehman Brothers. The SEC had seemed increasingly irrelevant during the post-Lehman panic, when Cox was routinely relegated to the edges of press conferences dominated by Secretary of the Treasury Hank Paulson and Federal Reserve chairman Ben Bernanke. Now it was clear that the agency had spectacularly failed to fulfill its core mission: investor protection. It was almost impossible to comprehend. Missing Madoff's crime, despite years of "credible" tips and warnings, began to look like the most appalling failure in the SEC's seventy-five-year history.

Cox, however, was on his way out. President-elect Barack Obama was just days away from announcing that he intended to appoint Mary Schapiro as Cox's successor as chairman of the SEC. Schapiro, a small, neat woman with chin-length blond hair and a warm, soft-spoken manner, had been president of FINRA, the self-regulatory agency that evolved from the NASD, since 1996. Bernie Madoff had become less active in the organization by the time she arrived, and she met him only a handful of times during her tenure; she had not seen him in years. Schapiro hadn't known that Madoff managed money on a large scale—there was no reason she would have, since neither the NASD nor FINRA had any jurisdiction over hedge fund managers or investment advisers. Nor had she noticed the articles that were published in 2001 about his mysterious prowess as an investor.

When the news about Madoff's fraud first broke, Schapiro was cleaning out her desk at FINRA's Washington office. She was distracted by the demands of the appointment process—the financial disclosure forms, the FBI questions, the preparation for her confirmation hearings. As she worked, she had her office television on and looked up when she heard the news about the arrest. She was shocked. But like the prosecutors who agreed to Madoff's bail arrangements, she did not immediately appreciate what a catastrophe Madoff would be for his investors—and for the agency she had just agreed to lead.

Obama announced Schapiro's appointment on Wednesday, December 17, the day after Cox's stunning disclosure. But she would not take office for more than a month; she could not be confirmed by the Senate until after Obama's January 20 inauguration. So she could only watch as Cox and his senior staff grappled with the early days of the devastating scandal.

It was clear to her that the agency's response needed to persuade the public that the SEC could restore competent and effective regulation to the marketplace—or it might not survive as an independent agency.

∞

Alone in the penthouse on Christmas Eve, Bernie and Ruth Madoff were sorting through some of their personal treasures. They had accumulated some lovely things over the years: a pair of antique diamond earrings from the early 1800s; graceful old Edwardian bracelets and earrings in combinations of black onyx, emeralds, and diamonds; dozens of new and classic wristwatches; and a remarkable rope of 320 baroque pearls that could be unclasped into sections to form chokers, bracelets, and necklaces.

Madoff surely knew that most, if not all, of his treasures had been purchased with stolen money. Indeed, the day after his arrest, he agreed to a court-imposed freeze on all his assets, although Ruth's jewelry was not yet as clearly under the court's control.

Ruth gathered four diamond brooches, a diamond necklace, an emerald ring, and a few other nice pieces. Bernie picked out two sets of cuff links, one of them an inexpensive gift from a granddaughter; some costly fountain pens; and more than a dozen precious wristwatches from his cherished collection. They packed the articles carefully and included small notes of remorse and affection. Guessing at the postage, Ruth covered the packages with stamps and mailed them to her sons, a daughter-in-law, her sister, Peter Madoff, and some close friends.

Ruth never considered the legal uproar these gifts would cause; she believed she and Bernie would be dead long before the presents were even delivered.

Life since her husband's arrest had been ugly, scary, and sad, filled with "hate mail and phone calls and lawyers," Ruth later recalled. Madoff said they were both in "a severe state of depression." At some point that day, Ruth told Bernie, "I don't know how I will ever get through this, nor do I want to." She felt they agreed that they would not continue living this nightmare.

After sending out their farewell gifts, they gathered all the Ambien tablets they could find in the apartment, swallowed handfuls of the tiny rose-colored pills, and climbed into bed. Ruth expected to die in her sleep.

"We woke the next morning very sick but alive," Madoff recalled. Ruth later described the suicide attempt as "very impulsive" and said she "was glad to wake up." But the world that awaited them outside the penthouse that morning was still filled with suspicion, isolation, and hate. Ruth began to simply tune out the news, building a cocoon to protect herself from a brutal new life so hurtful that she had been ready, for a moment, to leave it forever.

A few days later, one of their sons alerted prosecutors to his receipt of the valuable gifts. The ill-considered presents would hand Marc Litt one more opportunity to argue that Bernie Madoff could not be trusted free on bail.

A week later, at a meeting with one of her husband's lawyers, Ruth mentioned the gifts. The lawyer quickly warned her that she had to try to retrieve them—immediately. She sent urgent e-mails to her sons asking them to return the parcels.

There was no response.

12

RECKONING THE DAMAGE

As with every event of personal devastation, they remember exactly where they were and what they were doing when they learned that they were ruined.

Tim Murray, a property manager in Minnesota, whose family had first invested with Madoff through Mike Engler, was traveling and nearly drove off the road when he heard the news of Madoff's arrest. At first he thought it was just another of the jealous rumors that regularly surfaced about Madoff—always investigated, always disproved. Given Madoff's stature on Wall Street, he said, "I am supposed to believe that one day he gets up in the morning and does something to get arrested for? Not likely." But Madoff *had* been arrested, and all the money that Murray and his family had entrusted to him was gone.

Another second-generation investor was having her hair cut when her sister called with the news that "everything had vaporized." The realization that her elderly parents had lost everything "came quickly and hit hard. We were so worried."

The gray-white paper rolled out of Mary Thomajan's fax machine the day after she had returned from a soul-searching journey to India. She expected it to be the account statement that would confirm she had the money to build the dream life she'd planned to create in Santa Fe, New Mexico. The fax was from the small feeder fund she had trusted for eighteen years, telling her that all her money had been invested with Madoff, who had been arrested. "In the 50 seconds it took to read that fax, I went from being a multimillionaire to having my life savings wiped out and life as I knew it forever altered."

Ellen Bernfeld, a singer and songwriter with dreams of being an author, was having lunch with friends when she got the "life-shattering phone call that changed my world." She reflected sadly, "My father was not around to see this terrible disaster and to feel its aftermath, but my mother is, and she is a child of the Great Depression, so this is her worst nightmare."

Robert Halio's son called him at his retirement home in Boca Raton with the news. "I almost fell to the floor," he remembered. "I couldn't catch my breath and thought I might be having a heart attack. I was in total shock." A lifetime's savings, the cashed-out value of insurance policies—95 percent of his and his wife's modest wealth—had been entrusted to Madoff and was gone. His wife, Stephanie, was just entering a nearby movie theater with a friend, also a Madoff investor, when the friend got a call with the same dread news. Robert's call to her came a moment later. "I was hoping that it was all a terrible mistake," she recalled.

One investor was with her husband at her orthopedist's office in New York City, getting a cortisone shot for her sore hip. As she was pulling up her jeans, her husband got the news on his cell phone. He was devastated, almost hysterical. She had to help him to the car and make the drive to their home in suburban New Jersey. "Everything he worked for all his life was gone—'poof!'" When they finally walked into their house, she said, "I went into the bathroom and threw up."

Steven Norton of Fort Lauderdale had just driven quietly home from a memorial service for his life partner's brother. A voice-mail message from his broker delivered the news that their retirement savings were gone. Norton then called his partner's widowed sister-in-law in Miami to break the same awful news. Having just lost her husband, also a Madoff investor, she had now lost everything that he had set aside to keep her comfortable.

Kate Carolan heard the news when her husband, Gordon Bennett, shook her awake and said, "Kate, we just lost our house." Bennett had sold his successful natural foods business in 1988 to devote his time and money to environmental causes, and, on the strength of their savings, all invested with Madoff, he and Kate were working on a new half-finished home near the magnificent coastal preserve at Point Reyes, north of San Francisco. At first she thought he was joking. "Kate, I'm telling you—Madoff has been arrested for securities fraud," he repeated.

Another victim of very modest means said she felt as if a treasured talisman had suddenly fallen from her grasp. Knowing her money was invested with Madoff "was like Dumbo's feather," she said, reflecting on the classic Disney movie about a flying elephant who thinks his ability results from a magic feather he got from a friendly crow. "The feather doesn't enable you to fly," she said. "But [it] makes you think you've got some magic thing. . . . We felt like we had this nice safety net and now there's no net."

Frantic phone calls went out from nieces to aunts, from daughters to fathers, from grandsons to grannies, from one old friend to another: "Bernie Madoff—he's just been arrested!" And with his arrest, their worlds changed forever.

∽

On Tuesday, December 23, 2008, the anguish that had seized tens of thousands of invisible Madoff victims around the world suddenly became vividly and tragically evident to the public.

René-Thierry Magon de la Villehuchet, the aristocratic French financial salesman who cofounded Access International, had been personally warned about Madoff. One warning came in the spring of 2006, from the hedge fund analyst he and his partner had hired but did not heed. Another supposedly came from Harry Markopolos, who recalled in his memoir that he and the Frenchman traveled together in Europe to market a new financial product Markopolos had designed. Markopolos said he issued his warning before that trip, but the Frenchman became "extremely defensive" and rejected the possibility of fraud out of hand. Markopolos further claimed that de la Villehuchet ignored his offer to make his case to Access International's research director.

When the news broke on December 11 that Madoff had been arrested, the staff at Access International's Midtown office on Madison Avenue crowded around the television in their boss's office, slack-jawed and silent. "It was such a moment of eternity," one staff member later recalled. "A castle of cards falling down in one CNBC news flash."

De la Villehuchet, who was sixty-five years old, spent the days after the arrest frantically consulting with his partners and their lawyers about his funds' stake in Madoff—a total of about $1.6 billion, including $50 million of his own money. At the time, there seemed little hope of recovering anything. "It's a complete nightmare," he told a devoted client in Paris during an early morning phone call on Monday, December 22.

That day, de la Villehuchet calmly asked his young assistant to purchase a box cutter, as if it were just something he needed around the office.

"Leave it on my desk," he said.

Later, he asked to borrow the young man's office key, saying he would be working late that night and needed the key to lock up. He called his wife to tell her he had a late engagement and that she should not wait up for him, and then he hurried the cleaning staff out by 7:00 PM and locked the door behind them.

Sometime during that night, he positioned a trash basket to protect the carpet, slit his wrist and upper arm with the box cutter, and bled to death.

&

Irving Picard was a thoroughly prosaic man. He would raise an eyebrow at the fanciful notion that the legal drama surrounding the bankrupt brokerage firm for which he was the trustee was a heroic journey out of chaos or a mythic quest for lost treasure. At a rational level, where he preferred to operate, it was just a bankruptcy case under the Securities Investor Protection Act—the biggest, saddest, hardest, angriest, and possibly longest case ever litigated under that law. Nevertheless, a bankruptcy case.

This made it one of 10,629 cases pending before the ten federal bankruptcy judges in Manhattan, a tally that included the giant Lehman Brothers case and would soon include the bankruptcies of Chrysler and General Motors. And a bankruptcy case, which marks the death of a business enterprise, moves at the stately pace of a funeral march. It does not gallop, it does not sprint, and it does not take detours or shortcuts.

In a typical corporate bankruptcy, that dirgelike tempo is aggravating but tolerable. The debtor is reorganizing or liquidating a failed business and has work to do, and the banks, vendors, and other experienced creditors know what to expect. But in this bankruptcy, many of the creditors were desperate crime victims who had lost everything in a massive fraud, and some of them were relying on money from the debtor's estate to make their next mortgage payment or buy next month's medicines. The poetry of the judicial system may be that "justice delayed is justice denied," but the prose translation is that it takes a long time for justice to arrive in a complicated SIPC liquidation wrapped up in a continuing criminal investigation of a fraud that stretched around the world and affected millions of people.

The way Madoff organized his fraud magnified the complexities for SIPC, creating a knot of temper-fraying issues that would not be unraveled for years.

First, there was the question of who qualified as a "customer" eligible for SIPC's protection. Were Madoff's customers only the feeder funds such as Fairfield Sentry and Ezra Merkin's Ascot Partners, whose names were on the account statements? Or did all the various investors in those feeder funds qualify individually as customers? Over the long haul, it might not matter—any assets recovered should wind up in the right hands, whether directly or after a detour through the feeder funds. But in the short term, the answer determined whether a feeder fund would receive a single $500,000 cash advance from SIPC to share among all its investors—or whether *each* of those investors would be eligible for a cash advance of that size.

Second, and arguably far more significant, was the question of how much an eligible customer could claim as a loss. Was it the amount shown on the final statement, the one received a few weeks before Madoff's arrest? Or the amount of cash the customer originally invested from his own pocket, with no fictional profits added? Should a victim who had a sizable balance but who had already withdrawn the cash he originally invested be allowed to share in whatever assets Picard could recover? Or should every penny the trustee recovered be reserved for those who didn't get all their cash back before the scheme collapsed?

And what about the victims who had withdrawn millions of dollars more than they had put in, thinking they were only drawing out their legitimate profits? Could the trustee sue them to get that money back? If so, would he base his decision on how much they had taken out? On how much they had left? Or, somehow, on how much they might have known about what Madoff was doing?

Someone was going to have to play King Solomon with these questions, and every possible answer would leave someone enraged or bereft. And, as with the biblical precedent, getting the "right" answer would require wisdom about the human heart, not just knowledge about the rules of justice. The imperfect search for answers to these questions would impede the liquidation of the Madoff firm for more than two years and inflict bruises on everyone involved.

Picard and Sheehan believed that the law that applied to Ponzi schemes was clear: victims could recover only the cash they had put in, not the fictional profits allegedly generated by the fraud itself. Their view was shared by SIPC's lawyers, senior officials at the SEC, and a large number of bankruptcy lawyers.

It was also supported by rulings already coming out of the pending bankruptcy of the Bayou hedge fund, the Ponzi scheme whose collapse in mid-2005 nearly capsized Madoff's own fraud. As early as 2007, the judge in the Bayou case ruled that if a victim had withdrawn cash in excess of his original investment, those fictional profits had to be returned to the estate. Almost all of the Bayou fund investors who had withdrawn money within six years of the fraud's collapse—the statute of limitations under New York's creditor protection laws—were ordered to return their fictional profits.

But in adopting this view of how to calculate losses in the world's biggest Ponzi scheme, Picard and Sheehan became the lonely champions of some of Madoff's victims (those who had taken out none, or only some, of the cash they put in) and the bitterly despised adversaries of the others (those who had withdrawn all of their original cash stake and perhaps much more).

The Madoff investors who opposed Picard would soon argue that Bayou was different because it was not a SIPC case—and that SIPC was required to honor customers' "legitimate expectations," as reflected on their final account statements before the fraud collapsed. As they saw it, to do anything less was simply illegal.

Soon it was a sincerely held article of faith for some of them that

Picard and Sheehan were deliberately, heartlessly breaking the law to protect SIPC at the expense of thousands of devastated Madoff victims. As they saw it, anyone who argued otherwise had crossed over into the enemy camp.

༺༻

At a little past 2:30 PM on Monday, January 5, 2009, magistrate judge Ronald Ellis leaned forward on the bench and said, "Mr. Litt, why don't you tell me exactly what we're here for."

Federal prosecutor Marc Litt was there to try, once again, to get Bernie Madoff locked up.

By now, the public outcry against Madoff and his family had become a relentless, reverberating roar. Madoff's sons could not leave their homes without being dogged by photographers. Shana Madoff and her husband, former SEC lawyer Eric Swanson, expecting their first child, were under fierce scrutiny after the *Wall Street Journal* published an article suggesting that their relationship might have helped deflect the SEC's attention away from her uncle's hidden fraud.

As for Ruth Madoff, the consensus of the city's tabloids and the virulent Internet chatter was that she was the new Marie Antoinette, her husband's foolish pampered queen and, most likely, his outright accomplice. She could not leave the apartment for groceries without a paparazzi posse on her heels. The outcry against Madoff and his family was at a fever pitch.

At the hearing, Litt did his best to persuade Judge Ellis to change his mind about Madoff's bail. But he was pushing against the bedrock legal principle that all defendants are initially presumed innocent until their cases are adjudicated. Even if an accused person has confessed, he is still considered innocent in the eyes of the law, and it will be the prosecutor's burden to prove his guilt beyond a reasonable doubt. Because of this presumption, all defendants are entitled to bail unless they are a danger to the community or themselves or are likely to flee.

Litt argued that circumstances had changed since the magistrate's colleague, Judge Eaton, first approved bail for Madoff on December 11. The government's investigation was moving forward, and the extraordinary scale of the crime had been confirmed. Madoff would be facing a "very, very lengthy" jail term, Litt continued in his soft classroom voice. He concluded, "Given the defendant's age, the length of the likely sentence, the strength of the proof against the defendant, including his confessions—these facts present a clear risk of flight."

Judge Ellis mildly pointed out that all of those facts were known to the government when it last agreed to Madoff's bail conditions, those approved by Judge Gorenstein a week after Madoff's arrest. Moreover, Madoff had already surrendered his passport. So what had really changed?

What had changed, Litt explained, was that the Madoffs had mailed out those packages of valuable holiday gifts to their family and friends on Christmas Eve, in defiance of an asset freeze imposed in the civil case filed by the SEC. Though the items had all been quickly recovered, the episode was proof that Madoff "is not able to respect the limits imposed by the court."

When it was Ike Sorkin's turn for rebuttal, he pointed out that, even now, Litt was not claiming that Madoff had violated any of the bail conditions that had been imposed in the criminal case against him. Rather, Sorkin said, Litt was complaining that Madoff had violated an asset freeze that had been imposed by a different judge in a different case—a freeze that did not even apply to Ruth.

And how did Madoff do that? By sending out what "can best be described as some heirlooms," Sorkin said. Yes, some items had material value, but others had mostly sentimental value—some mittens, some cuff links. He portrayed the incident as an innocent mistake prompted by Madoff's awkward longing to make some gesture of reconciliation and connection toward his estranged sons, his brother, and his friends.

As close to visible anger as he had ever been in court, Litt protested: "The government is not here because of some mittens and cuff links." He continued, more calmly, "We're here because of hundreds of thousands of dollars, and perhaps millions of dollars worth of very expensive watches and other jewelry." The defendant violated a court order by mailing out those gifts, and "that is a change of circumstances. That's what brings us here."

Once again, Litt failed to persuade the court that Madoff should be locked up in advance of his trial. Judge Ellis ruled that the defendant could remain free on bail, confined around the clock to his penthouse apartment.

A month later, in a different courtroom with a different mandate, Judge Burton R. Lifland was getting worried.

One of the longest-serving judges on the federal bankruptcy court in Manhattan, Lifland, who was overseeing the liquidation of Madoff's assets, was also an expert on the complicated interplay between American bankruptcy laws and the rules that applied in foreign countries. When it came to the Madoff case, which spanned the globe, it was becoming evident that there were far too many cooks in this heated kitchen.

The Serious Fraud Office in London was investigating Madoff's British affiliate after receiving a confidential report from the accountants liquidating the firm under British law. But Lee Richards, the receiver whom the SEC had put in charge of the London affiliate, was not getting the cooperation he had expected from the London liquidators. Meanwhile, several other European governments had opened their own Madoff investigations. French prosecutors had begun a preliminary inquiry and were eying Madoff's property there—the town house, the $7 million yacht, and the $1.5 million slip where it was moored—as a source of compensation for local victims. Spanish regulators were examining losses in the Optimal funds. Austrian officials had begun an emergency examination of Bank Medici. Irving Picard had already sought Judge Lifland's permission to hire British counsel, and he was preparing requests for additional legal help in more than a half-dozen other countries.

There were vague hints of conflicts closer to home. David Sheehan was locking horns with federal prosecutors over subpoenas Sheehan wanted to serve on dozens of individuals the prosecutors did not want him to approach yet. Some forfeited Madoff property that Picard could sell on behalf of the victims was being earmarked for sale by the U.S. Marshals Service—which, unlike SIPC, would deduct its own expenses from the proceeds available for victims, irritating Picard and Sheehan. The SEC was trying to investigate the Madoff case while being investigated itself by its own inspector general.

And so on Wednesday, February 4, after a routine hearing in the case, Judge Lifland gestured for Picard and Sheehan to stay a moment.

"I think things are moving a little bit slower than some people would anticipate, at least on the public front," he said mildly. "I don't really know what is going on behind the scenes." But with "so many agents and agencies and units of government that are charged with maximizing recovery," Lifland was beginning to feel that "agencies are not pulling together."

He added, "I would like the word to get out for all parties to start working in harmony and not in disharmony."

He did not sound optimistic—for good reason. Disharmony was winning, hands down. A prime example was taking place that same day in Washington, D.C., where the House Financial Services Committee was holding its second public hearing on the Madoff scandal since the new year.

The Madoff victims had hoped to find justice in the halls of Congress, but this would prove to be a dead end for those seeking immediate practical help or swift legislative changes. For those demanding that the SEC be held accountable for its catastrophic failures, however, Congress was eager to oblige. On this day the star witness was Harry Markopolos, the oft-ignored whistle-blower from Boston. His testimony was spiced with folksy insults and energized by righteous anger toward the SEC that perfectly reflected the rage of Madoff's victims.

"'Denial' is not just a river in Egypt; it's the mindset that the SEC has adopted," he said.

"The SEC is a group of 3,500 chickens tasked to chase down and catch foxes," he observed. "Bernie Madoff, like too many other securities fraudsters, had to turn himself in because the chickens couldn't catch him, even when told exactly where to look."

There were plenty of spy thriller flourishes. "In order to minimize the risk of discovery of our activities and the potential threat of harm to me and to my team, I submitted reports to the SEC without signing them," Markopolos told the committee members. "My team and I surmised that if Mr. Madoff gained knowledge of our activities, he may feel threatened enough to seek to stifle us."

Since Madoff already faced life in prison, "there was little to no downside for him" to simply kill his accusers, Markopolos asserted. He added, "At various points throughout these nine years, each of us feared for our lives."

These dramatic disclosures simply reinforced the questions Markopolos was *not* being asked: Since he was convinced that Madoff was a dangerous criminal, why didn't he report him to the criminal authorities? Why had he persisted in sending his tips about this potentially murderous con artist to a civil agency—and always the *same* civil agency? Since the Boston SEC office saw Markopolos as a credible source, couldn't they have vouched for him at the FBI's New York office or at the Justice Department, and not just at the SEC? He never addressed these mysteries.

A few members of Congress looked a little uneasy, particularly when Markopolos described wearing latex gloves to prepare an anonymous package of information that he unsuccessfully tried to slip to Eliot Spitzer, who was then the New York State attorney general, during a speaking engagement at Harvard. No one asked the obvious question: Why not just put the package in the mail?

Mostly, however, Markopolos was lionized and applauded, after which came the public flogging of the SEC.

A panel of regulators filed up to the witness table, led by Linda Chatman Thomsen, the national director of enforcement for the SEC. The SEC team had apparently misread the occasion completely; they came armed only with legal technicalities and vague hints of executive privilege.

The congressional panel did not want to hear that an ongoing criminal investigation and an internal probe by the SEC inspector general made it legally impossible for these witnesses to give the candid details the committee demanded—although this was arguably true. Instead the committee members fired rhetorical questions at the SEC team, getting angrier with each inadequate answer. Their insults revealed a stunning degree of hostility.

The most merciless observation came from Representative Gary L. Ackerman, a Democrat from New York: "We thought the enemy was Mr. Madoff," he told the SEC officials lined up before him. "I think it is you."

Later that afternoon, the newly installed SEC chairwoman, Mary Schapiro, sent an apologetic letter to the committee's chairman and its ranking Republican member, promising to work with them in a collegial way going forward.

But the damage was done. Congress was taking up the issue of massive regulatory reform in the wake of the financial meltdown of September 2008. The SEC's failure in the Madoff case could erase all the other

accomplishments it might offer to justify its continued independent existence. The contempt and impatience on display at the hearing certainly
made this seem like an ominous possibility.

In his effort to speed the claims process along, Irving Picard needed to
locate as many Madoff investors as quickly as possible. SIPC had already
set up a Web site and a hotline, and now Picard decided to take a more
proactive approach, seeking out the victims himself, rather than waiting
for them to come to him. He instructed his forensic consultants to file a
public exhibit in bankruptcy court on February 6 that consisted of more
than thirteen thousand names found on account statements in Madoff's
files. As a public document, the list was available to anyone who wanted
a copy, and it was soon posted online.

The "Madoff names" became an instant worldwide sensation, a road
map to the stars and titans who had been swindled and also a roster
of the ordinary people who had—or might possibly once have had—a
Madoff account. In France, it was dubbed *la liste de pigeons*. In England,
the *Guardian* featured it prominently. The *Wall Street Journal* built a map
that showed the geographic concentrations of victims. The *New York
Times* created an online database that could be searched by name, town,
state, and zip code; it immediately attracted a nearly staggering number
of visitors. Virtually every regional publication in the country, if not the
world, had a feature story on the local "names" that had shown up on
"the list." Some accounts were active, some were not. Some people named
on the list insisted that they had never invested with Madoff, and some
had already disclosed that they had.

Among the surprises to be found on the list were the names of Nathan
and Rosalie Sorkin of Boca Raton, Florida—Ike Sorkin's deceased parents. The list also contained the name "Squadron, Ellenoff, Plesent &
Sheinfeld," the vanished law firm where Sorkin had once been a partner.

It seemed outlandish: Ike Sorkin's client had enticed Sorkin's parents
and former law partners into his Ponzi scheme. But it was true.

In such a closely watched case, prosecutors had to be sure that everything was done strictly by the book. And, by the book, a defendant's lawyer should not have such a close connection to the defendant's alleged

victims. It was a conflict that might cast doubt on how committed Sorkin was to his client's defense—and that could cause problems for the government if Madoff should appeal his conviction or sentence. Behind the scenes, prosecutors began to insist that Madoff waive any right to invoke these conflicts of interest on appeal; within a few weeks, he would publicly do so.

The list may have served its purpose. It certainly got the attention of the people whose names appeared on it, and it enabled Picard to quickly sift out the long-defunct or simply erroneous accounts. But for many shell-shocked Madoff victims, the publication of the list felt like a bruising invasion of their privacy—one more injury to blame on Irving Picard.

The list captured only direct customers, not those who had invested through feeder funds. So there was no record on the list of a Herald fund account in the name of William Foxton, a ruddy, ginger-haired man who was a retired major in the British army.

As his son Willard Foxton later recounted in a moving BBC documentary, Major Foxton spent his life serving bravely in dangerous places. He lost a hand in combat and earned the Order of the British Empire. He later joined humanitarian aid missions and testified against war criminals. By all accounts, Major Foxton was a courageous, ethical, and very private man.

His family's research indicated that Foxton invested roughly $3 million in the Herald USA fund and the Herald Luxembourg fund, both sponsored by Bank Medici in Vienna, sometime in late 2004 or early 2005. He had expected to live on those investments after his civilian retirement in November 2008.

Willard Foxton would later say that his father had no idea he was a Madoff investor—he believed that his money was invested in a safe, diversified fund at an established Austrian bank.

In early February, Major Foxton told his son he was having disagreements with the bank about his investments. Then his son received an erratically punctuated e-mail message:

> Dear Will, I will be brief. I had some in fact all my money in two
> funds Herald USA Fund and Herald Luxembourg Fund invested
> in Austria. I have now found out that the office is closed and

the money was invested in Hedge funds of Madoff of the Ponzi scheme. I have lost everything. I am now considering whether or not to get myself declared bankrupt. Feeling pretty low and depressed. Thats about it for the moment.

On February 10, Foxton carried his military handgun to a small enclosed park near his home in Southampton. He lay down on a long wooden bench under some leafless trees and, sometime later, shot himself.

೦೦

Normally there are no "creditor meetings" in a SIPC bankruptcy case. But there was nothing normal about this case, and the bankruptcy code allowed such informational meetings. So Irving Picard and David Sheehan decided they would hold one—not a "creditors" meeting, exactly, but a "customers" meeting. It was scheduled for Friday, February 20.

Investors began to queue up early at the Old Customs House, the classic-columned building that houses the federal bankruptcy courts in Lower Manhattan. Some victims still hoped that a remnant of the $64.8 billion they thought they had a few short months ago had been found.

Shortly after 10:00 AM, Picard and Sheehan walked onto the bare stage in the building's auditorium and sat at a metal folding table with a senior SIPC lawyer named Kevin Bell, a tall, taciturn man with a distinctive steel gray crew cut. Microphones were set up on the table and on both sides of the auditorium near the stage.

The audience, clustered near the front of the room, was a diverse crowd—some in sweaters or flannel shirts, others in suits and expensive ties. Many of them spoke to reporters about the hardships they or their family members were suffering since Madoff's arrest and expressed fury at the federal regulators who had failed to protect them from Madoff's crime.

Opening the meeting, Picard explained that he and Sheehan would brief investors and then field their questions.

"There are a couple of ground rules," Picard said. "Number one, this case—as you well know—involves a crime, so we are operating out of a crime scene." Although he and his team were working closely with federal prosecutors, FBI agents, and SEC investigators, he said, "there is a limit to what we can say." He asked investors "to respect the judicial system so that it can play out."

His briefing was detailed and legally precise, but possibly a little dense for the less sophisticated investors in the audience. He explained that victims would be paid from two sources of funds: cash advances from SIPC and whatever assets he could recover for the estate, which would take "some period of time. We can't, at this point, speculate how long."

He discussed the possibility of selling Madoff's market-making operation for the investors' benefit. He said he had hired a consultant to advise him about the sale of the Roy Lichtenstein prints and other artwork found on the premises. He had hired other consultants to reconstruct and digitize the account statements, an enormous task that had to be accomplished before customer claims could be paid. There was so much to be done.

Indeed, in the next four months, a hurricane of legal activity would spin out from the heirloom burl wood desk in Picard's office in Rockefeller Center.

He would serve more than 230 subpoenas as part of investigations being pursued in the Bahamas, Bermuda, the British Virgin Islands, the Cayman Islands, France, Gibraltar, Great Britain, Ireland, Luxembourg, Spain, and Switzerland.

He would grasp for assets anywhere he could find them, starting with the low-hanging fruit. He would cut a complicated deal to sell the Madoff market-making business. He would close all the firm's brokerage or banking accounts, taking in just over $37 million, and settle the pending securities trades for just over $297 million. His team would sell the firm's small stake in a charter airline. He would sell the firm's remaining tickets to New York Knicks and New York Rangers games and auction off its New York Mets tickets for the 2009 season.

Nothing would be too trivial. Picard would cancel insurance policies, collecting nearly $234,000 in premiums. He would suggest that politicians and charities return the almost $145,000 in contributions they'd received from the now-toxic donor. He would cash out the firm's stake in DTCC, Wall Street's cooperatively owned clearing corporation, for more than $200,000. As soon as the FBI permitted it, he would cancel the leases on all but the seventeenth floor of the Lipstick Building. He would even cancel the firm's magazine subscriptions, club memberships, and vehicle leases, netting another $54,000.

He only hinted at these plans as he briefed the Madoff victims. But he emphasized at the February 20 meeting that SIPC, financed by Wall Street, would pay all the expenses involved—including his and his law firm's bills. Despite widespread reports to the contrary, he explained, none of the trustee's bills were being paid with assets earmarked for the victims, as would have been the case in a normal bankruptcy. All of the legal bills and other expenses in the liquidation were paid by SIPC, at no cost to the victims.

There had been erroneous news reports a month earlier that Picard, as trustee, was entitled to be paid 3 percent of the assets he recovered through litigation. That arrangement was built into the federal bankruptcy code, but it did not apply in SIPC cases. Instead, Picard and his law firm submitted their bills to SIPC, which haggled a bit and sent them on to the presiding judge, who had the final say. Then SIPC paid them out of the membership assessments levied on Wall Street firms. The amount involved had nothing to do with how much Picard recovered from those he sued.

But it was too late to stamp out the misunderstandings. More than a year later, some angry victims would still rail against Picard's "3 percent fee" and oppose every bill he submitted on the grounds that he was getting money that would otherwise have gone to them.

In perhaps the first sign of how tangled the lines of communication with the victims would become, Picard presented the most stunning revelation of the meeting as a parenthetical aside during his arcane discussion about the appropriate deadline for filing claims.

Some lawyers were telling their clients that their claims had to be filed by March 4, while Picard said that the only meaningful deadline was July 2, 2009, six months after the official notice of the bankruptcy had been mailed to investors. The March 4 deadline, he explained, applied only in SIPC cases where investors wanted the option of being reimbursed with actual shares of stock, rather than the cash value of the securities in their account.

The March 4 deadline did not apply to the Madoff victims, he continued, because—as far his team could tell, going back at least thirteen years—no securities had ever been purchased for their accounts. So the only relevant deadline for them was July 2.

It was almost like that painful old joke about how a drill sergeant broke the news of a family bereavement to a private under his command: "Everyone with parents living, take a step forward. Not so fast, Private Jones."

Everyone who thinks that at least a few blue chips, some Treasury bills, a little cash might be left in their Madoff accounts, take a step forward. Not so fast, everybody . . .

"That means that for claims purposes, the November 30th statement that said you had various securities is not what we are going to rely on," Picard said. "This is going to be a case in which we're going to be looking at cash in and cash out."

The headlines the next day spread the news that Picard's team had searched all available records going back to 1995 and some records dating to 1993 and had found no evidence that Madoff had ever purchased any securities for his clients.

It had been a Ponzi scheme, pure and simple, the largest and most far-flung fraud in financial history—but, at heart, a classic Ponzi scheme, where Peter was robbed to pay Paul. And, as Picard saw it, there were clear rules for dealing with a Ponzi scheme, rules that had absolutely nothing to do with the calculations on the final account statements tucked hopefully into the handbags and briefcases propped beside seats in this bristling auditorium.

Many of the victims disagreed—and would disagree forever.

∞

Two and a half weeks later, on Tuesday, March 10, a silver sedan pulled up outside the north entrance to the federal courthouse on Worth Street in Manhattan. The side street off Foley Square was thickly lined with satellite trucks and television cameras. Photographers pushed against the metal barriers that created a walkway between the car and the building's entrance.

A security guard helped Bernie Madoff climb out of the rear of the car and hurried him toward the courthouse. U.S. marshals watched from the perimeter, their eyes darting, alert for danger, as Madoff's eyes remained fixed on the sidewalk five feet ahead of him. He was a study in gray—a soft charcoal suit, a dove-colored knit tie, his silver hair brushed back in wings framing his temples, his face ashen and empty.

A few minutes before 3:00 PM, he was ushered through a side door into the courtroom of Judge Denny Chin, a boyish-looking man in his mid-fifties. Born in Hong Kong but raised in New York, Judge Chin was the first Chinese American to have been named to the federal bench in Manhattan. He had drawn the Madoff case by lottery, and this was Madoff's first appearance before him.

Prosecutor Marc Litt, his colleague Lisa Baroni, and FBI special agent Ted Cacioppi, who had arrested Madoff three months earlier, were waiting at the table nearest Judge Chin's elevated bench.

At the crowded table behind them, Madoff's legal team was joined by a new attorney, Peter Chavkin. Wiry and alert, Chavkin bore a strong resemblance to the Las Vegas tycoon Steve Wynn—except that today, he was somber and unsmiling.

Chavkin was there to assure Judge Chin that Madoff had been independently advised about the conflicts facing Ike Sorkin, which included not only Sorkin's parents' investments with Madoff and his old law firm's ties, but also his representation of Avellino & Bienes in 1992.

Sorkin had been negotiating with prosecutors on Madoff's behalf since the day of the arrest. The previous Friday, March 6, the judge had been notified that Madoff had waived indictment and would be confronted only with a less detailed document called a "criminal information." The waiver was the first hint that Madoff would likely plead guilty at some point rather than stand trial.

But first Judge Chin had to be sure that Sorkin's conflicts of interest would not taint the plea process, which could hand Madoff a trump card for a successful appeal.

Madoff was sworn in, and Judge Chin began questioning him about the conflicts, repeatedly asking the same question with slight variations: Does Mr. Madoff understand that he is entitled to a lawyer free of any conflicts or divided loyalties? He does. And does he nevertheless wish to continue with Mr. Sorkin as his lawyer? He does. And does he understand that he is thereby waiving his right to cite these conflicts in appealing any aspect of his case? He understands.

Judge Chin was satisfied that Madoff had knowingly waived his right to change lawyers. He then quickly walked the defendant through the steps involved in waiving indictment and determining the amount of restitution that would be imposed.

Finally, he dropped the day's firecracker.

"Now, I gather that the expectation is that Mr. Madoff will plead guilty to the information on Thursday?" the judge said.

"I think that's a fair expectation, Your Honor," Ike Sorkin answered softly.

"And that would be to all eleven counts of the information?"

"Yes, Your Honor."

No one on the crowded courtroom benches had seen the charges or knew that a guilty plea was imminent. Judge Chin asked Marc Litt to review the felony counts in detail.

"Yes, Your Honor, I'm happy to do so," Litt said. "They are securities fraud, investment advisor fraud, mail fraud, wire fraud, three counts of money laundering, false statements, perjury, false filings with the SEC and theft from an employee benefit plan." He added, "There is no plea agreement with the defendant."

Judge Chin quickly pressed him: "And that means that if Mr. Madoff wishes to plead guilty on Thursday, as far as the government is concerned, he would have to plead guilty to the entire information?"

Litt answered, "That's correct."

The judge leaned back, still looking at Litt. "All right, would you tell us what the exposure is in terms of the maximum possible sentence of imprisonment, taking the eleven counts together?" he asked.

The prosecutor responded, "In total, it's 150 years."

Two days later, hundreds of victims gathered outside the federal courthouse well before dawn, waiting for seats in Judge Chin's courtroom on the twenty-fourth floor. A large overflow room had been set up on the first floor, where TV screens would display the proceedings live.

Security was tight. The streets and sidewalks were a circus of television cameras, satellite trucks, reporters, and photographers. Helicopters hovered above, tracking the progress of Madoff's SUV from his apartment.

When the courtroom was finally unlocked, several newspaper sketch artists, smudged with colored chalk and gripping giant clipboards, claimed the first row of the jury box. Reporters squeezed in behind them.

At 9:36 AM, prosecutors Marc Litt and Lisa Baroni arrived and took their seats at the table nearest Judge Chin's bench. Litt was wearing a navy suit and white shirt, with a dotted burgundy tie. Baroni wore a black skirt and jacket, her lanky dark blond hair pulled back from her face. Ted Cacioppi, his boss Keith Kelly (the head of the FBI's Madoff task force), and two other FBI agents in business suits joined the prosecutors at the table.

At 9:47 AM, Bernie Madoff and Ike Sorkin entered the well of the courtroom from a side door opposite the jury box. As on Tuesday, Madoff was dressed in gray. Unlike Tuesday, he wore no watch or wedding band.

The whole defense team was in attendance. At the center of the table, Madoff sat between the white-haired Sorkin and the young dark-haired Mauro Wolfe, who leaned over to pat his back softly. Madoff sat quiet and still, his hands clasped in his lap. Sorkin positioned a microphone in front of his client and leaned over to show him how to turn it on and off.

At 10:00 AM, Judge Chin swept in and took his seat. Introductions were made, and then Madoff was sworn in.

"Mr. Madoff," Judge Chin asked, "do you understand that you are now under oath and that if you answer my questions falsely, your untrue answers may later be used against you in another prosecution for perjury or making false statements?"

Madoff answered softly, "Yes, I do."

"Try to keep your voice up so that I can hear you, please," Judge Chin said.

In a stronger voice, Madoff repeated, "Yes, I do, Your Honor."

Sorkin asked if a court attendant could provide some water. Some was fetched and put within reach.

After a few preliminaries, Judge Chin reminded Madoff that he was waiving his right to be confronted with a formal indictment and had agreed to respond to the less detailed criminal information, laying out the government's case against him. "Correct?" the judge asked.

"Yes."

"And how do you now plead to the information, guilty or not guilty?"

Madoff answered, "Guilty."

The government lawyers described the charges, which took some time.

Finally, Judge Chin said, "Mr. Madoff, tell me what you did."

With Ike Sorkin standing by him, Madoff unfolded a typewritten statement and began to read it, fumbling slightly on the legal name of his firm: "Your Honor, for many years up until my arrest on December 11, 2008, I operated a Ponzi scheme through the investment advisory side of my business, Bernard L. Madoff Securities LLC. . . .

"I am actually grateful for this opportunity to publicly speak about my crimes, for which I am so deeply sorry and ashamed. As I engaged in my fraud I knew what I was doing was wrong, indeed criminal. When I began the Ponzi scheme, I believed it would end shortly and I would be able to extricate myself and my clients from the scheme. However, this proved difficult, and ultimately impossible, and as the years went by I realized that my arrest, and this day, would inevitably come."

His voice was flat, controlled. "I am painfully aware that I have deeply hurt many, many people, including the members of my family, my closest friends, business associates and the thousands of clients who gave me their money. I cannot adequately express how sorry I am for what I have done. I am here today to accept responsibility for my crimes by pleading guilty."

Although Madoff claimed to be explaining how he had carried out and concealed his fraud, parts of his statement were far from the truth.

"I want to emphasize today that while my investment advisory business, the vehicle of my wrongdoing, was part of my firm, Bernard L. Madoff Securities, the other businesses my firm engaged in, proprietary trading and market making, were legitimate, profitable, and successful in all respects. . . .

"To the best of my recollection, my fraud began in the early 1990s. . . ."

He alone had caused false documents to be created and mailed to clients and had wired money between New York and London to give the illusion of trading activity, he said.

Some of those statements—about the financial health of his firm, the starting date for his crime—would always be clouded by doubt. Others—such as the assertion that he had acted alone—would soon be revealed as outright lies.

When Madoff had completed his fanciful description of his crime and sat down, Judge Chin turned to Litt.

"Does the government believe that Mr. Madoff's admissions cover the elements of the crime of each count?"

"Yes, Your Honor," Litt answered. "The government does not entirely agree with all of the defendant's description of his conduct. However, the government does believe that his allocution does cover each of the elements of the charged offenses."

The government knew that Frank DiPascali was already in negotiations to plead guilty and to name names. Still, Litt was not yet free to dispute publicly Madoff's claim that he had carried out this crime alone. And, despite the obvious lies, it would be silly to waste resources prosecuting Madoff for perjury, given all the other work that needed to be done.

Madoff's version of his crime was clearly aimed at protecting his employees and preserving as much of his family's wealth as possible, since the government could not claim assets accumulated before the fraud began. His story was not the whole truth he swore he would tell. It was, instead, a clear declaration that he did not intend to finger anybody in this crime except himself.

Given a chance to speak, a Madoff victim named George Nierenberg insisted that the government should have charged Madoff with conspiracy, since it was obvious that Madoff could not have produced all the paperwork by himself. Maureen Ebel, a widow who had lost all her savings, urged the judge to reject Madoff's guilty plea and force him to stand trial so that "we have more of a chance to comprehend the global scope of this tremendous crime."

When the judge prompted Marc Litt to respond to the victims' statements, he asked for a moment to consider and then answered. "I think the only thing the government would say," he responded, "is that the government's investigation continues. It is continuing. A lot of resources and effort are being expended, both to find assets and to find anyone else who may be responsible for this fraud."

The man who could answer the government's questions was sitting silently at the defense table.

What then followed was a one-sided dialogue about bail. When Ike Sorkin described the security cordon set up around Madoff "at his wife's expense," victims in the courtroom laughed bitterly at the notion that Ruth had any money but theirs. Judge Chin called for order.

After Sorkin's long entreaty, Litt rose to his feet to respond. Judge Chin waved to him to remain seated.

"I don't need to hear from the government," he said. "It is my intention to remand Mr. Madoff."

A cheer erupted. "Ladies and gentlemen, please," Judge Chin said, with a sharp glance at the crowded courtroom. Silence returned, but it had a different quality now, no longer anxious and hostile but patient and relieved. The judge continued: "He has incentive to flee, he has the means to flee, and thus he presents the risk of flight. Bail is revoked."

After a few more procedural arrangements, he looked at the defendant and said, "Mr. Madoff, I will see you at sentencing. We are adjourned."

Madoff stood at the defense table, looking straight ahead as a U.S. marshal in a business suit approached him. At a soft word, Madoff brought his hands together behind his back. With a barely audible click, the handcuffs were snapped in place.

Bernie Madoff was led silently through a side door opening into the white-tiled corridor that led to a life behind bars.

13

NET WINNERS AND
NET LOSERS

On Wednesday, March 18, a week after the Madoff media circus, David Friehling and his lawyer arrived quietly and unnoticed at the federal courthouse in Manhattan.

Tall and trim in a pale taupe suit, Bernie Madoff's accountant was turning himself in to face the criminal fraud charges that had been made public that morning. After the usual processing by the FBI and the U.S. Marshals, Friehling was brought before a federal magistrate, where he pleaded not guilty and was released promptly on $2.5 million bail.

The previous Thursday, the day Madoff pleaded guilty, David Friehling's father-in-law and retired partner, Jerry Horowitz, died in Palm Beach Gardens, Florida, after a long battle with cancer. Horowitz had been Madoff's auditor as far back as the 1960s, when he worked in Manhattan alongside Saul Alpern, Frank Avellino, and Michael Bienes. Even after he set up his own practice, Horowitz continued to handle the independent audits that Madoff's firm submitted to the SEC each year. And he regularly invested a substantial portion of his own wealth, and that of many family members and friends, with Madoff.

It wasn't a strictly kosher arrangement. An accountant cannot be considered "independent" if he invests his money with the firm he audits. But everyone at Alpern's firm invested with Madoff.

In the early 1990s, as Jerry Horowitz focused more on retirement, Friehling took over the practice and moved it to a small office in New City, New York, about thirty miles north of Manhattan, where he and his wife had moved in 1986. He also took over as the independent auditor for

Madoff's brokerage firm—and continued to invest his own and his family's savings with Madoff, as his father-in-law had done.

Released on bail, Friehling strode quickly from the courthouse toward the black SUV waiting at the curb, ignoring questions shouted at him by several reporters. His defense lawyer, Andrew Lankler, platinum-haired and silent, climbed into the backseat with him, and the car sped away. Lankler had worked hard to avoid the media spectacle of an arrest at home by the FBI and a "perp walk" at the courthouse. But his negotiations with the prosecutors remained unsettled, as it was still unclear how much Friehling could help them in their search for Madoff's accomplices. The charges brought against Friehling on March 18 were just the first hand in this poker game.

The arrest, the first public development in the criminal investigation in three months, did not answer many questions about the fraud. Indeed, the prosecutors did not clearly assert that the forty-nine-year-old Friehling even knew about the Ponzi scheme. He was accused only of aiding and abetting Madoff's fraud by falsely certifying that he had done independent professional audits of the Madoff firm when he hadn't.

Neither the prosecutors' charges nor an SEC lawsuit filed the same day mentioned Friehling's curious meeting in November 2005 with the due-diligence team from the Optimal funds—the meeting, at the height of that near-death cash crisis, when he implausibly claimed to have verified Madoff's account balances with the DTCC.

But the SEC attorneys and the federal prosecutors said that their investigations were continuing.

Meanwhile, at SIPC, the question was still hanging in the air, confronting Irving Picard everywhere he went: "Where did the money go?"

It was a constant refrain on Web sites and talk show discussions, with participants firmly rejecting the notion that all those billions of dollars had just vanished. Wall Street sources would occasionally call reporters with intriguing tips and theories: Madoff had converted the billions into small-carat diamonds and stashed them in safe-deposit boxes around Europe; or he'd bought luxury real estate around the world through shell companies based in Panama; or he'd been blackmailed by Russian mobsters; or he'd been part of an illicit plot to secretly finance "black ops" missions by the Mossad, Israel's national intelligence agency. How else could one person consume so much money?

Even ignoring the fictional $64.8 billion on the final account statements, most of which had never actually existed in the first place, there still was an enormous amount of actual currency to be accounted for. Picard's experts estimated that the sum of all the out-of-pocket cash losses among Madoff's victims—money those victims paid in but never withdrew—was about $20 billion.

But Picard knew where most of that money had gone.

Aside from the hundreds of millions that Madoff diverted for his own use over the years, the cash handed over by investors had been paid out to other investors as bogus investment earnings. Picard had the bank records showing when the cash was withdrawn and by whom; and he knew whose account in which country received the money. By his estimate, more than $6 billion was withdrawn from the Ponzi scheme between the collapse of Lehman Brothers in September 2008 and Madoff's arrest in December. In the scheme's final year, withdrawals totaled nearly $13 billion—most of which had flowed in since early 2006.

Still, knowing where the money went was one thing, and getting it back was another.

While the federal bankruptcy code allowed Picard to seek the return of cash withdrawn within two years of the Madoff firm's bankruptcy filing, New York State law extended that window to six years. (The bankruptcy filing was actually made on December 15, 2008, but the court ruled that the official filing date would be December 11, the day of Madoff's arrest.) Withdrawals in the scheme's final three months were called "preference" payments, and those were relatively straightforward to recover. Withdrawals made in the preceding five years and nine months were generally known in bankruptcy court as "fraudulent conveyances," and recovering them usually involved a court fight.

As those who were well versed in bankruptcy law knew, the term *fraudulent conveyance* referred to Madoff's own fraudulent motives for conveying the cash to other people—namely, he did so to perpetuate his Ponzi scheme. The word *fraudulent* did not refer to the motives of the people to whom the cash was conveyed, those who had simply withdrawn what they thought was their own money. But many investors were not familiar with the legalese, and they were outraged when Picard's letters to them referred to their good-faith withdrawals as "fraudulent conveyances" and directed them to contact his office to discuss returning the money.

Under bankruptcy law, it didn't matter how pure an investor's motives were. Picard was allowed to sue to recover all "preference payments" and any money "fraudulently conveyed" to others by Madoff in that six-year window. In bankruptcy jargon, these lawsuits are known as "clawbacks," and for the small Madoff investors, they were just as frightening as they sounded.

Picard hated the term *clawback suits*, but by the end of June he would file eight of them against the giant investors and feeder funds whose individual withdrawals totaled hundreds of millions and, in some cases, billions of dollars.

He sued the Kingate funds, run by Carlo Grosso, for the return of $395 million, including nearly $260 million withdrawn in the last ninety days of the Ponzi scheme's life.

He sued to recover about $1 billion from dozens of accounts set up by Stanley Chais, who was now eighty-three years old. The first Madoff feeder fund entrepreneur had relocated from Los Angeles to New York, where he was undergoing medical treatment. Even after the Madoff scandal broke, Chais had been honored in absentia for his lifetime of generosity to a host of major Israeli nonprofits, including the Weizmann Institute of Science, Technion–Israel Institute of Technology, and the Hebrew University of Jerusalem.

Picard sought about $250 million from Cohmad Securities; its cofounder Maurice "Sonny" Cohn; his daughter and the firm's president, Marcia Beth Cohn; and a long roster of brokers who had worked there. He claimed that the brokerage firm had knowingly served as the sales force for Madoff's Ponzi scheme, allegations that the shattered firm and the Cohns themselves adamantly denied.

Picard sought another $3.5 billion from the Fairfield Sentry funds, operated by Walter Noel, Jeffrey Tucker, and their partners at the Fairfield Greenwich Group. With other smaller funds to operate, Fairfield Greenwich had not been completely wiped out by its Madoff losses. But the entire firm had denied any knowledge of Madoff's crime, and it had armed itself with lawyers, who were digging in for a long fight.

And on May 12, in the most ambitious of these initial lawsuits, Picard sued Jeffry and Barbara Picower for more than $6.7 billion—a staggering sum that, on further investigation by Picard's team, would be raised to $7.2 billion a few months later. No one else—not even Madoff and his entire family—had withdrawn anything remotely close to that sum of money from the Ponzi scheme.

The revelations in the Picower lawsuit were catnip for conspiracy theorists. Had Picower been pulling money out to hide it for the Madoff family? Madoff denied this—if it were true, surely he would have reclaimed the money to help keep his scheme afloat in those final months. Moreover, Madoff would have realized that his family's future sources of income would be scrutinized with a microscope by law enforcement for the rest of their lives. Others speculated that perhaps Picower was the actual mastermind of the Ponzi scheme all along and that Madoff was just his bagman. Madoff denied this, too—if it were true, certainly Madoff would have exposed Picower in exchange for leniency once he was confronted with that deadly 150-year jail term. There was simply no explanation that made much sense—except, as Madoff himself suspected, that Jeffry Picower was shrewd enough to know that he shouldn't leave his possibly fictional profits in Madoff's hands for very long.

By law, Picard had until December 11, 2010, to file his clawback suits. Before the end of the summer of 2009, he had gone to court to demand the return of $13.7 billion, all of it from giant feeder funds or enormously wealthy individuals whose lawyers were prepared for a long siege of motions and objections that would end either with a verdict in court or with a negotiated settlement. They could run out the clock and increase the cost of litigation, but actually filing the lawsuits cost Picard about the same whether he sued a giant or a midget. So it made no sense to start suing midgets when there were still so many giants walking around with so much Madoff money in their pockets.

Nevertheless, many small investors said they were terrified that he would come after them. Their fear was a signal of just how adversarial their relationship with Picard had become in the months since the February 20 meeting. The increasing hostility saddened him and frustrated his colleague David Sheehan. As they saw it, Picard was being as accessible, flexible, and sympathetic as the law allowed. He replied to thousands of e-mails and phone calls, or referred them to someone on his staff. It was a fiercely complicated international bankruptcy case, but Picard felt he was doing his best to explain those complexities to the people most grievously affected by them. He rarely lost his temper, despite the ugly accusations flung at him almost daily.

However, there were two bones of contention that he simply could not take off his plate: the slow pace at which claims were being paid and the way he was calculating losses.

By the end of June, after more than six months of work, fewer than 600 of 13,705 claims had been fully processed. It was an infuriatingly small number, and Madoff's more desperate victims were outraged by it.

This situation was not entirely the trustee's fault. Since most of Madoff's records were antiquated, Picard's team had spent hundreds of hours and tens of thousands of dollars converting millions of pages of paper and filmy microfiche into digital records that could be examined and distributed by computer. The FBI was carefully screening the records for possible accomplices hiding behind fictitious account names and had put a hold on payments to some claimants. The Justice Department had prohibited Picard's team from interviewing more than four dozen people, including nearly two dozen employees of the firm. Moreover, bankruptcy is not a speedy process in the best of times.

Yet Picard's adversaries blamed him personally for the slow pace of payment because they believed it was a direct result of how he was calculating investor losses. They argued that the costly and time-consuming reconstruction of customer accounts would not be necessary if he simply accepted the final account statements as the basis for SIPC claims, as they believed he was required to do by law. The best way for Picard to speed up the claims process, as they saw it, was to drop his insistence on the "cash in, cash out" approach.

Picard's team eventually would speed up the claims-paying process, creating a computer network that lawyers at several different locations could work on simultaneously. But the trustee and his adversaries were simply at an impasse over how he was calculating losses. He believed he was correctly interpreting the law, and thousands of investors believed he was dead wrong.

SIPC acknowledged that the delays were creating severe distress for some nearly destitute investors. Pressed by several investors' lawyers to craft some sort of interim relief, the organization established a novel "hardship" program in May that was supposed to fast-track especially urgent claims—the first time it had ever done this, or ever needed to. But the unfamiliar and cumbersome rules that applied to this new program only further infuriated some elderly investors who needed help.

Picard stuck to his guns. Claims were going to be calculated on a "money in, money out" basis. Under that approach, several thousand accounts, affecting unknown thousands of people, had no "net equity" because the owners of the accounts had already taken out more cash than they had put in. In the painful idiom of the bankruptcy court, they were "net winners" and were not entitled to get anything from the estate until after all the other investors had recovered their initial cash investment—which, in this case, seemed like legal shorthand for "never." More significantly for those in acute need, the net winners were not eligible for the cash advances of up to $500,000 from SIPC.

Many bankruptcy law experts had expected this outcome. In their view, it was the only court-tested way to calculate Ponzi scheme losses. But some Madoff investors were convinced that SIPC's involvement changed those established rules of Ponzi scheme liquidations, and a few were willing to ride into battle to prove it. One of them was a New Jersey attorney named Helen Davis Chaitman.

From her résumé, Helen Chaitman seemed an unlikely candidate for the role of Joan of Arc in this war over how to calculate net equity. She was a Bryn Mawr graduate who decided to go to law school in the mid-1970s. She was in private practice with the firm of Phillips Nizer, and she divided her time between its Manhattan offices and a small outpost in suburban New Jersey. Her specialty was lender liability, a substratum of bankruptcy law as arcane as SIPC liquidations; she had even written a respected textbook on the topic.

Tall, thin, and pale, with a short bob of strawberry blond hair, Chaitman looked much younger than her years and spoke in a soft, calming voice. But she was a tireless and fiercely tenacious advocate for her clients. In her pro bono work, she stood firmly with the underdog, and in all her legal battles she had a talent for powerful, persuasive language—inside the courtroom and out.

And, in this battle, she had skin in the game. On the recommendation of a friend, she had invested all her savings in 2004 with Madoff. The strategy looked "safe and conservative," she later wrote. "I told my friend the only risk was that Madoff was a fraud," she continued. "My friend laughed and said that Madoff had an impeccable reputation in the industry, had been chairman of the Nasdaq."

From the day of Madoff's arrest, Chaitman was determined to salvage whatever she could from the rubble and to hold somebody accountable. She focused her arguments on a knotty appellate case called *In re New Times Security Services*, which dealt with a much smaller Ponzi scheme liquidated by SIPC years earlier. It was a complex, muddled case that featured three sets of victims, each with distinctive circumstances; an internecine dispute between SIPC and its own trustee; and two separate visits to the appellate court.

For one set of *New Times* victims, those who thought their stolen money had been used to buy brand-name mutual funds, SIPC honored the final account statements—whose balances, unlike those in the Madoff accounts, accurately tracked the real-world fluctuations in the prices of the listed mutual fund shares, going up and down with the market tide. That decision was never challenged on appeal.

But the court upheld SIPC's refusal to honor the final account statements of another set of *New Times* victims who had purchased high-yielding securities that were actually invented out of whole cloth by the Ponzi schemer. "Treating . . . fictitious paper profits as within the ambit of the customers' 'legitimate expectations' would lead to the absurdity of 'duped' investors reaping windfalls as a result of fraudulent promises made on fake securities," the court decided.

So which aspect of the *New Times* rulings applied? The blue-chip stocks the Madoff customers thought they owned were obviously more akin to the real mutual funds than to the make-believe securities in the *New Times* case. But the values Madoff attributed to those stocks more resembled the unattainable fantasy values of the fictional *New Times* securities than the accurate up-and-down prices of the mutual funds. So it was a stretch to say that the rulings in *New Times* were crystal clear in favor of Chaitman's position—or, indeed, crystal clear about anything.

There were other court decisions that flatly contradicted her—*In re Old Naples Securities*, for example. In that case, decided in Florida in 2002, the court had acknowledged that "there is very little case law on point for determining what constitutes a customer's net equity in a situation such as this," another small Ponzi scheme being liquidated by SIPC. But the court nevertheless decided that letting the victims "recover not only their initial capital investment but also the phony 'interest' they received . . . is illogical."

So Chaitman also grounded her arguments against Picard on her reading of the 1970 law that created SIPC and the comments that lawmakers had made about their intentions. As she saw it, SIPC was an insurance program, created to restore investor confidence after the collapse of the wild go-go markets of the 1960s. Investor confidence could be maintained only if SIPC honored customers' "legitimate expectations." In this case, she argued, those legitimate expectations were based on the final statements they received just before Madoff's magic kingdom went up in smoke.

Again, this was not an undisputed thesis. The SIPC statute itself did not clearly address how a trustee should calculate net equity in a Ponzi scheme; nor did it flatly require the trustee to honor customers' final account statements, regardless of the circumstances. It did, however, define "net equity" in a convoluted way that might support Chaitman's position. It said the term meant "the sum which would have been owed by the [brokerage firm] if the [firm] had liquidated . . . all securities positions" of the customer, after subtracting any money the customer still owed the firm for those securities.

Irving Picard's response was that, for years, Madoff's victims had been paying for the "securities positions" shown on their account statements with play money—with the phony profits credited to them by Madoff. They had not actually given Madoff any real money with which to pay for the securities shown on their statements—except for the various cash payments they made, for which Picard was giving them credit.

Some previous legal rulings challenged Picard's reading of that portion of the statute, and it was certainly an issue that needed clarification from the courts or from Congress. However, it was not true to say that his definition of net equity was "invented," or that his position was indefensible or in clear contradiction of the law and prior court rulings.

But this is what Helen Chaitman did say—repeatedly, eloquently, widely, in any forum available to her. For her, this was not a topic about which reasonable people could disagree; this was not even a topic desperately in need of judicial clarification. She argued that she was correctly defining net equity and that Picard was deliberately ignoring the law to shortchange victims and protect SIPC and its Wall Street masters.

Her clients and admirers did not doubt her for a moment. For the tragically mischaracterized "net winners," who were denied any SIPC payment under Picard's analysis, she was a beacon of hope for a better outcome. They trusted her completely.

Chaitman's unequivocal opinions were amplified in the echo chamber of the Internet by an increasingly visible blog created and nurtured by another outspoken Madoff victim and Picard critic, a law school dean named Lawrence R. Velvel.

Like Chaitman, Velvel had been steered to Madoff by a trusted friend and had seen his nest egg crushed in the Ponzi scheme's collapse. But his résumé clearly suggested he would be an implacable foe of SIPC from day one—he was a self-defined radical, and had been since the antiwar movement of the 1960s. He also was a cofounder in 1988 of the Massachusetts School of Law in Andover, a small low-cost law school whose mission was to serve working-class students.

Velvel looked like a genial gnome, short and stocky with a chin-circling white beard and owlish spectacles. When aroused, however, he could employ his words like a blowtorch.

In his view, justice had to incorporate "the simple dictates of humanity," or it was not justice. This meant that the only just definition of net equity was one that provided SIPC money to Madoff victims who otherwise "will have to continue living on welfare or dumpster diving." If destitution was the result of Picard's net equity formula—as it would be for some as-yet-unknown number of victims—then Picard's formula could not possibly be just.

Chaitman and Velvel became two of the most visible champions of the unlucky "net winners." Their analysis of the *New Times* case was passed back and forth by e-mails and supplied to reporters as infallible doctrine. A few of their angriest supporters berated anyone—in the media or on victim chat sites—who did not agree with them.

It seemed impossible for them to shake free of the Wall Street vocabulary that Madoff had used to disguise his crime. His victims were "clients" who had been making "investments." He had been generating "profits," and they had been withdrawing them as "investment income"—even paying taxes on it, for heaven's sake. Thanks to those "profits," they still had money in their accounts when Madoff confessed. And that final account balance was the measure of what they had lost in Madoff's fraud, plain and simple.

But Irving Picard and David Sheehan did not see "investments" and "profits" and "account balances." Instead, they saw crimes and lies and stolen loot. In their view, Madoff was simply a thief. He had ridden into town and swindled everybody. Some people had been lucky enough to ask for their money back before he rode off into the sunset. He had given it back to them purely to forestall the cries of "Stop! Thief!" that would have broken out if he had refused. At the end of the day, those victims had dodged the bullet—they had narrowly avoided being robbed.

Other victims, the unlucky ones, had not retrieved a penny before Madoff galloped away. In their case, the bullet had hit home, the robbery had been consummated. As Picard and his posse saw it, any loot left in the crook's saddlebags when he was finally captured clearly belonged to those unlucky victims, to the thousands of "net losers," and to no one else.

But the net winners did not feel lucky. They felt as if they had been robbed, too—robbed of the wealth they thought they had. They felt betrayed by Madoff and by the SEC—and they were right; they had been tragically betrayed. But so had the "net losers," and at much greater cost, at least in terms of out-of-pocket cash. So the "lucky net winners" were not lucky and they were not winners. They simply were not eligible for immediate relief, under Picard's calculations, no matter how genuinely needy some of them might have been.

Picard's job, as the courts had long interpreted it, was to try to get all the innocent Madoff victims into the same boat, a boat whose occupants had sacrificed all their fictional profits but recovered all of the cash they originally invested. On the day Madoff was arrested, the net winners had already gotten all their cash back and the net losers had not. The net losers had never received any fictional profits, and the net winners had.

Madoff had robbed Peter to pay Paul; the only way to fix that was to take money back from Paul to repay Peter. Even if the trustee could find a way to repay Peter from some other source of money, Paul would still be better off than Peter because he had his fictional profits and Peter didn't. Unless everyone, somehow, could recover the full amount shown on their final account statements, the net losers would inevitably be treated worse than the net winners, which could not possibly be fair.

∽∾

Was there a moment immediately after Madoff's arrest when a different approach could have been applied to helping the neediest casualties of his crime?

The justice available through the bankruptcy court was blind. It would treat wealthy "net winners" such as the New York Mets' owners the same as nearly impoverished "net winners" such as retired schoolteachers or a struggling freelance writer. It would treat all "net losers" the same, whether they were rich hedge funds in the Caribbean or a retired small-town mayor in New Jersey. And this brand of justice was not only blind but slow, far too slow to deliver emergency relief.

There was a template for a different approach. After the 9/11 terrorist attacks, Congress recognized that the court system—the forum that would have to deal with lawsuits by victims' families against the airlines, the airports, and the Port Authority of New York and New Jersey—was a ruinous option. Thousands of breadwinners had been killed, and their families needed immediate relief, fairly distributed. So Congress created a victim compensation fund, whose special master was empowered to tailor compensation awards to reflect both justice and mercy, with financing from Congress—in exchange for an agreement not to sue the airlines or any other entity that could have been held negligent. The final distributions were made within two years and were generally considered fair.

More recently, when a massive oil spill inflicted enormous damage on the communities and businesses on the Gulf Coast of the United States in the spring and summer of 2010, a similar approach was taken, with the same special master appointed to make fast-track decisions to distribute funds set aside by British Petroleum for damage claims. The effort got off to a rocky start after the special master promised quicker decisions than he could produce. But while going to court remained an option for those dissatisfied by his rulings, the concept was still generally viewed as a faster route to recovery than a long trip through the judicial system.

Of course, a special master for some sort of "Madoff Victim Restitution Fund" would have faced all the same problems that the SIPC trustee confronted: the criminal investigation, the possibility that some Madoff victims were actually accomplices, the unreliable or nonexistent records. Taxpayers willing to finance compensation to 9/11 widows and orphans would no doubt have balked at reimbursing wealthy offshore hedge funds, and the only deep pocket that could have played the role of British Petroleum in paying claims was SIPC itself, which was institutionally committed to the bankruptcy process.

Still, some sort of global SIPC settlement or custom-tailored emergency relief for the neediest victims might have been possible if the SEC had immediately recognized the scale of financial devastation and had gotten the White House to persuade Congress to enact a more creative response.

But the reality of late 2008 was that the SEC was hamstrung by its history with Madoff and caught in a leadership change as a new administration moved into the White House. A divided Congress already was wrestling with failing banks, faltering insurers, near-bankrupt automakers, several endangered brokerage giants, a rising flood of home foreclosures, high levels of unemployment, and the paralysis afflicting most of the nation's sources of consumer and business credit.

In the absence of a more creative and flexible option, the default position was a blind, slow, and bitterly adversarial SIPC liquidation in bankruptcy court.

Clawback lawsuits were an integral part of bankruptcy court liquidation. Typically, the cash withdrawn before a Ponzi scheme collapses is the primary asset a trustee can find to settle claims. With luck, there may be some untapped bank or brokerage accounts, or some costly toys and pretty houses that can be seized and sold. In essence, though, a Ponzi scheme is simply a liar's bank account, with a stack of deposit slips at one end and a checkbook at the other. Its lifeblood is the money that flows in as "investments" and flows out again as "withdrawals."

To recover the investors' money that had flowed out, Picard needed to sue those who had withdrawn it, an obligation the net winners saw as a threat aimed directly at them, especially if they had taken out millions more than they originally invested. If Picard could be forced to acknowledge their final account statements as the basis for their claims, then they would still be owed money by the estate regardless of how much they had withdrawn. This would mean they would not be vulnerable to clawback lawsuits at all and, in turn, the recovery of many of the billions of dollars Picard had gone to court to claim would be impossible.

Picard's bedrock assumption was that there was a limited amount of money available to satisfy the claims of Madoff's victims. As he saw it, the net winners had already gotten back 100 percent of every dollar they had given Madoff. But, even on his optimistic days, he feared that net losers would get back just twenty cents on the dollar—maybe thirty cents if David Sheehan got very lucky with the big-ticket clawback lawsuits.

If that limited pool of cash were reduced by the invalidation of most clawback lawsuits and then had to be shared with every Madoff customer based on the final account balances, the payout could be pennies on the dollar, at best.

But what if the assets weren't limited? What if the saddlebags retrieved by the posse were bottomless? What if someone—such as SIPC or the SEC—somehow came up with the full $64.8 billion necessary to pay 100 percent of everyone's final account balance?

By law, SIPC could turn to Wall Street for the cash, and the SEC could get money from the U.S. Treasury. Perhaps that approach might have seemed fair to many Madoff victims—that the fat cats on Wall Street should deliver the fictional profits that Madoff had promised them, with something chipped in by the negligent regulators who had allowed this disaster to happen.

The debate over compensation escalated. Why rescue just the Madoff victims? Literally dozens of Ponzi schemes had fallen apart or were shut down in 2008 and the first half of 2009. And what about the legitimate profits the rest of America had lost in the same market meltdown that caused Madoff to implode? Why should the fictional profits promised by a crook magically reappear in people's bank accounts, while the reality-based profits created through honest trades by the rest of America just vanished? If Wall Street and the SEC were going to make Madoff's victims whole, why not make everyone whole?

It was going to be that kind of war, and the first shot was fired on June 5, 2009.

On that day, the small law firm of Lax & Neville filed a class-action suit against Picard on behalf of plaintiffs whose claims he had rejected. One plaintiff was a seventy-six-year-old New Yorker named Allan Goldstein, who had been one of the victims to testify before Congress soon after Madoff's arrest.

He had been an eloquent spokesman in his congressional testimony.

"I am a human face on this tragedy," he told the House Financial Services Committee on January 5. "I speak not only for myself but for the many people who have also lost everything because of this Ponzi scheme."

In a hardworking life, he had accumulated $4.2 million in retirement savings, all of it invested with Madoff. During twenty-one years of booming bull markets, Madoff had paid him steady annual returns ranging from 8 percent to 12 percent. "I was willing to forgo outsized gains in boom years in favor of greater security," he said. "We entrusted Mr. Madoff with all we had, and now everything that I worked for over a 50-year career is gone."

Since the collapse, he had cashed in his life insurance to pay his mortgage, was trying to sell his home in a dismal market, and feared he would be forced into foreclosure. "At this stage of our lives, I never could have envisioned the financial devastation that we are now suffering," he added. "In the blink of an eye, savings that I had struggled my entire lifetime to earn have vanished. . . . I sit before you today a broken man."

He urged Congress to set up a restitution fund and enact some sort of emergency legislation that would allow SIPC to "loosen the standards" and distribute money more quickly. He concluded, "We are not trust funds, hedge funds or banks. We are ordinary people who were victims of an incomprehensible crime and who have had their lives turned upside down. We are turning to you, our only hope, for relief we so desperately need."

But no emergency legislation or restitution fund was enacted by Congress; nor was either even considered. Appeals to the SEC did not produce any change in SIPC's policies, either. Privately, regulators might fume about how poorly SIPC was handling its escalating public relations problem. But the SEC had gigantic public relations problems of its own, and it did not commit itself in the net equity battle at all until just before it was required to do so in court.

The Lax & Neville lawsuit was followed almost immediately by a similar complaint by Helen Chaitman. She argued that Picard was wrong and conflicted, that clawback lawsuits were simply immoral, and that both clawbacks and Picard had to be eliminated from the Madoff claims process if the victims were ever to find justice.

Spurred by their tireless advocates, the "net winners" became more organized. In letters to the editor, Internet postings, media interviews, and letters to Congress and the courts, they honed their arguments against Picard's "cash in, cash out" approach. Some of them set up advocacy groups, forming alliances with other fraud-victim groups and lobbying Congress for legislative action to force Picard and SIPC to recognize their claims.

The net losers were less inclined to take a public stand. They found it less upsetting to remain silent—after all, Irving Picard and David Sheehan were fighting their fight, and they were loath to open themselves to attacks from the most vocal net winners. But in the absence of any public outcry from the thousands of net losers, Picard and Sheehan stood alone as the only visible defenders of the "cash in, cash out" approach.

14

THE SINS OF THE FATHER

A little before 3:00 PM on Wednesday, June 17, 2009, SEC inspector general H. David Kotz, an elfish-looking man with dark hair and deep-set eyes, entered the Metropolitan Correctional Center, a cocoa-colored building in the shadow of the towering federal buildings on Foley Square in Manhattan. With Kotz was his slender, blond deputy, Noelle Frangipane.

They came to ask Bernie Madoff how he had eluded dozens of SEC investigators for more than a decade.

Inside the MCC, they were shown to a small conference room furnished with only a handful of chairs—no table, no desk—where they were joined by Ike Sorkin and his colleague Nicole De Bello.

After a brief wait, Madoff arrived, escorted by a guard, who removed his handcuffs. Despite spending three months in jail, he looked much as he had on the newscasts and television specials over the past six months, except for his prisoner's uniform.

Kotz asked to swear in the witness, but Madoff declined to take the oath. He simply nodded when Sorkin reminded him of his obligation "to tell the truth."

Madoff immediately had some matters he wanted to set straight. He claimed that the prosecutors and Irving Picard had misunderstood some of the things he had said in his proffer session in December. "There's a lot of misinformation being circulated" about the case, he began, though quickly adding, "I'm not saying I'm not guilty."

He then spun out a true-false version of what had really happened, giving Kotz a firsthand look at how he had toyed with SEC lawyers for years.

He insisted that everything he had told the SEC about his split-strike conversion strategy and his computer algorithms had been true—in the very beginning, he'd actually been buying stocks and options and had been successful at it, he said. "Even with artificial intelligence, you still need to have a gut feel," he went on. "It's a combination of technology and trader's feel, and I was a good trader."

He repeated what he had said in court—that his fraud began in the early 1990s as a temporary measure. "I made commitments for too much money and then I couldn't put the strategy to work," he told Kotz, laying on the jargon and weaving fantasy and truth together. "I had a European bank, I was doing forward conversion, they were doing reverse conversion. . . . I thought I was going to be able to do it." When his profits fell short, he said, "I thought, 'Fine, I'll just generate these trades and then the market will come back and I'll make it back.'"

He added, "But it never happened. It was my mistake not to just be out a couple hundred million dollars and get out of it."

In an almost surreal way, Madoff kept assuring Kotz—accurately— that the investment strategy he pretended to be using all those years could have worked, could have been real, was "not that exotic." Big Wall Street firms might be claiming now that they saw through him, but his clients had included several former top executives at Merrill Lynch and Morgan Stanley, he said truthfully.

"Credible people knew it could be done or they wouldn't be clients . . . all you have to do is look at the types of people I was doing this for to know it was a credible strategy," he continued. Those people "knew a lot more than this guy Harry"—meaning Harry Markopolos. Madoff did not acknowledge that even if the strategy could have been used honestly, it could not have produced profits almost every month for nearly two decades—and it could not have been used honestly on a multibillion-dollar scale without overwhelming the markets.

His contempt for the SEC's failure to catch him was gentle but withering. "It all comes down to budgets, I guess," he said.

Madoff answered other questions posed by Kotz: He hadn't used a lawyer for his SEC testimony in May 2006 because he thought going in without one would suggest that he had nothing to hide. He hadn't been worried, either. "I had good answers for everything," he said. "Everything made perfect sense."

And, no, he hadn't been worried when Frank DiPascali was also questioned in early 2006, he said, lying as smoothly as ever: "He didn't know anything was wrong, either." And, no, he had never created fake DTCC records to show the SEC. In fact, he insisted that the SEC investigators who looked at Avellino & Bienes in 1992 had seen that his trades were real. He said he had had no idea the two men "had thousands of clients."

Madoff's opinion, which almost seemed to be taking shape as he answered Kotz's questions, was that the SEC's relentless focus on a crime he wasn't committing blinded it to the crime he was committing—otherwise, they could easily have caught him. They "asked all the right questions, but it was still focused on front-running," he said, adding, "It never entered the SEC's mind that it was a Ponzi scheme." Even after asking for his DTCC clearinghouse account number, the SEC never checked to see if the stocks and bonds on the client statements were actually there.

"If you're looking for a Ponzi scheme, it's the first thing you do," he told Kotz.

Madoff had been astonished at that. He remembered thinking, "After all this, I got away lucky."

In a rare reflective moment, Madoff observed: "I got myself in a terrible situation. It's a nightmare." Businesslike and composed until now, he lost his grip for a moment when he reflected on the "living hell" his family was facing: "It's a tragedy, it's a nightmare." But soon he regained his footing and asserted that he did a lot of good for the industry before he did anything wrong. "The thing I feel worst about, besides the people losing money, is that I set the industry back," he said.

By now, Kotz began to wonder if Madoff himself knew where the line between truth and lies was located. Months later, one exchange that day would remain sharp and suggestive in his mind.

Did you create false documents to give to the SEC?

No, Madoff answered, almost affronted. He said he gave the SEC the same documents he gave to his customers.

But weren't those customer statements actually false documents?

No, they weren't. Madoff paused for what seemed like thirty seconds, then gave a tiny nod to reality.

"I could see how you might see them as false," he said.

THE SINS OF THE FATHER | 273

On Monday, June 22, Ike Sorkin delivered a letter to Judge Denny Chin, who would sentence Madoff the following week. "We seek neither mercy nor sympathy," Sorkin wrote. "Respectfully, we seek the justice and objectivity that have always been—and we hope always will be—the bedrock of our criminal justice system."

His letter was one of the rituals of American justice. It was Sorkin's chance to persuade Judge Chin to ignore the demands the government was making—the 150 years tallied up when Madoff agreed to plead guilty—and the forever-after prison term that Madoff's victims demanded in the e-mails and letters the prosecutors were collecting to submit to the judge.

A confidential "presentencing report" by the federal probation office had just arrived at Judge Chin's chambers. It detailed the history of Madoff's crimes and the devastating human damage they had inflicted. The report recommended a prison term of fifty years.

In his letter, Sorkin urged the judge to consider a sentence of a dozen years. Given Madoff's age and the early age at which his parents died, that would allow at least for the thin possibility that Madoff would one day be released from prison—at age eighty-three.

Sorkin acknowledged the storm of justified anger and "heart-wrenching stories of loss and deprivation" reflected in the victims' letters to the court. Those letters uniformly demanded that Madoff be locked up for the rest of his life. The victims' fury, he wrote, was "no doubt justified in light of the circumstances" of a case that involved such grave injury to so many people. Sorkin promised that Madoff "will speak to the shame he has felt and the pain he has caused" at the sentencing hearing.

Sorkin observed that the messages the victims had submitted to Judge Chin were free of the anti-Semitic vitriol and death threats contained in some of the letters that Sorkin and his client had received. But these messages still disturbed Sorkin deeply. "The unified tone of the victim statements suggests a desire for a type of mob vengeance," he wrote. "It is the duty of the court to set aside the emotion and hysteria attendant to this case and render a sentence that is just and proportionate to the conduct at issue."

When word of Sorkin's request became public, it simply poured more fuel on the fiery outrage of Madoff's victims.

On Friday, June 26, a fax machine came to life in the law office of Peter Chavkin, disgorging a legal document's signature page. When Chavkin and his client, Ruth Madoff, signed this page, she would be handing the government more than $80 million worth of property—a portfolio of municipal bonds, the Manhattan penthouse, the beach home in Montauk, the Palm Beach house, the three-bedroom apartment on the French Riviera, the boats and cars, the furniture and artwork, the Steinway piano her son Andrew had played, her fur coats, her well-worn designer handbags, the vintage jewelry, the Wedgwood china and Christofle silver, even Bernie's class ring from Hofstra, class of 1960.

She would be signing away every treasured thing she had thought was hers—until that December day when her husband revealed that her dream world had been built entirely from dreams he had stolen from other people, many of them people she had known and loved all her life.

In offering Ruth Madoff this civil settlement, the prosecutors were making some significant admissions—publicly and implicitly. Publicly, they were conceding that they might not be able to prove in court that they had a valid claim to the $14.5 million in equity that Ruth held in the Manhattan penthouse and the beachfront home in Montauk, properties purchased before the date Madoff claimed his fraud began. They were also acknowledging that, if she decided to, she could fight them in court over the other $70 million she would be handing over.

But the unspoken message behind the settlement was that the prosecutors had no criminal charges to file against Ruth Madoff. If they had had any, then this civil settlement would have been unnecessary. If she were to be indicted and convicted, they could seize every penny she had under the criminal forfeiture laws, and there would be nothing she could do to stop them.

So in exchange for agreeing to sign over these assets without a fight, Ruth was allowed to keep $2.5 million in cash to furnish herself with a new home, a new life, some kind of future.

It was perhaps the only personal exoneration she could hope for, even though it protected her only from further claims by the prosecutors. It didn't protect her from claims filed by anyone else—including Irving Picard, the bankruptcy trustee. And it certainly didn't protect her from the suspicion and insults she faced every day in the world outside this quiet law office in a tower attached to the Chrysler Building.

She signed the settlement anyway, in a firm hand, as did Chavkin. At some point, the page was faxed to Judge Chin and the federal prosecutors downtown.

The stage had now been set for Monday's performance. On June 29, spectators squeezed elbow to elbow on every polished bench in the richly decorated ceremonial courtroom on the ninth floor of the federal courthouse, with its wood-paneled walls and gilded coffered ceiling. The marshals scanned the crowd, alert for any outburst.

As was his style, Judge Chin swept gracefully onto the high, carved bench, the prosecutors and defense lawyers already positioned at tables before him. Just minutes before 10:00 AM, Bernie Madoff was brought in and seated at Ike Sorkin's side. He appeared thinner, no longer looking as carefully tailored in the familiar gray suit, white shirt, and gray tie that Ruth had been allowed to send from his apartment the previous week. He looked haggard and gray, his once-silvery hair now a lank pewter.

The four-act drama of a criminal sentencing was about to begin.

After a few curtain-raising procedures, Judge Chin invited Madoff's victims onstage. Hundreds of them had sent in letters and e-mails, and many were present in the court on this day. Nine had asked to address the court, and a microphone had been placed at the ornate rail that divided the spectators' benches from the area reserved for the lawyers and the judge.

Dominic Ambrosino, a retired New York City corrections officer, squeezed out of a crowded bench near the front. He described the life-altering decisions people had made because they believed their money was safe. His pension payout, his retirement, the proceeds from his and his wife's sale of their house, their purchase of a motor home to pursue a dream of travel—all were decisions they could not undo, decisions made only because they had trusted Madoff.

Maureen Ebel, the petite sixty-one-year-old widow who spoke at the plea hearing, aimed her first arrows at the SEC, which, "by its total incompetence and criminal negligence, has allowed a psychopath to steal from me and steal from the world." She was now working three jobs and had sold her home and many of her possessions. "The emotional toll that this has taken on me has been devastating," she said.

Multiple jobs were all that sustained Thomas Fitzmaurice and his wife, both sixty-three. Madoff "cheated his victims out of their money so that he and his wife Ruth and their two sons could live a life of luxury beyond belief," he said—a life "normally reserved for royalty, not for common thieves."

Fitzmaurice read his wife's message to Madoff. Her children have provided "constant love and support," she wrote. "You, on the other hand, Mr. Madoff, have two sons that despise you. Your wife, rightfully so, has been vilified and shunned by her friends in the community. You have left your children a legacy of shame. I have a marriage made in heaven. You have a marriage made in hell, and that is where you, Mr. Madoff, are going to return."

Carla Hirschhorn described the loss of her daughter's college tuition fund in the middle of her junior year and the frantic uncertainty of how to pay bills. "Since December 11, life has been a living hell," she said. "It feels like a nightmare we can't wake from."

Sharon Lissauer, a fragile blond model in a pale summery dress, was near tears before she began. She had trusted Madoff with everything, and he stole everything. "He has ruined so many people's lives," she said in a soft, oddly gentle voice. "He killed my spirit and shattered my dreams. He destroyed my trust in people. He destroyed my life."

Burt Ross, a charismatic older man supporting himself on two walking sticks, tallied his losses at $5 million. He then eloquently addressed Madoff's life. "What can we possibly say about Madoff?" he asked. That he was a philanthropist? "The money he gave to charities he stole." A good family man? "He leaves his grandchildren a name that mortifies them." That he was a righteous Jew? "Nobody has done more to reinforce the ugly stereotype that all we care about is money." Ross invoked Dante's *Inferno* and condemned Madoff to the lowest circle of hell.

A young man named Michael Schwartz explained that part of a trust fund Madoff had stolen from his family had been "set aside to take care of my twin brother who is mentally disabled." He concluded: "I only hope his prison sentence is long enough so that his jail cell becomes his coffin."

The next speaker was Miriam Siegman, who repeated a wish made during Madoff's plea hearing—that he be publicly tried, that the full truth come out in a courtroom before a jury, that he acknowledge "the murderous effects" of a crime that had already driven a few people to suicide.

The final speaker was Sheryl Weinstein, a well-spoken accountant and the former chief financial officer of Hadassah. In two months, her pale heart-shaped face framed by sleek blond hair would be on the cover of a memoir she was secretly writing, in which she would claim to have had a brief extramarital affair with Bernie Madoff. On this day, she said, "I felt it was important for somebody who was personally acquainted with Madoff to speak." She described "this beast who I called Madoff. He walks among us. He dresses like us. He drives and eats and drinks and speaks. Under the façade, there is truly a beast."

It was a wrenching recital, punctuated by soft sobs and steadied by anger. Whether eloquent or clumsy, each victim testified to a profound sense of betrayal—by Madoff, by the SEC, by the courts, by life.

In an earnest tone, Judge Chin thanked them and tilted his head: "Mr. Sorkin?"

The defense counsel, under the circumstances, is often little but a diversion between acts. Who could defend the man who caused all the heartbreak that had mesmerized the courtroom for nearly an hour? Yet, somehow, Sorkin had to try.

"We cannot be unmoved by what we have heard," he said. "There is no way we cannot be sensitive to the victims' suffering. This is a tragedy, as some of the victims have said, at every level. . . . We represent a deeply flawed individual—but we represent, Your Honor, a human being."

Sorkin closed simply by urging a sentence free of vengeance, free of rage. "We ask only, Your Honor, that Mr. Madoff be given understanding and fairness."

Now it was time for act two, Bernie Madoff himself.

He had a prepared speech, like his statement in March, but this one sounded more authentically like the man who existed before December 11, 2008.

"Your Honor, I cannot offer you any excuse for my behavior," he began, facing the judge. "How do you excuse betraying thousands of investors who entrusted me with their life savings? How do you excuse deceiving 200 employees who have spent most of their working life working for me? How do you excuse lying to a brother and two sons who have spent their whole adult life helping to build a successful and respected business?"

There was a breath-long pause. "How do you excuse lying and deceiving a wife who stood by you for 50 years—and still stands by you?"

He inched toward a smudged sketch of what he had done. "I believed when I started this problem—this crime—that it would be something I would be able to work my way out of, but that became impossible. The harder I tried, the deeper I dug myself into a hole." He was accustomed to making trading mistakes, he said. They were part of his business; he could forgive himself for those. But he had made more than a mistake in this instance, he'd made "a terrible error in judgment. I refused to accept the fact—could *not* accept the fact that for once in my life, I had failed. I couldn't admit that failure and that was a tragic mistake."

On paper, his words seemed deeply remorseful, although they were delivered in a bleak, leaden voice: "I am responsible for a great deal of suffering and pain. I understand that. I live in a tormented state now, knowing of all the pain and suffering I have created. I left a legacy of shame, as some of my victims have pointed out, to my family and grandchildren. That's something I will live with for the rest of my life."

He tried, too late, to repair the damage caused by months of standing mute. "People have accused me of being silent and not being sympathetic. That is not true," he said. "People have accused my wife of being silent and not being sympathetic. Nothing could be further from the truth. She cries herself to sleep every night knowing of all the pain and suffering I have caused—and I am tormented by that, as well."

He said that he and Ruth had remained silent on the advice of their attorneys. But he added that Ruth would release a written statement later in the day expressing her anguish and sympathy for his victims. "I ask you to listen to that," Madoff said. "She is sincere, and all I ask [of] you is to listen to her."

In a way, the sheer impossibility of making anything better or different seemed to suck the life out of his final sentences. He almost acknowledged this: "Nothing I can say will correct the things that I have done. . . . There is nothing I can do that will make anyone feel better."

He concluded: "But I will live with this pain, with this torment, for the rest of my life. I apologize to my victims"—and now he abruptly turned in place and looked at the crowded courtroom, his face haggard with deep gray triangles under his eyes—"I will turn and face you and say I am sorry. I know that doesn't help you."

He turned back to the bench. "Your Honor, thank you for listening to me." He sat down.

The government's case, too, was a short familiar solo before the final act. Everyone knew that the prosecutors wanted a sentence of 150 years; they had laid out their reasons in a memo made public a few days earlier. "For more than 20 years, he stole ruthlessly and without remorse," said Lisa Baroni, one of the prosecutors. "Thousands of people placed their trust in him and he lied repeatedly to all of them."

But the climax in this drama could come only from Judge Chin.

"Despite all the emotion in the air, I do not agree with the suggestion that victims and others are seeking mob vengeance," he observed. He agreed with Sorkin that Madoff was entitled to a sentence "determined objectively, and without hysteria or undue emotion."

But he did not linger there. "Objectively speaking, the fraud here was staggering," the judge went on. "It spanned more than 20 years." Perhaps Madoff did not begin to mingle his fraud's cash with his firm's assets until the late 1990s, the judge continued, "but it is clear that the fraud began earlier."

Judge Chin found no mitigating factors. "In a white-collar fraud case such as this, I would expect to see letters from family and friends and colleagues. But not a single letter has been submitted attesting to Mr. Madoff's good deeds or good character or civic or charitable activities. The absence of such support is telling."

Given Madoff's age, Judge Chin acknowledged that any sentence above twenty years was effectively a life sentence. "But the symbolism is important," he added. Madoff's betrayal had left many people, not just his victims, "doubting our financial institutions, our financial system, our government's ability to regulate and protect, and, sadly, even themselves."

The victims were not "succumbing to the temptation of mob vengeance," he concluded. "Rather, they are doing what they are supposed to be doing—placing their trust in our system of justice. . . . The knowledge that Mr. Madoff has been punished to the fullest extent of the law may, in some small measure, help these victims in their healing process."

He paused. "Mr. Madoff, please stand," he instructed.

Madoff and Sorkin stood together.

"It is the judgment of this court that the defendant, Bernard L.

Madoff, shall be and hereby is sentenced to a term of imprisonment of 150 years—"

A cheer from the benches stopped him but was quickly stifled. He continued to itemize the sentence for each felony count. "As a technical matter," he added, "the sentence must be expressed . . . in months; 150 years is equivalent to 1,800 months." A few details were then added to the record, and Madoff was advised that he had limited rights to appeal.

The curtain came down: "We are adjourned."

Madoff was once again handcuffed and led out a side door. At seventy-one, even if he had two more lifetimes ahead of him, he would spend them both in prison.

∽

Just three days after Madoff's sentencing came the closing of another chapter in the story of his fraud. Five miles uptown from the U.S. courthouse, a female U.S. marshal stood in the closet of the master bedroom in the penthouse apartment on East Sixty-fourth Street, as Ruth Madoff negotiated what she could pack into cartons and take with her.

She was leaving behind the appliances, the furniture, the artwork, the designer clothing, the gowns, the top-end fur coats—all the "insured and readily saleable personal property" in what was once her home. She had been told that she could keep items that could not be readily sold, and she hoped to keep the well-worn, thirty-year-old fur coat she was holding, which was arguably too old to have any resale value.

Maybe we could get a dollar for it, the marshal replied. The fur coat stayed.

So did her used golf shoes, three used golf gloves, thirty miscellaneous used golf balls, several crocheted golf club covers, seven Ella Fitzgerald commemorative euro-denominated postage stamps found in a coin purse, and a 1967 quarter fished out of a no-name black leather shoulder bag.

Meanwhile, the television cameras had settled outside the apartment building, somehow alerted to the fact that the U.S. Marshals would be taking over today. Ruth Madoff discovered the gauntlet and managed to slip out of the building, for the last time, through a back entrance.

The day before, the *Wall Street Journal* had reported online that after six months of investigation, there was no evidence that Ruth had been involved in her husband's fraud.

∞

Much remained a mystery about Bernie Madoff's crime, even after he pleaded guilty in March 2009. But one thing, it seemed, that everybody knew was true was this: his wife and sons were guilty, too.

From the first weeks after his arrest, unidentified "former prosecutors" and "criminal lawyers who have followed the case" and "legal sources" were repeatedly quoted in various media outlets asserting that Ruth, Mark, and Andrew Madoff were under investigation and would soon be indicted. Glossy magazine articles would speculate carefully; garish Internet blogs would accuse recklessly; television commentators would wink and nod knowingly. All that fierce, smug certainty about their guilt—unsupported by any cited facts—effectively drove Madoff's immediate family into exile.

In an era of hypermedia, with cell phone paparazzi and self-defined Internet commentators constantly on the alert for ways to attract attention, it is worth noting that these attacks on the Madoff family were a sharp departure from the typical public reaction to cases of white-collar crime, going back more than a century.

Of course, such criminals—confidence men, embezzlers, crooked politicians, fraudsters of all kinds—were attacked savagely by the press and the public when their crimes came to light. But their wives and children were almost never included in those attacks; rather, they were almost always ignored or, at the very least, quickly left alone. There were a few exceptions where criminal charges were actually filed against a close relative, who was then pulled to the whipping post of public attention. In general, however, even the wives and children of executed murderers were left to rebuild their lives in relative obscurity, unless they sought the spotlight themselves.

The treatment over the years of organized-crime defendants is instructive. Despite widespread fascination with the murderous escapades of so-called "Mafia dons" and crime-family "capos," it was extremely rare for any attention to fall on the elderly Mrs. Mafia Don or the capos' children—even though a realist might have wondered how much they knew about why their husband or father had asked all his closest buddies to wear guns and sleep on mattresses in the garage. On rare occasions, a mobster's relatives actively courted publicity. (The Gotti family comes to mind.) But those who didn't were routinely ignored by the media and certainly were never publicly and repeatedly accused of complicity in their husbands' or fathers' crimes.

Yet the public outcry against Ruth Madoff and her sons began almost from the instant of Madoff's arrest and did not cease. By the time he pleaded guilty, it was deafening.

From the beginning, however, there were facts in the Madoff case that just didn't seem to be consistent with the family's guilt.

First, there was the fact that none of them fled the country. Perhaps Bernie Madoff, seventy years old at the time of his confession, felt too old and tired to live as a wealthy fugitive; and perhaps Ruth, even if she were guilty and faced arrest and a lifelong imprisonment, would not leave without him. But his two sons, if they were guilty, had the opportunity, the means, and the motive to flee. The end was clearly in sight weeks in advance, there was still a princely sum in the bank, and they and their families were young and relatively portable. Surely Madoff, before turning himself in, would have handed his sons the keys to the company jet and enough cash to let them live comfortably beyond the reach of the law for the rest of their lives. After all, if they were his accomplices, their only other option would have been to stay and go to prison.

And yet Madoff did not flee—and neither did his wife or sons.

Then, there was his confession. Some hostile theorists immediately argued that Madoff and his guilty sons staged his confession so they could turn him in and thereby deflect suspicion from themselves. But this would have been a worthless gesture unless they all could have been absolutely sure that no incriminating evidence would surface later and none of their other low-level accomplices would finger the sons in a bid for leniency—assumptions that were not remotely realistic if the sons were actually guilty. Moreover, if Madoff truly believed anyone could be insulated from suspicion simply by turning him in, wouldn't he have arranged for that to be Ruth?

Logic aside, assumptions about the family's guilt began to run up against the fact that, as the Madoff investigation progressed, the predicted arrests of his wife and sons simply did not happen.

It is true that the legal bar for proving that Ruth, Mark, or Andrew Madoff shared Bernie Madoff's guilt was high. To tie them to the Ponzi scheme, prosecutors had to do more than prove that they had somehow suspected the fraud, or had stumbled across it, and looked away. It is almost never a federal offense to fail to report a crime one merely observes. Instead, prosecutors would have had to prove that they knowingly helped plan the fraud, carry it out, or cover it up.

Yet for two years into the investigation, with other suspected accomplices quietly trying to negotiate deals with prosecutors and earn a little mercy from the courts, neither the government nor those accomplices made any public (or artfully leaked) accusations against Ruth, Mark, or Andrew. Indeed, the family members were never even formally notified by prosecutors, as would be required, that they were the subject or the target of a criminal investigation.

Of course, all those accumulating details do not mean that prosecutors will not act against Madoff's family at some point in the future; new evidence could surface, even years from now. And, apart from the fraud, the family remains vulnerable to federal tax charges arising from their casual use of company cash, credit cards, and low-cost loans. But what those accumulating details *do* mean is that there was insufficient evidence to support even a formal notification that they were the subjects of a criminal investigation during the months and years when they were being repeatedly accused in public of being Bernie Madoff's accomplices.

Another fact, visible very early in the case, suggests that the prosecutors did not believe that Madoff's sons, at least, knew anything about the crime before their father's confession: Mark and Andrew Madoff continued to be represented by the same lawyer, Martin Flumenbaum.

Typically, no two suspects in a criminal investigation can be represented by the same attorney, for reasons so obvious that most people don't even need to reflect on them. What if Suspects A and B are sharing a lawyer when Suspect A decides to cut a deal and testify against Suspect B? Who will help him negotiate with the prosecutors—the same lawyer who also is honor-bound to look out for Suspect B's best interests? Definitely not.

It would have been unethical for Flumenbaum to represent both brothers if he had known they were under criminal investigation and might best be served by turning on each other and seeking a deal with prosecutors. Even if the two brothers had sworn a guilty allegiance to each other behind some cover story, it would have been irregular for prosecutors to permit Flumenbaum to represent both sons if a criminal case were secretly in the works against either or both of them.

Yet Flumenbaum remained on duty, alone. Experienced defense lawyers understood the implications; the public, by and large, did not.

As early as December 16, 2008, the *New York Times* reported that investigators had found no evidence linking the sons to Madoff's Ponzi scheme—except as victims and as witnesses to their father's confession. Nevertheless, Mark and Andrew Madoff were vilified on the Internet, insulted in public, sued in court, accused in books and magazine articles, and pursued by photographers wherever they went.

The brothers had grown up in the shadow of an autocratic, controlling father whom the whole family considered a genius and to whom their mother constantly deferred. Despite the difficulties his personality created in their relationship, they apparently loved and admired him. At the same moment their father's crime had destroyed that relationship, it had shoved both of them from lives of near anonymity into a blistering media spotlight, where nothing could be protected as private.

Andrew Madoff's seventeen-year marriage to his wife, Deborah, had already broken apart, and they had been separated for more than a year. The divorce papers were filed on the same day as his father's arrest, a coincidence that provided tabloid fodder for days. There were news reports—untrue, his friends would later insist—that some parents of his two young children's friends grew leery of including them on playdates, allegedly worried that their own children might get caught in any ugly verbal cross fire from angry victims. At the time of the arrest, Andrew was living with his fiancée, Catherine Hooper, an accomplished woman whose background as a fly-fishing guide was promptly dissected down to the bone on the gossip circuit.

One of Andrew's early expeditions out of their apartment after his father's arrest was to pick up a take-out meal. It ended in a sidewalk scuffle with an angry former Madoff trader, who recognized him, accused him loudly of being a criminal, and shouted crude sexual insults at Hooper. At that, Andrew exchanged punches with the trader and drove away in fury. Later, when he calmed down, he turned himself in to the police. No charges were filed.

Andrew's battle with cancer, which had begun with the discovery of a swollen lymph node in his neck in March 2003, seemed to mark a break with his former life at the firm. At thirty-seven, he had lymphoma, tentatively diagnosed as a rare and almost always fatal form called mantle cell lymphoma, although a firm diagnosis would prove elusive. He underwent six weeks of treatment and "came out of the experience with a shaved head, a newfound interest in yoga and an outward soulfulness I hadn't seen before," his younger cousin Roger noted in a posthumously published memoir about his own losing battle with cancer. After his diagnosis and treatment, Andrew took more vacation time, spent more time with his two children, embraced his lifelong piano study, and talked openly about the importance of enjoying each day because "life is short."

Mark Madoff's life also became a fishbowl. All of tabloid New York knew that he and his second wife, Stephanie, had a new baby in February 2009, Mark's fourth child and their second child together. Everyone in the Madoff blogosphere knew that neither Ruth nor Bernie had seen their new grandson because Mark, like Andrew, had avoided any contact with his parents since the day of the confession. In months to come, everyone with a television set or computer would know that Mark's wife petitioned the court to change her own and their children's last names to "Morgan," to avoid the stigma and danger of the Madoff name—a name her husband could not shed so easily.

Most people who knew the family thought that Bernie felt closer to Mark, who was warmer and less cerebral than Andrew, although each son always got a hug and kiss from his father whenever Madoff returned to the trading floor after an extended vacation. One longtime friend recalled going to dinner with Ruth and Bernie one evening in 1999, when Mark's first marriage was splintering apart after nearly a decade. "Bernie spent 90 percent of the dinner outside talking with Mark, sort of holding his hand," this friend remembered. Also, Mark was more likely than Andrew to join their father in glad-handing the crowd at securities industry events and the annual employee parties at Christmas and on the beach at Montauk.

Whatever their personal dramas, though, both sons had official titles at the Madoff firm, titles that gave them legal responsibilities as licensed Wall Street professionals. So both of them were sitting ducks for civil litigation by the SEC, which could accuse them of a failure to adequately supervise the business, especially after the firm began to receive such steady infusions of capital from their father's secret fraud. But as late as the fall of 2010 federal regulators had not made even that anticipated accusation against the Madoff sons.

To be sure, the regulators who might make that accusation had failed to detect Madoff's devious strategies, too. This was the curious paradox in the public's certainty about the family's guilt: no one seriously disputed that Madoff had successfully and repeatedly hidden his crime from regulators, foreign accounting firms, hedge fund due-diligence teams, and his savviest professional investors. Why was it so implausible that he had hidden it from his wife, who had no official role at the firm, and from his sons, who worked in a separate part of the business and learned only as much about his private, closely held investment management business as Madoff chose to tell them?

Even so, there was nothing to prevent regulators from accusing the Madoff sons of failing to supervise their father's business.

There would be a certain irony if they were held responsible for what happened in the bowels of their father's brokerage firm, because their father had never even made them his partners. They were simply at-will employees, albeit extremely well-paid ones. Their father was the sole owner of Bernard L. Madoff Investment Securities; nobody disputes that he had always been almost obsessively in charge.

With their father's confession and arrest, any of their assets that had not been consumed in their father's crime were certain to be claimed for his victims—on the grounds that everything they got from the firm over most, if not all, of their years of employment had been their father's ill-gotten gains. The business they expected to inherit had been destroyed, along with the personal and professional reputations on which they might have built new careers. Half the world thought they were criminals, and the other half thought they were too naïve or lazy to discover that their father was one.

Although neither the SEC nor the U.S. attorney filed any court cases against Mark or Andrew in the first two years after their father's arrest, almost everyone else did. It increasingly began to seem that personal bankruptcy would be the only way they would be able to preserve any assets at all for their families. Whatever their skills or experience, it would be a brave employer indeed who openly offered a job on Wall Street to one of Bernie Madoff's sons.

&

Ruth Madoff was in an even more precarious situation in the months after her husband's arrest. Her sons at least still had their young families, their in-laws, their closest friends. But her decision to stand by Bernie had cut her off from her sons and almost everyone else in her world except her husband's lawyers.

Within a week, she was being insulted in print, caricatured in cartoons, and openly accused of criminality by some of Madoff's victims. She was badgered by crowds of photographers on the few occasions she left the apartment to shop or, later, to pay a weekly visit to her husband in jail. The attacks on the Internet were especially virulent. One cultural anthropologist memorably observed that Ruth was "perceived as the succubus to Bernie's incubus"—in plain English, a life-sucking female demon working hand in hand with an equally evil male demon.

Her only proven offense? Not walking out on her husband after his confession. According to a confidential source, she later explained her decision like this: "I had a love affair with someone for fifty years— I couldn't abandon him, even though he had committed this terrible crime. If you had a grown child who committed a terrible crime, what would you do? Would you abandon him?" So she stayed, apparently staggered by the crime but somehow unable to desert the man who had committed it.

Some of her relatives and a few close confidantes privately stood by her, even though her husband had robbed them, but none could step up to defend her in public. Many lifelong friends shunned her, some because of constraints imposed by their lawyers and others out of justifiable fury over Madoff's betrayal of them. She was unwelcome at her hairdresser's, shunned by her florist, turned away at a favorite restaurant. Her own sons blamed her for not walking out on their father, although they did not believe she was his accomplice.

Overnight, a woman whose peers had never considered her lifestyle garish or vulgar found herself accused of greedy, gaudy, nearly criminal excess—as if the East Sixty-fourth Street apartment suddenly had become a full marble-clad floor at Trump Tower, and Montauk had started parading its wealth with more swagger than any of the Hamptons. There were frequent breathless stories predicting her imminent arrest even after the civil forfeiture deal leaving her $2.5 million was approved by Judge Chin.

By then, it looked as if she would lose even that. On July 29, 2009, Ruth Madoff was sued personally by Irving Picard, who demanded the return of $44.8 million that he claimed she had received from the Madoff firm in the six years before it was bankrupted by her husband's crime. The complaint detailed more than a hundred wire transfers from the firm to her personal accounts or to companies in which she had invested. It did not cite any evidence that she had participated in the fraud or had even known about it.

After forfeiting $80 million to her husband's victims, Ruth Madoff could not possibly meet the trustee's demands. She did not have $44.8 million—she had exactly $2.5 million and now feared most of that would be required to settle the case with Picard.

Picard was not trying to get blood from a stone. He simply wanted a judgment against Ruth Madoff that would obligate her to pay any future earnings—from a memoir, for example—into the victims' asset pool. Her lawyer, Peter Chavkin, was outraged and said so. Bernie Madoff could not comment publicly, but he was equally furious. Any inclination he might have had to cooperate with Picard—and, admittedly, little had been evident—nearly evaporated the day he learned that his wife had been sued. It would be more than a year before he would even meet with Picard's legal team.

Could Ruth's life become more humiliating? It could. In August, one of her husband's victims, Sheryl Weinstein, the accountant and former chief financial officer of Hadassah who had spoken so eloquently about Madoff's beastliness at his sentencing, published the memoir in which she claimed that she had had a brief sexual affair with him in the mid-1990s. The tell-all was studded with hurtful comments about Ruth and her sons—that she "had Bernie on a short leash" and "was intimidated by the social circles in which they were traveling," and that Bernie's comments about his sons made them seem "spoiled and obnoxious."

Of course, it is possible that Madoff had affairs; he was an attractive, seductive man, and every marriage encounters some rocky terrain at times that can tempt spouses to stray. But, in a less hysterical environment, even this might have been seen as proof that Ruth did not know about her husband's crime: What lunatic would risk cheating on a wife who knew he was a crook and could turn him in with one phone call, a wife whose lawyers certainly could have cut her a pretty good deal in exchange for nailing him? If Ruth were Madoff's accomplice and caught him cheating, he risked far more than the mere fury of a woman scorned.

Time and again, Ruth Madoff's lawyers tersely denied or refused to comment on the more outlandish allegations about her. But when Weinstein's memoir was published, Chavkin saw a teachable moment and seized it. He said that Ruth had been totally unaware of both her husband's crime and the purported affair.

If the affair really happened, Chavkin continued, it "stands as a powerful reminder to those who say Ruth must have known of her husband's criminal scheme, that there are some things that some spouses—however close they are—do not share with each other."

Still, the public's appetite for dirt about this fragile sixty-eight-year-old woman seemed bottomless. More than eighteen months after Madoff's arrest, ABC News ran a news story and a brief Web site video segment, complete with telescopic camera footage, trumpeting a hot new discovery: Ruth Madoff had changed her hair color from blond to light auburn, perhaps because she thought that would allow her to move incognito through Manhattan. Little chance of that, obviously.

There is absolutely no denying that Ruth, Mark, and Andrew Madoff would have deserved all these hardships—and worse—if they had indeed been guilty of participating in the vicious crime that shattered so many people's lives, or even of suspecting it and keeping quiet. If they were accomplices, they deserved to be more than vilified in the media; they deserved to be indicted, convicted, sued, ruined, and imprisoned for life.

But in the oceans of ink and galaxies of cyberspace devoted to Ruth Madoff and her sons, few, if any, commentators asked the obvious question: What if they were innocent?

Perhaps they simply trusted Bernie Madoff, without question—as all his victims did. Perhaps they honestly assumed they were the lucky beneficiaries of his obsessively private but hugely successful hedge fund business, as the heirs of any Wall Street billionaire would. Perhaps, if they did ask him, he bamboozled them with the same phony paper trail that had fooled regulators for years.

That would be an uncomfortable truth.

Thousands of Madoff's victims suffered enormously from his betrayal of their financial trust—indeed, their lives were nearly ruined. Although most still had their families and friends, they had lost their money, their place in society, their sense of security about the future, their confidence in their own judgment—they had lost it all in an instant, in a heartbeat.

Ruth, Mark, and Andrew Madoff lost all of those things, too—all their money, their social position, their sense of security, their confidence in their own judgment, any hope for a better future. And in the same heartbeat, they also lost almost every cherished relationship in their lives, including their connections to one another.

If Ruth Madoff was innocent, she learned in an instant that she had been married for nearly fifty years to a living, breathing lie. She lost every happy memory, every scrapbook moment of their life together. Behind his mask, the husband she still adored, her sweetheart since she was thirteen years old, was actually an accomplished criminal who had been stealing for decades from thousands of people, including almost every member of her family and virtually all of their friends.

If it was true that Mark and Andrew Madoff were innocent, they learned in a heartbeat that their father had lied to them with every lecture about life, every pretense of honesty, every gift, every holiday. He had lied with every luxury he presented as the harvest of his genius and hard work, when it actually was all just loot from his crimes, some of it stolen from them and from people they all loved. The firm they thought they were helping to build was the scene of a historic fraud. Some of the employees they had trusted may have been their father's accomplices. He had destroyed their future, and he had also destroyed their past. They had nothing left of their father, not even their memories.

Overnight, they all became social pariahs, scorned, slandered, sued, even physically threatened. No one but hired hands would defend them in public and few would publicly admit feeling any pity for them at all. And that might well be the case for as long as they lived—even if prosecutors never filed any charges against them. Without a single documented fact placed into the record, the supreme court of public opinion had already indicted, convicted, and banished them all, without appeal.

And that was exactly what they deserved, if they were guilty.

Yet if Ruth, Mark, and Andrew were innocent, then all three of them were Bernie Madoff's victims, too—just possibly, his most damaged victims. But this was not a possibility anyone was willing to acknowledge in public in the summer of 2009. It was not something many of Madoff's victims would ever acknowledge.

15

THE WHEELS OF JUSTICE

The fog of suspicion that engulfed the Madoff family would be especially thick around Peter Madoff.

Peter worked at his older brother's shoulder for almost forty years, filling his gaps and constructing the framework of technology that had made his firm so admired in the industry. Their offices were never more than a dozen steps apart. They supported each other through dreadful tragedies and celebrated great achievements together.

The intimacy of Peter Madoff's relationship with his brother, both in and out of the office, left him more vulnerable to civil lawsuits and criminal investigation than any other member of the Madoff family. He had been a senior executive and the chief compliance officer for the Madoff firm, and the SEC could conceivably hold him accountable for failing to prevent or discover his brother's crime, even if he was never officially accused of knowing about it. Regulators would argue that, as a lawyer and licensed securities professional, he could not have failed to discover the crime if he had been doing his job properly.

Peter had signing authority for one of the firm's bank accounts until about 1985. Although he was not an accountant by training or a partner in the firm, he could have gotten access to the firm's general ledgers and might have seen the creative accounting and emergency loans arranged during the cash crisis in 2005 and early 2006, despite the awful distraction of his son's illness during those frantic months. And, as chief operating officer of Madoff's investment advisory business, he arguably should have made it his business to know what was happening on the seventeenth floor, however much his brother tried to shoo him away.

Like everyone else in the family, Peter was the target of lawsuits by Madoff victims. In late March 2009, he was sued by Andrew Ross Samuels, the grandson of Martin J. Joel Jr., the longtime Madoff broker and friend. Peter was the trustee of the college fund that Joel set up for his grandson, a trust fund totally wiped out by Bernie's fraud. Peter settled that lawsuit by midsummer, but by then he was tangled in court in New Jersey in a lawsuit filed by U.S. senator Frank Lautenberg's two grown children and their family foundation, which had lost about $9 million in the Ponzi scheme.

That lawsuit argued that Peter, by virtue of his position at his brother's firm, was responsible for the damage done by the fraud, whether he knew about it or not. The paperwork in the Lautenberg litigation revealed that Peter Madoff had repeatedly asserted his Fifth Amendment rights at a civil deposition, saying that the prosecutors had advised him that he was the subject of a criminal investigation. The most serious status prosecutors assign in a criminal case is to identify someone as a "target" of an investigation; being identified as a "subject" is less conclusive but, for Peter Madoff, no less worrisome.

How could Peter not have known? Sure, he was the perpetual kid brother, and he was never made a partner in the business. Still, how could Bernie have hidden his crimes from Peter for so many years? Even people who knew Peter Madoff and trusted his integrity had a hard time finding plausible answers to that question in the weeks and months after Bernie's arrest.

Peter's lawyer, John R. "Rusty" Wing, answered every inquiry by repeating what he had said from the first: that his client had not known about or participated in his brother's fraud.

By the time the criminal investigation entered its third year, no criminal charges had been filed against Peter, nor had the SEC lodged a civil complaint over his handling of his supervisory duties at his brother's firm. But, of all the Madoffs, it was Peter whose legal fate was surely the most uncertain.

The seesaw of the Lautenberg case perfectly captured that persistent uncertainty.

In September 2009 the presiding federal judge denied Peter's motion to dismiss the case, citing factual disputes about whether he had exercised enough control within the firm to bear some of the blame for his brother's fraud. Yet, in November 2010, the same judge denied the Lautenbergs' motion for a summary judgment in their favor. It wasn't enough, the judge said, to argue that Peter Madoff simply could not have been deceived or misled about what his brother was doing. The judge recognized that Peter's position at the firm, "his many years of close association with his brother," and the "gross nature" of the fraud "would cast substantial suspicion about Defendant's culpable involvement in those activities." But, he concluded, "suspicions based upon titles without specific evidence of conduct and responsibilities cannot be the basis of legal judgments." So far, the judge said, that specific evidence had not been presented.

After suing Ruth Madoff for $44 million in July 2009, Irving Picard filed a clawback lawsuit on October 2 against Peter Madoff, Mark and Andrew Madoff, and Peter's daughter, Shana, also a compliance officer at the defunct firm.

But that carefully drafted lawsuit—written by people who had issued hundreds of subpoenas for documents, conducted dozens of interviews, and examined more of Madoff's internal records than anyone with the possible exception of the FBI—did not provide any evidence that Peter or any of the other family defendants had been Bernie Madoff's accomplices. To the contrary, the suit flatly said that the trustee was *not* accusing them of knowing about the fraud until Bernie Madoff confessed—although this careful phrasing was ignored by those convinced of the family's guilt. Rather, the lawsuit simply asserted that the Madoff family executives should have discovered the fraud and could have prevented it had they not been "completely derelict" in their professional duties. "Simply put, if the family members had been doing their jobs, honestly and faithfully, the Madoff Ponzi scheme might never have succeeded, or continued for so long," the trustee's brief argued.

In a subsequent court filing, David Sheehan made the trustee's position even clearer. The trustee "has not taken on the burden of proving criminal complicity or common law fraud by these defendants," he wrote. "By so strenuously denying [that] they knowingly participated in the Ponzi scheme, the defendants have moved to dismiss a case the trustee did not bring." Peter Madoff's lawyers were quick to point out in court that "the trustee's concession is significant: in his year-and-a-half investigation, he plainly has uncovered no evidence that Peter Madoff was aware of or involved in his brother's fraud."

It made no difference. Armchair analysts without access to any of the evidence available to Picard still assumed that all the family defendants, including Peter, had been Bernie's accomplices, and they regularly predicted their arrest. Some victims publicly referred to the Madoffs as an organized-crime family.

Picard's lawsuit sought the roughly $200 million that had been withdrawn from Madoff family accounts, as well as unspecified damages and the rejection of any claims the family might have for SIPC relief.

At the same time, all over the world, the giant feeder funds were being sued by their own investors—although Picard insisted he had first claim on any of those funds' assets. The same was true for the minor feeder funds, smaller pension advisory firms, and individual investment managers, who were being sued across the country, in Europe, and in the Caribbean. As the stack of lawsuits mounted, the allegation was always the same: "You knew, *or you should have known*, that Madoff was a fraud."

These lawsuits cited Harry Markopolos's red flags and the early warnings that a few alert bankers and hedge fund consultants had shared with their clients. They cited the 2001 article in *Barron's*, the occasional errors in the account statements, the impossibly consistent returns. Given all those warning signals, how could any financially sophisticated person have failed to suspect Madoff's fraud?

But the line dividing those who should have been suspicious from those who couldn't have been expected to detect Madoff's fraud was extremely difficult to draw. It became a bitter joke on Wall Street that the Madoff case proved there was no such thing as a "sophisticated investor." Even financially astute people could look at worrisome facts and draw reassuring conclusions, and even a worrisome conclusion could be explained as sloppy paperwork or obsessive privacy. It did not automatically point to a massive fraud. Apparently, trust in Bernie Madoff could blind a hedge fund manager as easily as it could blind a retired retailer's widow.

Without doubt, there were signs that should have made even unso-phisticated investors pause before investing with Madoff. The firm's Web site did not mention his advisory services, his "hedge fund," or his customer accounts. As the years went by, his account statements remained primitive, printed and mailed, while customers at Fidelity or Merrill Lynch could check their accounts online. Some were warned by Madoff not to talk about being his investors. For most of his career, he was not registered with the SEC as an investment adviser, surely something a small pension plan trustee or IRA investor would have noticed. True, he paid relatively modest returns—roughly equal to an S&P 500 index mutual fund—but his results were far less volatile and, hence, much safer than an index fund. How was that possible? If he was a lot safer than an index fund, shouldn't his returns have been a lot lower?

As Madoff's victims sought redress, the question of who should have known would split the world cleanly into two groups. One group looked at Madoff's stature in the industry, his long track record with his investors, his obvious wealth, and his phony but immensely convincing paper trail—voluminous account statements, simulated DTCC screens, bogus trading terminals for conducting fake trades—and asked, "How could his victims have ever figured it out?" The other group looked at the red flags—the anomalies, the impossible scale, the implausible consistency, the secrecy, the whispered warnings on Wall Street—and asked, "How could his victims *not* have known?"

In truth, the answer to whether you should have known depended on who you were, what your personal circumstances were, how much you trusted Wall Street—indeed, how much you trusted life in general. The world wanted a single answer; in fact, there were thousands, each different, each debatable, and each utterly academic in the aftermath.

It was indisputable that the SEC should have caught Madoff, and would have, except for its woefully inadequate investigative skills. But it is equally true that all his middle-income victims could have protected themselves from ruin simply by sticking with familiar heavily regulated investments, such as mutual funds and bank CDs, and avoiding the less regulated hedge fund environment—not to mention the totally undocumented promises of casual feeder funds such as Avellino & Bienes.

Still, all investors who are honest with themselves will realize that Madoff's less sophisticated middle-class victims probably were no less diligent in doing their financial homework, or any more trusting in picking their investments, than most investors were in those galloping, giddy days before the 2008 meltdown. So many people were trying to manage their retirement savings in their spare moments, with too little training and too many other things to do. So they substituted trust and gut instincts for the fine print and legalese that regulators expected them to study. Some trusted Vanguard and Citibank, and others trusted Madoff—but it was a leap of faith for everybody.

That should have worried everyone much more than it apparently did.

∽

At 2:45 PM on Tuesday, August 11, 2009, Frank DiPascali entered a federal courtroom in downtown Manhattan. Smiling and seeming relaxed, he embraced members of his legal team, led by Marc Mukasey, and shared a few wisecracks with one of the attorneys.

At 3:05 PM, Judge Richard J. Sullivan strode to his high-backed black leather chair on the bench. Tall and attractive, Sullivan had a deep, mellow voice that must have mesmerized juries when he was a federal prosecutor. In simple terms, he explained the purpose of the hearing to the two dozen Madoff victims in the courtroom.

"On Friday, I received notice that Mr. DiPascali was waiving indictment," he said. The defendant had agreed to plead guilty to ten separate criminal counts, including conspiracy to commit securities fraud and tax evasion.

The judge walked DiPascali through the litany of questions designed to show that he understood what he was doing. He did; his mind was "crystal clear," he said.

Prosecutor Marc Litt summarized the government's case, which accused DiPascali of having conspired with Bernie Madoff "and others" to violate the law. He had misled regulators with faked records, had given perjured testimony to the SEC, had wired money around to simulate phony commission income, and had aided and abetted other unnamed people in carrying out these crimes, Litt said.

DiPascali was facing a prison term of 125 years, but Litt explained that the government had agreed that if he provided "substantial assistance," prosecutors would ask the court to be lenient in imposing a sentence.

DiPascali then stood and read a statement describing his crimes.

"From the early 1990s until December of 2008, I helped Bernie Madoff and other people carry out a fraud," he said.

He recalled having been hired by Madoff in 1975, right after high school. "By 1990 or so, Bernie Madoff was a mentor to me, and a lot more. I was loyal to him," DiPascali said. "I ended up being loyal to a terrible, terrible fault."

For years, he continued, he had handled inquiries from Madoff's investors. But there was "one single fact" that he did not tell clients or regulators. "No purchases or sales of securities were actually taking place in their accounts. It was all fake, it was all fictitious."

He took a breath. "It was wrong and I knew it was wrong at the time, sir," he said.

"When did you realize that?" Judge Sullivan asked.

"In the late '80s or early '90s," he said—slightly amending his earlier statement that the fraud had begun in "the early 1990s."

He admitted that he had created a lot of the false paperwork that had fooled the SEC so many times, and that he had lied directly to the regulators during his testimony in January 2006.

Why did he lie to the SEC lawyers?

"To throw them off their tracks, sir," DiPascali answered.

"Did you have the sense that they were on the track?" the judge asked, with evident skepticism about those hapless investigations.

"Yes, sir."

DiPascali concluded, his voice breaking, "I don't know how I went from an eighteen-year-old kid who needed a job to where I am standing before you today. I never intended to hurt anyone. I apologize to every victim. I am very, very, very sorry."

Litt quickly explained that the fraud had started "at least as early as the 1980s," but he offered no evidence for this. As the prosecutor addressed the court, DiPascali, seated at the defense table, wiped away a tear, and Mukasey put a steadying hand on his shoulder.

All that was left was for the judge to hear from the victims. The only speaker was Miriam Siegman, who once again urged that the judge reject the plea agreement and send the case to trial to satisfy "the public's quest for truth."

"I am sensitive to the points you've made," Judge Sullivan responded, "but there's a difference between a criminal trial and a truth commission." He added, "I don't believe the quest for truth ends today."

He accepted DiPascali's plea—but he stunned Mukasey and Litt by refusing to accept their deal to let DiPascali remain free on bail.

The defendant was facing a "fairly astronomical" prison sentence, the judge said. And his participation in a twenty-year fraud "doesn't give me great confidence." Was there enough cooperation in the world to trim a meaningful amount off a 125-year prison term? "I am not persuaded," he said.

He ordered DiPascali to jail. At 5:18 PM, Madoff's protégé, in obvious shock and distress, was handcuffed and taken from the courtroom. Months would pass before his lawyers and the government could finally come up with a bail package the judge would accept.

The investigations of Madoff's crimes in Europe were announced with great fanfare in the weeks immediately after his arrest, but by the summer of 2009 they had produced few results.

Official interest in Sonja Kohn's once-prestigious Bank Medici remained high. In April, Kohn was questioned privately in a Viennese court for three hours, with officials from the U.S. Justice Department, the SEC, and the FBI in attendance. And, in May, Austria's senior financial regulator revoked Bank Medici's banking license. But Kohn continued to deny that she had been anything but another of Madoff's trusting victims, and there was little public evidence of a formal case being developed.

The Serious Fraud Office in London launched an investigation of Madoff's British affiliate within days of his arrest. But for months there was no news of any indictments. In the early months of 2010, the SFO would quietly announce that it was closing its examination without filing charges against anyone.

Acting on complaints from investors, Swiss prosecutors were looking into the role of Banco Santander's Optimal hedge fund unit in Geneva, and that of other fund managers who invested with Madoff or one of his feeder funds. But they filed only preliminary fraud charges against a handful of executives, who all denied any wrongdoing.

In France, the examiners focused on banks involved in derivative investments linked to Madoff. But no criminal charges were filed.

The Paris prosecutors' office was investigating specific complaints from defrauded investors. In November, an investigating judge would accuse Patrick Littaye, the cofounder of Access International, of a criminal breach of trust for putting a client's money in his firm's Madoff feeder fund, but those charges would later be dropped after the judge determined that Littaye himself was a victim of the fraud and no charges against him were warranted.

The official investigations and private lawsuits in Luxembourg, an emerging European hub for hedge funds and other pooled investments, were piling up almost as rapidly as in New York. At least twenty Madoff-related civil disputes were filed with the Luxembourg courts.

All these cases were closely watched by lawyers hired by Irving Picard, who was trying to ensure that any feeder fund that had made major withdrawals from the Ponzi scheme held on to the money long enough for him to claim it for Madoff's victims.

Ultimately, much of the private investor litigation against banks and feeder funds in Europe would be settled out of court by the summer of 2010, shedding no light on what had happened there or who was responsible.

In the United States the civil courts were not making much progress either. The limits on securities lawsuits that had been enacted by Congress in the late 1990s made it difficult for investors to sue the bankers, accountants, hedge fund consultants, and feeder funds that had left them in Madoff's hands, and many such cases were being thrown out of court. One of the cases dismissed was the SEC's lawsuit against Cohmad Securities, the tiny brokerage firm that Madoff founded with his longtime friend Sonny Cohn.

The SEC lawsuit was able to assert only that Cohmad and its executives "*knew or should have known*" that they were dealing with a Ponzi scheme. But in a ruling that cast doubt on a number of similar pending cases, U.S. District Court judge Louis L. Stanton declared that the SEC's assertion simply wasn't enough to sustain the case, even after he examined the agency's assertions in the most favorable light possible.

"Nowhere does the complaint allege any fact that would put defendants on notice of Madoff's fraud," Judge Stanton observed. There were no references to revealing e-mails, no affidavits about overheard conversations, no allegations from Madoff himself that the Cohmad team had been in on the fraud.

"Rather, the complaint supports the reasonable inference that Madoff fooled the defendants as he did individual investors, financial institutions, and regulators"—including the plaintiff, the SEC.

The judge, who had handled key elements of the case since the day of Madoff's arrest, refused to dismiss a few technical violations relating to the accuracy of Cohmad's annual filings with the SEC, and he gave the agency a chance to try again by dismissing the complaint without prejudice. Nevertheless, the decision was a warning that, even for federal regulators, the question that mattered to the courts was not "who should have known?" but "who actually *did* know?" And the answer to that question would remain elusive.

By the late summer of 2009, the SEC had filed only two other Madoff-related lawsuits—against Madoff's accountant David Friehling and Madoff's first feeder fund manager, Stanley Chais.

As civil regulators, SEC officials necessarily had to defer to the criminal investigation being conducted by the Justice Department—although it was not making much visible progress either. Its only arrests by October 2009 were Madoff, who'd confessed; Friehling, who wasn't clearly charged with knowing about the Ponzi scheme; and DiPascali, who'd turned himself in.

The Madoff case had landed in the U.S. Attorney's Office in Manhattan when it was in the middle of a massive investigation of insider trading in the hedge fund industry, and manpower had been strained from the beginning. Moreover, the case was an upside-down version of the typical criminal investigation. Instead of the classic process of working up the chain and getting the small fry to nail the mastermind, prosecutors had locked up the mastermind and now had to work back down the chain, largely without his help.

Even so, the SEC's Mary Schapiro felt it had built a strong enough roster of important regulatory actions to reclaim some of its lost respect. It had sued Halliburton, the giant oil services company, accusing it of violating laws against foreign bribery. It had accused the Swiss banking giant UBS of helping thousands of U.S. citizens evade federal income taxes. It had sued three major banks for allegedly misleading investors about the risks of a disastrous product called "auction rate securities." And it had sued the high-profile chief executive of a major subprime lender, asserting that his company's notorious practices had not only helped to undermine the nation's credit markets but had also undermined the company itself. Behind the scenes, it had a major investigation under way against Goldman Sachs.

In a warm and relaxed speech to a bar association group in New York in early August, the SEC's new enforcement chief, Rob Khuzami, disclosed that the commission had dismantled restrictions put in place in previous regimes and had agreed to let him issue subpoenas on his own authority—an authority he intended to delegate to other appropriate senior staff members.

There would be no more limp tolerance for stonewalling suspects, he warned the defense lawyers in his audience. If they resisted requests for documents or witnesses or dragged their feet on responding, "there will very likely be a subpoena on your desk the next morning."

It was the kind of tough talk that should have been used with Madoff but wasn't—as the entire world learned in great detail a few weeks later, on August 31, when the SEC's inspector general, H. David Kotz, sent Mary Schapiro the final report on his monumental eight-month investigation of the agency's failures in the Madoff case. Four days later, the full report became public.

The only good news in it for the SEC was that Kotz had not found any evidence that Madoff had corrupted the previous investigations by paying bribes or that agency officials had deliberately tried to protect him and cover up his crime. Shana Madoff's romance with the former SEC lawyer Eric Swanson, whom she married in 2007, was closely examined—even his former girlfriends were interviewed—but Kotz concluded that the relationship had not influenced the SEC's handling of Madoff or his firm, although it looked dreadful in hindsight.

The rest of the report was a humiliating litany of well-documented incompetence and bungled opportunities. In the years leading up to Bernie Madoff's arrest, the agency received at least six complaints suggesting that he was operating a Ponzi scheme. A basic step in detecting a Ponzi scheme is to verify trades or confirm the existence of assets. "Yet, at no time did the SEC ever verify Madoff's trading through an independent third-party," Kotz concluded. In fact, it "never actually conducted a Ponzi scheme examination or investigation of Madoff" at all. This failure persisted in the face of frequent, blatant evidence that Madoff was a liar.

Perhaps worst of all was Kotz's finding that Madoff deliberately exploited the SEC's bungling to reassure his victims of his honesty. "When potential investors expressed hesitation about investing with Madoff, he cited the prior SEC examinations to establish credibility and allay suspicions," Kotz observed. Thus, the SEC's failure to detect the fraud lent credibility to Madoff's criminal operations.

Braced for a new storm of criticism, Mary Schapiro immediately issued a statement apologizing again for the agency's past failures. The inspector general's report, she said, "makes clear that the agency missed numerous opportunities to discover the fraud. It is a failure that we continue to regret, and one that has led us to reform in many ways how we regulate markets and protect investors."

Schapiro and her senior staff were already implementing a sweeping reorganization of the agency's structure and procedures that would address many of the shortcomings cited in the report, she said, and those reforms were being willingly embraced "by the dedicated men and women" at the SEC. The 477-page report left no doubt, however, that those who "should have known" that Madoff was a fraud included many of the dedicated men and women at the SEC.

Six weeks later, on Wednesday, October 14, the Madoff victims' demands for compensation and accountability came together when lawyers for two victims held a press conference in New York to announce that they were suing the SEC, seeking compensation for the investors' losses in the Madoff swindle. The lawsuit contended that the SEC was liable for compensating the plaintiffs because its well-documented negligence had caused their losses.

The lawsuit was a long shot. It has always been extremely difficult to win even the right to sue the U.S. government, much less to win the lawsuit itself. As in most countries steeped in English common-law traditions, citizens cannot sue the federal government over its official actions—the sovereign is immune from litigation. The logic behind "sovereign immunity" is simple: the appropriate place for citizens to challenge the actions of their elected government is at the polls, not in the courts.

There are a few exceptions to this bedrock principle. One of them is the Federal Tort Claims Act, which allows a citizen to sue if a negligent or deliberately improper action by a government employee causes damage to that individual. But that loophole does not apply to policy decisions or discretionary steps taken by federal employees carrying out their official duties.

The Madoff victims argued that they had been injured by the negligence of the SEC, not by its discretionary policy decisions. As they saw it, opening multiple investigations of Madoff may have been a policy decision protected by sovereign immunity, but bungling almost every detail of those investigations was negligence and was not protected from litigation.

The Justice Department argued for the dismissal of the case with almost poignant logic. "Plaintiffs' losses are undeniably tragic," it said in one legal memorandum. "And, for the purpose of this motion, the Court may assume that they were preventable—if only the SEC had shut down Madoff's scheme; or if only it had employed better-qualified and more-experienced investigators, been more persistent in its pursuit of the facts, or devoted additional time and resources to its examinations." Still, the department asserted, the plaintiffs nevertheless were barred from using the courts "to revisit such judgment calls by federal agencies."

In the months to come, at least a dozen similar lawsuits would be filed, including one class-action case seeking redress for all Madoff victims. But even with the inspector general's report mustered in support of their arguments, the plaintiffs faced a steep uphill fight. More than two years after Madoff's arrest, they were still bogged down in the federal courts, waiting for a key ruling on whether they had the right to sue the government at all.

If this was the path toward justice, it would be a long journey to a nearly inaccessible destination.

∽

Given the fate of private lawsuits at home and abroad, it became clear before the first anniversary of Madoff's arrest that the most promising avenue for finding money to compensate victims was going to be through litigation by the bankruptcy trustee, Irving Picard.

The deadline for filing SIPC claims had come on July 2, 2009, and Picard's offices in Rockefeller Center stayed open late to accommodate the mail and messenger deliveries. By the time the clock ran out, the number of claims had exceeded 15,000; the final total would be 16,518.

Many of those filings were from victims who had invested through feeder funds or partnerships, people who did not meet SIPC's definition of a customer and thus were not eligible for SIPC relief at all.

The battle over who was and was not a customer in SIPC's eyes would likely take years to resolve. For now, the first order of business was for the courts to resolve how Picard should calculate victim losses. So, on August 28, Picard officially petitioned the federal bankruptcy court to schedule a hearing devoted exclusively to the so-called "net equity" dispute. The journey toward that hearing would entail months of briefs and reply briefs and briefs replying to the reply briefs. But at least the issue was on the calendar, and the "net winners" would have their day in court, their chance to demand their definition of justice.

Over the course of the summer and fall of 2009 the government auctioned off Madoff's property—the beach house in Montauk sold for more than $9 million; the penthouse went for about $8 million; the Palm Beach home was still on the market for $7.25 million. The Mercedes sedans were sold, and the yachts and power boats were auctioned off. In November the U.S. Marshals held a sort of public flea market to sell a hodgepodge of personal belongings from the Madoff homes—from Bernie's personalized New York Mets jacket to some antique duck decoys. All told, with a storehouse of items destined for future sale, the U.S. Marshals raised just under $900,000 at that auction—an impressive figure in almost any other case but a mere rounding error in the Madoff fraud.

By the fall of 2009, Picard had separately collected roughly $1.5 billion from the firm's brokerage and bank accounts, asset sales, and a few out-of-court settlements, including a $234 million settlement with the family of the late Norman Levy. He had also pressed ahead with his $7.2 billion lawsuit against Jeffry Picower and his wife, Barbara. The Picowers insisted that they had known nothing about Madoff's fraud, but they had recently started talking about a settlement.

However, on Sunday, October 25, Barbara Picower discovered her husband's body drifting motionless near the bottom of the swimming pool on the grounds of their Palm Beach estate. With help from her housekeeper, she was able to get Jeffry out of the pool, but they could not revive him. He was pronounced dead at around 1:30 PM. There were immediate rumors of suicide or foul play, but a prompt autopsy showed that Picower had suffered a massive heart attack and drowned. He was sixty-seven years old and had suffered from heart problems and Parkinson's disease. The family's longtime lawyer, William D. Zabel, said that the settlement talks with Picard would continue on behalf of the estate.

By late October, Picard had approved 1,561 claims and denied 1,309 on the grounds that more had been withdrawn from the holders' Madoff accounts than had been deposited. Already SIPC was obligated to pay more in cash advances to the so-called "net losers" than the total it had paid out since its inception in 1970: $535 million. The sum of approved claims was roughly $4.4 billion, well shy of the $18 billion to $21 billion in "net loser" losses the trustee ultimately expected.

The preliminary arithmetic looked more hopeful than anyone could have imagined on the day of Madoff's arrest. If the total claims and total assets increased at roughly the same rate in the months to come, Picard might be able to pay out as much as thirty cents on the dollar to eligible net losers—most of whom had hopelessly but firmly expected to get nothing.

But those numbers were just placeholders. No one would know what the actual equation would be until the courts decided whether Picard had been wrong to deny the claims of thousands of "net winners."

That process would begin in earnest on Tuesday, February 2, 2010, the day for oral arguments on the dispute over Picard's calculations of victim claims. The queue to get through security at the courthouse that day included more than three dozen lawyers. Among them was Helen Chaitman, who had been tirelessly demanding this day in court for more than a year.

The small courtroom was filled, and latecomers were detoured to an overflow room. The cheap metal coatrack near the door had long since disappeared under a mountain of down parkas and winter wool.

After a forty-five-minute delay to allow more lawyers to get through the crowded security checkpoint downstairs, Judge Burton Lifland took his seat in the plain, low-ceilinged chamber, which was graced only by a view of the New York Harbor through its deep old-fashioned windows.

Colleagues spoke of Judge Lifland as a jurist "of the old school," and it was not hyperbole—he was born in 1929, got his law degree in 1954, and had been on the bankruptcy court bench since 1980. Even at age eighty, he was a diligent judge, studying all thirty-three legal briefs submitted in this case and twenty-two letters from individual investors. A small bespectacled man with an easy smile, he rarely raised his voice, much less lost his temper.

At the judge's nod, David Sheehan, who was presenting Picard's case, carried a three-inch stack of notes and references to the boxy lectern between the two counsel tables.

Sheehan was blunt and direct, as usual. Most of his opponents had argued that Madoff's Ponzi scheme was different from other Ponzi schemes simply because it was a SIPC case. "They are wrong," he said. They were ignoring the fact that the cherished final account statements were simply the artifacts of a fraud. "No one in their right mind would say you have to use the last statement," he said in a flash of passion.

Sheehan was quickly drowned out by jeering laughter from the courtroom. He fell silent for a moment, flushed with embarrassment or perhaps anger. Then he continued softly. "It's really sad that some of my colleagues have led people down this path."

Judge Lifland looked startled at the outburst; it was not the sort of thing that typically happened in bankruptcy court. He nodded to Sheehan to continue.

A few moments later, when Sheehan referred to some detail in the convoluted *New Times* case, the basis for so many conflicting claims about the adjudication of Ponzi scheme losses, there was another outburst of scornful laughter.

This time, Lifland did not let it pass. The crowd was "not here as a cheering section," he said sternly. "Let's have some decorum in the court." As he spoke, there were red faces among the opposing counsel. It did not help their case if their clients' boorish behavior insulted the judge, even-tempered as he was.

Sheehan's opponents included the lawyers for baseball's Wilpon family and for the millionaire Carl Shapiro in Palm Beach. However, they focused on their most sympathetic clients, those middle-class victims who had been living off the proceeds from their Madoff accounts, arguing that Picard's stand on net equity was denying those clients the SIPC cash advance of up to $500,000 that many of them needed desperately to meet their daily expenses.

Helen Chaitman told the judge that her clients included both net winners and net losers, "but every single one of these people believes that SIPC guarantees to them $500,000." Calmly intense, she moved eloquently through her argument—that it would cost SIPC's Wall Street members just $700 million more than was already in its reserve fund to pay all the direct investors $500,000 apiece, regardless of their net equity status. "To SIPC's members, $700 million is not a lot of money," she said, but for some of her clients the SIPC payment "is the difference between living with bleeding ulcers or living without them."

To Sheehan, Chaitman's proposal was unjust; it would mean that many people who had already recovered all of their initial investment would now get more—up to $500,000 more. Meanwhile, those victims who had not recovered any of their initial investment might never do so. "At the end of the day, they still wouldn't be as well off as those who got all their money out," he said.

After nearly a year of opposition, six months of court filings, and four hours of argument, there was not a lot left to say. Judge Lifland thanked the lawyers on both sides but reminded them, "No matter how I come down and rule, it is going to be unpalatable . . . to one party or another."

Precisely one month later, on March 2, Judge Lifland affirmed Picard's "cash in, cash out" definition of net equity in the Madoff Ponzi scheme. In a carefully drafted opinion, the judge recognized that there was some fuzziness in the law, but he concluded that "a thorough and comprehensive analysis of the plain meaning and legislative history of the statute, controlling . . . precedent, and considerations of equity and practicality" all supported the trustee's approach.

Judge Lifland's reasoning closely tracked Sheehan's arguments: after the initial cash investment, all the securities supposedly purchased for customers were actually paid for with fictional profits, so they were not legitimate "securities positions" as defined in SIPC statute. "Given that in Madoff's fictional world no trades were actually executed," he noted, "customer funds were never exposed to the uncertainties of price fluctuation, and account statements bore no relation to the United States securities market at any time."

Consequently, "the only verifiable transactions" were the deposits and withdrawals of cash, not the balances shown on the final account statements, which were "entirely fictitious, do not reflect actual securities positions that could be liquidated, and therefore cannot be relied upon to determine net equity."

He concluded, "It would be simply absurd to credit the fraud and legitimize the phantom world created by Madoff."

The judge and the lawyers on all sides agreed to seek a fast-track review by the Second Circuit Court of Appeals, the next stop in the net winners' long, unsatisfying search for justice.

৩৩

Meanwhile, the criminal cases ground on slowly. On November 3, 2009, David Friehling changed his plea from not guilty to guilty, but only to the crimes involving the filing of falsely certified audits and financial statements with the SEC. When Friehling stood to speak to the presiding judge in his own behalf, he was emphatic. "First and foremost," he said, "it is critical for Your Honor to be aware that at no time was I ever aware that Bernard Madoff was engaged in a Ponzi scheme." In fact, he pointed out, he and many members of his family had put their savings and retirement funds into Madoff's hands and had lost it all.

After pleading guilty, Friehling was released on bail, promising to cooperate with the continuing investigation.

The next defendants to come before the court were Jerome O'Hara and George Perez.

When the FBI agents came to arrest the forty-six-year-old O'Hara on November 13, he was at his home in Malverne, New York, a compact, tree-studded Long Island suburb about six miles due east of Madoff's original hometown of Laurelton, Queens. A big ruddy man with salt-and-pepper hair, O'Hara had worked as a computer programmer for Madoff since he was in his twenties. Now, in an indictment unsealed that morning, he was accused of using his computer skills to help Frank DiPascali create the fictional paper trail that had concealed Madoff's Ponzi scheme for years.

His officemate on the seventeenth floor, George Perez, was arrested the same morning, on identical charges. The FBI arrived early at his home in East Brunswick, New Jersey, one of the suburban bedroom towns that are strung like beads along the turnpike in central New Jersey. The forty-three-year-old Perez, a muscular man with a thick neck and small, somewhat pugnacious features, had joined the Madoff firm about a year after O'Hara.

The SEC was suing the two men as well, echoing the accusations in the indictment, the most intriguing of which was that O'Hara and Perez, uneasy after helping Madoff through his cash crisis in 2005 and the SEC probe that followed, had allegedly confronted him in September 2006 and refused to help anymore—telling him to "ask Frank" the next time he needed his dirty work done, the SEC asserted.

According to the indictment and the SEC complaint, Madoff—flush with cash again and out from under the SEC's unfocused microscope—had simply told DiPascali to offer the two men as much money as it took to keep them quiet.

O'Hara and Perez were brought before a magistrate at the federal courthouse in Manhattan, and each was released on $1 million bail. Their lawyers said that they were innocent and would vigorously fight the charges, which carried prison terms of up to thirty years.

On February 25, 2010, on a day of slush and spitting snow, a team of FBI agents pulled up at 6:00 AM outside an apartment building on East Seventy-ninth Street, near the East River. They went directly to Dan Bonventre's apartment and advised him that he was under arrest.

It was the usual drill. He was allowed to dress, advised of the wardrobe restrictions, handcuffed, escorted downstairs, and eased into the rear passenger seat of the waiting government sedan. Once, Bonventre had so closely resembled Bernie Madoff that employees joked that they were twins separated at birth. The similarity was lost now. Bonventre had grown a neatly trimmed white beard and lost weight since he last showed up for work at the Lipstick Building. Photographers clustered around him as he sheltered under an umbrella at Foley Square. He looked bereft and terrified.

He had been one of Madoff's senior executives for more than thirty years, but now he stood accused of having conspired to sustain and conceal the Ponzi scheme, notably by helping Madoff survive the late 2005 cash crisis. As with O'Hara and Perez, the SEC was filing a parallel civil case against him, too.

Bonventre's lawyer, Andrew J. Frisch, quickly arranged bail and then responded to media calls. The case is "a prosecutorial 'Hail Mary'" effort, he said. "I'm not just saying he is not guilty or that they can't prove it. I'm saying Dan Bonventre is absolutely innocent."

As 2010 opened, none of the arduous journeys that began in the aftermath of Madoff's arrest were anywhere near an end—except for Madoff's own journey to a life behind bars. Criminal cases were still moving steadily toward distant trial dates as the government's investigation continued to inch forward amid frequent changes in personnel. Civil lawsuits were still aiming for the appellate courts, where both sides would wait and pray for vindication. And regulatory reform within the SEC was gaining as much ground as budget and congressional constraints allowed.

Thousands of victims had actually been paid by SIPC and had begun to put their lives together again. Meanwhile, in the summer of 2010, more than two dozen victims, largely net winners, collaborated to publish *The Club No One Wanted to Join*, a moving collection of essays that bore witness to the heartbreak and the quiet heroism that Madoff's crimes had drawn forth. And the advocacy groups that had formed in opposition to Irving Picard continued to seek tax relief for victims and constructive reforms at SIPC, which would be considered at congressional hearings that fall.

Behind the scenes, the spring and summer of 2010 were marked by almost relentless activity at Irving Picard's offices, as he and David Sheehan pushed their staff to meet the December 11 deadline for filing their biggest and most sensational clawback suits. But these months also brought unexpected strain and continuing backstage friction between their staff and the U.S. Attorney's Office over the handling of the assets forfeited by Madoff and other criminal defendants. From the beginning of the case, Sheehan had argued that the asset sales should be left to the trustee, since SIPC would pay all the expenses and thus leave more money for victims. The prosecutors preferred to handle the sale of seized assets through the U.S. Marshals Service, a process more familiar to them and more advantageous to their own budgets.

The conflict came to a head in the spring of 2010, when prosecutors stepped into the protracted negotiations between Irving Picard and Jeffry Picower's estate. Inches away from a settlement agreement requiring the estate to pay $5 billion to the trustee, the senior Picower lawyer, Bill Zabel, balked when the U.S. Attorney's Office threatened to file a civil forfeiture action to claim additional assets on top of any settlement with Picard. Zabel politely but implacably insisted on a global settlement or none at all.

Sheehan would later say that the day he heard that news from the prosecutors' office was, for him, the worst moment in the entire tortured case.

16

HOPE, LOST AND FOUND

David Sheehan was racing against time.

Under bankruptcy court rules, he had until midnight on December 11, 2010, the second anniversary of Madoff's arrest, to file lawsuits aimed at retrieving cash withdrawn from the Ponzi scheme. By late September, nearly a thousand clawback lawsuits were still making their way through his firm's pipeline. They included little ones against Madoff cousins and in-laws, midsize ones against elite hedge funds and former Madoff employees, and giant ones against Madoff's earliest backers and some of the world's biggest financial institutions.

Nearly four dozen lawyers in Baker & Hostetler's offices in Rockefeller Center were working almost around the clock. The lawsuits against smaller investors had been farmed out to dozens of lawyers scattered among the firm's offices in Orlando, Houston, Denver, and Los Angeles. Forensic accountants and private investigators were working alongside the legal teams—as were paralegals, courthouse computer specialists, and multitasking secretaries. In addition, a small battalion of foreign lawyers had been hired to monitor and respond to more than 275 lawsuits in courts spread from Luxembourg to the Cayman Islands.

Sheehan, who relished complexity, had divided the work among several specialized teams. Some teams were devoted to investigating and framing lawsuits against a single high-profile defendant, such as a major bank or a feeder fund. Others were handling the vast list of "good faith" withdrawals—the excess cash taken out by the modest net winners who opposed Irving Picard's effort to recover any money from them. Another large team was focusing on what Sheehan called "bad faith" withdrawals, large sums of money taken out by sophisticated investors who might arguably have had solid grounds for suspecting fraud at the time they removed their cash.

Finally, representatives from all of these teams formed a "complaint review" task force that met several times a week to read one another's drafts for consistency and accuracy.

The scene at the firm was like law school finals writ large: soggy pizza boxes, discarded take-out food containers, an increasingly pungent gymnasium smell in conference rooms used as "war rooms" by the rumpled people working on one case or another. As in a war, all leaves were canceled until further notice. One day, feeling a momentary lull in the pressure, Sheehan asked a colleague if she would like to strike a blow for civilization by going down to the lobby for a sandwich; she replied, "No, thanks—my priority is personal hygiene." If she had time for a sandwich, she'd spend it on a shower.

By mid-November, Sheehan was ready to file a half-dozen cases to recover money from former Madoff employees, some of them with résumés that went back to the earliest days of the firm.

He sued Irwin and Carole Lipkin, whose association with Bernie Madoff dated to 1964, when Irwin Lipkin was hired as Madoff's first employee. A letter Lipkin wrote in 1998, which was found on a computer at the firm, described Madoff as "the brother I never had." Carole Lipkin had first worked for the stockbroker Marty Joel, Madoff's officemate in the early 1960s, but she eventually joined the firm as well. Their son Eric had been hired in 1992 and was still on the payroll on the day of Madoff's arrest. Among the checks Madoff had prepared in the final hours of his fraud was one for almost $7 million to be mailed to the Lipkins at their Florida home, according to the lawsuit.

Other lawsuits were filed the same day against Enrica Cotellessa-Pitz, a perky young woman with dark corkscrew curls who had worked for Madoff since 1978 and had been listed as the firm's controller since the late 1990s, and David Kugel, a distinguished-looking Wall Street veteran who was hired by Madoff in 1970 as an arbitrage trader and who was accused by the trustee of helping to falsify arbitrage trades in the early years of Madoff's fraud. Sheehan also sued Daniel Bonventre, Madoff's operations director, who was already facing criminal charges in the case.

Two other Madoff employees—JoAnn "Jodi" Crupi, in her late forties with two young children, and Annette Bongiorno, a short, heavyset woman in her early sixties—were also named in lawsuits filed by Sheehan's team on November 11. But a week later, those lawsuits became the least of Crupi's and Bongiorno's worries.

Shortly before dawn on Thursday, November 18, FBI agents arrived at Jodi Crupi's white gabled home on a tree-darkened street in suburban Westfield, New Jersey, and arrested her on criminal charges of conspiring with Madoff and others to sustain his Ponzi scheme. She was driven into Manhattan for a bail hearing on Foley Square. Far to the south, other FBI agents were navigating past the shadowy fairways and ponds of the Woodfield Country Club community in Boca Raton, pulling up outside Annette Bongiorno's pastel Spanish-style home. Also arrested on criminal conspiracy charges, she was driven a short distance north to the modern federal courthouse in West Palm Beach, where a bail hearing would be held that afternoon.

The two women's names were added to the indictment that prosecutors originally filed in November 2009 against the two computer programmers, George Perez and Jerome O'Hara, and amended in February to include Dan Bonventre. All three men had denied the charges and vowed to fight them in court.

Now there were five defendants, all accused of having helped Bernie Madoff and Frank DiPascali construct and maintain the elaborate charade on the seventeenth floor of the Lipstick Building. Crupi, who faced a possible jail term of sixty-five years, was accused of maintaining the daily record of cash flowing in and out of the Ponzi scheme's bank account, researching fake trades, and helping to maintain the computer programs that generated the account statements. Bongiorno, facing a seventy-five-year term, was accused of creating fake trades and phony account statements for several hundred individual accounts, including those Madoff set up for his biggest clients and family members.

Like their codefendants, both women denied the charges and asserted their innocence. Their trial is expected sometime in 2012.

〰️

The general public barely noticed Sheehan's early lawsuits or the two new indictments and arrests. But a week earlier, on Wednesday, November

10, the hunger for Madoff news was on full display as the U.S. Marshals Service invited reporters to examine the personal belongings from the homes of Ruth and Bernie Madoff. These items would be auctioned off at the end of the week.

The pending auction was an instant sensation. Film crews from local television stations and news Web sites jousted with foreign documentary teams for the best-lit angles amid the arrangements of furniture and tightly packed racks of clothing. Reporters scribbled and photographers snapped as the marshals who had seized the goods provided anecdotes about where the items had once fit in the Madoff homes. Hundreds of items—from the couple's ornate canopy bed to Ruth's personalized Mother's Day coffee mug—had been swept from the rooms and closets and drawers of the Manhattan penthouse and the Montauk home and were now spread out in a vast unused space at the Brooklyn Navy Yard.

It was the second auction of personal items seized from the Madoffs. The 2009 auction, a year earlier, had been dominated by Bernie's fabled wristwatch collection, some of Ruth's important jewelry, and garish oddities such as Bernie's personalized silk New York Mets jacket, which was sold for $14,500. That sale raised just under $900,000.

This time, the marshals were selling off much more intimate relics from the private life the Madoffs once had—the most photographed item was a pair of black velvet bedroom slippers, lined in red and adorned with Madoff's monogram embroidered in gold thread. Another object of fascination was Bernie's pleated-front boxer shorts, neatly pressed and laid out among representative items of clothing being put up for sale.

But where were the bits of appalling excess and gaudy grandeur that people expected from the Ponzi king and his scorned queen?

Well, they were clotheshorses, those Madoffs—no doubt about it—although they apparently bought classics, lots of them, and wore them for years. The racks of Bernie's custom-tailored Savile Row suits went on forever, but some were more than a dozen years old. His towering stacks of custom-made shirts and seven dozen unworn pairs of shoes in the same Mr. Casual Belgium style drew snickers—but sold for more than the marshals expected. Ruth's designer handbags were a big hit, but some had worn linings and well-rubbed corners. Her iconic collarless Chanel jackets, all in size two, had seen a lot of seasons, and her evening gowns were few and elegantly modest.

The chintz hangings on the canopy bed were faded. There were small holes in the side of a gray leather sofa. The living room furniture looked well used and comfortable. Many of the rugs were frayed, mended, or marred; one catalog listing cautioned: "Note: cigarette burns on bottom."

The art was by minor artists, the most recognized name being Thomas Hart Benton. The treasures here were small or subtle, in some cases too modest to have impressed the marshals. They expected no more than $12,300 for an oil painting by the American artist Ernest Lawson—it would sell for $40,000. But then they estimated that a beautiful early Georgian drop-front secretary, in figured walnut and rosewood, would fetch as much as $22,500, yet it would be hammered down for $9,500.

An atmosphere of faint embarrassment arose as people thumbed through the more modest household items on display at one end of the Navy Yard showroom. Oh, look over there. Isn't that . . . a latke platter?

It was not surprising that Ruth Madoff had forfeited the designer clothing, the elegant Edwardian bracelets, and the magnificent 10.5-carat diamond ring with its custom platinum setting—it sold for $550,000. Those luxury items could generate substantial amounts of money for her husband's victims. But the auction catalog was evidence of just how thoroughly she had been dispossessed. It listed eight pairs of her panty hose, her cosmetic brushes, two dozen pairs of her socks (used), her "assorted workout clothes," including her well-worn tank tops and yoga pants, T-shirts from the Gap, and two laundered hankies—along with "a box of new hankies." The contents of all her bathroom and kitchen cabinets had been swept out and put up for sale—shampoo and hand cream, pot holders and dish towels, a salad spinner and a tissue-box cover, anything and everything.

Lot number 448 included a fishing trophy Bernie had won with a 350-pound blue marlin in 1975 and an assortment of toys from the Montauk home—jacks, a kite, board games, decks of cards. It also included "two (2) partial boxes of light bulbs," a box of staples, and ten size-D batteries. Another lot included pliers and other hand tools, several extension cords, gardening equipment, and a dozen packages of assorted screws and nails. The trays of costume jewelry included a tarnished Eagle Scout medal inscribed "Be Prepared."

The bidding, in person at a Midtown hotel and online, was a headline event. As expected, there was fierce interest in the monogrammed slippers, which went for $6,000 in a lot that included one of Ruth's mono-grammed Ascot Chang shirts. Fifteen pairs of used slacks and jeans from Bernie's closet went for just $25.

All told, the two Madoff auctions raised just under $3 million. The proceeds from the sale of their three homes, three boats, and a car brought the total from forfeited assets to about $27 million, not counting an estimated $10 million in future proceeds from the French town house and the eighty-eight-foot yacht that Madoff kept moored nearby, which were being haggled over in bankruptcy court in London.

This was a drop in the bucket against the "net loser" claims, which Picard estimated to run as high as $20 billion. The only way to raise that kind of money was through litigation. As Thanksgiving neared, Sheehan's team announced lawsuit after lawsuit, sometimes electronically filing several major cases and dozens of smaller cases on a single day.

On November 24, UBS, the giant Swiss bank, was sued for a minimum of $2 billion in a complaint that accused it of lending its prestige to vari-ous Madoff feeder funds without taking any steps to protect investors. The case also named Access International, the company whose aristo-cratic French founder, René-Thierry Magon de la Villehuchet, commit-ted suicide after Madoff's arrest. A few days later, UBS would be named in a second suit involving another set of feeder funds, bringing Picard's total claims against it to $2.5 billion.

Early December brought a lawsuit seeking $6.4 billion in recovered fees and damages from JPMorgan Chase, the primary bank used by Madoff during his decades-long fraud. The case was filed under seal, but Sheehan said publicly that it would show that the bank had been "willfully blind" in its dealings with Madoff and had ignored its own executives' "clear, documented suspicions" about him over the years. The lawsuit would remain sealed until early February, when its detailed documenta-tion of the bank's growing doubts about Madoff would become public. The formidable bank said the accusations were preposterous and vowed to fight them in court.

Three days later, on Sunday evening, December 5, Sheehan's team filed a massive lawsuit seeking $9 billion from HSBC, the global bank based in London, and dozens of hedge funds and individual defendants

it had dealt with during the Madoff years. The allegations were familiar—
that people at the bank had suspected Madoff but looked the other way
to preserve the fees he generated for them. These allegations, too, were
stoutly denied.

On Tuesday, December 7, two more high-profile cases were filed—
both under seal. One was against Tremont Group Holdings, Madoff's
second-largest feeder fund complex after Fairfield Greenwich. The other
was against a host of companies and partnerships affiliated with the Wilpon family, the owners of the New York Mets baseball team. This time,
Sheehan offered no details—but he did disclose that the trustee's lawyers
were "currently engaged in good-faith negotiations" with lawyers for the
Wilpons, aimed at settling the case out of court. By the end of January
2011, the *New York Times* would have uncovered some key details about
the sealed lawsuit. On the day Fred Wilpon disclosed that the New York
Mets were seeking new investors, the *Times* would report that the trustee
was suing the Wilpons for hundreds of millions of dollars.

There was a case against the directors of Madoff's bankrupt British affiliate, filed under seal in London. There was a claim for $1 billion
against seven major banks that had sold derivatives linked to Madoff
feeder funds. There were multimillion-dollar lawsuits against smaller but
notable hedge fund managers in Manhattan, Europe, and the Caribbean,
including the pension specialist Sandra Manzke and her Maxam Fund
Group in Connecticut. And there were nearly nine hundred lawsuits
against individual Madoff investors and their family partnerships and
trust funds—the cases the "net winners" in the vast fraud had expected
for almost two years.

By now, the trustee's sprint toward the December 11 deadline for
filing clawback suits had become a fixture in the hourly headlines on
Internet news sites. Given the ambient exhaustion and the possibility of
something breaking down or going astray in the complex process, Picard
and Sheehan agreed that it would be foolish to risk a last-minute glitch in
the electronic filing system at the federal courthouse, so they established
midnight Friday, December 10, as their internal deadline. At least that
would give them a cushion of time if something went wrong.

Each half of this legal odd couple stayed in character. While Sheehan was busily and publicly filing new lawsuits, Picard was negotiating
behind closed doors to settle old ones.

On Monday, December 6, he landed a $500 million settlement with Union Bancaire Privée, the elite family-run Swiss bank that had set up its own feeder fund to invest with Madoff. The next day, he and the U.S. government announced a sweeping settlement with Carl Shapiro and his family in Palm Beach, including the former Cohmad executive Robert Jaffe, Shapiro's son-in-law. Although Picard had named Jaffe in his lawsuit against Cohmad, the trustee had not sued Shapiro, and neither he nor the government accused Shapiro of any wrongdoing in connection with the settlement. The deal added $624 million to the pool of cash for Madoff victims. A few days later, the trustee announced smaller settlements with some important charities, including Hadassah. The settlements almost doubled the amount of cash Picard had raised; it now approached $2.5 billion.

But all the earlier lawsuits and settlements were eclipsed by a case filed on Friday evening, December 10. In an ambitious 161-page complaint, Sheehan's team sued the Austrian banker Sonja Kohn, members of her family, her flagship firm Bank Medici, her major European banking partners, and a battalion of trusts, partnerships, shell companies, and individuals—more than three dozen defendants in all. Those defendants who chose to comment denied the allegations. Uniquely among the lawsuits filed on Picard's behalf, this case asserted civil racketeering charges against the defendants, claiming that Kohn had knowingly helped steer $9 billion into Madoff's hands, introducing him to new sources of cash for his Ponzi scheme in exchange for tens of millions of dollars in secret fees.

The lawsuit sought nearly $20 billion in recovered cash and damages. But since the court could order the losing defendants in a racketeering case to pay triple damages, the Kohn case had the potential to produce up to $60 billion for Madoff's victims. Lawyers for Kohn promptly denied that she had ever known, or even suspected, that Madoff was operating a Ponzi scheme and said that she and her family would vigorously contest the trustee's claims in court.

Later that night, just hours before midnight, the last big case was filed—a case rooted in the first days of Madoff's fame as a market wizard. Its primary defendants were Frank Avellino and Michael Bienes, the two accountants whose lives had intersected in the accounting firm run by Madoff's father-in-law. Picard now sought $900 million from them, their wives, and a host of family partnerships and trust funds. The lawsuit accused the two accountants of knowingly pocketing millions of stolen dollars that Madoff had paid as their reward for bringing investors back to him after the SEC shut down the Avellino & Bienes operation in 1992. Their lawyers did not comment but prepared to battle the accusations in court.

One tiny flake in the blizzard of litigation that week was a case seeking money from various trust accounts set up for the benefit of Bernie Madoff's grandchildren, the children of his sons, Mark and Andrew.

The lawsuit had not been unexpected, a person close to Mark Madoff said later. It came as the renewed publicity about the December 11 litigation deadline and the approach of the scandal's second anniversary were shoving the Madoff sons back into the spotlight.

It was not a place where Mark Madoff had ever felt comfortable.

By this time he was a defendant in at least nine federal lawsuits, including several others filed by Picard—who had publicly characterized him as negligent, derelict, and incompetent. Picard's scorn hadn't hurt as much as the enforced silence of those former Wall Street colleagues who might have publicly defended him, a friend said. Others recalled that Mark had always been sensitive to criticism and inclined to brood over his grievances, to visibly fret over problems. "That's why I never believed he knew about the fraud," one family friend and former business associate said. "He was always a nervous wreck. He could never have stood it—keeping a secret like that would have torn him apart."

Neither he nor his brother, Andrew, had spoken to their parents since the day of their father's arrest. Still, Mark's estrangement from his gilded past seemed to cut deeper than his brother's. Within a short time, Andrew was unfazed by the inevitable raised eyebrows of waiters looking at his credit card and airport security guards examining his driver's license; yes, he would shrug, he was *that* Andrew Madoff. He told friends he had never met anything but courteous sympathy. But Mark did not seem willing to risk the ill will of strangers; he had agreed with his wife's decision to change her own and their children's last name from Madoff to Morgan.

"He had always been so proud of his name and being the guy who was Bernie Madoff's son," another friend recalled. "And then afterwards all anyone ever saw in him was that he was Bernie Madoff's son."

On October 14, 2009, Mark checked into a hotel and took several dozen Ambien, leaving a suicide note for his father: "Now you know how you have destroyed the lives of your sons by your life of deceit. Fuck you." He survived and sought medical treatment. Over the next year, he seemed to regain his balance. A friend in the financial world let him use a free desk in his office; others met him regularly for lunch. Picard still held the purse strings under an asset freeze, but Mark was finding new ways to support his family.

His primary focus was a new business, an online real estate newsletter called Sonar Report, which he hoped would be the first in a fleet of specialty online financial publications. Each day he would rise at 4:00 AM to scour the Internet for relevant news items, assemble the newsletter, and, at around 9:00 AM, send it out electronically. It was a smart and useful service, and some of its regular readers were willing to sign up for paid subscriptions. But most of his readers had no idea there was a Madoff involved—he felt he had to purge his name from the newsletter's pages and incorporation records.

The issue for Friday, December 10, was sent out a few minutes past 9:00 AM, as usual. Mark's wife, Stephanie, and their four-year-old daughter were in Florida with his mother-in-law, visiting Disney World, leaving him to care for their twenty-two-month-old son and the family dog, an engaging Labradoodle named Grouper. As the day went on, Mark talked with friends and kept scheduled appointments. He seemed fine—or, at least, no more upset than usual about the fresh media attention focused on him that week. He nodded graciously when an employee at the garage that housed his family cars thanked him for his annual Christmas tip. He walked the dog for about ten minutes that evening, his doorman later said, and returned to the apartment for the night.

Awake at 4:00 AM, as usual, on Saturday—the second anniversary of his father's arrest—he sent a series of e-mails. One went to his lawyer, Marty Flumenbaum: "Nobody wants to believe the truth. Please take care of my family." He wrote his wife, telling her, "I love you," and urging her to "please send someone" to take care of their son.

When Stephanie saw the notes several hours later, she called her stepfather in New York and asked him to go to the apartment immediately. He arrived to find Mark's body hanging from a black dog leash attached to a metal beam in the living room ceiling.

It clearly was suicide—an autopsy would later confirm it, but evidence at the scene was proof that Mark had been determined to end his life. Police found a snapped vacuum cleaner cord suspended from the same metal beam, and a discarded noose fashioned from that cord was on a table nearby. Mark's son and the family pet were found in another room in the apartment—"unharmed," in the vocabulary of police reports.

A person who had remained close to Mark since childhood said he believed that the approaching anniversary, and the attendant surge in speculation about Mark's guilt or innocence, had "reopened the wounds. It must have just been more than he could bear."

Mark Madoff's suicide, at age forty-six, was another blow for a shattered family. Ruth was heartbroken, her lawyer said. Bernie wept at the news, his lawyer said later. Neither could attend a funeral—even if they had been welcome, the fierce media clamor made it impossible to hold one. Mark's cousin Shana and uncle Peter would have been welcome, but their lawyers still advised against any contact. Mark's wife and brother arranged a private cremation and a quiet gathering with their families and a few friends; Ruth was not included.

Still standing in the rubble was Andrew Madoff, a cancer survivor at age forty-four who seemed to be less haunted by the past than his brother had been. Just a few weeks before his brother's death, Andrew and his fiancée, Catherine Hooper, had gathered friends for a Thanksgiving dinner at their apartment on the Upper East Side of Manhattan. Music had always been part of his life, and he spent more time at the piano, working with his longtime instructor. Hooper had launched a new business advising families on strategies for dealing with disastrous disruptions in their lives. As she described it, she and Andrew were determined to deal wisely with the disastrous disruption called the Madoff scandal. "When all of this happened, we decided that we weren't going to sit around all of the time with our laptops on our laps reading blogs," Hooper later told a reporter. "We were not going to sit around talking about how horrible this is."

Perhaps it all came down to the habits of mind revealed in that first searing confrontation two years earlier. When Bernie Madoff confessed, as he recalled in one prison interview, Andrew wept and gave his father a last embrace, but Mark's almost inarticulate anger burned white hot from that moment on. While Andrew's lawyers dealt with lawsuits and weighed settlement negotiations with Picard, Andrew seemed to get on with his life—still willing to be a Madoff, but not willing to be defined by his father's crime.

∽

By the time the litigation deadline arrived, Picard had filed claims seeking more than $90 billion—although it could take years of litigation to collect even some fraction of that amount. That formidable pursuit of assets was encouraging to the net losers in the case—and the occasional Wall Street speculator who had bought up valid claims for twenty or thirty cents on the dollar, hoping to recover more when the case was finally settled. But the blizzard of big-ticket lawsuits brought a bitter chill to the net winners, who, under prevailing law and court decisions, seemed unlikely to share in a penny that Picard might retrieve. Unless and until all the net losers recovered all their lost cash, the net winners simply had no place at the table.

With their claims denied by Picard, and his action upheld in the bankruptcy court and not yet reviewed in the Court of Appeals, some net winners turned to Congress for help. Since early in the year, they had been seeking legislation to require SIPC to accept the final account statements of Ponzi scheme victims as proof of the amount they had lost, regardless of how much cash they had paid in or had taken out.

By summer, some net winners were lining up, reluctantly, behind a bill called "The Ponzi Victims Bill of Rights." The bill was, at best, half a loaf for them because it did not include the "final account statement" rule that was at the heart of their demands. But the leaders of one organized group of victims argued that it would at least spur hearings and an investigation that, "combined with our extensive lobbying efforts, will enable us to pursue necessary modifications."

Despite their lobbying, the bill did not emerge from committee before the end of the congressional term. But, in late December, a few supportive members of Congress promised to introduce a stronger replacement for the bill after the new term began in January 2011.

As written, this new bill would prohibit a SIPC trustee from filing any clawback cases against innocent Ponzi victims and require him to honor the investors' final account statements, unless they were Wall Street professionals who "knew . . . or should have known" about the fraud but did not warn regulators about it.

This proposed "Equitable Treatment of Investors Act" did not prohibit all clawback lawsuits. But the bill, submitted in February 2011, would bar a trustee from trying to recover money that an innocent investor withdrew from a Ponzi scheme before it collapsed. The ban would shrink the universe of investors from whom the trustee could recover cash, thereby reducing the odds that net losers could be made whole. Most intriguingly, the bill codified the notion that only brokers and investment advisers belonged in the category of those who "should have known" that Madoff was a crook.

Under the bill, Picard would have been barred from suing some of Madoff's richest and most sophisticated investors, who were neither brokers nor money managers. Moreover, these "civilian" investors had final account statements showing huge balances; they could have filed claims for hundreds of millions of dollars, further reducing the cash available for net losers. Picard would have had to honor those claims unless he could prove the individuals actually knew about Madoff's fraud. By contrast, if a newly licensed mutual fund salesman was a net winner in a Ponzi scheme, the bill seemed to offer him little protection against clawbacks, no matter how unsophisticated he might be.

Some of the net winners could justifiably argue that Picard should not try to recover money they didn't have or could not repay without beggaring themselves. But if a net winner qualified under SIPC's hardship program, Picard left him alone. Within weeks of the litigation deadline, more needy net winners had applied and qualified, and the cases against them were dismissed. By December, Picard had foregone his claims against more than two hundred net winners who could not afford to repay their fictional profits.

This anti-clawback bill, however, did not seek to extend SIPC protection to indirect investors in a Ponzi scheme. The thousands of people who had invested through Madoff feeder funds were as frustrated with SIPC as the net winners. Their claims, too, had been denied by the trustee, not because they had received fictional profits but because they hadn't had accounts in their own name at Madoff's brokerage firm. The feeder fund that took their money was the "customer" eligible for SIPC relief. To recover any money from the bankruptcy, they would have to get it from their feeder fund, assuming the feeder fund had a valid claim.

More than ten thousand indirect investors filed claims with Picard and were turned down. Whether Picard was entitled by law to deny their claims was one of the knotty problems that remained before the courts two years after Madoff's arrest. Indirect investors had trusted the feeder funds with their initial investments—and, under prevailing law, would have to trust them, or some corporate parent standing behind them, for any recovery from the Madoff bankruptcy. In the case of many small or bankrupt feeder funds, unfortunately, that was a bleak hope that assured investors of little except years of litigation.

In the days and weeks after Madoff's arrest, the search for his accomplices dominated the public's attention. By the second anniversary of that arrest, he and two other men—the indispensable Frank DiPascali and the negligent accountant David Friehling—had confessed. Five other people stood accused of sustaining the Ponzi scheme, but all had proclaimed their innocence and were preparing to fight the accusations in court. Prosecutors insisted at every opportunity that the criminal investigation was continuing, but they also explained that the burden of proving guilt "beyond a reasonable doubt" was far heavier than the burden of proof required in civil cases filed in bankruptcy court, no matter how conclusive and dramatic the allegations in those cases seemed.

The days and weeks after Madoff's arrest also ignited angry demands for reform—at the SEC, at SIPC, and in the courts where the two agencies' work was carried out. Under Mary Schapiro's chairmanship, the SEC had undergone one of the most sweeping reorganizations in its history. Its enforcement branch was given new tools—an expanded bounty system for whistle-blowers, a streamlined process for serving subpoenas, a simpler management structure that put more boots on the ground in the fight against fraud, improved training programs for its lawyers and investigators—and more money to deploy them. Future budget cuts could undermine these gains, but there was clearly a new fearlessness in the agency's enforcement agenda and broader support for its mission in Congress—where, just two years earlier, one congressman had condemned the SEC as "the enemy."

Schapiro sat on a Fordham Law School panel in late September 2010 with two former SEC chairmen—both Republican appointees—who publicly praised her for almost single-handedly preserving the commission's independence when it was most at risk. "If you didn't do anything else but save the agency, it's a pretty good start," said Richard Breeden, who headed the commission from 1989 to 1993. Harvey Pitt, the chairman from 2001 to 2003, seconded the compliment, saying that Schapiro had stepped in "at a time of real crisis."

At SIPC, change came far more slowly but seemed inevitable. Prodded by congressional committees weighing various legislative proposals, some wiser than others, the organization itself set up a task force to study and address the many weaknesses the Madoff scandal exposed. As for the bankruptcy and litigation process, the questions posed by the Madoff case would take years to resolve. How should losses be calculated? Who had the right to file claims? What responsibility, if any, did hedge fund managers, accountants, bankers, and financial advisers have for failing to detect this massive fraud? Could the SEC itself be held accountable in the courts?

Finally, in the days and weeks immediately after Madoff's arrest, recovering anything for his victims looked like something only a real wizard could achieve.

Just over 16,500 claims had been filed by the end of 2010. About two-thirds of those were from indirect investors who could not collect anything unless the courts ultimately decided otherwise. About 120 of the claims were withdrawn. More than 500 claims remained in the pipeline—these were the largest net losers, with combined losses that Picard estimated at $14 billion, although he knew that this figure could change as disputes were resolved. About half of those thorny cases were already in litigation, and many more probably would be.

Of the remaining claims, by year end Picard had denied more than 2,700 claims from net winners and approved just over 2,400 claims from net losers, whose verified cash losses totaled just under $6 billion.

So, on the second anniversary of Madoff's arrest, Picard had about $2.5 billion to cover losses he estimated conservatively at $20 billion—

a dime on the dollar. He had hopes of paying more, of course, but you can't put hope in the bank and write checks on it. Sheehan's indefatigable legal team had sued various defendants for $90 billion, but actually collecting more than a modest fraction of that would take another act of wizardry.

Still, a dime on the dollar—even twice or three times that, if Sheehan won as much in court as Picard thought possible—was far more than anyone had expected in the dark spring of 2009.

⚭

A week after that second anniversary, the arithmetic for the net losers changed dramatically—indeed, it changed so dramatically that it made history, as so much about Madoff's saga did.

Friday, December 17, was a day that David Sheehan had sometimes feared would never arrive—and a day that federal prosecutors had delayed for months in their determination to get the best outcome possible for Madoff's victims. It dawned bright and very cold, with a bitter wind whipping around the towers of Foley Square in downtown Manhattan. Even before U.S. attorney Preet Bharara announced that he would hold a press conference at noon to announce a settlement with the estate of longtime Madoff investor Jeffry Picower, the news broke on the Internet. Lawyers for Picower's widow had reached a global settlement with the government and the trustee totaling $7.2 billion. It was the entire amount Irving Picard had sought in his original lawsuit; it was $2.2 billion more than the trustee might have gotten without the prosecutors' intervention in the negotiations months before.

And it was the largest single forfeiture in American judicial history.

The press conference was held in a small, oddly shaped area in the lobby of the U.S. attorney's headquarters, the gritty corrugated concrete walls partially lined with deep blue velvet drapes. Overhead, a giant mobile of spatter-painted metal tubes and spheres dangled from the two-story ceiling. Four rows of cheap metal folding chairs had been set up in front of a picket line of television cameras. At 12:15 PM, a door framed by the velvet drapes opened and a fleet of people entered and lined up a little awkwardly along the walls: David Sheehan, looking pugnacious; Irving Picard, in a bland gray suit; two SIPC executives, in a dim corner; senior officials from the New York offices of the FBI and the IRS; and a host of young prosecutors led by their boss, the U.S. attorney for the Southern District of New York.

Preet Bharara, a striking man with thinning dark hair and an eloquent, confident manner, stepped immediately to the lectern as photographers crouched and scuttled from side to side, looking for a camera angle that would capture him with Irving Picard over his shoulder.

"Today's truly historic settlement with the estate of Jeffry Picower is a game-changer for Madoff's victims," Bharara said, reading from a bracing script. "By returning every penny of the $7.2 billion her late husband received from [Madoff's firm] to help those who have suffered most, Barbara Picower has done the right thing."

The amount that Barbara Picower had handed over represented the difference between the cash her husband had withdrawn from his Madoff accounts and the amount he had put in—which was estimated at just under $620 million. But it did not represent all of her immensely wealthy husband's estate. What was left would be used to create a new Picower Foundation, which would continue the couple's philanthropy. Their longtime lawyer and adviser, Bill Zabel, had spent more than a year forging a global agreement that would allow Barbara Picower to get on with her life and her charitable work. As the press conference was being held downtown, Zabel's Midtown office released a statement on the widow's behalf: "I believe the settlement honors what Jeffry would have wanted, which is to return this money so that it can go directly to the victims of Madoff. I am absolutely confident that my husband Jeffry was in no way complicit in Madoff's fraud. . . . I was a witness to his integrity in our marriage and in his life during our 40 years together."

It got little attention in the uproar, but a passage in a statement released by SIPC that day quoted Irving Picard on the topic of Jeffry Picower's relationship to the massive Ponzi scheme—and, in the process, offered a quick glimpse of the strategy that produced so many fierce accusations against various Madoff insiders and big investors in the lawsuits that had been filed over the previous two years.

"When we filed suit against Mr. Picower and others in the spring of 2009, the records available led us to allege that Mr. Picower might have or should have known of Mr. Madoff's fraud," Picard acknowledged. "With the benefit of additional records, I have determined that there is no basis to pursue the complaint against Mr. Picower and we have arrived at a business solution instead."

It would certainly not be the last such "business solution" to the lawsuits in which Picard accused various defendants of deliberate misconduct or knowing complicity in the biggest swindle of the age. But it was the biggest solution so far, and while it did not shed any light on Picower's role in Madoff's fraud, it immediately improved the prospects for both the net losers and the net winners.

With nearly $10 billion in hand, Picard seemed on course to restore roughly half of the cash the net losers had invested with Madoff. If Sheehan had even modest success in the courts, the recovery could be even larger—and Sheehan himself began to say privately that he thought they could get the net losers close to that Holy Grail for bankruptcy trustees: a hundred cents on the dollar.

If that happened, then it would be a new ball game for the net winners. While they did not have valid customer claims, they certainly had fraud claims they could file against the Madoff estate—all the defrauded investors did, although that fact had seemed futile and academic until now. If Picard's clawback blitz produced substantially more than the estimated $20 billion he needed to repay the net losers—and he already had almost $10 billion in hand—then the payment of fraud claims would become a real possibility.

And if this occurred, then this historically large, long, far-flung crime would have achieved another superlative. It would have produced the most remarkable Ponzi scheme recovery ever. For the Madoff victims, the record-setting Picower settlement delivered something that for two years had been even more elusive than justice: hope.

Oddly enough, Picard and Sheehan were not the only ones who thought some sort of historic recovery would be possible in the case. Bernie Madoff thought so, too.

In several e-mails from prison after the Picower settlement, Madoff wrestled almost obsessively with Picard's arithmetic, protesting that it looked as if the trustee would "recover at least 24 billion in claw backs against 20 billion in valid loss claims." He was certain that some European banks and hedge funds had reached confidential settlements with their investors in late spring 2010 that fully covered $15.5 billion in claims. "I know it's 100% reliable and that's all I can say," he added. So it looked to him that Picard could wind up with much more money than he would need to repair the damage Madoff himself had caused.

The $20 billion would only cover the cash lost in his scheme, of course, not the accumulated wealth his investors had counted on for their future security—comfortable fortunes that turned out to be cruel fantasies. And no amount of money could repair all the broken hearts, bereaved families, and disrupted lives he left in his wake, or restore the trust his betrayed victims once had in themselves and the world around them. Even on a purely monetary level, the foreign investors who were supposedly made whole by those confidential settlements in Europe might not even have filed claims with Picard. And the foreign banks and hedge funds that paid those settlements might still have valid claims in their own right, even if they had paid off their investors.

Still, Madoff was calmly confident about the eventual outcome: "I have to assume that if the foreign claims were 100% settled in one form or the other, and the other domestic claims will be made whole from the recovered assets, everyone's principal will be returned."

17

THE LONG ROAD FORWARD

After a short stay in a federal jail cell in Atlanta, Bernard L. Madoff arrived at the seven-hundred-acre Federal Correctional Complex in Butner, North Carolina, on Tuesday, July 14, 2009, two weeks after being sentenced by Judge Denny Chin.

The facility had housed a number of prominent white-collar criminals over the years, and its current notable inmates included the convicted Israeli spy Jonathan Pollard, the aging gangster Carmine Persico, and one of the executives convicted in 2004 of cooking the books at Adelphia Communications.

Madoff was taken to FCI-1, one of two medium-security prisons in the complex. Now officially designated as Inmate Number 61727054, he was issued the standard inmate uniform, a khaki shirt and slacks, and began several weeks of orientation.

The inmate handbook advised him that all his personal property had to fit within a single storage locker, although the space under his bunk might be used with permission. His jewelry was limited to a single inexpensive watch and a wedding band without gemstones. His normal purchases at the prison commissary could not exceed $290 a month.

His links to the world outside would now consist of monitored handwritten letters, a few monitored e-mails from people on a preapproved list, and occasional visits with Ruth and his lawyers.

At first, he worked in the prison library and education department. Then he was assigned to the commissary, a well-paid and coveted job among inmates. He did not mop floors or scrub toilets, as some published reports would later claim. By his own account, he remained in relatively good health and was always "treated well by the inmates and staff here," in contrast to "all the absurd stories that have appeared in the media." As for the reports that he had made disparaging remarks about his sons or victims, he was emphatic: "I have never said the slightest negative thing about my sons, who I love and miss terribly. I feel great remorse for my victims."

ᕣᕤ

Ruth Madoff looked out the window of the taxi carrying her to Butner for her first visit with her husband since his arrival at the prison there.

She had driven to Charlotte from Boca Raton, Florida, where she was house-sitting a friend's condominium near her sister Joan's home. Her niece in Charlotte drove her as far as Durham, where this quintessentially urban woman hailed a cab for what turned out to be a forty-five-minute drive and a $35 fare. Ruth had reached a settlement with the government but had been sued by the bankruptcy trustee and was afraid to spend a single unnecessary penny. The taxi was far more expensive than she'd expected; she still had to buy gas for the trip back to Florida.

The taxi slowed, turned into the Butner complex, and circled around to the top of a small hill dominated by a tall gray-stone building at one edge of a large parking lot. The taxi left her at the door; she entered and was directed by a guard to put her handbag and sweater into a locker that could not, in fact, be locked. Few visitors used them; they left their valuables in their locked cars. What if her purse were stolen here? It had all her identification, her cash, her car keys, everything. Ruth hesitated, then stowed her purse and got in line for the security check.

That was when she learned that the taxi had dropped her at the wrong facility—Bernie Madoff was housed in the one-story prison at the foot of the hill. It wasn't far by city-walking standards. But the guard said she could not walk; she would have to go by car. Bernie was waiting; he was expecting her. She dug out her cell phone and called for another taxi. As she waited, she looked bleakly across the parking lot. There were people pulling out, maybe prisoners' relatives or employees leaving after a shift change. She could flag someone down and ask for a lift. But she was afraid to do that.

This once-carefree child had become an anxious, fragile woman; fear was her constant companion today. Bernie had told her that inmates were feeding bits of gossip about him to the New York tabloids. They could have tipped a reporter that she was coming. She could be heading into a swarm of paparazzi. Or she could miss visiting hours completely because of this taxi delay, wasting all that money and disappointing Bernie.

In this summer of 2009, she still cared about that. Bernie needed her, craved her attention, clung fiercely to their fifty-five-year connection. His sons had angrily rejected him and thought she should, too; they could not understand the lifelong habits of loyalty and pity that tied Ruth to her husband. His brother Peter, on notice that he was under criminal investigation, had been warned by his own legal team that he should stay away. There was nobody else for Bernie but Ruth. He had been intensely anticipating her visit.

Finally the taxi returned—and charged her another $35 to drive her down the hill. She was too frantic about the time to argue. She got in line, stowed her purse without thinking, and made her way through the security screening and into the busy visiting room. She found Bernie, sitting a little apart. They could touch, could hug each other—it was awkward, this unfamiliar etiquette.

Bernie talked about the other prisoners he'd met, his living situation, the job he'd been assigned, the daily routine. Using a stack of quarters, he got a hamburger from a vending machine and warmed it in a nearby microwave, chatting with her as if they were in some casual bistro. She listened but said little; it was a blur, almost surreal. She had never known anyone who had gone to prison. Yet here was her husband, in his crisply pressed prison uniform, locked up for life with all these criminals—all these *other* criminals.

※

On March 3, 2011, the ceremonial courtroom at the federal courthouse in downtown Manhattan—the elegant, soaring chamber where Bernie Madoff had been sentenced nearly two years earlier—was once again packed to the walls.

This time, though, the benches and more than a dozen extra leather armchairs were filled with lawyers and reporters. A three-judge panel of the United States Court of Appeals for the Second Circuit was hearing arguments on the stubbornly divisive "net equity" issue, the core dispute over Irving Picard's formula for calculating investor claims. David Sheehan and his colleagues sat at the same table where Madoff had been seated. To their left were their opponents, including Helen Davis Chaitman and Karen Wagner, the petite spiky-blonde lawyer representing the owners of the New York Mets, the most visible of the "net winners" challenging Picard. At an aisle seat in the back row sat Mario Cuomo, the former governor of New York, who had been asked by Judge Lifland to mediate the trustee's dispute with the Mets owners. "Just here to observe," he explained softly.

The arguments from both sides were newly phrased but familiar: Chaitman and her team argued that there was no Wall Street safety net—that SIPC protection was meaningless—if their clients could not rely on their final account statements, even if they were lies. Sheehan argued that reality mattered and that those account statements reflected a fantasy world in which Madoff could buy and sell blue-chip stocks and customized options in enormous volume without ever incurring a loss or moving the market. Investors who thought they had made money in their Madoff accounts had actually received money stolen from other investors; the trustee's first obligation was to recover that stolen money, Sheehan said.

The three judges, seated on an elevated polished-wood dais, interrupted these carefully crafted statements after a few sentences.

Judge Pierre Leval challenged Picard's adversaries. Imagine two Madoff customers, one a friend and one an enemy, he said. Madoff chews on his pencil and magically turns his friend's $1 million in cash into a $2.5 million balance and reflects that on his friend's final account statement. But with another flick of his pencil, Madoff creates fictional losses that wipe out all but $50,000 of his enemy's $1 million cash investment; that, too, is shown on the final account statement. If the final account statement governs, the trustee would have no choice but to approve a $2.5 million claim for Madoff's friend and a $50,000 claim for Madoff's enemy, although both men had lost $1 million in cash. Was that fair?

The lawyers struggled to find an answer that did not disadvantage their clients or insult the judge's intelligence.

Judge Dennis Jacobs, the chief judge of the Second Circuit, posed his own conundrum. Suppose any broker created a fraudulent account statement that reduced a $20 million balance by $5 million, and then went bankrupt. Would that customer have a SIPC claim for $20 million, or just for the $15 million shown on that phony final account statement?

No, in that case the customer would have a $20 million claim, answered Barry Lax, one of Picard's adversaries.

How could that be? The judge's skepticism was obvious.

The three-judge panel answered its own questions on Tuesday, August 16, 2011. Its decision, written by Chief Judge Jacobs, unequivocally supported Picard's decision to limit investor claims to the actual cash they had lost, not the fictitious balances shown on their final statements.

The judges rejected Chaitman's assertion that SIPC was intended to be an insurance plan for investors, saying "it is clear that the obligations imposed on an insurance provider under state law do not apply" to SIPC. Indeed, the ruling cited the Securities Investors Protection Act of 1970, the law that created SIPC, and noted: "It is not at all clear that SIPA protects against all forms of fraud committed by brokers." And it firmly corrected Chaitman's contention that SIPA gave the trustee no choice but to honor an investor's final account statement. Rather, the judges said, every trustee was required to exercise discretion in the pursuit of fairness based on the facts in each case.

"The question presented by this appeal," they concluded, "is whether the method Mr. Picard selected for carrying out his responsibilities under SIPA is legally sound under the language of the statute. We hold that it is." In this case, to rely exclusively on the final account statements would be "impermissible" and "legal error" because it "would have the absurd effect of treating fictitious and arbitrarily assigned paper profits as real and give legal effect to Madoff's machinations."

The ruling vindicated Picard and freed him to make a first, small distribution of cash to the net losers. But his victory did nothing to reduce the hostility of the net winners. Their lawyers appealed for reconsideration and lost; in February 2012, they filed a long-shot appeal to the United States Supreme Court.

∽

It was not coincidental that the owners of the New York Mets were at center stage at the "net equity" hearing. In the city's sports pages, the trustee's courtroom battles with Fred Wilpon and his brother-in-law

Saul Katz vied for space with stories about their team's lackluster performance on the field.

Wilpon had been deeply wounded by Madoff's fraud. "I had a personal relationship with the Madoffs . . . not an everyday personal relationship but a friendship . . . [a] very trusting relationship," he said. "There is no person that you will talk to—none—that is more betrayed than I am." His memory of that last Gift of Life board meeting at the Lipstick Building in December 2008, just a few days before Madoff's arrest, was "like a dagger in the heart."

But the trustee's lawsuit asserted that Katz and Wilpon should have become suspicious of their trusted friend years before his fraud collapsed for a host of reasons—all of which the Wilpon family denied or disputed as misleading.

Looming large in the trustee's case was the issue of fraud insurance. In the early 1990s, Katz had encouraged a wealthy friend and longtime business associate to invest with Madoff. The friend, a Wall Street veteran whose clients included the Sears Roebuck heirs, was skeptical at first but in 1996 finally decided to invest. In early 2000, according to the trustee's lawsuit, he arranged for an AIG subsidiary to sell him a costly one-of-a-kind insurance policy that would protect his clients from loss if Madoff turned out to be a fraud. In early 2001, this friend urged Katz to explore a similar policy, the trustee asserted. Katz did, consulting the same insurance broker his friend had used. He ultimately decided that the insurance was too expensive for too little coverage—he had many millions more invested with Madoff than the Sears heirs did, and besides, he later recalled, "it was a waste of money . . . because Bernie's not going to do anything wrong." But the trustee argued that Katz's inquiries to the insurance broker showed that he had at least some doubts about whether Bernie would, in fact, do something wrong.

The trustee's case cited numerous other instances in which the Wilpon family allegedly turned a blind eye to specific warnings about Madoff.

The trustee quoted e-mails that executives at a Wilpon-affiliated hedge fund called Sterling Stamos allegedly exchanged after Madoff's arrest, claiming they had repeatedly warned the Wilpons that Madoff's lack of transparency was worrisome and that his returns were "too good to be true." The trustee claimed that the Wilpon executives knew Madoff had misled them in 2002 about the nature of his hedge fund clientele and should have become suspicious about that. Moreover, the Wilpons had invested indirectly in the Bayou fund, the high-profile fraud that collapsed in mid-2005, and the trustee argued they should have recognized the ways it resembled Madoff's operation.

According to the trustee, a Merrill Lynch executive had cautioned Katz in 2007 that Madoff did not conform to his firm's due diligence standards and had reminded Katz of the persistent rumors that Madoff was engaged in illegal front-running. As early as 1996, according to the trustee, several banks had refused to act as the custodian for some Wilpon employee retirement plans because their Madoff investments lacked transparency. The trustee further claimed that Katz had been warned about Madoff in 2002 by a cofounder of Ivy Asset Management, an allegation that Katz flatly denied. (Ivy was later sued by the New York State attorney general, who accused the firm of allowing its pension-fund clients to remain invested with Madoff for almost a decade after it had urged its private clients to close their Madoff accounts. The firm and its founders denied that accusation.)

Picard sought $1 billion from Wilpon and Katz, who already were in debt and would have trouble paying that sum without selling the Mets. The team owners insisted they had never suspected Madoff was running a Ponzi scheme but they were fighting an uphill battle for their most beloved possession until a federal district court judge named Jed S. Rakoff determined that their case—and a growing docket of other important Madoff cases pending before Judge Lifland—warranted district-court review because it raised issues that went beyond the purview of the bankruptcy court. Rakoff would tackle these complex legal issues himself.

Beginning in the summer of 2011, Judge Rakoff made several highly damaging rulings against Picard that will take many months, if not years, to resolve. He ruled that Picard had no legal right to sue the big banks and other third parties that had provided financial services for Madoff's feeder funds. He specifically ruled that Picard could not sue HSBC for damages, and a few weeks later, another federal judge similarly barred Picard's $19.6 billion claim for damages against JPMorgan Chase, Madoff's own banker.

The reasoning in both cases was that Picard, as trustee of the Madoff estate, stood in the shoes of the criminal Bernie Madoff, who had no right to sue the banks because he clearly had not been harmed by their actions. If the banks had done any harm, they had done it to Madoff's investors, so only those investors had the right to sue for damages. These rulings were well grounded in the prevailing case law, but they made little sense to Madoff's investors. Picard wasn't Madoff, so why should he be barred from suing the banks just because Madoff couldn't do so? And what was the point of giving the right to sue to the defrauded investors? Few had the money to file individual lawsuits against such formidable defendants, and federal securities laws sharply limited their ability to sue the banks collectively through class-action cases. It sounded like a Catch-22: Picard could afford to sue the banks but wasn't allowed to, and the investors were allowed to sue but couldn't afford to.

In late September 2011, Judge Rakoff unexpectedly ruled that there was a "safe harbor" provision of the bankruptcy law—a clause that had rarely if ever been applied in Ponzi schemes—that could bar Picard from recovering any of the fictitious profits the Mets owners had withdrawn from their Madoff accounts, and threw out all but two of the trustee's claims against them. This ruling would also affect hundreds of other clawback cases pending in the Madoff case. In the same opinion, Judge Rakoff raised Picard's burden of proof for his claims that Katz and Wilpon had been willfully blind to Madoff's fraud. This ruling, too, would affect a host of similar cases pending in the courts.

The two opinions that denied Picard the right to sue third parties for damages were pending before the federal appeals court at the end of 2011. In mid-January 2012, Judge Rakoff refused to let the trustee immediately appeal his far-reaching opinion in the Mets case. Instead, he scheduled the trustee's remaining claims against the Mets owners for trial in the spring of 2012.

∞

Over the years, Ruth Madoff had occasionally suspected that her husband was cheating on her. He "was always a flirt," she said. "It hurt me, terribly." Bernie always denied it and, in time, she decided simply to trust him. In any case, she was certain that Bernie loved her as intensely as she loved him. In her first days alone in the penthouse after he was locked up, as she started packing up decades of her life, she had come across their wedding album. She looked at the black-and-white images of that day: Ruth, an eighteen-year-old bride in white, Bernie a Hollywood-handsome groom in his tuxedo. In an impulsive gesture of anguish, she pulled out all the photographs, tore them up, and threw them away, along with the album. A stack of cherished love letters from Bernie followed. "I just couldn't bear to look at those," she explained later. This marriage, this love she felt for her husband, had been "my lifetime, my entire memory," she said.

Then she learned about Sheryl Weinstein's memoir, published in August 2009, in which the former Hadassah executive claimed to have had an affair with Bernie in the mid-1990s. "I didn't doubt that he'd slept with her," Ruth said. She visited the prison soon after the book was published and angrily confronted Bernie. "Tell me what happened," she demanded. "I can't stand the thought of you lying to me about this."

Bernie calmly reassured her that the memoir's claim was "totally not true." There had been no affair.

"I didn't believe him," she said.

To others, Madoff's betrayal of his marriage vows may seem trivial compared to his betrayal of every other promise he'd made to the world. But for Ruth, the topic was so painful that, years later, her eyes filled with tears talking about it. After Weinstein's memoir came out, she couldn't put the issue out of her mind.

It hurt her so much, she told him on her next visit. "I'm miserable to think that you have done this to me," she said. For several long moments, she waited, willing him to answer.

"He said, 'I'm sorry.' That's all," she recalled sadly. So he had apologized, perhaps tacitly admitting his faithlessness. "Did it make me feel better? No." Nothing could make her feel better.

❧

By the summer of 2011, Mary Schapiro and her management team at the Securities and Exchange Commission had the agency's new "whistle-blower" office up and running, with an expanded bounty program that allowed tipsters to profit if their tips produced successful cases. Even the implacable Harry Markopolos, the Boston analyst whose tips about Bernie Madoff had been bungled by the SEC for a decade, had become a fan of the agency's new leader.

"The woman's on fire," Markopolos said in 2009. "She has changed that agency. I'm really impressed."

He was even more impressed two years later when what he called "a great whistleblower program" went into operation. In an interview in 2011, he said, "The SEC is on the right track in developing a world-class system." The agency "is now highly responsive, and is getting back to people within three days or less of their filing a report. It's working." He added, "With the whistleblower program in place, the SEC is well on track to bringing the biggest cases in its history."

But his praise for the still-beleaguered agency was lost in a hurricane of controversy. At the eye of that storm was a quiet, bespectacled lawyer named David M. Becker, an SEC veteran with a lucrative private law practice and a sterling reputation. In early 2009, Schapiro had asked Becker to help her deal with the agency's post-Madoff crisis; despite what he later called a 90 percent pay cut, he agreed.

When he reported for work at the end of February 2009, he mentioned to the harried new chairwoman that his late mother had been a small-scale Madoff investor. One of his brothers had liquidated her account after her death in 2004, withdrawing about $2 million. He also shared this information with the agency's chief ethics officer. None of them—not Becker, the ethics officer, or Schapiro—saw the Becker family's Madoff connection as a reason to bar Becker from any role in Madoff matters. In fact, the ethics officer would advise Becker that the situation was "neither a conflict of interest nor an appearance of a conflict within the meaning of the applicable ethics statutes and rules."

This decision would come back to haunt the agency in February 2011, when news reports surfaced that in the last weeks of 2010, Sheehan's lawyers had sued the Becker estate to recover $1.5 million in fictitious Madoff profits. And at a congressional hearing in March, Helen Chaitman speculated that the reason the SEC had failed to force SIPC to honor Madoff's final account statements was "the conflict of interest of its general counsel."

But at the SEC, Becker hadn't acted like a man trying to protect his own wallet. His family might have saved $1.5 million if he had done what Chaitman wanted and used his influence to force SIPC to honor Madoff's final account statements. Instead, he advised the SEC to do just the opposite and support the "cash in, cash out" formula under which Picard would sue his family.

Similarly, in October 2009, Becker was asked to review a piece of long-shot legislation favored by Chaitman and other Picard critics. The bill would have prevented a SIPC trustee from filing any clawback lawsuits against innocent investors. Clearly, Becker's family would have benefited from such a ban—but his guidance to the SEC's legislative-affairs staff was that the bill was "incomprehensible" and did not "seem fair."

There was one point on which the SEC, under Becker's influence, differed with SIPC: The agency argued in court that victims' claims should somehow be adjusted for inflation. SIPC opposed that approach; the issue was scheduled for argument before Judge Lifland sometime in 2012. This "constant dollar" approach would benefit unknown numbers of long-time Madoff investors facing clawback lawsuits. It also would marginally reduce the amount of money the Becker family might owe Picard.

Becker's position clearly infuriated senior executives at SIPC, who later told the SEC's inspector general, incorrectly, that the SEC had agreed to support SIPC's position before Becker showed up and that he had then pushed it to reverse itself—an assertion, attributed to unidentified sources, made in a number of articles about the Becker issue. In sworn testimony, Becker disputed that claim, and in time the inspector general conceded that the SEC had voted only once on which position to take on the SIPC claims issue—in November 2009, when it agreed to support Picard but also to seek an inflation adjustment for claims.

Of course, Becker should have recused himself from the Madoff issues dominating the agency's workload. It was poor judgment or wishful thinking on everyone's part to believe that any relative of a Madoff investor working in the top ranks of the SEC, even one with a marked tendency to support positions at odds with his personal interests, would be given the benefit of the doubt in a case with the emotional valence of this one. That alone was reason enough for Becker to have steered clear of Madoff matters, despite the green light from the ethics office.

The bill that Becker found incomprehensible in October 2009 was not the last effort by the Madoff net winners to enlist help from Congress. In February 2011, Representative Scott Garrett, a New Jersey Republican, introduced a bill that would require SIPC trustees to base claims on the final account statements of innocent investors and would shield those investors from clawback lawsuits.

As 2012 opened, the bill was stalled in committee with only eight cosponsors, but its supporters were confident that hearings later in the year would give it a boost.

In 2009, without his lawyer's knowledge, Mark Madoff sent a few short e-mails to his mother, expressing love and encouragement. But her continued visits, calls, and letters to Bernie were the Berlin Wall in their relationship. "Ruth still didn't see that there was no such thing as neutrality in this particular war," Mark's widow, Stephanie, later recalled in a memoir.

After Mark's suicide attempt in October 2009, he became more insistent in demanding that Ruth cut her ties to Bernie. "I kept e-mailing him," Ruth recalled. "I told him I had visited Bernie maybe four times in two years—it wasn't as if I had put a tent up outside the prison and visited him daily. I had no idea it affected Mark so cruelly." Ruth loved her son and wanted to visit him, she said, but he would not let her into his life while Bernie was still in her life. Andrew's position was just as implacable: You can see Bernie or you can see your children and grandchildren, but not both.

In the fall of 2010, Ruth paid one last visit to the federal prison in Butner.

"I'm losing my family because I keep coming here," she told her husband as they sat together in the visiting room. "I have to stop."

He seemed to understand, she later recalled. He knew that she had few friends and family connections left. Joan and Bob Roman, her sister and brother-in-law, had embraced her with love and not a trace of blame, although they had lost much of their savings in Bernie's fraud and now ran an airport taxi service to make ends meet. The Romans' children had been supportive, too. But Ruth's own sons and their children were her most precious connections, and the nonnegotiable price of restoring those ties was to cut off Bernie. It was a price she was finally ready to pay, if she could. "I have to stop," she told him again, "and you have to *help* me stop—you can't keep writing and calling."

He agreed, and she left the prison for the last time. But he kept writing and calling. "It was as if he couldn't *not* call," she said. She could ignore the letters and the e-mails but not the calls. After a few weeks, she changed her phone number.

She spoke with him one last time, the day she learned that their son Mark was dead. "I called the prison and was connected to the chaplain," she said. "He got Bernie, and he told Bernie before I spoke to him." When Bernie called her back, she recalled, "I could barely get it out . . . everyone was crying." In his grief, Bernie tried to reach her again, but she wouldn't take his calls or e-mails. "Mark's suicide was the end of it for me," she said.

She built a life. She did volunteer work, delivering food for the Meals on Wheels program near Joan's home. She made a few new friends. When Andrew called and asked her to visit his family in early 2011, she rejoiced and went.

That was when she learned that Andrew was cooperating with an author, Laurie Sandell, who was writing a biography of the Madoff family; Andrew wanted Ruth to cooperate as well.

Sandell, in fact, was one of Andrew's houseguests when Ruth arrived. "I didn't realize at first that she was taking notes," Ruth said, regretting that she had not considered more carefully how her wry memories and earthy humor would look on paper. She would have a few glasses of wine and forget that this wasn't just one of Andrew's smart young friends; this was an author taking notes and making constant observations.

Ruth had heard rumors that Mark's widow, Stephanie, was also working on a memoir—it would be published a few weeks before Sandell's book. Ruth couldn't imagine actually seeking public attention by pitching a book; she had spent two years trying to escape the harsh glare of the public spotlight. But regarding Andrew's request, she didn't see that she had a choice. "Andrew asked me to do it—and I had decided to do what he wanted me to do." She would sacrifice her privacy, her peace, anything to "make a better relationship between Andy and me."

She stared into space for a moment. "I hadn't done that in Mark's case. And I will regret that until my dying day."

For the federal prosecutors, the Madoff criminal case gained a little ground in 2011, although the five defendants indicted the year before were still awaiting trial at year-end.

On Monday, June 6, Eric S. Lipkin, the former payroll manager at the Madoff firm, pleaded guilty in federal court in Manhattan. Lipkin's parents, Irwin and Carole, had both been early Madoff employees, and Eric had worked there since he was a teenager in the mid-1980s, doing clerical chores for his father, the firm's controller. Lipkin confessed that he had conspired to create false records for Madoff investors, regulators, and auditors; had padded payroll records to conceal "no-show" jobs; and, just weeks before Madoff's arrest in 2008, had lied on a $1.4 million mortgage application. At age thirty-seven, he faced a possible sentence of seventy years in prison.

On Wednesday, November 16, prosecutors quietly disclosed that another longtime Madoff employee, David L. Kugel, would plead guilty the following Monday. This letter contained a little bombshell: It noted that Kugel would confess to faking arbitrage-trade records as part of "a conspiracy beginning in the early 1970s." No other criminal cases had cited such an early starting date for Madoff's crimes.

When Kugel, a bland but well-groomed man in his mid-sixties, appeared in court on November 21, he told the judge he was "ready to accept responsibility for what I have done" and was "deeply sorry for my actions and the harm suffered by the victims." He admitted he had provided "historical trade information" to other Madoff employees "which was used to create false, profitable trades" for Madoff's investors.

"Specifically," he said, "beginning in the early '70s, until the collapse of [Madoff's firm] in Dec. 2008, I helped create fake, backdated trades" that "gave the appearance of profitable trading when in fact no trading had actually occurred." He knew that these faked arbitrage trades would show up on monthly customer statements, he added, although they had been "executed only on paper." And like Lipkin, he also confessed to committing bank fraud involving false mortgage applications.

The prosecutor provided a few more details, asserting that Kugel had supplied the false arbitrage-trading data to Annette Bongiorno through the 1970s and 1980s, and to Jodi Crupi thereafter. Both Bongiorno and Crupi have denied any knowledge of Madoff's Ponzi scheme.

Some of the trading data mirrored legitimate trades for the Madoff firm's own account, but Kugel said he had known the data was being used to create fake trades. The prosecutor claimed that Bongiorno would tell Kugel precisely how much cash she needed to appear to be investing for a client, and he would tell her how much trading volume had occurred so that her faked trades would always look plausible. Kugel allegedly followed the same routine with Crupi after she took over from Bongiorno. The goal was to "meet the rate of return predetermined by Madoff for that client," the prosecutor said.

Kugel, facing eighty-five years in prison at age sixty-six, promised to contribute to the continuing investigation. "I want the Court and everyone to know that I will do all I can to cooperate with the government," he said.

On Monday, December 19, Enrica Cotellessa-Pitz, a petite brunette in her early fifties who was hired by the Madoff firm in 1978 and named its controller in 1998, became the third Madoff executive to plead guilty in 2011. Cotellessa-Pitz admitted that she had filed false documents with the SEC over several years. She also confessed to conspiring with others to help Bernie Madoff cheat on his income taxes for more than fifteen years by understating his profits from the firm. And she said she helped doctor the firm's books to hide the transfer of millions of dollars from the investment-management business to Madoff's legitimate trading operation. Facing a possible sentence of fifty years, Cotellessa-Pitz agreed to cooperate with the continuing investigation.

Like Lipkin, Kugel and Cotellessa-Pitz were released on bail until their work for the government was done.

❧

His voice on the phone was soft but intense. Bernie Madoff was clearly agitated by reports of Kugel's confession. In a collect call on November 29, he insisted that Kugel would have had "no clue as to whether they were real trades or not" back in the 1970s. He repeated that assertion in an e-mail he wrote that night—one of seven he wrote the week of Kugel's confession.

He seemed most upset by the suggestion that he had been faking arbitrage trades back in the 1970s. Each e-mail added new flourishes to his bedrock claim that he was a legitimate success until 1992. The claim by the prosecutors and the trustee that he had never been a successful money manager "drives me crazy," he said. He regretted pleading guilty without a trial at which he could have refuted "all of this speculation."

For Madoff, the year had opened with the grief of his son's death and the loneliness of Ruth's rejection, and it closed with the wounded pride and impotent anger triggered by Kugel's confession. But the most potentially significant development came in the summer, when he became ill and underwent a battery of medical tests. The prison doctors found he had stage-four chronic kidney disease, one step short of the worst diagnosis for that condition.

The doctors warned Madoff that he would probably need dialysis sometime in the foreseeable future. But a few weeks after the diagnosis, he told a visitor he didn't see the point of trying to prolong a life spent behind bars, rejected by his wife and family.

By the fall, he was clearly stronger. Asked about his health during a phone call in early September, he said, "I'm okay. I have this kidney issue—I mean, it's going to kill me some day. But it's not too bad. I'm managing."

He managed, indeed. He traded e-mails with a Fox Business News correspondent; conversed with a Harvard business professor researching a case study; enjoyed a few visits from the *Today* show host Matt Lauer, a former neighbor; and talked for two hours off-camera with Barbara Walters, who visited him in prison in October.

As the third anniversary of his arrest approached, Madoff grew reflective. From his vantage point, "the real tragedy" of those years was the death of his son and "the loss of my wife Ruth, son Andy and all my grandchildren." But, he added, "this in no way diminishes the pain and suffering I have caused to my friends and [many] clients whose trust I betrayed."

By January 2012, his reflections had grown even darker. Asked about his physical health, he responded, "My health is as good as can be expected for now." But the severe depression that afflicted him "is doing me in," he continued. "As you can imagine I miss my family so much I find it unbearable. After more than fifty years of constant togetherness both emotional and physical it's as if I have no soul left. I blame myself for so much."

∽

The two books about the Madoff family were published in late October, and after the publicity ebbed, Ruth Madoff decided to move north, closer to the grandchildren she could now visit freely. A relative offered her a home in shoreline Connecticut, and she gratefully accepted.

Ruth piled her belongings—not a large collection—into her small black Honda, said farewell to her faithful sister in Boca Raton, and set out on the 1,300-mile, twenty-two-hour drive. It would have been an ordeal for most solo seventy-year-old drivers in a light-weight sedan. But Ruth said she loved every minute. She could go where she wanted, stop whenever she liked, never worrying about being hassled or recognized.

Looking back on the trip from the winter solitude of her new home, she said, "There's this sense of freedom you get driving yourself. It was wonderful."

EPILOGUE

On August 24, 2010, more than a year after his arrival at Butner, Bernie Madoff grants his first on-the-record interview, sitting in the prison's nearly empty visitor room and spinning tales about his long career on Wall Street and the fraud that will forever be associated with his name.

The first question demanding an answer is: Who else knew?

He insists that his family knew nothing about his fraud. "I knew it was going to be a disaster; I had to take the blame," he says. "I felt I deserved to be punished—it was almost a relief—but I had to spare my family." So he faced the firestorm of his arrest, and he says he was horrified when his wife, brother, and sons were vilified anyway. There were no witnesses, no records, no bits of evidence that would implicate his family members, he continues, because they were not involved in any way. "I didn't see how they could have been found guilty," he asserts. "I knew there was nothing anyone could find."

Then who else might have suspected he was a fraud?

"Picower was the only one that might have," he says. "I mean, how could he not?" Jeffry Picower had promoted dubious tax shelters to his clients and had been a client of the corrupt arbitrageur Ivan Boesky in the red-hot 1980s. "He had pushed a lot of envelopes," Madoff says of Picower, but he does not concede that the other giant feeder funds or major investors knew that they were investing in a Ponzi scheme. The worst he will say is that some of them were "lacking in sophistication."

The second most compelling question must be: When did it start?

Madoff continues to insist, as he did in court, that his vast fraud did not start until 1992. Until then, he says, he was making legitimate investments. He claims that the government and the bankruptcy trustee are simply wrong when they assert that the fraud began earlier, or that it was a fraud from the beginning.

Of course, so much is riding on the answer to that question, "When did it start?" The earlier the fraud began, the more of the Madoff family's remaining assets the government can claim for his victims. So the answer to this simple question will remain elusive at least until the Madoffs have settled all the financial claims now facing them. Even then, Madoff himself is unlikely to jeopardize those settlements by answering this question any differently than he does today.

Prosecutors have said at every opportunity that the Ponzi scheme began "at least by the 1980s." The bankruptcy trustee claims that only a minimal amount of trading was done in a few big client accounts during all the years for which they have reconstructed Madoff's in-house records—back to the late 1970s. But the account statements for those years do show investment holdings in client accounts. Banks and clearinghouse records go back only to 2002, so there are no records from independent sources that verify whether Madoff was actually making those investments. After nearly two years of investigation, there is nothing in any of the legal filings that proves precisely when the Ponzi scheme began. The records that would answer the question no longer exist, and the people who can answer the question either won't do so, or they echo Madoff's own story.

It could have been a Ponzi scheme from day one, but Madoff flatly denies that supposition. He says he was successful enough as a trader to build the visible, legitimate side of his business in the first two decades of his career, a period rich in arbitrage opportunities. It is not naïve to think that someone as successful as he was in public could have been equally successful as a private money manager pursuing commonplace arbitrage strategies, at least at first—before so much money started pouring in.

There is a slight tilt on the seesaw of probability toward the notion that the Ponzi scheme itself began on a large scale sometime in the middle or final years of the 1980s. Many investors recall being told that Madoff was shifting away from his arbitrage strategy around that time, a shift that may have been designed to cover his tracks. He told Mike

Engler in Minneapolis soon after 1986 that he was opening his "institutional" money management business to individual investors for the first time, another plausible cover story. Until 1985, Peter Madoff occasionally signed redemption checks for Ruth's relatives, but no one recalls him doing so after that date. It was during the mid-1980s that the "friends and family" accounts originally set up by Saul Alpern began their astronomical growth under Avellino & Bienes, perhaps funneling more money to Madoff than he could deploy in legitimate arbitrage. Even Madoff concedes that a rise in withdrawals after the 1987 market crash put him under intense pressure, just as an abundance of cash started to flow in from his first hedge funds clients.

But it is clear from Madoff's answers today that he has drifted across the border between truth and lies since the earliest days of his career. He talks about getting into trouble as a young broker in 1962, when he lost money for his "friends and family" clients but made them whole by borrowing money from Alpern—allowing them to think he was a genius. He talks about the foreigners who used him to evade their home country's currency controls in the 1980s—clearly across the bright line of their local laws—but he never blinked at helping them.

So even if Madoff were to take a lie-detector test, the odds are he could not be pinned down as to precisely when he became a crook. Was it a decision he made on a single red-letter day, or was it a destination he reached after a decades-long journey along the edges of right and wrong?

What is also evident in Madoff's answers is that he clearly feels betrayed by the big clients who abruptly started to pull money out of his hands after the 1987 crash—men listed now among the victims of his own vast betrayal.

"Part of the agreement I had with them was [that] the profits would be reinvested—not withdrawn," he says, sounding disappointed rather than angry. "They were the only ones who didn't abide by that. Picower and Shapiro were the worst; Chais and Levy were not so bad." But he concedes that "there was nothing I could have sued them over." And he acknowledges that Carl Shapiro, Jeffry Picower, and Norman Levy did put in fresh cash when he desperately needed it during the SEC investigation in 1992. But he still believes that these men "changed the deal on me. I was hung out to dry."

Without a trace of irony, Madoff says, "Picower claimed he had lost a lot of money on bonds with Goldman Sachs. It turned out he lied—he didn't lose money; that wasn't why he withdrew [money] from me." Madoff's other big customers took money out, too, though nowhere near as much. In fuzzy language, he suggests that their holdings included paper profits on long-standing securities positions that were offset by counterparty positions held by his foreign customers, positions that he claims he could not liquidate without huge losses.

Like so much that Madoff says, it is a plausible, detailed, credible-sounding explanation that starts to fray after it is handled a few times. What kind of legitimate positions would have created such a problem for him? If there were paper profits on real securities, surely at least some of those profits could have been realized. Why didn't his sophisticated customers understand that rapidly unloading huge amounts of stock would drive the prices down and reduce or even eliminate their profits?

Before any such questions can arise, Madoff moves swiftly to the punch line about those unwelcome post-1987 withdrawals: "Before I realized it, I was in the hole for a few billion dollars."

To have simply admitted his losses at that point "would have been a total scandal," he continues. So he covered up the losses with money stolen from other people, some of them relatives and lifelong friends whose faith in him grew with each year of impervious success.

Asked to explain his relationships with a long list of big investors and feeder fund managers, he veers off on a tangent, sounding almost defensive for the first time. "People are greedy," he says, apparently unaware of the chutzpah required for Bernie Madoff to express that opinion about anyone. "I told everyone, 'Don't put more than half of your money with me—you don't know, I could go crazy.'" But he took their money anyway, and thousands of them were ignoring his sage advice and betting their entire family's future on their faith in him.

"Somehow [at first], I assumed it would work out," he says, returning to his explanation of why he started to steal from his big institutional clients. "That's when I started taking money in from all of those hedge funds. And I said, 'Well, I'll just get myself out of a hole.'"

But he couldn't. "I got trapped in this hole. I never set out to just steal money," he says.

But he was stealing money; he was running an enormous inescapable

Ponzi scheme. If he didn't plan to kill himself or go into hiding, how did he think it would end?

"It was almost like—it sounds horrible to say it now, but I just wanted the world to come to an end." He pauses, glances at his lawyer, and shrugs. It does sound horrible to say it, but he continues, struggling to explain. "When 9/11 happened," he went on, "I thought that would be the only way out—the world would come to an end, and I'd be dead and everyone would be gone."

He knew that sort of oblivion wasn't really possible, of course, unless he took his own life or fled, and either exit ramp would have left his family to face the scandal alone. And he could not do that, he says. "It never entered my mind," he adds.

Implausibly, against the weight of the available evidence, he claims that he could have kept his gigantic fraud going if he had wanted to. He insists he had not been beaten by the market maelstrom of the summer and fall of 2008; he had simply decided to quit. "I could have covered everything," he says. "I had commitments of cash that would have come in. So I could have—but I got tired. . . . I knew by Thanksgiving that I was going to give it up. I was going to stop."

He backs up. "For sixteen years, I kept this secret from my wife, my brother, my sons. How I was able to do that and maintain any degree of sanity—well, that worries me, when I think about it," he says, shaking his head slightly as if he is still baffled.

Even at the end, he says, "I always expected that the people who would take the big losses would be the hedge funds"—not the friends, relatives, foundation directors, college administrators, and trusting investors who fawned over him for years. He recalls all the fund-raising galas and charity dinners that were a common feature of his calendar: "I hated going to those events. I hated having everybody falling over me, telling me how wonderful I was, when I knew it was not true. It was all a charade."

He adds, "It was like the emperor's new clothes."

The one time his control slips is when he is asked about the wisdom of Ruth's decision to stay with him after his arrest, the one topic he cannot seem to tackle with any fluency.

"I never told Ruth that she couldn't leave me. I said to her, 'You could leave me.' Friends advised her to [leave]. It's hard to understand." He pauses. "You have a relationship of fifty years," he says, staring out the window and pausing again. "It would have been better for her if she'd left." Their sons "are still furious with me," he acknowledges. "They don't understand why she doesn't hate me, why she isn't as angry as they are."

She is fiercely angry, he says, his voice breaking. "But somehow she was still able to find some compassion for me."

He wipes away his tears with some stiff paper napkins his lawyer finds somewhere and gradually regains a grip on his emotions.

Steadier now, he deflects a question about how he and his wife spent their last night together in their home, before he pleaded guilty in March 2009. "There was always the hope" that he would remain free on bail until he was sentenced, he says. They watched a little television, he thinks, or maybe she read something. "Ruth held herself together—and I tried to hold myself together for her." That is what they do, apparently.

Despite his initial anger over the lawsuit the trustee filed against Ruth in 2009, Madoff has recently begun cooperating with the trustee's efforts to compensate victims of his Ponzi scheme. He reports—and his lawyer confirms—that members of the trustee's legal team interviewed him at the prison for almost sixteen hours during the summer. He thinks he was helpful, he says.

When the allowed interview time is over, Madoff stands, shakes hands, and thanks his visitor for listening and trying to understand— although his explanations have created as many questions as they have answered. The guard waiting in the corner unlocks the small door at the back of the visiting room; the associate warden who escorted him to the interview gestures for him to go ahead. He steps through the door into the courtyard and, in a moment, is out of sight.

❧

With its global scope and its generational reach, the Madoff case gave the world some new and unsettling lessons about a very old crime. Throughout history, Ponzi schemes have always been profoundly ambiguous. Like a robbery, a Ponzi scheme is a transfer of wealth. But unlike a robbery, the transfer is not just from victim to villain; it is also from victim to victim. It is a crime that the past inflicts on the future; in the present, in the heyday of its success, a Ponzi scheme is amazingly painless.

Perhaps that has always made it easier to live with yourself when you're running one. It's not like sticking a knife in someone to steal a wallet, or bashing someone's skull to grab a luxury car, or kidnapping someone's child at gunpoint. You don't see the terrified faces, the blood, the horror, the loss. At first, you just see gratitude.

It seems to be such a gentle crime—until the awful day when the music stops. Until then, anyone who needs to withdraw money for necessary comforts or philanthropy can do so. And the others, those who don't take their money out, nevertheless feel secure in their wealth, safe from the financial anxieties of the world. Until the money runs out, people love the Ponzi schemer; they are grateful to him. Why should that cause him any pain?

No doubt that is how Bernie Madoff lived with his crime every day. He did not see any "victims"; he saw only "beneficiaries." It's easy to see how seductive that would be. Who has not fantasized about winning the lottery and playing God by giving vast sums away—the delicious rush, the sense of joyful power that this would produce? Until the end, there was only the possibility that, someday, others would be hurt. He might die before he had to face that, after all. Or the world might end, as he imagined.

Or, better still, he might figure a way out. Elie Wiesel spoke of the criminal's capacity to imagine crimes that are unthinkable to his victims. True—but perhaps he can also imagine an escape from the consequences of his acts. If Madoff had the imagination to sustain his historic crime, he certainly had the imagination to dream of getting away with it; every Ponzi schemer does. "Everyone here always asks me why I never ran," he wrote in an e-mail from prison. "I certainly had the opportunity over the last few years to stash money somewhere with all the connections I had. . . . The truth is that it never was something I ever gave any thought to. I never wanted to think of what I was doing as stealing, I guess. Somewhere in my head I allowed myself to believe that I was going to make things work out, as crazy as that seems now." Criminals are not tethered to logic; if they were, there would be no Ponzi schemes, whose only logical outcomes for the schemer are suicide, prison, or life as a fearful fugitive.

If Bernie Madoff could be admired everywhere and still see only a crook when he looked in the mirror, he would have been much more honest with himself than most of us are—much more honest with himself than he was with anyone else. Like every Ponzi schemer, he was able to face his victims every day because they didn't look like victims, not until the final days and weeks—and the evidence is that, in those days, he was as tormented by fear and grief as any guilty, cornered human being would have been.

Such is the Ponzi scheme. It is the crime of the egotist, not the sadist. One need not enjoy others' pain to run a Ponzi scheme. Until the final moments, there is no pain. One is helping, not hurting. That delusion, based on a lie, is reinforced every day by every thankful customer who says, "Bless you, Bernie!"

But Madoff's Ponzi scheme didn't simply reinforce what we always knew about this sort of crime. It etched new lessons into our hearts.

All Ponzi schemes transfer wealth from victim to victim. But because of the nature of so many of Madoff's victims—charities, endowments, major philanthropists, generous people on all rungs of the economic ladder—this Ponzi scheme transferred wealth from victims to the larger community, too. In effect, Madoff robbed Peter to pay Paul, and Paul gave the stolen money away to help the rest of us.

The problematical role of Jeffry Picower is extreme but telling.

Like so many of Madoff's investors, Picower built up enormous wealth, at least partly with Madoff's help. And then he used some of that wealth to support hospitals, scientific research, education—in short, to make the world better.

So did Carl Shapiro, the Palm Beach philanthropist. Like the early investors in every Ponzi scheme, he received money that was taken from later victims and he used that money to endow hospitals, art museums, charitable services for needy people.

Norman Levy died leaving a fortune in fictional profits in Madoff's hands, and his daughter used some of that phony fortune to create a foundation dedicated to the fight for human justice and equality. The family foundations of Madoff victims such as the New York Mets owner Fred Wilpon and the famed movie director Steven Spielberg supported a host of worthy causes. Even Madoff's family foundation contributed to leukemia research.

A common thread in the hundreds of individual stories about Madoff's victims at every socioeconomic level is their generosity to others. A typical example is Gordon Bennett, the natural foods entrepreneur who retired on his Madoff savings; with his modest nest egg generating a comfortable income, he was able to devote the second half of his life to conservation causes and making a notable difference in his community. Modest family foundations in towns and cities all across America are scattered through the Madoff victim list, and each one of them made small, precious improvements in the lives of those they touched.

Rich and possibly selfish hedge fund managers invested with Madoff—and he paid out their money as investment income for Hadassah, which dedicated it to charity and good works. Rich Arab sovereign wealth funds invested with Madoff—and he paid their money out as profits and management fees to Stanley Chais, who gave it away to educational institutions in Israel. Rich investors living lavishly gave money to Madoff—and he used it to make reassuring, steady payments to modest investors who consequently lived in greater comfort and died with greater dignity than they might have enjoyed otherwise.

These generous ends do not remotely justify the viciously criminal means that empowered them, of course. But they add a new facet to our understanding of how Ponzi schemes work in society and why they gain such traction in people's lives and dreams.

This particular Ponzi scheme delivered another new and unwelcome message to those wise enough to see it. With his ability to disarm even the most sophisticated institutional investors, Bernie Madoff revealed how diabolically difficult it is for regulators to protect the public in the twenty-first century.

If the Madoff story proves nothing else, it proves that regulators are living in a dream world, one that is very different from the dream world populated by investors. Indeed, if any gap in perception justifies dusting off the tired old dichotomies between Mars and Venus, it is this one. Regulators, even very good ones, are from Mars; investors, even very rich ones, are from Venus.

Good regulators believe in skepticism, but most investors crave simplicity. If regulators run across someone claiming to have a safe, high-yield investment that always goes up even when everything else goes down, they want to take him to court. Investors want to take him to dinner. They are desperate for an easy answer to the immensely difficult problems that have confronted them since the slow demise of the "gold watch" company pensions and the rise of do-it-yourself retirement plans. That need for something simple always seems to strangle skepticism before it can speak up.

For regulators, the most important attributes of an investment are clarity and liquidity, and they believe that any attractive investment should have both. For investors, the only important attributes of an investment are safety and yield—and they stubbornly insist, against all logic, that any attractive investment should have both. Somewhere out there, they are certain, there is a wizard who can produce a totally safe investment yielding at least 8 percent a year.

Regulators believe in the fine print. Investors never, ever read the fine print—never.

Because of this culture clash, the Madoff scandal prompted almost everyone in Washington to ask the wrong questions: How can we improve the world that regulators live in? How can we make a regulatory regime based on fine print work better? The questions that should have been asked are: How can we improve the world that investors live in? What kind of regime will work in a world where nobody reads the fine print, where investing is almost always a blind leap of faith?

The Madoff lesson is crystal clear: The "full-disclosure" regime that had been generating fine print for investors for more than seventy-five years didn't work—and not just because the SEC failed to act on the credible tips it received. It didn't work because it doesn't reflect the way today's investors make their decisions.

Inadequate disclosure was not what inflicted the catastrophic losses that so many of Madoff's victims sustained. What inflicted those losses was their failure even to ask for some fine print, much less read it. What went wrong was their rejection of basic bedrock principles of investing— that high returns are leg-shackled to high risks; that you should never put all your eggs in one basket; that you should never invest in something you cannot understand. They failed to see that no one should hand *all their money* over to anyone simply because they trust him, or because someone they admire trusts him.

Yet that is what so many millions of people do. We do not consult the fine print to decide if we can trust someone. We consult our friends, our relatives, our coworkers, our sons, our fathers, our richest acquaintances, our past experiences, and, ultimately, our gut. And as Bernie Madoff learned, once trust is earned, it will protect a con man from every red flag. After all, "con man" is short for "confidence man," someone who inspires enough confidence to blind his victims to his crime.

More rules and more fine print aren't going to do much to stop the next Bernie Madoff. What would? That could be a creative parlor game for future generations, to design a regulatory scheme that works on Venus, not just on Mars. Perhaps someone will propose borrowing a lesson from the medical world and developing a "formulary," a roster of approved investments that are the only ones the public can buy with any official assurance of safety. Regulators could designate several large, well-regulated categories of investments as safe for investors—mutual funds, annuities, bank CDs, real estate investment trusts—and then watch those categories like hawks to ensure that no con artists slip in. Investors would still be free to invest in everything else, of course, but purely on a "caveat emptor" basis. If it wasn't on the protected list when you bought it, don't go running to the regulators if it turns out to be a fraud.

Or maybe the answer is to require individual investors to be licensed, the way drivers are licensed—after they've passed tests on all the basic rules of the road. They could be quizzed on how to recognize a fraud, how to choose the best investment out of a multiple-choice test, and how to pick the Ponzi schemer out of a lineup. Running a do-it-yourself pension fund (which is what each of us is doing with our IRAs and 401(k) plans) is far more difficult than driving a car, so perhaps we should make investors study and pass a test before they steer their life savings off a cliff.

Or perhaps the answer is to make the penalties for even the smallest fraud infractions so draconian that Wall Street will actually police itself, blowing the whistle on those it suspects of chicanery and protecting investors from their worst instincts. Fines are just money—Wall Street makes money like clouds make rain. Serious penalties, such as a serious loss of liberty or a meaningful career setback, might be more effective than a few more emphatic rules enforced by a few more inexperienced inspectors.

The point here is not to advocate one particular reform or another, but to look for out-of-the-box solutions that actually address what went wrong in the Madoff scandal and that are not simply improvements to the "fine print" regime. Without training, we all wildly overestimate our capacity to detect risks and recognize criminals in the market-place. This is the hard lesson of the Madoff case that none of us wants to accept. We all invest on faith. We all believe that trust is all we need—indeed, most of us don't have enough time or information to rely on anything but trust. If regulators and policymakers don't acknowledge this, their approach to the chronic problem of market fraud will be limited and ineffective.

☙

On February 15, 2011, Bernie Madoff sits for a second interview at the prison in Butner. The security maze is the same, the associate warden as gracious as before, and the visiting room still clean, dimly lit, and slightly shabby. But the man waiting there alone is shockingly changed. He is thin, almost fragile. His loose-fitting khaki uniform is a little rumpled, its collar oddly pressed. The excess length of the webbed belt at his waist is folded under to keep it from flapping at his side. Halfway through the conversation, he notices that one shirt button is undone and quickly buttons it. What had been confident magnetism has weakened into a troubled intensity.

He still believes that Jeffry Picower was the only investor who might have suspected his fraud, he says. But he also believes that the big banks and funds who dealt with him were somehow "complicit" in his crime. Pressed to square the contradiction, he accuses the banks and funds of "willful blindness" for failing to investigate the discrepancies between his regulatory filings and other information available to them.

"They were deliberately ignoring the red flags," he says. "They had to know. But the attitude was sort of, 'If you're doing something wrong, we don't want to know.'" As in the August interview, he claims he has tried to help the trustee recover assets for his victims from those giant institutions.

He again insists that his family knew nothing about his crime, but he dodges any discussion of his son's suicide, saying only that he never expected his arrest would cause so much personal devastation. For the first time, he discloses that he is working with a therapist to dig into the psychological roots of his life of lies.

"I always wanted to please people; that was a weakness that I had," he says. "I had been successful in a business, taking on the New York Stock Exchange—so, I figured, why can't I manage money? Why can't I do this, too?" He shakes his head and gazes down at the bare floor. "How did I live with myself? My counselor says people 'compartmentalize.' I never believed that I was stealing. I thought I was taking a business risk, like I did all the time. I thought it was a temporary situation."

He adds: "It starts as a very simple thing and then becomes complicated."

When the associate warden calls time, Madoff stands and moves toward the courtyard door. He pauses to comment bleakly on a recent *People* magazine article about his wife. "I was sorry to see they used that photo of her with Mark when he was a boy," he says, shaking his head. Then he bids an awkward good-bye and follows a uniformed guard out of the room.

∞

The Madoff case demonstrated with brutal clarity another truth that we simply do not want to face about the Ponzi schemer in our midst: He is not "other" than us, or "different" from us. He is just like us—*only more so.*

Even the lawyers at the SEC thought that an apparently trustworthy, apparently successful Wall Street statesman like Bernie Madoff did not fit the profile of a Ponzi schemer. But that is *exactly* the profile of a Ponzi schemer. Any number of crimes may be committed by a seedy-looking, shifty-eyed, inarticulate grifter in a cheap suit and scuffed shoes, but a Ponzi scheme is *never* going to be one of them. Yet almost every Madoff victim, including the SEC, trusted him precisely because he seemed so trustworthy, a mistake that Ponzi scheme victims make over and over again.

Why? Perhaps because they refuse to accept the exposed Ponzi schemer as fully human.

Of course it's comforting to think that only a soulless, heartless monster could have inflicted such pain on those he knew and supposedly cared about, that no human being could construct a life of such brazen, destructive lies.

We flatter ourselves. All human beings have the capacity for deceit. We all damage and disappoint people we love. We all delude ourselves about ourselves, every single day. *I'm not going to get cancer even though I smoke. I can drive better after a few drinks. I'll pay off that credit card debt next month.* Most of us are born knowing how to tell lies. By definition, we cannot see our own blind spots.

So to insist, as so many of his victims have, that Bernie Madoff was not fully human, that he was a beast, a psychopath, is a facile cop-out, one last comforting delusion that will leave us forever vulnerable to the seductive spells that all Ponzi schemers cast.

Madoff was not inhumanly monstrous. He was monstrously human. He was greedy for money and praise, arrogantly sure of his own capacity to pull it off, smugly dismissive of skeptics—just like anyone who mortgaged the house to invest in tech stocks, or tapped the off-limits college fund to gamble on a new business, or put all the retirement savings into a hedge fund they didn't understand, or cheated a little on the tax return or the expense account or the spouse.

Just like us—only more so. His imagination constructed a soaring scaffold of deceit that towered over the simple cover stories we occasionally hammer together. His lies were massively larger than ours, and they lasted longer, survived more scrutiny, were more ambitiously conceived and elaborately documented. As a result, tens of thousands of trusting victims believed that Madoff's genius could defy markets, year in and year out.

And they sustained their belief in exactly the same way he sustained his belief that he could get away with it; the belief was reinforced by daily experience, *selectively observed.* He ignored the fact that he didn't have any investment earnings to pay to his customers. His customers ignored the fact that his results were increasingly implausible and his operations were suspiciously secret. While the money was rolling in, the victims did not torture themselves daily, minute by minute, wondering if it was somehow possible that all their wealth and status would vanish in a puff of smoke on a single day. While the money was rolling in, Madoff probably didn't either.

But this wizard behind the curtain—pumping the bellows and pushing the buttons and working the microphone to create his utterly convincing illusions, even after the prison doors had clicked shut behind him—was able to build his Emerald City only because such an extraordinary number of people decided to believe him. His accomplices believed they could go along for the ride and enjoy the wealth without facing a day of reckoning. Add in the friends and family members, the bureaucratic or inexperienced regulators, the smart accountants and lawyers, the sleek feeder fund salesmen, the international bankers, the charity investment committee members, the brilliant hedge fund due-diligence experts—they all told themselves that while it didn't exactly make a lot of sense and was a little unusual and possibly even a little suspicious, it would turn out fine.

Time and again, people caught Madoff in an obvious lie and gave him the benefit of the doubt. They didn't do this because he seemed so different from them, but because he seemed so much like them, only better: smarter, more experienced, more confident, more in control. Because he was fundamentally human and seemed to live in the same world they did, they could believe that somehow it would all work out, that they could ignore unpleasant realities without incurring unpleasant consequences.

So, like every philandering spouse, every opportunistic cheat, every impulsive risk-taker—like so many of us, only more so—Bernie Madoff thought he could avoid the implacable dead-end finale of the Ponzi scheme and somehow get away with it.

The next Bernie Madoff expects to get away with it, too.

No matter when you are reading this, the next Bernie Madoff is working in secret somewhere in the country, somewhere in the world. A world immune to Ponzi schemes is a world utterly devoid of trust, and no one wants to live in a world like that. Indeed, no healthy economic system can function in a world like that. So right now, some new Bernie Madoff is exploiting our need for trust to build another world of lies.

We will read about him next month or next year. Until then, his victims are telling themselves how generous and respected he is in the community. They are admiring his life of quiet luxury, they are flattered when he includes them, they are a little envious of the money he is making for their more successful friends, those sophisticated folks who speak so highly of him. They are telling themselves that he is an excellent person, a gentleman, a mensch.

Whatever their niggling doubts, they are reassuring themselves right this minute about how trustworthy he is, as he spins out his vibrant, beautiful web of fantasy.

Later, when that new world of lies is torn apart, they will rage at the pain and devastation he caused and brand him an evil, inhuman monster. But if they are honest with themselves, they will have to admit that he was recognizably, shamefully human every step of the way—just like the last Bernie Madoff and the first Bernie Madoff.

That is the most enduring lesson of the Madoff scandal: in a world full of lies, the most dangerous ones are those we tell ourselves.

NOTES

Except as specifically noted, all the civil lawsuits and criminal cases cited in the text and notes were still pending in the courts as of February 2011, the deadline for revisions before hardcover publication.

PROLOGUE

xx the guards here act "starstruck": *American Greed: Madoff Behind Bars*, produced by Kurtis Productions (Mike West, executive producer) for CNBC (Charles Schaeffer, executive producer), premiered Aug. 25, 2010.

xx he was beaten up in an argument with another inmate: Dionne Searcey and Amir Efrati, "Madoff Beaten in Prison," *Wall Street Journal*, Mar. 18, 2010.

xx he told a visitor he "didn't give a shit" about his sons: Joseph Cotchett, a lawyer, quoted in Brian Ross and Kate McCarthy, "First Madoff Interview: Can't Believe I Got Away with It," ABC News, July 28, 2009.

xx Madoff blurted out, "Fuck my victims": Steve Fishman, "Bernie Madoff, Free at Last," *New York*, June 14–21, 2010, p. 32.

xx he had hidden away billions of dollars: Dan Mangan, "Madoff's Hidden Booty," *New York Post*, June 21, 2010.

xxiii 50 percent bigger than the banking giant JPMorgan Chase: Based on *Institutional Investor*'s Hedge Fund 100 ranking for 2008, JPMorgan Chase topped the list with $44.7 billion in assets under management. Goldman Sachs ranked seventh, with $29.2 billion, and Soros Fund Management ranked eighteenth, with $17 billion.

xxiii he said in one prison interview: Interview with Bernard L. Madoff (hereafter BLM) on Feb. 15, 2011 (hereafter Second BLM Interview).

1. AN EARTHQUAKE ON WALL STREET

1 He is ready to stop now: This chapter draws on the author's interviews with BLM, Eleanor Squillari, Irving H. Picard, David J. Sheehan, and Lee S. Richards III; on fourteen confidential interviews with people familiar with the events of the week; on e-mail messages and letters from BLM; on the author's personal inspection of many of the scenes involved, including the FBI building and the Lipstick Building

lobby and suite; and, where noted, on court records, actual transcripts, and other published accounts.

2 Fairfield Greenwich has to replace the redemptions: E-mail from Jeffrey Tucker, Dec. 8, 2008, 12:22 PM, *In the Matter of: Fairfield Greenwich Advisors LLC and Fairfield Greenwich (Bermuda) Ltd.*, Commonwealth of Massachusetts, Office of the Secretary of the Commonwealth Securities Division, Docket No. 2009-0028 (hereafter *Galvin Fairfield Greenwich* Complaint), Exhibit 44. (Direct quotes are used only for those passages designated as such in the e-mail itself.) Without admitting or denying the state's allegations, Fairfield Greenwich settled with Galvin on September 8, 2009, paying $500,000 in state investigative expenses and agreeing to pay an estimated $8 million in restitution to its Massachusetts investors.

2 "My traders are tired of dealing with these hedge funds": Ibid.

2 Madoff scoffs at the notion: Ibid.

3 "Just got off the phone with a very angry Bernie": Ibid.

3 can withdraw $35 million from one of his accounts: *In re: Bernard L. Madoff Investment Securities, Debtor; Irving H. Picard, Trustee for the Liquidation of Bernard L. Madoff Investment Securities v. Stanley Chais, et al.* (hereafter *Picard v. Chais*), filed as Adversary Proceeding No. 09-01172 (BRL) in U.S. Bankruptcy Court for the Southern District of New York, Declaration of Matthew B. Greenblatt, Oct. 1, 2009, p. 3.

3 Jay Feinberg, the foundation's executive director: Interview with Squillari.

4 they manage to link in Norman Braman: Ibid.

4 Feinberg passing around copies of the foundation's conflict-of-interest policy: Gift of Life Bone Marrow Foundation, Boca Raton, Fla., Internal Revenue Service Form 990 for 2008, Schedule O, p. 2.

4 Madoff has planned to meet with the son of his friend J. Ira Harris: Interview with Squillari; BLM appointment calendar; e-mail message from BLM, Feb. 20, 2011.

5 He tells Mark to draw up a list of the trading desk employees who should get checks: Interview with BLM on Aug. 24, 2011 (hereafter First BLM Interview); David Margolick, "The Madoff Chronicles, Part III: Did the Sons Know?" *Vanity Fair*, July 2009, p. 72.

5 Troubled, Mark consults his brother, Andrew: Margolick, "Madoff Chronicles, Part III," p. 72.

5 Madoff walks across the oval area where the secretaries sit and enters Peter's office: First BLM Interview.

5 asks his brother if he had "a moment to talk": Andrew Kirtzman, *Betrayal: The Life and Lies of Bernie Madoff* (New York: HarperCollins, 2009), p. 229.

5 "I have to tell you what's going on": First BLM Interview.

6 "You've got to tell your sons": Ibid.

6 he still isn't certain about when to do it: Ibid.

7 Madoff initially tries to reassure them: *U.S.A. v. Bernard L. Madoff*, criminal complaint by FBI special agent Theodore Cacioppi (hereafter *Madoff Criminal Complaint*), U.S. District Court, Southern District of New York, Dec. 11, 2008, p. 3.

7 The sons stand firm: Ibid.

7 he isn't going to be able to "hold it together" any longer: First BLM Interview.

7 Eleanor Squillari recalls asking Bernie where they were going: Interview with Squil-

lari; Mark Seal and Eleanor Squillari, "The Madoff Chronicles, Part II: What the Secretary Saw," *Vanity Fair*, June 2009, p. 103.

8 it took nearly ninety minutes to return with the sedan: Kirtzman, *Betrayal*, p. 231.

8 sits between his two worried sons: Interview with Andrew Madoff on Oct. 17, 2011 (hereafter Andrew Madoff Interview); Laurie Sandell, *Truth and Consequences: Life Inside the Madoff Family* (New York: Little, Brown, 2011), p. 177.

8 a dark refuge of rich burgundy leather and tapestry fabric: First BLM Interview; confidential interview, a U.S. Marshals video tour of the room, and the author's inspection of its furnishings at auction in November 2010.

8 "basically, a giant Ponzi scheme": *Madoff Criminal Complaint*, p. 4.

8 he plans to pay that money out to certain loyal employees: Ibid.

8 She asks her weeping husband: Interview with Ruth Madoff on Oct. 10, 2011 (hereafter Ruth Madoff Interview); Andrew Madoff Interview.

8 with a tenderness that sears itself into Madoff's memory: First BLM Interview; confidential interviews.

8 "a father-son betrayal of biblical proportions": Andrew Madoff Interview.

8 The brothers leave the apartment: Ibid.

9 London is a formidable litigator: Margolick, "Madoff Chronicles, Part III," pp. 72–73. London handled the criminal defense for the disgraced U.S. vice president Spiro Agnew when bribery accusations led to his resignation in 1973.

9 He immediately tries to reach a younger colleague at Paul Weiss: Ibid.; confidential interviews.

9 Flumenbaum calls and learns: Andrew Madoff Interview; Sandell, *Truth and Consequences*, pp. 183–85.

9 Mark calls and tells him to go on to the office party: Kirtzman, *Betrayal*, p. 235.

9 Mark and Andrew repeat the story of their shocking day: *Madoff Criminal Complaint*, p. 3; Andrew Madoff Interview.

10 Is that *billion* with a *B*?: Confidential interviews.

10 He recalls returning to the office: First BLM Interview.

11 "You are our most important business partner and an immensely respected friend": *In re: Bernard L. Madoff Investment Securities, Debtor; Irving H. Picard, Trustee for the Liquidation of Bernard L. Madoff Investment Securities v. Fairfield Sentry Fund LLC, et al.* (hereafter *Picard v. Fairfield Sentry*), Amended Complaint, Adversary Proceeding No. 09-01239 (BRL) in U.S. Bankruptcy Court for the Southern District of New York, Exhibit 78.

11 Without even removing his coat, he lies motionless on his bed for hours: Margolick, "Madoff Chronicles, Part III," p. 73.

11 They are on autopilot, trying just to function: First BLM Interview.

11 One person recalls that Madoff surprised the staff: Erin Arvedlund, *Too Good to Be True: The Rise and Fall of Bernie Madoff* (New York: Portfolio, 2009), p. 265.

11 "a look of death on his face": Margolick, "Madoff Chronicles, Part III," p. 73.

11 "out of it": Jerry Oppenheimer, *Madoff with the Money* (Hoboken, N.J.: John Wiley & Sons, 2009), p. 11.

11 "as if they didn't have a care in the world": Seal and Squillari, "Madoff Chronicles, Part II," p. 104.

12 "for a couple of hours": First BLM Interview.

12 "a taco station, a guacamole station": Kirtzman, *Betrayal*, p. 235.

12 He feels confident that he still has several days to settle matters: First BLM Interview.

13 Madoff had been about to get dressed for work: Ibid.

13 "There is no innocent explanation": *Madoff Criminal Complaint*, p. 4.

13 "money that wasn't there": Ibid.

13 Squillari hears Ruth say to someone else: Seal and Squillari, "Madoff Chronicles, Part II," pp. 104–5.

14 When Squillari first notices him: Ibid., p. 106.

14 DiPascali also tries to delete sensitive information: *U.S.A. v. Frank DiPascali Jr.*, filed in the U.S. District Court for the Southern District of New York (hereafter *DiPascali Criminal Information*), p. 32.

15 to take his granddaughter to her nursery school class: Confidential interviews; similar details are provided in Kirtzman, *Betrayal*, pp. 236–37; Ross, *Madoff Chronicles*, p. 1.

16 He quietly reports what has happened: First BLM Interview.

16 They quiz him as politely as they can: Ibid.

19 "took no extraordinary measures and sat there and waited to be arrested": Mark Hamblett, "Dreier Remains Jailed as Court Imposes Bail Beyond His Reach," Law.com, Jan. 23, 2009. The comments were made on the record at a subsequent bail hearing for Marc Dreier.

21 They arrange for guards to monitor the office: *Securities Investor Protection Corp. v. Bernard L. Madoff Investment Securities LLC* (hereafter *Initial SIPC Filing*), 08-CV-10791 (LLS), U.S. District Court, Southern District of New York, "Report of the Receiver Lee S. Richards and Application to Terminate the Receivership" (hereafter First Richards Report), Feb. 26, 2009, pp. 8–10.

21 Yesterday, Richards was getting off his commuter train: Interview with Richards.

22 By the afternoon, he will be sitting in the office of one of the city's top criminal defense lawyers: *DiPascali Criminal Information*, transcript of plea hearing on Aug. 11, 2009, p. 85.

22 Madoff, too, will spend this day: E-mail message from BLM, Jan. 4, 2011.

22 The members of Richards's law firm have already curtailed access: *Initial SIPC Filing*, First Richards Report, pp. 4–9.

23 Richards's staff has to try to unwind or complete the deals: Ibid.

23 At about 10:00 AM, two New York City police officers: Interview with Richards.

2. BECOMING BERNIE

24 immortalized later as the "go-go years": It's not clear who first coined the phrase and applied it to the stock market of the 1960s, but it was etched into Wall Street's vocabulary by John Brooks, a gifted financial writer for *The New Yorker* and the author of *The Go-Go Years* (New York: Weybright and Talley, 1973).

25 as five times higher than the Dow Jones Industrial Average: Frank K. Reilly, "Price Changes in NYSE, AMEX and OTC Stocks Compared," *Financial Analysts Journal* (March–April 1972): 54–59. Reilly based his calculations on the National Quotation Bureau average of thirty-five industrial stocks, which he said were "consistently described as the blue chips of the OTC market." Those robust returns, which did not

include cash dividends, were challenged in Paul F. Jessup and Roger B. Upson, *Returns in the Over-the-Counter Stock Markets* (Minneapolis: University of Minnesota Press, 1973), which argued that the total return on OTC stocks did not significantly outperform New York Stock Exchange returns after adjusting for transaction costs and including cash dividends. Jessup and Upson's findings were too arcane to have shaped public opinion about the OTC market, however, and their methodology was occasionally quite odd. For example, for some reason they decided to exclude banks and insurance companies from their sample of OTC stocks, although virtually all such companies traded only in the OTC market and virtually all of them paid cash dividends. The rapid evolution of the OTC market can be tracked by comparing the third edition of Leo M. Loll Jr. and Julian G. Buckley, *The Over-the-Counter Securities Markets* (Englewood Cliffs, N.J.: Prentice Hall, 1973), with the fourth edition, published in 1981.

25 "I thought, when we started up our company": Editors of *Institutional Investor, The Way It Was: An Oral History of Finance: 1967–1987* (New York: William Morrow, 1988), pp. 270–71.

26 "the manufacture of The Sheets": Martin Mayer, *Wall Street: Men and Money*, rev. ed. (New York: Harper & Brothers, 1959), p. 142.

26 he relied on day-old Pink Sheets: E-mail message from BLM, Jan.17, 2011.

27 a little outfit called A.L.S. Steel: Ibid.

28 Madoff violated long-standing market rules: The National Association of Securities Dealers, which regulated member brokers such as Madoff, had imposed a "suitability rule" on its members since 1939. It required brokers to tailor their investment recommendations to the individual circumstances and goals of each customer. As one historical review of the rule noted, any broker caught violating the rule was subject to "license suspension and/or monetary sanctions." (See Nelson S. Ebaugh and Grace D. O'Malley, "Picking Your Battles," *Journal of Texas Consumer Law* [Jan. 24, 2009].)

28 its worst weekly loss in more than a decade: Brooks, *Go-Go Years*, pp. 56–58.

28 "the hot-issue boys, the penny-stock plungers": Ibid., pp. 57–58.

28 "I realized I never should have sold them those shares": First BLM Interview.

28 He simply erased those losses from his clients' accounts: Ibid.

28 "I felt obligated to buy back my clients' positions": Letter from BLM to author, Oct. 3, 2010.

29 "a large amount to me in those days": Ibid. In 2009 dollars, Madoff owed his father-in-law more than $200,000.

30 high-risk "short sales": In its orthodox form, short-selling is the practice of borrowing shares of stock (specifically, ones you think are going to decline in price) and selling them. If the price falls as you anticipated, you can buy cheaper shares to replace the ones you borrowed and pocket the difference as your profit. If the price goes up, you wind up buying more expensive shares to replace the borrowed ones and you incur potentially open-ended losses. For example, if you borrow and sell shares priced at $10 each and the price falls to $1, your profit is $9 a share. But if the price goes up and up without limit, to $20 or $40 or $100 a share, your losses climb right along with it. Being wrong about whether a stock is going up or down can ruin a short-seller overnight. This game is risky enough when you first borrow

the shares from some brokerage house willing to lend them for a fee. But as a bona fide market maker, Madoff was allowed to sell short without borrowing the shares first—a practice known as "naked shorting," which he said he sometimes deployed for clients. Without the stock-borrowing fee, the potential profit was greater. But without an assured supply of stock to cover the borrowed shares, the risks were even higher. A short-seller might find that there simply are no shares to be had except at an astronomical price—a ruinous situation known as a short squeeze. Another form of short-selling Madoff said he frequently employed was "shorting against the box." In this strategy, a trader shorts the shares of a stock he himself already owns. His holdings protect him against a short squeeze if the price goes up; if the price goes down, his short sale locks in his accrued profits without his actually having to sell the shares, which could have tax consequences. Legislation later reduced the tax benefits of this strategy.

30 His grandparents on both sides: The most extensive research into Madoff's genealogy is included in Arvedlund, *Too Good to Be True*, pp. 14–15. Their move to the Bronx was noted in the 1930 census.

30 Ralph Madoff described his employment as "credit": Several of the 2009 biographies of Madoff cite this entry; see especially Kirtzman, *Betrayal*, p. 17.

30 Madoff himself said his father attended college: First BLM Interview.

30 the nation's leading source for professional boxing equipment: See the obituary for Everlast's founder, "Jacob Golomb, 58, a Manufacturer," *New York Times*, Aug. 25, 1951.

31 the popular "Joe Palooka" comic strip character: Interviews with BLM and a confidential source who knew Ralph Madoff and was familiar with his family's history. Ham Fisher's "Joe Palooka" comic strip, about a virtuous prizefighter, made its newspaper debut in 1930. It migrated from newspapers to comic books, radio plays, and movies and became one of the most popular wartime comic strips.

31 In April 1946, he and Sylvia and their three children moved: Kirtzman, *Betrayal*, pp. 17–18.

31 The young Bernie Madoff attended Public School 156 and became a Boy Scout: Brian Ross, *The Madoff Chronicles: Inside the Secret World of Bernie and Ruth* (New York: Hyperion, 2009), p. 26.

31 it was nearly $90,000 in debt when it made its bankruptcy court filing: In 2009 dollars, the Dodger Sporting Goods Corp.'s debts exceeded its assets by more than $725,000. Its bankruptcy filing was reported in an agate section on business records in the *New York Times* on Jan. 23, 1951. In that report, its business was described as "manufacturing toys, sporting goods and kindred leather goods," and it was located at 345 Carroll Street in Brooklyn. Its liabilities were approximately $150,000 and its assets were approximately $61,000. The company was listed in a 1949 edition of the Industrial Directory of New York State, but it was not included in the 1946 directory, according to researchers at Princeton University's Firestone Library, where an archival copy was located. So the company's life span was at least two years but probably less than five.

31 a tax lien was imposed on the family home: Kirtzman, *Betrayal*, p. 35. According to Andrew Kirtzman, citing "the real estate records kept by the Queens County clerk," a government lien for $9,000—about $70,000 in 2009 dollars—was placed on the fam-

ily home in 1956, Bernard Madoff's senior year of high school, after Ralph Madoff and his business partners failed to pay withholding taxes. According to Madoff, this problem arose in connection with a second short-lived sporting goods venture his father launched after Dodger folded.

31 **a one-man brokerage firm:** There is no relationship between the firm founded by Ralph Madoff and any prior or current firm using the Gibraltar Securities name.

31 **it was the firm through which he conducted his sporadic work as a finder:** First BLM Interview.

32 **their own junior high school fraternity:** Oppenheimer, *Madoff with the Money*, pp. 30–31.

32 **Bernie joined the swim team and was a decent competitor:** Kirtzman, *Betrayal*, p. 24.

32 **If you had a little savings, you kept it in the bank:** Robert Sobel, *Inside Wall Street* (New York: W. W. Norton, 1977), pp. 103–4.

33 **the executives at most of the top WASP firms on Wall Street:** Editors of *Institutional Investor, Way It Was*, pp. 551–53.

33 **he decided he'd like to sell sports equipment as a "manufacturer's rep":** First BLM Interview.

33 **the second son of Benjamin Alpern, a skilled watch repairman:** Arvedlund, *Too Good to Be True*, p. 21.

35 **the son of an early stock market success story:** Michael Lieberbaum's father was Louis B. Lieberbaum. According to SEC archives, the senior Lieberbaum founded Lieberbaum & Company at 50 Broadway in New York in January 1961; in 1963, Louis B. Lieberbaum d/b/a L.B. Lieberbaum & Co., was registered at 40 Exchange Place. Madoff had rented space at 40 Exchange Place in 1961, but by 1963, he was at 39 Broadway. In an interview, Madoff confirmed that Louis Lieberbaum was one of the first Wall Street figures to come to his notice, and that his close friendship with Michael Lieberbaum was a factor in turning his attention from sporting goods to Wall Street. Michael's brother, Sheldon, would later introduce Madoff to one of his first big clients, Carl Shapiro.

35 **the single best stock tip of his life:** Oppenheimer, *Madoff with the Money*, pp. 98–100.

36 **"would break up the trades into individual transactions":** Letter from BLM, Oct. 3, 2010.

37 **in a green plastic loose-leaf notebook:** Michael Bienes interview for "The Madoff Affair," a RAINmedia production for *Frontline*, WBGH Boston, Program No. 2714, aired on May 12, 2009, hereafter cited as Bienes *Frontline* interview.

37 **"No, I cannot handle small accounts like this":** Ibid.

38 **"I'm taking the green book down to Florida":** Ibid.

38 **"50 to 75 investors":** Letter from BLM, Oct. 3, 2010.

38 **That pair of CPAs set up a separate fund to invest with Madoff:** The account was set up by Edward Glantz and a partner, Steven Mendelow, who solicited investors under the name of the Telfran fund.

38 **It was called riskless arbitrage:** "Riskless" arbitrage was not really free of any risk; glitches in trading or delays in paperwork processing could derail a profit opportunity. The term was used to describe the lightning-fast strategies in which a security or its nearly exact equivalent, such as a convertible bond or a warrant, were almost simultaneously bought at one price and sold at a higher price.

39 changing hands in the so-called "when issued" market: Most commonly, these arbitrage opportunities involved stock splits by a company with shares already trading. For example, a company may authorize a stock split, effective on a given day. The not-yet-issued shares may trade in the "when issued" market at prices that don't precisely reflect the arithmetic behind the stock split. Say a company has announced that, on a certain date, it will split each share of its stock into two shares. After that announcement but before the effective date of the split, the not-yet-issued shares should trade in the "when issued" market for precisely half the price of the pre-split stock. For example, if that stock is trading at a particular moment for $100 a share, "when issued" shares should be trading at that moment for exactly $50 each. But they don't always do so. If a trader can buy one pre-split share for $100 and sell two shares of the "when issued" stock for $51 each, he can lock in a $2 profit.

39 Sometimes he took on more risk: E-mail from BLM, Jan. 13, 2011.

39 arcane securities called "warrants": A warrant entitled its owner to buy the related common stock at a specified price, which could be higher or lower than the trading price for the stock. By buying stocks with warrants attached to them, a trader could exercise the warrant to buy shares at one price while simultaneously selling shares at a higher price, locking in an arbitrage profit.

39 actively and visibly pursuing warrant arbitrage: Peter Chapman, "Before the Fall: Bernard L. Madoff," *Traders Magazine*, March 2009.

41 the returns on convertible bonds were slightly higher: Scott L. Lummer and Mark W. Riepe, "Convertible Bonds as an Asset Class: 1957–1992," *Journal of Fixed Income* (September 1993), from an undated reprint by Ibbotson Associates, Inc., Chicago, Ill.

41 falsifying convertible bond arbitrage profits: *In re: Bernard L. Madoff Investment Securities, Debtor; Irving H. Picard, Trustee for the Liquidation of Bernard L. Madoff Investment Securities v. David L. Kugel, et al.* (hereafter *Picard v. Kugel*), pp. 19–21. The civil lawsuit asserts that because numerous pairs of convertible bond arbitrage trades produced highly consistent returns in Kugel's account, the trades must have been phony. But consistency alone is not proof of fraud; Madoff could simply have closed out real trades as soon as they had produced a targeted rate of return. On Nov. 21, 2011, Kugel pleaded guilty to federal criminal charges that he helped concoct phony arbitrage trades for Madoff in the late 1970s. The analysis cited here was by Bruce G. Dubinsky; an expert witness in the trustee's lawsuit against the New York Mets owners, *infra*. It is Document No. 107 in that case, filed on Jan. 26, 2012.

3. THE HUNGER FOR YIELD

43 the SEC suspended him from the brokerage business for seventy-five days: SEC release dated Aug. 15, 1970; disciplinary records of the National Association of Securities Dealers, now known as the Financial Industry Regulatory Authority, or FINRA.

43 the first outside employee of Bernard L. Madoff Investment Securities: Irwin Lipkin would remain with the Madoff firm for the rest of his career, and his son Eric was a Madoff employee at the time of Madoff's arrest.

43 Madoff and Joel socialized frequently: Their relationship has been confirmed by

BLM and was described in Oppenheimer, *Madoff with the Money*, who cited interviews with the Joel family. It was also confirmed in post-arrest litigation filed by various Joel family members against the bankruptcy trustee, Irving Picard. In 1981, Joel went to work for Madoff, and his daughter Amy followed him to the firm in 1989. He died in 2003, but Amy Joel was still on staff at the time of Madoff's arrest.

44 Congress established the Securities Investor Protection Corporation: The law that set up the corporation and amended the bankruptcy code was the Securities Investor Protection Act of 1970.

45 "Often as not, Madoff's firm did not get called": Chapman, "Before the Fall."

45 "We felt, as a small market-making firm": Eric J. Weiner, *What Goes Up: The Uncensored History of Modern Wall Street as Told by the Bankers, CEOs, and Scoundrels Who Made It Happen* (New York: Back Bay Books, 2007), pp. 188–92.

45 "you had to show your hand, and they didn't want to do that": Ibid., p. 189.

46 the NASD's own security measures: Created under the Maloney Act of 1938, the NASD was known legally as a "self-regulatory organization," with the power to enact rules and enforce them, subject to the SEC's oversight.

46 an automated system built for the NASD: Chris Welles, *The Last Days of the Club* (New York: E. P. Dutton, 1975), pp. 6–8, 286–87.

46 At least one former employee later thought so: *Andrew M. Cuomo, the Attorney General of the State of New York v. Ivy Asset Management LLC, Lawrence Simon and Howard Wohl* (hereafter *Cuomo v. Ivy* Complaint), filed May 11, 2010, in the Supreme Court of the State of New York, County of New York, pp. 22–23, 36–37. The lawsuit covers events that occurred after even Madoff acknowledged he was operating a Ponzi scheme, but it provides secondhand quotes from a former Madoff employee whose experience with the firm predated that period.

47 he applied and was admitted to Brooklyn Tech: The Brooklyn Tech High School Network Web site shows him as a member of the class of 1963.

47 the family's golf games improved: By 2000, Madoff had a 12 handicap and consistently shot in the mid-80s—more consistently than many golf experts could credit when they were questioned after his arrest by reporters for CNBC, who relied on online records of the scores players reported to the Florida State Golf Association. Madoff's suspiciously steady golf scores were also cited in Robert Frank and Tom Lauricella, "Madoff Created Air of Mystery," *Wall Street Journal*, Dec. 20, 2008.

48 "was almost universally liked": Chapman, "Before the Fall."

48 "were just great, great people": Ibid.

48 his only ownership stake in the primary Madoff firm: Peter Madoff would later hold a 9 percent stake in Cohmad Securities, formed by his brother and Maurice J. "Sonny" Cohn in 1985. But, unlike Bernard L. Madoff Investment Securities, that firm was not under Bernie Madoff's control; he himself owned only a minority stake in it.

48 he and Sylvia would sometimes help Bernie by riding out to inspect some company: Confidential interview with a person familiar with the Madoff family history.

48 She was just weeks shy of her sixty-third birthday: First BLM Interview.

49 "Bernard (who founded the firm) and Peter (the company's computer genius)": Marshall E. Blume, Jeremy J. Siegel, and Dan Rottenberg, *Revolution on Wall Street: The Rise and Decline of the New York Stock Exchange* (New York: W. W. Norton, 1993), p. 221.

49 credited Peter with developing the trading technology: *The Lautenberg Foundation, Joshua S. Lautenberg and Ellen Lautenberg v. Peter Madoff* (hereafter *Lautenberg v. Madoff*), filed in U.S. District Court for the District of New Jersey on Feb. 24, 2009, p. 4.

49 "And it was that decision": Chapman, "Before the Fall."

50 had gotten far too cumbersome, according to Bienes: Bienes *Frontline* interview.

51 "Four words: Let's pay them interest": Ibid.

52 the accounting firm "always stood behind it": Ibid.

52 "If the first crash was a dramatic leap from a sixty-story building": Adam Smith (George J. W. Goodman), *Paper Money* (New York: Summit Books, 1981), pp. 271–72.

52 "Inflation this high during peace time was unprecedented in American history": Carl E. Walsh, Visiting Scholar, Federal Reserve Bank of San Francisco Economic Letter, Number 2004-35, Dec. 3, 2004, p. 1.

55 the Madoff investment operation made up more than a third of the accounting firm's business: Bienes *Frontline* interview.

55 Four people in the firm's New York office handled calls and applications: The testimony of Avellino and Bienes before the SEC on July 7, 1992 (hereafter Avellino-Bienes SEC Transcript) was part of the file "In the Matter of King Arthur, MNY-1490." See U.S. Securities and Exchange Commission Inspector General H. David Kotz, "Investigation of Failure of the SEC to Uncover Bernard Madoff's Ponzi Scheme—Public Version," Case No. OIG-509, Aug. 31, 2009 (hereafter Kotz Report), Exhibit 117, pp. 33–34.

55 "never advertised, we never promoted, we never sent out a Christmas card": Bienes *Frontline* interview.

55 "That's all we'd say. We were very tough": Ibid.

55 "We had medium-sized, small clients, individual clients": Ibid.

55 "All I could say to you is, at one point in time": Avellino-Bienes SEC Transcript, p. 53.

56 "I don't like to give out financial statements": Ibid.

56 "Michael Bienes and Frank Avellino . . . have their own assets": Ibid.

4. THE BIG FOUR

57 typically did no better than a portfolio of stocks chosen utterly at random: See Burton G. Malkiel, *A Random Walk Down Wall Street* (New York: W. W. Norton, 1973).

57 Chais was a courtly gentleman: *Picard v. Chais* Complaint, Declaration of Stanley Chais in support of his request for a temporary restraining order, p. 3.

57 her "peaches-and-cream complexion" and "tidily coiffed" blond hair: Lewis Funke, "News of the Rialto: Inside Musicals," *New York Times*, Apr. 27, 1969.

57 the daughter of a Broadway playwright and was a promising playwright herself: Louis Calta, "News of the Rialto: A Guest Shot Back Home," *New York Times*, July 24, 1966.

58 decided to invest some of his own money in arbitrage: First BLM Interview.

58 including his father-in-law, Saul Alpern: The retired Saul Alpern set up a shell business in 1983 in Florida called the Onondaga Investment Company. The unusual "Onondaga" name is one that Stanley Chais applied to a few of his Madoff accounts—and both names echo the title of the campus yearbook at Syracuse, Chais's alma mater. Alpern had no known relationship with the school or with Onandaga County, in which it is located. That shell was one of three that Alpern created at the time, all of them terminated in 1986. All three had the same corporate officers: Saul Alpern as

president, treasurer, and director, and a prominent Los Angeles tax lawyer named Bruce M. Stiglitz of the firm Loeb & Loeb as the second director. Stiglitz, who died in 2004, was an entertainment law specialist and a tax expert catering to the creative community in Hollywood. There is no evidence, aside from the Florida business records, that Stiglitz even knew Saul Alpern, but he certainly knew Stanley Chais; they were neighbors and close friends. And Stiglitz clearly knew Madoff: one of the trustees for his family's trust funds was Irwin Lipkin, Madoff's longtime employee, and Stiglitz was an indirect Madoff investor, through Chais. It is possible that Alpern, like Madoff, met Chais directly through Marty Joel, who was a client of Alpern's accounting firm.

58 It was called the Lambeth Company: *The Securities and Exchange Commission v. Stanley Chais* (hereafter *SEC Chais* Complaint), filed in U.S. District Court for the Southern District of New York on June 22, 2009, pp. 4–5. The case against Chais himself was dismissed after his death in September 2010.

58 He did not believe he needed to: Confidential interviews.

59 matches the memories of a few early Madoff investors and other sources familiar with the accounts: A state senator in New Jersey recalled that her family called its Chais account "the arbitrage partnerships," and had always believed that Chais himself was making the investment decisions that were producing the steady 10 percent to 14 percent returns, according to an account of her experience in "Victims of Scandal Reflect on a Shocking Turnabout," *Wall Street Journal*, Dec. 20, 2008.

59 "He supposedly had come up with this computerized system": Confidential interview with a longtime Madoff investor.

59 disappeared quickly if too much money was thrown at them too fast: Consider the example described earlier involving a convertible bond that should have traded at $150 that actually traded for just $130. If a lot of people tried to buy up those convertible bonds at $130, the increased demand would push their price back to the appropriate level of $150 and the arbitrage profits would disappear.

60 that he directed Madoff to backdate trades: First BLM Interview; confidential interviews with several people familiar with interviews with Madoff by bankruptcy trustee Irving Picard's legal team.

61 "When Kay Windsor was formed": Carl Spielvogel, "'Work Horse' Dress Builds a $22,000,000 Business," *New York Times*, Jan. 27, 1957.

62 Mike Lieberbaum's brother, Sheldon, worked for a larger brokerage firm: Although regulatory records show Sheldon Lieberbaum's employment going back only to 1967, Madoff recalled that he worked at the time for D.H. Blair, which was a member of the New York Stock Exchange but which underwrote a number of OTC stocks.

62 "was interested in doing arbitrage": First BLM Interview.

62 "In those days, it took three weeks to complete a sale": Kirtzman, *Betrayal*, p. 41.

62 he staked Bernie Madoff at the arbitrage table: Ibid., p. 42.

63 within two years, he had scraped together enough: Dee Wedemeyer, "At 12% Rates, a Housing Boom," *New York Times*, Aug. 29, 1982.

63 a country club friend of Levy's named Arthur Schlichter: Schlichter may have become a Madoff investor himself, as his estate showed up on the list of accounts filed by the Madoff bankruptcy trustee. More significantly, he was a close friend of Gladys Luria, a steel industry heiress whose family became substantial Madoff investors.

63 Madoff seemed to bask in the warmth: Mark Seal, "Madoff's World," *Vanity Fair*, April 2009; confidential interview with a longtime Levy family friend.

63 Levy's "close friend and trader": Confidential documentation provided to the author.

63 his balance would grow to $1.5 billion: Ibid.

63 a stunning $35 billion: Letter from Stephen P. Harbeck, president and chief executive officer of SIPC, to the Honorable Scott Garrett, chairman, Subcommittee on Capital Markets and Government-Sponsored Enterprises, House Financial Services Committee (hereafter SIPC-Garrett Letter), Jan. 24, 2011, pp. 14–15. In his second prison interview, Madoff hinted that Levy was "kiting" money between his various bank accounts and his Madoff account to make his cash flow look more impressive to creditors.

64 Madoff recalled that Alpern was Picower's personal accountant: First BLM Interview.

64 Picower's father was a Polish immigrant: Nathan Ward, "Madoff's Mystery Man," *Forbes*, Oct. 11, 2010, corrected in confidential interviews.

64 wound up at Laventhol & Horwath: Michael Amon, "The Jeffry Picower File," *Newsday*, Oct. 25, 2009.

64 a brassy and persuasive Broadway producer: Ward, "Madoff's Mystery Man." The producer was Adela Holzer, a producer of the musical *Hair*, who was convicted on fraud charges in 1979. See Charles Kaiser, "Adela Holzer Is Given 2-to-6-Year Sentence for Investment Fraud," *New York Times*, May 4, 1979.

64 "started out as a professional relationship": Responses from Jeffry and Barbara Picower to questions submitted by the author in the summer of 2009.

65 building up a big stake in the Shopwell supermarket chain: "French Investor May Seek Shopwell," *New York Times*, May 5, 1979. Amsellem's stock plays were also documented in various *SEC News Digest* issues in the late 1970s.

65 Igoin had a remarkable résumé: These details were provided by BLM and confirmed by an excellent French account, "Les discrets amis français de Bernard Madoff," published on the Web site Eco89, June 12, 2009, accessible at eco.rue89.com/2009/06/12/les-discrets-amis-francais-de-bernard-madoff.

66 Peter Madoff traveled around the country: Specifically, Peter Madoff was selling the Madoff firm's services as "corresponding broker" to these smaller firms, offering to process their New York Stock Exchange trades for a small commission.

66 Engler's business partner liked Peter and agreed to shift the firm's business to Madoff: Telephone interview in 2010 with Steven Engler, Mike Engler's son and former employee.

67 Engler himself had founded a liquor store: Obituary of Mike Engler, Minneapolis *Star Tribune*, Dec. 20, 1994.

67 Madoff invited him to sign on: Telephone interview with Steven Engler.

67 more and more of Engler's country club friends: Dave Kansas, "Madoff Does Minneapolis," Fortune/CNNMoney.com, Jan. 16, 2009.

67 "I called it my 'steady Eddie' investment": Telephone interview in 2010 with Madoff investor Renee Soskin.

69 the Madoffs bought a handsome weekend house: Many sources date this purchase to 1980, but an inventory of assets Madoff filed with the court after his arrest dated the purchase to 1979.

69 He was part of a group of adventurous Wall Street executives: The saga of the Cessna seaplane has been cited in various sources, including Arvedlund, *Too Good to Be True*, pp. 51–52. These details were confirmed with three confidential sources familiar with the Madoff family during the years when the seaplane was in use.

5. THE CASH SPIGOT

71 a bright red phone in the rear window: Confidential interview with a former Roslyn neighbor.

71 "never had a losing day": Confidential interviews.

71 He grew increasingly restless: *In the Matter of: Cohmad Securities Corporation*, administrative complaint filed Feb. 11, 2009, by the Commonwealth of Massachusetts, Office of the Secretary of the Commonwealth Securities Division (hereafter *Galvin Cohmad* Complaint), Exhibit 3.

72 the historic Harmonie Club: The private social club, at 4 East Sixtieth Street, was founded in 1854 by New York's German-Jewish aristocracy, and for years German ancestry was a requirement for membership. Over time, it became a choice venue for Jewish weddings, receptions, and charitable events. When the Wall Street division of the American Jewish Committee honored Bernie Madoff in 1999, the reception was held at the Harmonie Club.

72 after six years at Cowen & Company: Central Registration Depository (CRD) records for Marcia Beth Cohn, maintained by FINRA.

72 The remaining 25 percent was lopsidedly split: *SEC v. Cohmad Securities Corporation, et al.* (hereafter *SEC v. Cohmad*), filed as Case No. 09-cv-5680 (LLS) in U.S. District Court for the Southern District of New York, p. 6.

72 He began his Wall Street career in 1969: CRD record of Robert M. Jaffe, maintained by FINRA.

72 More significantly, he was married to Ellen Shapiro: *In re: Bernard L. Madoff Investment Securities, Debtor; Irving H. Picard, Trustee for the Liquidation of Bernard L. Madoff Investment Securities v. Cohmad Securities Corporation, et al.* (hereafter *Picard v. Cohmad*), filed as Adversary Proceeding No. 09-01305 (BRL) in U.S. Bankruptcy Court for the Southern District of New York, p. 15.

73 subsequent lawsuits would claim that the firm's compliance officer was Peter Madoff's daughter, Shana: Ibid., p. 14.

73 several hundred clients with traditional brokerage accounts: It cleared those customer trades through Bear Stearns until that firm was taken over in early 2008.

75 Some options traders called his new strategy a "bull spread": Harry Markopolos, *No One Would Listen: A True Financial Thriller* (Hoboken, N.J.: John Wiley & Sons, 2010), p. 27.

75 the right (the "option") to buy or sell that stock at a specific price: The right to buy a stock was called a "call option." The seller of a call option is promising to let the buyer purchase the shares at a specified price for the term of the option. The right to sell a stock is called a "put option." The seller of a put option is promising to let the buyer sell him a stock at a specified price for the term of the option. Traders typically shorten these terms to "puts" and "calls," and Madoff used both forms of options in his strategy.

76 Madoff's new strategy was to buy a broad portfolio of stocks: Madoff was supposedly

buying a representative sample of thirty to thirty-five blue chips in the S&P 100 index and then selling call options that entitled the buyer of the options to purchase the stocks from him if they rose to a specified price. (Essentially, this was a "covered call," a strategy familiar to many individual investors.) The call option limited his potential profit, but he supposedly used the money he got from selling that option to buy a put option giving *him* the right to sell the portfolio at a specified price a bit below its current value. The put option established a floor under his potential losses if the value of the stocks declined sharply. Thus, both his upside profits and downside losses were limited by the use of options.

76 its monthly returns bounced around: Morningstar data, compiled for the author with the help of *New York Times* chief financial correspondent Floyd Norris.

77 "a simplistic, and most important, a very conservative strategy": *Galvin Cohmad* Complaint exhibits, letter from Maurice J. Cohn dated Nov. 21, 1991.

77 a scorching courtroom battle over some audits they had done: The case, *In re: M. Frenville*, was cited in bankruptcy court battles for years.

77 Bienes later said the litigation was an enormous expense and distraction: Bienes *Frontline* interview.

77 Frank Avellino felt utterly burned out: Avellino-Bienes SEC Transcript, p. 36.

77 devote themselves exclusively to their Madoff business: Bienes *Frontline* interview.

78 But they were still remarkably casual about maintaining the paperwork: An affidavit filed by Frank Avellino in his 1993 bankruptcy court dispute over the accounting fees he had to pay as part of the SEC's 1992 investigation.

79 the SEC's fabled Enforcement Division director, Stanley Sporkin: David A. Vise and Steven Coll, *Eagle on the Street* (New York: Charles Scribner's Sons, 1991), pp. 1–20.

79 John Shad, a lifelong veteran of Wall Street: Shad, who was vice chairman of E.F. Hutton at the time of his appointment, was the first Wall Street executive to head the commission since President Franklin Roosevelt tapped Joseph P. Kennedy, the father of President John F. Kennedy, as the first SEC chairman in 1934. Reagan moved Sporkin to the post of general counsel at the Central Intelligence Agency, and four years later appointed him to the federal bench.

79 Shad was less hostile to the SEC's mission: Joel Seligman, *The Transformation of Wall Street: A History of the Securities and Exchange Commission and Modern Corporate Finance* (Boston: Northeastern University Press, 1995), p. 576.

79 "was essentially an honest place": Vise and Coll, *Eagle on the Street*, p. 128.

79 a general view in Congress that the NASD had fallen down: See Senate Report No. 94-75, at 2 (1975), as reprinted in 1975 U.S.C.C.A.N. 179, 181: "The Committee believes . . . the self-regulatory organizations must display a greater responsiveness to their statutory obligations and to the need to coordinate their functions and activities. In the new regulatory environment created by this bill, self-regulation would be continued, but the SEC would be expected to play a much larger role than it has in the past to ensure that there is no gap between self-regulatory performance and regulatory need."

79 "a competent but cautious commission": Seligman, *The Transformation of Wall Street*, p. 577.

81 a quiet prestige: The building, designed by Kenneth Murchison, "has most of the

trademark elements of the type: an elegantly finished lobby of very modest dimensions, a sun-washed site—well away from the blocky ranges of tall apartment buildings to the west—and an elegant run of bronze storefronts," wrote Christopher Gray in "Streetscapes: 133 East 64th Street: If a Building Could Blush," *New York Times*, Sept. 16, 2009.

81 made some minor renovations: Ibid. Howard R. Goldin, who was the architect for the work, "said some clients were so prominent that he was asked not to list their names on the building permit, but the Madoffs had no such worries at the time. As the clients were not demanding, and paid promptly, 'it went without a hitch,' Mr. Goldin remembered."

82 Bernie Madoff became a go-to figure for the industry press when international issues arose: In December 1986, for example, he talked with *Securities Week* about a two-day meeting he attended in Washington between officials of the Singapore Stock Exchange and other NASD leaders. The topic was the possibility of building an electronic link between their markets similar to the one the NASD maintained with the London Stock Exchange.

82 "Madoff's sole proprietorship, founded 26 years ago": The article also reported, incorrectly, that Madoff "did, however, found North Shore Hospital in Manhasset, Long Island, near one of his three homes." According to the hospital's successor institution, he played no role in the hospital's founding, although his friend Sonny Cohn was a substantial benefactor to the hospital for many years.

83 The OTC market was "in shambles": Tim Metz, *Black Monday: The Catastrophe of October 19, 1987 . . . and Beyond* (New York: William Morrow, 1988), p. 198.

83 "This added to the confusion and panic in the markets": General Accounting Office, "Financial Markets: Preliminary Observations on the October 1987 Crash," GAO/GGD-88-38, p. 6.

83 "We're scared. Of course we're scared": As quoted in Metz, *Black Monday*, p. 199. In fairness, the computer technology at the New York Stock Exchange had broken down, too. Later, NASD leaders would argue that NASDAQ's technology failures were overstated in a government study of the 1987 crash.

84 Mike Engler, Madoff's friend and associate in Minneapolis, would tell his son later: Telephone interview in 2010 with Steven Engler.

85 only seven losing months: Morningstar data compiled for the author.

85 the expectation that they would be rolled over year after year: Second BLM Interview.

85 "I felt they weren't sham transactions": First BLM Interview.

86 an influential voice in putting NASDAQ back together: As chairman of one of the key committees looking at automated order flow, Bernie Madoff was one of the men the media sought out for comment. On Nov. 16, 1987, the newsletter *Securities Week* headlined the news that the NASD board was ready to vote on four items to improve market making. The story noted: "The first item on the plate will require all OTC market makers to participate in the NASD's small order execution system (SOES), according to Bernard Madoff, chairman of the SOES committee and founder of the New York broker/dealer bearing his name."

86 the consequences of the NASD's flabby discipline: The NASDAQ market's own

official history later acknowledged that traders soon learned how to use the rhythm of posting and boosting their quotes on the newfangled automated system to manipulate stock prices in old-fashioned ways.

86 a new standard for speed in handling customer orders: In its issue of July 10, 1989, *Forbes* took note of how revolutionary the Madoff system was by describing the system's automatic purchase of some proffered shares of IBM: "Once the computer has that IBM stock it just bought, it shows the trader various ways of hedging his position and the costs. It even shows the carrying costs for not hedging. That hedging is done by Peter Madoff's software. The Madoffs' computer hedging is far ahead of anything that the specialists [on the New York Stock Exchange's trading floor] have."

87 "although the Madoff firm isn't technically a stock exchange": Blume, Siegel, and Rottenberg, *Revolution on Wall Street*, p. 221.

88 By one popular measure: The measure is the S&P 500 index, adjusted for inflation and dividends.

88 Squadron had once been the boy wonder: Hedy Shulman, "Prominent Attorney Howard M. Squadron to Be Honored on June 10 at Benjamin N. Cardozo School of Law Dinner," Yeshiva University press release, May 10, 1999. Madoff cochaired the event with the media mogul Rupert Murdoch, a Squadron law partner named Stanley Plesent, and an owner of the New York Mets, Fred Wilpon.

88 Squadron was instrumental in the rescue of the New York City Center: Ibid. See also a paid death notice placed under Squadron's name by the City Center board in the *New York Times*, Dec. 28, 2001.

89 a former SEC lawyer named Jeffrey Tucker: Tucker's original connection with investment management was through a client, an options trader named Fred Kolber, with whom he formed an options trading fund. Tucker became a general partner in Fred Kolber & Company, which formed the Greenwich Options fund.

89 Noel thought Tucker's new fund might have promise for his foreign investors: *Picard v. Fairfield Sentry* Complaint, p. 80.

89 "Walter was very impressed with their trading": Interview with former Fairfield Greenwich employee Sherry Shameer Cohen.

89 Tucker's father-in-law, a retired knitwear manufacturer: *Picard v. Fairfield Sentry* Complaint, pp. 81–82.

89 One associate called it "an aura": Bienes *Frontline* interview. Bienes said: "He had an aura about him. Not charisma, an aura about him—a confidence, the way he was set up, the way he looked, the way he spoke, the self-confidence. He just evoked confidence in you, that he knew that he was in control and if he was around, everything was fine."

90 almost literally "the world," as it turned out: The worldwide distribution of the firm's clients is documented in "Fairfield Greenwich Group: Firm Profile," a confidential document provided to the author, dated Nov. 15, 2007, p. 5.

90 Madoff had caught the attention of a few other young offshore hedge funds: First BLM Interview. Madoff recalled that Fairfield Greenwich was the first hedge fund to invest with him, and he identified the Kingate funds, run by Carlo Grosso and Federico Ceretti in London, and the Thema fund, guided by the Austrian-born banker Sonja Kohn, as the other earliest investors. But his relationship with Kohn dated to

1985, and she was allegedly instrumental in steering several other European hedge funds to him in these early years, so Madoff's version may be less than accurate. See *Irving H. Picard v. Sonja Kohn, et al.,* filed as Adversary Proceeding No. 10-05411 (BRL) in U.S. Bankruptcy Court for the Southern District of New York, Dec. 10, 2010 (hereafter *Picard v. Kohn*), pp. 6, 9, and 65.

91 he wrote in an e-mail from prison: E-mail from BLM, Dec. 26, 2010.

6. WHAT THEY WANTED TO BELIEVE

92 a legitimate and apparently successful brokerage firm: National Association of Securities Dealers comment letter on an oversight examination of Madoff's firm for the period ending Sept. 30, 1994, dated Jan. 26, 1995. The exam showed that by mid-1994, the Madoff firm's annual income was just under $125 million a year, so this estimate seems likely.

92 a remarkable 10 percent of the total daily trading volume: Ibid.

92 considered among the best on the Street: Chapman, "Before the Fall." According to Chapman, Dennis Green, former head trader at Legg Mason, gave this assessment of the Madoff firm: "They always had the best technology. They always did. Even when none of us could afford that technology. . . . They always had the best systems."

92 whose accounts now totaled at least $8 billion: Letter from BLM, Oct. 3, 2010. Madoff estimated that client account balances totaled $5 billion in 1987; if so, the annual investment returns he claimed to be producing would have pushed that number, conservatively, to about $8 billion by the early 1990s.

93 the harder it would be for savvy investors to believe: Indeed, as early as 1991, the pioneering quantitative analyst Edward Thorp looked at the results Madoff was producing for a pension fund client and found some red flags, including a day in April 1991 when Madoff's reported trades in Procter & Gamble options were more than ten times the total number of P&G options traded that day. See Scott Patterson, *The Quants: How a New Breed of Math Whizzes Conquered Wall Street and Nearly Destroyed It* (New York: Crown Business, 2010), p. 63.

94 a pair of skeptical investors had sent two documents: Kotz Report, pp. 42–44, and Kotz Report, Exhibit 113, p. 1.

94 The fact sheet was on the letterhead of a financial adviser in San Francisco: Ibid., p. 43.

95 "relatives, friends and former clients": Ibid.

95 he had received a call from his friend Richard Glantz: Avellino-Bienes SEC Transcript, pp. 12–14.

95 one of the earliest subcontractors: The elder Glantz was a partner with accountant Steven Mendelow in the Telfran fund, an indirect Madoff feeder fund that invested through Avellino & Bienes. Since at least 1985, Mendelow had been a principal in Paul Konigsberg's accounting firm, Konigsberg Wolf.

95 The younger Glantz had shared in that business and steered others to it: Richard Halstead, "San Rafael Lawyer Helped Friends and Family Invest Money with Madoff," *Marin Independent Journal,* Feb. 12, 2009, and interviews with Glantz investors. Glantz did not deny that he set up funds through which people invested with Madoff, but noted that he was as victimized as they were, having lost all his wealth in the Ponzi scheme.

95 Glantz explained why he had called: Avellino-Bienes SEC Transcript, p. 14.

95 Avellino promptly phoned Michael Bienes, who recalled the conversation years later: Bienes described the conversation in Bienes *Frontline* interview.

96 he called his friend and longtime investor Howard Squadron: Bienes recalled that Madoff himself recommended Ike Sorkin, but Sorkin disputes this, saying the request came through Squadron.

96 In 1992, Ike Sorkin knew Bernie Madoff only slightly: Interview in 2009 with Ira Lee Sorkin.

96 "When asked what he does with the money borrowed": Kotz Report, Exhibit 112, p. 1.

96 "We do not deal in real estate or anything other than securities": Ibid.

96 someone from the SEC team got a call from Ike Sorkin: Kotz Report, p. 45.

97 They listened patiently and directed more questions at Frank Avellino: Avellino-Bienes SEC Transcript, p. 35.

97 Eventually, he explained how the "very private group": Ibid., p. 67.

98 "$400 million": Ibid., pp. 61–62.

98 One of those creditors was Telfran Associates: See *SEC v. Telfran Associates Ltd., Telfran Associates Corp., Steven Mendelow, and Edward Glantz*, filed as 92-cv-8564 in the U.S. District Court for the Southern District of New York, included in Kotz Report, as Exhibit 126.

98 "in the late '80s or early '90s": Transcript of DiPascali Plea Hearing before U.S. District Court Judge Richard J. Sullivan, Aug. 11, 2009, p. 46.

99 it was almost $30 million short: *In re: Bernard L. Madoff Investment Securities, Debtor; Irving H. Picard, Trustee for the Liquidation of Bernard L. Madoff Investment Securities v. Frank J. Avellino, et al.* (hereafter *Picard v. A&B*), filed as Adversary Proceeding No. 10-05421 (BRL) in U.S. Bankruptcy Court for the Southern District of New York, pp. 3, 39. Specifically, the lawsuit claimed that Avellino & Bienes gave the SEC a list showing that investors were owed $399,819,455, but Madoff's account statements reported that their six accounts held only about $364 million. As of publication, lawyers for Avellino and Bienes were contesting the trustee's allegations in court.

99 the fraudulent use of the investors' money: Ibid., p. 40.

99 elaborately concealed hush money: Ibid., pp. 51–54.

99 assisted by other close associates on the small staff devoted to Madoff's investment clients: The criminal charges to which DiPascali pleaded guilty in 2009 acknowledged that others were involved in the effort and knew it was fraudulent. The government subsequently filed criminal charges against Annette Bongiorno, JoAnn Crupi, Daniel Bonventre, George Perez, and Jerome O'Hara, accusing them of helping Madoff and DiPascali carry out and cover up the fraud. All denied the charges. Similar accusations were made in civil suits filed by the Madoff trustee in bankruptcy court against Bongiorno, Crupi, Bonventre, Eric Lipkin, Lipkin's father and mother, and David Kugel, a trader at the firm. Eric Lipkin and Kugel pleaded guilty to criminal charges in 2011; the other defendants denied the trustee's allegations.

99 A footnote showed that Madoff had fluently explained it all to them: Specifically, the SEC memo in the Kotz Report's Exhibit 114 noted in footnote 10 on page 9 that "Madoff hedges A&B's portfolio primarily by purchasing long-term equity anticipation securities ('LEAPS'), which are essentially long-term options (two year expira-

tion) on underlying stocks or stock indexes. During the time period reviewed by the staff (i.e., May through October 1992), Madoff purchased puts on the S&P 100 Index and utilized a 'short [against] the box' trading strategy designed to lock in trading profits." A "short against the box" is a short sale of stock that an investor already owns—a way of reaping profits on the stock's current selling price without actually selling the shares and incurring capital gains taxes.

100 "I was actually doing the trades": First BLM Interview.

100 "Shapiro, Picower, and Levy all sent in actual money, new money": Ibid.

101 "I am not a cash cow and I will not be milked": Affidavit of Frank J. Avellino dated Mar. 10, 1993, filed in *SEC v. Avellino & Bienes, Frank J. Avellino and Michael S. Bienes* (hereafter "the 1992 SEC Case"), filed as 92-cv-8314 (JES) in U.S. District Court for the Southern District of New York, p. 1.

101 "I personally oversaw Avellino & Bienes' books and records": Ibid., p. 2.

101 "I don't believe your client": Transcript of a hearing in the 1992 SEC Case, held before federal district judge John E. Sprizzo on April 21, 1993, p. 147.

102 They denied that they were involved at all: Bienes *Frontline* interview.

102 laid out a very different scenario: *Picard v. A&B* Complaint, p. 51.

102 the "schupt" payments: Ibid., p. 55. In a separate complaint, the trustee would assert that Steven Mendelow of Konigsberg Wolf profited to a lesser degree from both the guaranteed profits and the "schupt" payments for allegedly steering his former Telfran investors back to Madoff. See *In re: Bernard L. Madoff Investment Securities, Debtor; Irving H. Picard, Trustee for the Liquidation of Bernard L. Madoff Investment Securities v. Steven B. Mendelow, et al.* (hereafter *Picard v. Mendelow*), filed as Adversary Proceeding No. 10-04283 (BRL) in U.S. Bankruptcy Court for the Southern District of New York, p. 25. In a telephone interview in January 2011, Stanley Arkin, a lawyer for Mendelow, denied the allegations and said his client "was a victim like many others, and had no idea that Mr. Madoff was conducting a Ponzi scheme."

103 DiPascali, in turn, allegedly relied on two computer programmers: As of February 2012, the programmers, Jerome O'Hara and George Perez, had denied the allegations and were awaiting trial.

103 "I could not have operated in view": E-mail from BLM, dated Dec. 27, 2010. In the e-mail, Madoff insists the move occurred when "the problems started with crime," denying again that his Ponzi scheme started before the SEC investigation. What is more likely is that the scale of his fraudulent operation was compact enough to be hidden on the eighteenth floor until the enormous increase in the number of individual accounts that followed the SEC's action against Avellino & Bienes.

104 The theory behind hedge funds: As one scholar noted: "High leverage, management expertise, performance fees, and absolute return strategies are the hallmarks of the industry. [Hedge fund managers] share a belief that markets are not strongly efficient, and that adroit managers can take advantage of superior information, analysis, and minimization of trading cost to achieve absolute returns under any market conditions." J. W. Verret, "Dr. Jones and the Raiders of Lost Capital: Hedge Fund Regulation, Part II, a Self-Regulation Proposal," *Delaware Journal of Corporate Law* 32, no. 3 (2007): 803.

104 The hedge fund was pioneered: Carol Loomis, "Personal Investing: The Jones Nobody Keeps Up With," *Fortune*, April 1966, p. 237.

104 even the fabled Jones fund: Carol Loomis, "Hard Times Come to the Hedge Funds," *Fortune*, January 1970, p. 134.

104 its partners "aren't rocket scientists": Kotz Report, Exhibit 104, p. 5.

105 Born in Nashville and educated at Vanderbilt University: These and other personal details, unless otherwise noted, are drawn from his engagement announcement, "Monica Haegler Will Be Married to an Economist," *New York Times*, Apr. 8, 1962. As in all society page announcements, the details were provided by the engaged couple and were not independently verified by the newspaper.

105 He later helped develop an international private banking operation: Official biography for Walter Noel contained in promotional material from Fairfield Greenwich Group.

105 four of them would marry into influential European and Latin American families: Lisina Noel's husband, Yanko Della Schiava, was the son of a prominent Italian textile executive active in the fashion industry and his wife, the editor of the Italian edition of *Cosmopolitan* magazine. Daughter Alix's husband, Philip J. Toub, had family ties to a major shipping company in Switzerland, where he was raised. Andrés Piedrahita, Corina's husband, was the ambitious Boston-educated son of a commodities trader in Bogotá, Colombia. Ariane Noel married Marco Sodi, an investment banker born in Florence. The fifth Noel daughter, Marisa, was the only one to accept a domestic suitor: she married Matthew Brown, whose father had been an IBM executive and whose mother was briefly the mayor of San Marino, California. These details are all drawn from the daughters' wedding and/or engagement announcements in the *New York Times*.

105 Monica Noel had her own wealthy family connections: Kristina Stewart, "Golden in Greenwich," *Vanity Fair*, October 2002; Sarah Medford, "Easy in the Islands," *Town & Country*, May 2005, p. 207.

109 "Mustique is the antithesis of Palm Beach": Medford, "Easy in the Islands."

109 it probably totaled more than $45 million in 1998: The estimate is based on comparisons of the fees collected on total Sentry fund assets of $4 billion in 2002, which totaled $87 million, according to exhibits filed in connection with lawsuits by the Madoff trustee, Sentry fund investors, and Massachusetts securities regulators. Since the Sentry fund's assets were just under $2 billion in 1998—about half the 2002 level—it is reasonable to conclude that the firm's fee income was likewise about half the 2002 level.

109 the firm would collect nearly $920 million between 2002 and 2008: For example, see *Picard v. Fairfield Sentry* Amended Complaint, p. 34.

110 J. Ezra Merkin was to the intimate, fraternal world of Jewish philanthropy: Steve Fishman, "The Monster Mensch," *New York*, Mar. 2, 2009, p. 18. Fishman noted that "Ezra took Bernard L. Madoff Investment Securities places Bernie couldn't have dreamed of going by himself. The list of people and institutions that Ezra Merkin put with Bernie Madoff is a kind of Jewish social register. There was Mort Zuckerman, the media and real-estate mogul, and Ira Rennert, chairman of Fifth Avenue Synagogue and owner of a 68-acre oceanfront Hamptons estate. Over 30 charities invested with Ezra, many of them with a Jewish affiliation" (p. 77).

110 One of them recalled the ritual of lunching with Hermann Merkin: Confidential interview with a former business associate of BLM.

111 the synagogue became the spiritual home of a number of wealthy congregants: Reporting notes contributed to the author by Alison Leigh Cowan, a reporter at the *New York Times*, based on her extensive coverage of Merkin's role in the Madoff affair.

111 "a voracious reader": Ibid.

111 "pious, prayerful and profound": Douglas Feiden, "Famed for Piety, Jacob Merkin Put Faith and Funds in Bernie Madoff," New York *Daily News*, Jan. 18, 2009, quoting Rafi Weiss, "a retired investor who worshiped with Merkin at Orthodox synagogues in Manhattan and Long Island." The same quote was included in Fishman, "Monster Mensch," p. 20, attributed to "a fellow congregant."

111 his sometimes harsh dismissal of those he considered his intellectual inferiors: Fishman, "Monster Mensch," p. 24.

111 After briefly practicing law at an elite New York firm: *In re: J. Ezra Merkin and BDO Seidman* (hereafter *NYLS v. Merkin*), filed in U.S. District Court for the Southern District of New York as 08-Civ.-10922 (DAB), p. 23 of the Amended Complaint. An identical chronology is laid out in *The People of the State of New York, by Andrew M. Cuomo, Attorney General v. J. Ezra Merkin and Gabriel Capital Corp.* (hereafter *Cuomo-Merkin* Summons), filed as Index No. 450879/09 in Supreme Court of the State of New York, County of New York, on Apr. 6, 2009, p. 24, based on testimony by Merkin and others involved.

111 far less involved in actually managing the money: *NYLS v. Merkin*, pp. 4, 12–18, 25–32. Again, these allegations were echoed in *Cuomo-Merkin* Summons, notably on p. 29.

111 almost exclusively by a young man named Victor Teicher: *Cuomo-Merkin* Summons, pp. 26–27.

111 According to Teicher, he continued to advise the two Merkin funds: Ibid.

112 Merkin started thinking about putting a portion of the Ariel and Gabriel money: Excerpts from deposition of J. Ezra Merkin on Jan. 30, 2009 (hereafter Merkin Transcript), filed as Exhibit 1 in *Cuomo-Merkin* Summons, p. 8.

112 "a kind, *haimish* sort of guy compared to my father": Fishman, "Monster Mensch," p. 77.

112 One of Merkin's associates would later theorize: Ibid.

112 Merkin would later argue in court that many investors were aware: *Cuomo-Merkin* Summons, Opinion Denying Defendants' Motion to Dismiss by Justice Richard B. Lowe III (hereafter Lowe MTD Opinion), Feb. 8, 2010, p. 11.

112 According to Merkin, his father first introduced him to Madoff: Merkin Transcript, p. 8.

113 it apparently carried great weight with his eldest son that he spoke well of Madoff: Ibid.

113 "described Madoff in terms of what he was doing": Deposition of Victor Teicher, filed in *Cuomo-Merkin* Summons, pp. 39–45.

113 Merkin got similar warnings from John Nash: Arvedlund, *Too Good to Be True*, pp. 252–53, 258–59.

113 Later lawsuits would calculate that Merkin collected nearly $170 million: Lowe MTD Opinion, p. 3.

114 "We did not speak about markets": Author's notes of Portfolio seminar featuring Wiesel.

114 "Everybody we knew told us we could do so much more": Ibid.

114 It was widely known that prospective members had to demonstrate: Confidential interview with a person in Palm Beach familiar with the club's membership rosters and practices since the late 1980s. This person said that the club's initiation fee was $125,000 in 1990–91 and was about $400,000 in 2010. Assuming that the $275,000 increase had been spread evenly across the nineteen-year period, the fee in 1996 would have been $197,500.

7. WARNING SIGNS

117 a lengthy article by writer Michael Ocrant: The article is reproduced in Markopolos, *No One Would Listen*, p. 288.

117 "considered somewhat high for the strategy": Ibid.

117 "experienced far greater volatility and lower returns": Ibid., p. 289. The Gateway fund actually tracked the Fairfield Sentry fund fairly closely from 1993 until about 1997; thereafter the disparity between the two funds widened sharply as Gateway became more volatile and less profitable.

118 "Never in my wildest dreams did I think I would have partners like these": Michael Carroll, Hal Lux, and Justin Schack, "Trading Meets the Millennium," *Institutional Investor*, January 2000, pp. 36–53.

118 "Market timing and stock picking are both important for the strategy to work": The Ocrant article in Markopolos, *No One Would Listen*, p. 292.

119 The following week, a similarly skeptical view: Erin Arvedlund, "Don't Ask, Don't Tell," *Barron's*, May 7, 2001.

119 "Much of it I thought was, frankly, just irresponsible journalism": *Galvin Fairfield Greenwich* Complaint, transcript excerpts from interview with Jeffrey Tucker, Mar. 12, 2009, p. 97. (Excerpts were also cited as Exhibit 85 in *Picard v. Fairfield Greenwich* Amended Complaint.)

119 "Come up this afternoon": According to Tucker's testimony, Madoff extended a similar invitation that day to Carlo Grosso, a principal of the Kingate funds based in London, who was visiting New York.

119 Wall Street's central clearinghouse, the Depository Trust & Clearing Corporation: Originally named the Depository Trust Company, the clearinghouse later combined with a separate clearinghouse called the National Securities Clearing Corporation, on whose board Madoff served in the late 1980s, and was renamed the Depository Trust & Clearing Corporation, or DTCC. According to the official DTCC history, the clearinghouses were "both created in response to the paperwork crisis that developed in the securities industry in the late 1960s and early 1970s. At that time, brokers still exchanged paper certificates and checks for each trade, sending hundreds of messengers scurrying throughout Wall Street clutching bags of checks and securities."

120 Tucker later told regulators about this pivotal visit: *Galvin Fairfield Greenwich* Complaint, transcript excerpts from interview with Jeffrey Tucker, Mar. 12, 2009, pp. 97–100.

121 "This is a great exam for us!": Kotz Report, p. 89.

121 Congress broadened the loophole: Previously, hedge funds restricted themselves to

fewer than one hundred partners; the National Securities Markets Improvement Act of 1996 allowed them to have an unlimited number of partners, provided each was a "qualified purchaser" with at least $5 million in invested assets.

121 In a 2001 report: The General Accounting Office issued three reports and provided congressional testimony on SEC staffing issues: GAO-01-947, GAO-02-302, GAO-03-120 and GAO-02-662T. None reported any meaningful progress toward resolving the agency's profound personnel problems.

121 left the agency between 1998 and 2000: General Accounting Office, "Securities and Exchange Commission: Human Capital Challenges Require Management Attention," Report No. GAO-01-947, p. 1.

122 Markopolos had become interested in Madoff's returns a few years earlier: Harry Markopolos, Testimony Before the House Committee on Financial Services, Feb. 4, 2009, p. 5

122 The son of immigrant Greek restaurant owners in Erie, Pennsylvania: These personal and career details are drawn from Markopolos, *No One Would Listen.*

122 "We settled for a carat and a half": Ibid., pp. 65–66.

123 "Sometimes Harry is not too smooth": Kotz Report, Exhibit 18, pp. 18–19.

123 "could count to 21": Markopolos, *No One Would Listen*, p. 161.

123 "That would be equivalent to a major league baseball player batting .966": Markopolos testimony, p. 9.

123 only fourteen losing months in the same period: Morningstar data compiled for the author, analyzed over the same period Markopolos used in his 2000 submission to the SEC. See Kotz Report, Exhibit 134.

124 "And Harry would say: See, there it is, you know": Kotz Report, transcript of interview with Ed Manion, Exhibit 18, p. 24.

124 could tell that Ward's eyes had glazed over: Kotz Report, p. 64.

124 "Returns can't be coming from net long exposure to the market": Ibid., Markopolos 2000 Submission, Exhibit 134, p. 2.

124 the official report concluded that this, too, was untrue: See Kotz Report, p. 67: "Based on [then-Boston regional administrator Juan] Marcelino's testimony and [Ward's predecessor Jim] Adelman's corroborating statement, Ward's testimony to the OIG was not credible regarding: (1) whether he recalled meeting with Markopolos or hearing concerns about Madoff's hedge fund in 2000; and (2) the substance of his February 4, 2009 conversation with Marcelino. Accordingly, the OIG concludes that, based upon the preponderance of the evidence, Ward met with Markopolos in 2000 and told Manion that he had referred the complaint to NERO, but never actually did."

124 "These numbers really are too good to be true": Kotz Report, p. 67.

125 "I don't think we should pursue this matter further": Ibid., p. 27.

125 "My impressions are that this is a document": Ibid., pp. 72–73.

126 A fund of hedge funds was the same idea: Funds of hedge funds that were not publicly registered as mutual funds had been available in the international market since at least 1990, when there were approximately four dozen of them, according to Van Hedge Fund Advisors International. By August 2005 the advisory firm estimated that there were three thousand such funds, constituting about 40 percent of the industry's assets.

126 "Funds of hedge funds raise special concerns": William H. Donaldson, "Testimony Concerning Investor Protection Implications of Hedge Funds," U.S. Senate Committee on Banking, Housing and Urban Affairs, Apr. 10, 2003.

126 had already moved their "self-directed" IRAs into the hands of Bernie Madoff: Diana B. Henriques, "Questions for a Custodian After Scams Hit IRAs," *New York Times,* July 24, 2009.

127 a small firm called Retirement Accounts Inc.: In 2008, the unit handling self-directed IRAs was spun off from Fiserv and divided, with the self-directed services going to a private company set up by the unit's former president and the rest going to TD Ameritrade. Fiserv was sued on behalf of its customers in 2009 for "facilitating" Madoff's fraud, and the case was still moving slowly through the courts more than eighteen months later.

127 By 2008 it would be handling roughly eight hundred self-directed IRAs: Henriques, "Questions for a Custodian." Three other convicted Ponzi schemers steered their IRA investors to Fiserv for support services. Regulatory gaps and inconsistent court rulings about the duties of support firms left the legal landscape fairly foggy; litigation arising from the Madoff case may clarify their responsibilities.

127 they maintained a relationship with him for more than a decade: *Cuomo v. Ivy* Complaint, p. 12.

127 Some new limited partnerships were formed solely to invest with Madoff via the Ivy firm: Ibid., pp. 1–4.

127 By 1991 some Ivy partners had heard disquieting rumors: These details and the ones that follow are drawn from several sections of the *Cuomo v. Ivy* Complaint, which cites contemporaneous e-mails and letters from Ivy's files.

128 "compensation for the use of their money": *Cuomo v. Ivy* Complaint, p. 23.

128 The Ivy executive described the conversation in an internal memo: Ibid., p. 36.

129 "You omitted one other possibility—he's a fraud": Ibid., p. 42. The Ivy case is pending, but the partner filed a formal answer in court contesting the attorney general's accusations and denying that he suspected Madoff was running a Ponzi scheme during these years. See *Cuomo v. Ivy*, Answer and Affirmative Defenses of Howard Wohl, Aug. 28, 2010.

129 In the early 1970s she developed methods for measuring fund performance: Official biography in Maxam fund prospectus; Greg Newton, "A Talented Talent Scout," *Barron's,* Aug. 2, 2006.

130 legendary fund managers such as Peter Lynch, Fred Alger, and Mario Gabelli: Newton, "Talented Talent Scout."

130 Madoff himself identified Kingate as one of the first hedge funds to invest with him: First BLM Interview.

131 a public forum in 2003: The transcript for this session, held May 14–15, 2003, at SEC headquarters in Washington, D.C. (hereafter May 2003 Hedge Fund Forum), is posted on the SEC's Web site without page numbers but in a form that can be searched. In February 2011, it could be found at www.sec.gov/spotlight/hedgefunds/hedge2trans.txt.

131 "It's very difficult to get answers out of managers": Ibid.

132 warned its clients away: Kevin E. Lynch, Charles Colfer, and Tomas Kukla, "Flash:

Rogerscasey's Buy-Rated Hedge Fund Managers Have No Exposure to Madoff Investment Securities LLC," Rogerscasey Inc. internal publication, December 2008.

132 Rogerscasey's rating for the Madoff-related Tremont funds was "sell": The warnings surfaced in the course of lawsuits filed in Colorado by Madoff victims against units of Fiserv that provided IRA custodial services to more than eight hundred retirement savings accounts invested with Madoff.

132 "The Madoff exposure is a potential disaster": Lynch, Colfer, and Kukla, "Flash," p. 2.

133 he invested about $620 million: Diana B. Henriques, "Deal Recovers $7.2 Billion for Madoff Fraud Victims," *New York Times*, Dec. 17, 2010.

133 the model for the Gordon Gekko character in Oliver Stone's 1987 movie *Wall Street*: James B. Stewart, *Den of Thieves* (New York: Simon & Schuster, 1991), pp. 202–3. Stewart noted that a Boesky aide, Reid Nagle, "had no idea where Picower's money came from; he occupied an unmarked office suite in an anonymous Manhattan tower."

133 Picower's trading account at Goldman Sachs: Henriques, "Deal Recovers $7.2 Billion," and reporting notes made available to the author by her colleague Peter Lattman.

133 Available records show that Picower and his wife withdrew $390 million: Jake Bernstein, "Madoff Client Jeffry Picower Netted $5 Billion—Likely More Than Madoff Himself," ProPublica.org, June 23, 2009 (subsequently updated), and the accompanying graphic, Dan Nguyen and Jake Bernstein, "Chart: The Picower-Madoff Transfers, from 1995–2008."

135 a posthumous memoir called *Leukemia for Chickens*: Roger Madoff, *Leukemia for Chickens: One Wimp's Tale About Living Through Cancer* (New York: privately published, 2007).

135 One hospital staff member would poignantly recall Peter gently rubbing ointment: Ibid., pp. 273–74. The scene, two days before Roger's death, was described in Roger's book by counselor Larry Dyche of Albert Einstein College of Medicine: "I wound my way through long corridors to Roger's area. Through the door of his room, I could see a man putting ointment on Roger's feet. . . . He was Roger's father, a man renowned on Wall Street. Apologizing for not taking my hand, he rose to let us have the room to ourselves. He looked as if he would give all he owned to keep his son."

138 twice the value reported just five years earlier: Based on self-reporting to the *Securities Industry Yearbook* for those years.

138 had written him off and warned their clients to get out: In one lawsuit against a Madoff feeder fund, the bankruptcy trustee noted: "Based on all of the foregoing factors, many banks, industry advisors and insiders who made an effort to conduct reasonable due diligence flatly refused to deal with BLMIS and Madoff because they had serious concerns that their [investment advisory] business operations were not legitimate. On information and belief, included among these were Société Générale, Goldman Sachs, CitiGroup, Morgan Stanley, Merrill Lynch, Bear Stearns, and Credit Suisse." See *In re: Bernard L. Madoff Investment Securities, Debtor; Irving H. Picard, Trustee for the Liquidation of Bernard L. Madoff Investment Securities v. Thybo Asset Management Ltd.* (hereafter *Picard v. Thybo*), filed as Adversary Proceeding No. 09-01365 (BRL) in U.S. Bankruptcy Court for the Southern District of New York, p. 18.

8. A NEAR-DEATH EXPERIENCE

139 "What are you looking for?": Kotz Report. These details are drawn from transcripts of Kotz's interviews with Lamore, Exhibit 48, and Ostrow, Exhibits 36 and 37, and his report on his interview with Madoff himself, Exhibit 104, and from confidential interviews with people familiar with SEC operations. Where direct quotes are used in this passage, they are the phrases recalled in official transcripts by the participants.

139 insisted on being their only contact in the office: Kotz Report, Ostrow Transcript, Exhibit 36, pp. 22, 34.

139 Frank DiPascali on the seventeenth floor had been busy: *Securities and Exchange Commission v. Frank DiPascali Jr.* (hereafter *SEC v. DiPascali*), filed as 09-cv-7085 in U.S. District Court in the Southern District of New York on Aug. 11, 2009, p. 16; and *DiPascali Criminal Information*, pp. 14–15.

139 On December 18, 2003, Madoff was walking through the Lipstick Building lobby: Kotz Report, Exhibit 104, Madoff interview, p. 3.

140 "Bernie, it's Lori": According to the Kotz Report, Richards recalled talking with Madoff in advance of a 2003 examination and agreed that it might have developed along the lines Madoff described, but she could not confirm the exact dialogue. See Kotz Report, p. 87.

140 The records from that exam were piled into a pair of boxes and forgotten: Kotz Report, pp. 136–37.

140 Lamore was okay, a smart kid: Kotz Report, Exhibit 104, Madoff Interview, pp. 1–3, 6.

140 Ostrow and Lamore tried to calm Madoff: Kotz Report, e-mail on Apr. 20, 2005, Exhibit 233.

140 a belated response to a set of e-mails: Kotz Report, p. 145.

140 an indirect stake in Madoff through its Meritor hedge fund: Meritor had entered into a total return swap with another party, who promised to pay Meritor a rate of return equal to the performance of one of the Madoff-linked hedge funds. See Kotz Report, p. 145.

140 The Renaissance e-mails, written in late 2003: Kotz Report, internal Renaissance executive e-mails contained in Exhibits 211, 212, and 213.

141 "First of all, we spoke to an ex-Madoff trader": Ibid., Exhibit 211.

141 "where there was some chatter about Madoff": Ibid., Exhibit 215, p. 2.

141 "Despite the fact that we are kind of smart people": Ibid., p. 151.

142 on May 20, 2003, a hedge fund managing director: Ibid., pp. 77–78.

142 But the request was never sent: Ibid., pp. 97–98.

143 "Front-running—aren't you looking for front-running?": Ibid., Lamore Transcript, Exhibit 48, p. 77.

143 reassuring to those who thought they knew Bernie best: Confidential interviews with people familiar with Madoff's trading desk operations.

144 "the possibility that Madoff is using": Kotz Report, p. 131.

144 they would later vehemently deny this allegation: This argument was made in numerous lawsuits against various feeder funds, based on Affidavit of Edward H. Siedle, filed Mar. 26, 2009, in *Retirement Program for Employees of the Town of Fairfield, et al. v. Bernard L. Madoff; Tremont Partners, Inc., et al.* (hereafter *Town of Fairfield* Complaint), filed in Connecticut State Superior Court, Judicial District of

Fairfield at Bridgeport, p. 6. Siedle was a financial consultant offered by plaintiffs as an expert witness in the case.

144 one Italian money manager said *market intelligence* was the code word: Confidential interview.

144 an illegal practice known as "cherry-picking": Kotz Report, p. 146.

144 The supervisor did not share the response with Lamore or Ostrow: Ibid., pp. 189–90.

145 "We do a few trades on behalf of brokerage firms and institutions": Ibid., Exhibit 104, p. 2; Exhibit 244; and Exhibit 245.

145 The news was a shock: Kotz Report, Exhibit 36, p. 24.

145 Recovering, Ostrow said something about the SEC being a large organization: Kotz Report, Exhibit 104, p. 4.

145 Madoff conceded that perhaps there were as many as fifteen entities: Kotz Report, Exhibit 245. In the e-mail that opens the exhibit, Lamore writes his colleagues that "Bernie's fessing up." His supervisor would later say that the obvious lies Madoff was telling did not overly concern him: "it's hard to get inside someone's head about why they're saying what they're saying" (Ibid., pp. 194–95).

145 But the model stopped using options about a year ago: Kotz Report, Exhibit 104, p. 4.

146 They'd cleared up the whole thing back in 2003: Kotz Report, Exhibit 48, p. 103.

146 "We are hoping that if what he is saying has any truth at all to it": Kotz Report, Exhibit 247, p. 2.

146 they were stacked in a hallway, heading for the archives: Kotz Report, p. 136.

146 the staff had never even drafted a closing report: Ibid., p. 137.

146 he told the two examiners that they needed to wrap things up: Ibid., pp. 222–23.

146 She expected some of her clients would leave Tremont: Newton, "Talented Talent Scout."

146 $175 million in redemptions in April, another $85 million in July, and $30 million in early September: Confidential "Fairfield Greenwich Group: Firm Profile" dated Nov. 15, 2007, and apparently prepared as part of the partners' effort to find a buyer or major investor for the firm (hereafter FGG 2007 Profile), pp. 13–14.

147 not willing to accept profits of less than 7 percent a year: Ibid.

147 The Bayou Group was founded in the mid-1990s: Letter from Samuel Israel III to U.S. District Court Judge Colleen McMahon, Apr. 9, 2008, p. 1.

147 assets totaling $411 million: Gretchen Morgenson, Jenny Anderson, Geraldine Fabrikant, and Riva D. Atlas, "What Really Happened at Bayou," *New York Times*, Sept. 17, 2005.

147 In mid-August the skeptical investor arrived at Bayou's offices: Ibid.

147 accused of running a $400 million Ponzi scheme: Gretchen Morgenson, "U.S. Sues Bayou; Fraud Cited," *New York Times*, Sept. 2, 2005.

147 He and Israel would subsequently plead guilty: Both Samuel Israel III and the CFO, Daniel E. Marino, were charged, pleaded guilty, and were sentenced in the U.S. District Court, Southern District of New York. Each was sentenced to twenty years in prison. The case is number 1:05-cr-01036-CM-1.

148 One of his last calls from his deathbed: Confidential interview with a longtime friend of the Levy family.

148 "Bernie Madoff, trust Bernie Madoff": Fox Business News interview with Francis

Levy, "Bulls and Bears," January 2009, from a transcript of *Money for Breakfast*, Jan. 9, 2009, posted on CEOWire and retrieved from BNET.

148 He had named Madoff as the executor: *SIPC v. Bernard L. Madoff Investment Securities, Debtor; In re: Bernard L. Madoff, Debtor* (hereafter *Main Madoff Liquidation*), case number 08-01789-BRL in U.S. Bankruptcy Court, Southern District of New York, "Motion for Entry of Order Pursuant to Section 105(a) of the Bankruptcy Code and Rules 2002 and 9019 of the Federal Rules of Bankruptcy Procedure Approving an Agreement by and Among the Trustee and Jeanne Levy-Church and Francis N. Levy," dated Jan. 27, 2010, p. 4.

148 some of the people defrauded in the Bayou scam also had money with Madoff: These connections were identified and documented by the author, matching investor claims in the Bayou Group LLC bankruptcy case, filed as case number 06-22306 (ASH) in U.S. Bankruptcy Court in the Southern District of New York, with the records in the Madoff case.

148 e-mailed the firm after the Bayou scandal to ask explicit questions: *Picard v. Fairfield Sentry* Amended Complaint, pp. 100–102; actual e-mail exchanges are Exhibit 18 in *Galvin Fairfield Greenwich* Complaint.

149 had most, if not all, of their money with Bernie: Transcript, Plea Hearing in *U.S.A. v. David Friehling* (hereafter *Friehling Plea Transcript*), filed as Case No. 09-cr-700 (AKH), U.S. District Court, Southern District of New York, Nov. 3, 2009, pp. 34–35.

149 "We would question Bayou's obscure auditing firm": *Picard v. Fairfield Sentry* Amended Complaint, Exhibit 56, "Fairfield Greenwich Group Investment Team Presentation, November 2, 2005," p. 15.

150 "250 hours in a year-long process": July 2006 memo by Jonathan Clark, filed as an exhibit in the case *In re: Optimal Strategic U.S. Equity Fund Securities Litigation*, Multi-District Case No. 2073, U.S. District Court, Southern District of Florida, pp. 6–7.

150 "David seemed surprised to hear Madoff Securities described": Ibid.

150 coached DiPascali in the role: *U.S.A. v. Daniel Bonventre*, Sealed Complaint, sworn by Special Agent Keith D. Kelly before Magistrate Judge Theodore H. Katz and filed as Case No. 10-MAG-385 on Feb. 24, 2010, p. 22. The complaint, the basis for the arrest warrant in the case, was replaced a month later by a formal indictment that combined the case against Bonventre with an indictment already pending against two other Madoff employees, Jerome O'Hara and George Perez, as noted below. Bonventre denied all charges filed against him.

151 the amount of custom-designed software serving the Ponzi scheme: There is no legal dispute that these computer programs existed and were used to deceive regulators, accountants, and investors. The dispute is over who created them and why. DiPascali admitted ordering that they be designed and putting them to use; the two computer programmers he accused of creating them, George Perez and Jerome O'Hara, have denied any wrongdoing and demanded a jury trial. Details of the charges against them are contained in a civil complaint, *SEC v. Jerome O'Hara and George Perez* (hereafter *SEC v. O'Hara and Perez*), filed in U.S. District Court for the Southern District of New York, Nov. 13, 2009, and a related criminal indictment against Perez and O'Hara made public the same day. As noted hereafter, a superseding indictment adding Daniel Bonventre as a defendant was filed Mar. 24, 2010; Bonventre also denied the charges and demanded a jury trial.

151 There were programs that generated random numbers: *SEC v. O'Hara and Perez.*

151 the balance in Madoff's slush fund account: *U.S.A. v. Daniel Bonventre, Jerome O'Hara and George Perez* (hereafter *First Superseding Bonventre Indictment*), filed on Mar. 24, 2010, as S1-10-cr-228 (LTS), U.S. District Court, Southern District of New York, p. 29.

152 the firm's proprietary trading desk: *In re: Bernard L. Madoff, Debtor; Irving H. Picard, Trustee for the Liquidation of Bernard L. Madoff Investment Securities LLC. v. Peter B. Madoff, Mark D. Madoff, Andrew H. Madoff and Shana D. Madoff* (hereafter *Picard v. Madoff Family*), filed as Adversary Proceeding No. 09-01503 (BRL) in U.S. Bankruptcy Court, Southern District of New York, "Declaration of Martin Flumenbaum in Support of Mark and Andrew Madoff's Reply Memorandum of Law in Further Support of Their Motion to Dismiss," Exhibit A: Memorandum by Lazard Freres & Co., dated Dec. 23, 2008, p. 1.

152 A subsequent criminal indictment asserted that it was Dan Bonventre: Bonventre was arrested on a criminal complaint by the U.S. Attorney's Office for the Southern District of New York on Feb. 25, 2010, three months after the indictment of two computer programmers who allegedly helped DiPascali construct phony records for the fraud. The reference here is to the formal charges that were filed against Bonventre in the *First Superseding Bonventre Indictment*, pp. 28–30.

153 Prosecutors and regulators at the SEC later claimed: On the same date as Bonventre's arrest, the SEC filed related civil fraud charges against him, *SEC v. Daniel Bonventre* (hereafter *SEC v. Bonventre*), in U.S. District Court, Southern District of New York, providing additional details about his alleged role in the Ponzi scheme.

153 making the cash look like legal profits: Ibid., p. 14.

153 phony ledger entries were created: Ibid., p. 2.

153 "The World's Largest Hedge Fund Is a Fraud": Kotz Report, Exhibit 268, p. 1.

154 "Very few people in the world have the mathematical background needed": Ibid.

154 They were impressed—indeed, alarmed: Kotz Report, p. 240.

154 the SEC office in New York would have to investigate him: Kotz Report, p. 242.

154 "The informant believes that Madoff may be running one giant Ponzi scheme": Ibid., p. 243.

154 had virtually no experience investigating Ponzi schemes: Ibid., pp. 245–46.

155 she had been "hamstrung by a lack of resources and personnel": Ibid., Exhibit 281, p. 4.

155 "she thought he was kind of condescending to the SEC": Kotz Preport, pp. 250–51.

155 He said later that she seemed "offended" by this: Ibid., p. 251, note 174. In a statement on Cheung's behalf, her lawyers argued to Kotz that, while the failure to uncover Madoff's crime "is a burden Ms. Cheung carries daily and will continue to carry for years to come," she and her colleagues conducted "a meaningful and good faith investigation" of Madoff that was "consistent with SEC rules, policies, and practices." The lawyers complained that she was being unfairly blamed for "what appears to be a systemic failure." See ibid., Exhibit 281, pp. 1–2.

156 he approached John Wilke in the Washington bureau of the *Wall Street Journal*: Markopolos, *No One Would Listen*, p. 152.

156 where he wrote about corrupt congressmen and the companies that corrupted them: Joe Holley, "John Wilke, 54: Acclaimed Investigative Reporter," *Washington Post*, May 4, 2009.

156 Some of Markopolos's allies urged him to approach other reporters: E-mails Markopolos submitted as part of his congressional testimony in 2009 included several messages in which friends urged him to contact other reporters.

156 Markopolos wanted to work only with Wilke: Markopolos, *No One Would Listen*, p. 154.

156 "that someone high up at the *Journal* had decided": Ibid.

156 flatly denied that anything was behind Wilke's decision: Joe Strupp, "Former 'WSJ' Editor Does Not Recall Madoff Tip," the Market Rap blog, Feb. 5, 2009. See also Richard J. Tofel, "Bookshelf: Shadowing a Swindler," *Wall Street Journal*, Mar. 8, 2010.

156 "basically some of the same issues": Kotz Report, p. 255.

156 "I think he is on a fishing expedition": Ibid., p. 256.

157 "There is still a little mystery as to what Madoff does": Ibid.

157 There did not seem to be any explanation: Ibid., pp. 271–72.

158 "any *real* reason to suspect some kind of wrongdoing": Ibid., p. 292.

158 conducted after the SEC gave him permission to consult with Madoff before testifying: The conversation the witness had with Madoff hit the headlines when a partial transcript of it was released as Exhibit 1 in the *Galvin Fairfield Greenwich* Complaint. According to the transcript, Madoff opened the conversation by saying to Fairfield Greenwich general counsel Mark McKeefry: "Obviously, first of all, this conversation never took place, Mark, okay?" (See Exhibit 1, p. 30.) Lawyers for Fairfield Greenwich responded that the call, however Madoff described it, was made with the SEC's permission and was disclosed to the SEC after it took place.

158 using another $54 million in government bonds from Carl Shapiro's account: *SEC v. Bonventre*, pp. 18–19.

158 On January 30, 2006, they interviewed Jeffrey Tucker: Kotz Report, p. 293.

158 Two days later they sent a letter to Tremont Partners: Ibid., p. 269, note 189.

159 Madoff . . . produced a six-page list of the financial entities: The list included Madoff's own firm; the DTCC; the Bank of New York; Barclays Capital of London; forty-two overseas broker-dealers, thirty-six in the United Kingdom, two in Ireland, and one each in Belgium, Germany, the Netherlands, and Spain; and twelve counterparties for his options trades, including UBS and one other institution in Switzerland, the Royal Bank of Scotland (RBS), the Bank of Bermuda in London, four entities in Germany, and one each in Austria, France, the Netherlands, and Spain. See Kotz Report, Exhibit 334.

9. MADOFF'S WORLD

160 nearly 20 percent of its assets: FGG 2007 Profile, p. 13.

160 emptied their Madoff accounts in the spring of 2006: *SEC v. Bonventre*, p. 22. All three men denied government allegations that these withdrawals reflected knowledge of the Ponzi scheme.

161 They simply continued to tap Bernie's piggybank: Ibid., p. 17. The SEC calculated that Madoff made $50 million in loans to family members between 2001 and 2008.

162 decided to delay sending the letters: Kotz Report, p. 304.

162 Madoff had done no options trading at all on that date: Ibid., pp. 307–8.

163 too large to fit into the agency's limited imagination: A history professor who read

an early draft of this book observed that the SEC's reactions in the Madoff case were reminiscent of the response of U.S. leaders in the years before Pearl Harbor to reports that the Japanese were planning an air assault on Hawaii. Given the disparity in the military and economic power of the two nations, the reports just seemed too far-fetched to be credible—except in hindsight.

163 "If I was talking to a brain surgeon": Kotz Report, Exhibit 267 (an excerpted transcript of the interview), p. 47.

163 "Everybody goes to the over-the-counter market on options": Ibid., pp. 64–65.

164 "I'd like to go over this list": Ibid., pp. 88–89.

164 "I thought it was the end, game over": Kotz Report, Exhibit 104, pp. 3–4.

164 "if you're looking at a Ponzi scheme": Ibid., p. 3.

165 "Do you recall telling Peter": Kotz Report, Exhibit 267, pp. 103–5.

165 Lamore was furious: Kotz Report, Exhibit 48, p. 182.

165 "I just remember sitting there": Ibid., p. 250.

165 "I mean, 'lying or misleading' to 'fraud, Ponzi scheme' to me was a huge step": Ibid., p. 184.

165 despite all the lies they had discovered, there was no evidence of fraud: Kotz Report, Exhibit 390. The Case Closing Memorandum, which relayed this conclusion, was apparently written in January 2007, but its author, Simona Suh, went on maternity leave and the final report officially closing the case was not completed until she returned. It was then delayed while she followed up on an anonymous tip reporting (quite accurately) that Madoff was looting the estate of Norman F. Levy; Madoff denied managing money for Levy, and the matter was dropped.

166 The turnaround in Europe was nothing short of spectacular: One good proxy for the growth in the overall hedge fund market was the popular cross-border funds called UCITS, an acronym for Undertakings for Collective Investments in Transferable Securities. Sales of stock-based UCITS—the best comparison to the funds Madoff serviced—increased 25 percent in the first nine months of 2006, compared with the same period in 2005.

166 "I said, 'I want to sell'": Confidential interview.

166 Sonja Blau: In litigation filed by the Madoff trustee in December 2010, she is described as having been known by two other maiden names: Sinja Blau and Sonja Türk. The latter maiden name is also cited in Miriam Shaviv, "Could This Frum Lady Be Madoff's $40m Agent?" *Jewish Chronicle*, July 9, 2009; and Haig Simonian and Eric Frey, "Profile: Bank Medici's Sonja Kohn," *Financial Times*, Jan. 7, 2009. Kohn's mother, also sued in the trustee's case, was identified as Netty Blau.

166 an importing business in Milan and Zurich: *Picard v. Kohn*, p. 61.

167 by 1985 she had obtained her broker's license: Central Depository Records for Sonja Kohn, maintained by FINRA.

167 the firm paid more than $125,000 to settle the disputes: Ibid.

167 Kohn was introduced to Madoff: *Picard v. Kohn*, p. 62. The trustee asserted that Madoff paid Cohmad "at least $526,000" over the years for this introduction.

167 suggested he talk with a dynamic Austrian woman: Confidential interviews.

167 worked with some of the top money managers in Europe: Arvedlund, *Too Good to Be True*, p. 130; New York secretary of state corporate records.

167 commonly identified as being from Eurovaleur: Interview with Squillari.

168 Infovaleur was "a sham": *Picard v. Kohn*, p. 23.

168 "over tea at the Ritz or Claridge's in London": *In re: Bernard L. Madoff Investment Securities, Debtor; Irving H. Picard, Trustee for the Liquidation of Bernard L. Madoff Investment Securities v. Leon Flax, et al.* (hereafter *Picard v. Flax*), filed as Adversary Proceeding No. 10-05267 (BRL) in U.S. Bankruptcy Court for the Southern District of New York, pp. 19–20. Flax was also among the directors and executives of Madoff's London affiliate who were sued by Picard in the British courts. No lawyer had entered an appearance for Flax in bankruptcy court or responded to the trustee's claims at the time this book was sent to production.

168 Through her lawyers, Kohn insisted that she never had any knowledge of Madoff's fraud: David Crawford, "Madoff Kickbacks Alleged in Austria," *Wall Street Journal*, July 3, 2009, and a telephone interview with Andreas Theiss, Kohn's Viennese lawyer, on Dec. 12, 2010.

169 She also reportedly introduced Madoff to Charles Fix: "Taki" Theodoracopulos, "Madoff's Make Away," *Taki's Magazine*, published online at www.takimag.com, Jan. 12, 2009. Theodoracopulos was an investment client and social friend of Charles Fix.

169 "Austria's woman on Wall Street": Nelson D. Schwartz and Julia Werdigier, "Austria's 'Woman on Wall St.' and Madoff," *New York Times*, Jan. 7, 2009.

169 the aristocracy of European banking: Unlike Kohn's Bank Medici boutique, Creditanstalt had a corporate pedigree that really did include the legendary Medici banking family of Italy.

169 the Herald fund, which opened for business in April 2004: *In re: Bernard L. Madoff Investment Securities, Debtor; Irving H. Picard, Trustee for the Liquidation of Bernard L. Madoff Investment Securities v. Herald Fund SPC, et al.* (hereafter *Picard v. Herald Fund*), filed as Adversary Proceeding No. 09-01359 (BRL) in U.S. Bankruptcy Court for the Southern District of New York, p. 10.

169 none sent more fresh money to him during his 2005 cash crisis: Pierre Clauss, Thierry Roncalli, and Guillaume Weisang, "Risk Management Lessons from Madoff Fraud," as posted online on Apr. 8, 2009, p. 10. Electronic copies of the study are available at: www.ssrn.com/abstract=1358086.

169 would pump more than $1.5 billion into Madoff's hands: *Picard v. Herald Fund*, p. 10.

170 Littaye insisted that no one at Access deal with Madoff except through him: *In re: Bernard L. Madoff Investment Securities, Debtor; Irving H. Picard, Trustee for the Liquidation of Bernard L. Madoff Investment Securities v. UBS AG, et al.* (hereafter *Picard v. UBS*), filed as Adversary Proceeding No. 10-04283 (BRL) in U.S. Bankruptcy Court for the Southern District of New York, p. 53.

170 the connection was through a French bank executive: Benjamin Masse-Stamberger, "Revelations: Affair Madoff: Le rapport secret qui accuse JPMorgan," *L'Express*, Oct. 7, 2010.

170 he first met Madoff in 1985: Alan Katz, "Madoff Investor Awaits 'Imbecile' or 'Dupe' Verdict (Update 1)," Bloomberg news service, Jan. 5, 2009.

170 Madoff was impressed by Littaye's European connections: Alan Katz, "Madoff Investor's Suicide Was an 'Act of Honor,' Brother Says," Bloomberg news service, Jan. 2, 2009.

170 the beautiful provincial estate near St. Malo: Ibid.

170 an Access executive confirmed an odd fact: The details of this 2006 episode are taken

from *Picard v. UBS*, pp. 55–57. According to that complaint, the account was based on internal records subpoenaed by the trustee from Access International and sworn interviews with the Access employee, identified as Theodore Dumbauld, and the independent analyst, identified as Chris Cutler, the founder of Manager Analysis Services LLC.

170 "I did my best to inject doubt in a courteous yet effective manner": The description of Cutler's approach and Littaye's reaction is from e-mails between Dumbauld and Cutler, quoted in *Picard v. UBS*, p. 57.

171 a small investment from a multinational development bank in Central Africa: Auditors' General Report, Central African States Development Bank (CASDB), Year ended December 31, 2008, p. 73.

171 Madoff feeder funds based in the Cayman Islands: *In re: Bernard L. Madoff Investment Securities, Debtor; Irving H. Picard, Trustee for the Liquidation of Bernard L. Madoff Investment Securities v. Harley International (Cayman) Limited* (hereafter *Picard v. Harley*), filed as Adversary Proceeding No. 09-01187 (BRL) in U.S. Bankruptcy Court for the Southern District of New York, p. 11.

171 In the course of raising a total of $4.5 billion: *Picard v. Fairfield Sentry* Original Complaint, p. 13.

171 would ultimately raise at least $1.5 billion: *Main Madoff Liquidation*, "Motion for Entry of Order Pursuant to Section 105(a) of the Bankruptcy Code and Rules 2002 and 9019 of the Federal Rules of Bankruptcy Procedure Approving an Agreement by and Among the Trustee and Optimal Strategic U.S. Equity Limited and Optimal Arbitrage Limited," p. 4.

171 Many of the feeder funds paid "retrocession fees": *Picard v. Kohn*, p. 96.

172 its largest individual account was under $750,000: These details are drawn from *Main Madoff Liquidation*, "Affidavit of Gregory J. Adams in Support of Anchor Holdings LLC's Claim."

172 "These investors did not wish to be protected from risks": Mark Jickling, "Hedge Funds: Should They Be Regulated?" Congressional Research Service, updated July 2, 2007, p. 6.

172 the concept of "hedge funds for everyone": See Franklin R. Edwards, "Hedge Funds and Investor Protection Regulation," Federal Reserve Bank of Atlanta quarterly review, Fourth Quarter 2006; and Franklin R. Edwards, "New Proposals to Regulate Hedge Funds: SEC Rule 203(b)(3)-2," presented at the Conference on New Initiatives to Regulate Hedge Funds, at Columbia University, Oct. 21, 2004. In the latter at p. 15, Edwards writes, "Rather than focusing exclusively on restricting access to hedge funds as a way of protecting investors, the SEC should explore ways to make at least some hedge fund strategies *more* available to investors" (emphasis in the original).

174 sold $20 million worth of these derivative contracts: FGG 2007 Profile, p. 64.

174 Soon, Nomura Bank International: Sales brochure for Fairfield Sentry Ltd. USD 3X Leveraged Version.

175 would soon be offered by HSBC, Citibank, Fortis, Merrill Lynch: See "Press Release of Irving H. Picard: Trustee for Liquidation of Bernard L. Madoff Investment Securities Seeks $1 Billion from Seven Global Financial Institutions in Madoff Ponzi Scheme," Dec. 8, 2010. The actual complaints against the banks were filed under seal in U.S. Bankruptcy Court for the Southern District of New York.

176 the return on the Fairfield Sentry fund in 2006: The Sentry fund produced a return of 6.44 percent in 2004 and 7.26 percent in 2005, but in 2006 its rate of return was 9.38 percent.

177 "there is a well-known cloud over the head of Madoff": *In re: Bernard L. Madoff Investment Securities, Debtor; Irving H. Picard, Trustee for the Liquidation of Bernard L. Madoff Investment Securities v. J.P. Morgan Chase & Co., et al.,* filed as Adversary Proceeding No. 10-04932 (BRL) in U.S. Bankruptcy Court for the Southern District of New York, p. 31. The bank vigorously denied the trustee's allegations in this case, which remained under seal until Feb. 2, 2011.

178 pledging $1 million to the school: Confidential interviews.

178 doubled Frank DiPascali's annual salary: *DiPascali Criminal Information*, p. 44.

178 a new sixty-one-foot fishing boat: Ibid.; "The United States of America's Application for a Preliminary Order of Forfeiture (Final as to the Defendant) etc.," filed Apr. 21, 2010. Many of DiPascali's possessions were auctioned off by the U.S. Marshals Service on June 24, 2010. The boat and three family cars fetched just under $1 million.

178 He did not file his personal income tax returns for 2002 and 2006: *DiPascali Criminal Information*, pp. 43–45; *SEC v. DiPascali*, p. 15.

179 She emphatically denied the charge: In a telephone interview, Roland Riopelle, a lawyer for Bongiorno, said she was "very vigorously contesting" both the criminal and civil cases filed against her and "wants to try her best to vindicate herself, because she is innocent."

179 no evidence it had any impact on the unwise decisions: Kotz Report, pp. 408–9.

179 he hadn't even known Shana was dating an SEC lawyer: Kotz Report, Exhibit 104, p. 10.

179 appearing on a panel at the Philoctetes Center: A transcript of the session (hereafter Philoctetes Transcript) was obtained from the Web site of the Philoctetes Center. The page references are to the PDF version of the transcript.

179 "You have to understand, Wall Street is one big turf war": Philoctetes Transcript, pp. 7–8.

180 "which sometimes the regulators lose sight of": Ibid., p. 8.

180 "Wall Street—just so you understand the scale of it": Ibid.

180 "Now, no one is going to run a benefit for Wall Street": Ibid.

180 "Today, basically the big money on Wall Street is made by taking risks": Ibid.

180 "By and large, in today's regulatory environment": Ibid., p. 9.

10. THE YEAR OF LIVING DANGEROUSLY

181 chief compliance officer for the private money management business: SEC Public Filings, Form ADV, Uniform Application for Investment Advisory Registration filed by Bernard L. Madoff Investment Securities in February 2005.

181 an annual interest rate of 4.13 percent: *Picard v. Madoff Family*, p. 29.

182 the firm's office holiday party: This passage is based on the *Securities Industry Yearbook*, a review of Bernard L. Madoff Investment Securities employee lists, and interviews with Squillari, BLM, three confidential sources who attended the 2007 office party, and confidential sources familiar with the operation of the Madoff firm.

183 On Madoff's calendar, this evening belongs to New York City Center: BLM appointment calendar for 2008.

183 Bernie Madoff catches a night flight to Palm Beach: Ibid.

183 the touching moment when Shapiro takes the microphone: Shannon Donnelly, "He's 95, and He'll Sing if He Wants To," *Palm Beach Daily News*, Feb. 20, 2008.

184 his successful application to the Palm Beach Country Club: *Picard v. Cohmad*, p. 15.

185 Some HSBC units have been recommending various Madoff feeder funds: *In re: Bernard L. Madoff Investment Securities, Debtor; Irving H. Picard, Trustee for the Liquidation of Bernard L. Madoff Investment Securities v. HSBC Bank PLC, et al.* (hereafter *Picard v. HSBC*), filed as Adversary Proceeding No. 09-01364 (BRL) in U.S. Bankruptcy Court for the Southern District of New York, as amended, p. 106.

185 As early as 2001 a few bank executives were expressing doubt about Madoff: Ibid., p. 16.

185 a chilling list of what could go wrong: Ibid., pp. 107–11.

185 the bank will ask KPMG to do yet another assessment: Ibid., p. 111.

186 When the Wall Street division of the American Jewish Committee honored Madoff: Program for the event, held at the Harmonie Club on Nov. 15, 1999, provided to the author. The list of donors to this event, "A Tribute to Bernard L. Madoff," was a Who's Who of the Madoff victims. The "patrons," those who contributed $10,000 or more, included Edward Blumenfeld, the real estate developer; Stanley Chais, the early feeder fund operator; Maurice J. "Sonny" Cohn, cofounder of Cohmad Securities; Sonja Kohn of Bank Medici; Robert I. Lappin, whose foundation lost millions; Norman F. Levy, whose children's fortunes were caught in the scandal; Mr. and Mrs. Peter Loeb, members of a fabled Wall Street family; Walter M. Noel Jr. and Jeffrey Tucker of Fairfield Greenwich Group; Jeffry M. Picower, the biggest winner in Madoff's Ponzi scheme; Carl Shapiro, one of Madoff's earliest investors; and Sterling Equities, an investment vehicle for Fred Wilpon and the Wilpon family, which owned the New York Mets. The ranks of lesser donors is packed with Madoff victims—Jerome Fisher of Nine West; Mrs. Martin Joel, the widow of Madoff's onetime officemate; Paul Konigsberg's accounting firm; the Bernard A. Marden family; Ivy Asset Management; Madoff's high school friend Michael Lieberbaum; steel industry heiress Gladys C. Luria; Mike Engler's widow, Marja Engler; Carl Shapiro's son-in-law, Robert Jaffe; prominent New York lawyer Howard Squadron and his wife, Anne; and artist management impresario Howard Thau.

187 pension funds and other institutional investors will demand more information: E-mails between Fairfield Greenwich and the fund management company Unigestion in August 2008 cite the "new set of rules that Pension funds have put in place after the Bear Sterns [*sic*] collapse" as the reason Unigestion is withdrawing its money from the Fairfield Greenwich hedge funds invested with Madoff.

187 "many investors use Sentry like a checking account": *Galvin Fairfield Greenwich* Complaint, Exhibit No. FAI 00005367, e-mail from Charles Murphy dated Friday, Apr. 25, 2008, at 12:37 PM.

188 "I don't know why I agreed to see you": This passage is based on interviews with the retired businessman and his accountant, supported by records maintained by the businessman's secretary and BLM appointment calendar.

189 it has five bedrooms and baths: The online real estate listing by Killen Real Estate described and provided photographs of the home, at 51 Wanoma Way, when it was put on the market for $7.5 million after Madoff's arrest.

190 the financial consultant in Boulder, Colorado: The passage is based on *Picard v. Fairfield Sentry* Amended Complaint, pp. 133–36 and Exhibits 76 and 77.

191 Bernie Madoff is meeting with four visitors from Florida: Details of the visit and its aftermath are contained in *MorseLife Foundation Inc. v. Merrill Lynch, Pierce, Fenner & Smith, Inc.*, filed in the Circuit Court of the Fifteenth Judicial Circuit in and for Palm Beach County, Florida, on July 16, 2009; and Kathleen Chapman, "Merrill Lynch Negligent on Madoff, Lawsuit States," *Palm Beach Post*, July 28, 2009. The firm denied the allegations. The case was subsequently moved from state court to the U.S. District Court for the Southern District of Florida, where Merrill Lynch Bank & Trust Company was substituted for Merrill Lynch as the defendant. In an opinion dated July 21, 2010, the court ruled that the dispute had to be submitted to arbitration, as required in the foundation's contracts with the Merrill Lynch entities. The federal case was stayed pending the outcome of the arbitration process.

192 one client is pulling $74.5 million out of the Sentry fund: *Galvin Fairfield Greenwich* Complaint, Exhibit 27.

192 "there are certain aspects of BLM's operations that remain unclear": Ibid., Exhibit 19.

193 "the biggest single counterparty exposure risk we have at FGG": Ibid., Exhibit 28.

194 the Madoffs' small stucco town house: Details about the town house are from Alan Katz, "Madoff's Three-Bedroom Riviera Retreat Belied Ponzi Scheme Role," Bloomberg news service, Jan. 8, 2009. The rest of the passage is based on confidential interviews.

195 a reassuring "Dear Investor" letter: *Galvin Fairfield Greenwich* Complaint, Exhibit 49, p. 1.

196 "looking to do an orderly exit tomorrow": Ibid., Exhibit 13, p. 1.

196 DiPascali has not confirmed his "orderly exit": *Galvin Fairfield Greenwich* Complaint, p. 89, paragraph 254 reports that the chief risk officer and another partner at the firm both acknowledged in sworn testimony that the investor letter was not accurate.

196 Madoff will not reach the safe harbor of Treasury bills until Friday: Ibid., Exhibit 49, pp. 2–16.

196 The account statements are all lies: Regulators in Massachusetts summed it up this way: "Investors experienced a double falsehood: Madoff was sending fake records to Fairfield that Fairfield claims it did not detect and Fairfield misrepresented what those records said to customers." *Galvin Fairfield Greenwich* Complaint, p. 89, paragraph 255.

196 "not providing risk capital to anyone": Ibid., Exhibit 33.

197 all records of his dealings with Kohn be destroyed: *Picard v. Kohn*, p. 8.

197 More than a half-billion dollars in cash is about to pour out: *Picard v. Herald Fund*, p. 11.

198 a modern seven-story boutique building on East Seventy-fourth Street: The new building, called LUX 74, was also home to Ken Starr, a Ponzi schemer to the stars who pleaded guilty in September 2010.

198 The one thing he has no intention of doing: *Madoff Criminal Information*, p. 22.

199 Tucker, Noel, and McKeefry file into Madoff's offices: The passage is based on details in *Galvin Fairfield Greenwich* Complaint, Report on "BLM Operational Due Diligence" visit on Oct. 2, 2008, included as Exhibit 35.

200 Stanley Chais is in town from Los Angeles: BLM appointment calendar; First BLM Interview.

200 in June he wrote investors in his partnerships: *SEC Chais* Complaint, p. 12.

200 Madoff privately wonders if Chais suspects his fraud: First BLM Interview.

201 the amounts he has wired recently to the Kingate Euro fund: *In re: Bernard L. Madoff Investment Securities, Debtor; Irving H. Picard, Trustee for the Liquidation of Bernard L. Madoff Investment Securities v. Kingate Global Fund et al.*, Second Amended Complaint in Adversary Proceeding No. 09-01161 (BRL) in U.S. Bankruptcy Court for the Southern District of New York, p. 13.

201 The day gets off to a bad start for Amit Vijayvergiya: This passage is based on e-mails filed as Exhibit 30, *Galvin Fairfield Greenwich* Complaint.

202 JPMorganChase is revving up to pull $250 million: Claudio Gatti and Diana B. Henriques, "JPMorgan Exited Madoff-Linked Funds Last Fall," *New York Times*, Jan. 28, 2009. A bank spokeswoman acknowledged that the bank "became concerned about the lack of transparency to some questions we posed as part of our review." A source close to the bank recalled being told at the time that the bank's "due-diligence people had too many doubts" about the performance of the underlying funds, which were operated by Fairfield Greenwich Group. "They felt the consistency of its performance wasn't any longer credible" given the downturn in the overall market, the source said.

202 J. Ezra Merkin's office in the black granite tower at 450 Park Avenue: Details in this passage are drawn from *New York University v. Ariel Fund Ltd., Gabriel Capital Corp., J. Ezra Merkin et al.*, Supreme Court of the State of New York, County of New York, filed Dec. 24, 2008, and from Attachment B in that lawsuit, the Affidavit of Maurice Maertens.

202 For some reason, Ezra Merkin does not say: His failure to do so would be cited among the complaints in the civil fraud case filed against him in 2009 by the New York State attorney general, Andrew M. Cuomo. The case was pending in state court in February 2012. Lawyers for Merkin, who denied that he had any knowledge of the Ponzi scheme, also denied in court filings that he had misled his investors or misrepresented the way his hedge funds operated, as Cuomo asserted.

203 "which is so consistently and significantly ahead of its peers": These details are drawn from copies of these documents posted online by Benjamin Masse-Stamberger, author of "The Madoff Affair: The Secret Report Accusing JPMorgan," *L'Express*, Oct. 7, 2010. (The documents themselves were posted in English, although the article was published in French.)

203 "I can see the price you want": These quotations are based on a certified translation of the conversation provided to the author.

204 "we are simple people from Switzerland": The Swiss banker quoted in the conversation was identified in the *L'Express* account as Laurent Mathyson-Gerst, a director of Aurélia Finance, an investment firm in Geneva. He and the four other directors of the firm were named in criminal charges related to their alleged mismanagement of client assets invested with Madoff. As of publication, that case was pending, and the directors had denied any wrongdoing. No separate actions had been filed citing this recorded conversation. See Silke Koltrowitz and Emma Thomasson, "Swiss Judge Allows Charges in Madoff Losses Case," Reuters, April 24, 2009.

204 a worried businessman in Dubai arrives for a meeting: Details of this meeting are drawn from *Jitendra Bhatia et al. v. Standard Chartered International, et al.*, originally Case No. 1:09-cv-02410 (LTS) in U.S. District Court for the Southern District of New York; the case was consolidated with *Anwar et al. v. Fairfield Greenwich Limited, et al.*, Master File No. 09-cv-0118 (VM), also for the Southern District of New York, pp. 5, 7–8, 10–12.

205 a staggering $850 million: *Picard v. Fairfield Sentry*, Exhibit 2.

205 Madoff is sure he can forestall disaster: First BLM Interview; e-mail from BLM, Feb. 20, 2011.

205 Increasingly, he is inclined to say no: Ibid.

205 It is Thanksgiving Day: This passage is based on cited news accounts, comments by the chairman of Grupo Santander (the bank's holding company), confidential notes and interviews, and lawsuits filed against the bank.

206 He is surprised that Madoff scheduled it on the holiday: Confirmed by a bank spokesman, based on comments by the bank chairman at the company's annual meeting, February 2009.

206 Echenique Gordillo is here at the request of the CEO of the holding company: Ibid.

206 Optimal's analysts have written memos citing weaknesses: *In re: Santander–Optimal Securities Litigation* (hereafter *Santander Litigation*), Consolidated Amended Class Action Complaint, Case No. 09-cv-20125 (PCH), U.S. District Court, Southern District of Florida.

206 always managed to persuade themselves that Madoff was still safe: See Jonathan Clark, "Madoff Securities," Optimal Investment Securities, an internal report dated July 2006, and a memo "To: Manuel Echeverria, From: Karine Courvoisier, Re: Meetings with Bernard Madoff and lawyers in New York—September 18–19, 2002," p. 4, both filed as exhibits in *Santander Litigation*.

206 the mood becomes tense, maybe even threatening: Terrence Owen Jones, a former Optimal executive, told plaintiffs' lawyers in the *Santander Litigation* (at p. 116) that the reason for the meeting was that Optimal was withdrawing $400 million from Madoff, but he did not indicate when Madoff was told about the planned redemption. According to the bank, the redemption request was not made until Echenique Gordillo returned to Madrid, although *El Confidencial*, a Spanish publication, reported that Echenique Gordillo delivered the news, prompting Madoff's angry response. (Charles Penty, "Santander Sought to Withdraw Madoff Funds, *El Confidencial* Says," Bloomberg news service, Dec. 24, 2008.) But in a subsequent report, the *Financial Times* said that "what happened at the meeting is disputed," with one "banker with knowledge of the meeting" saying it was a "routine" inspection. (Joanna Chung, Victor Mallet, and Brooke Masters, "Santander Praised Madoff Weeks Before His Arrest for Alleged Fraud," *Financial Times*/FT.com, Jan. 23, 2009.) The bank confirmed to the author that the meeting was scheduled because its chairman was concerned about the Madoff investment, and the visit was not routine, so the *El Confidencial* account seems more likely to have captured the mood of the meeting, if not all the details.

207 Bernie Madoff sits down for a talk with Frank DiPascali: These details are drawn from *DiPascali Criminal Information*, p. 19.

207 Madoff is tired of the relentless struggle: First BLM Interview.

207 He wants to use this money: Prosecutors, in criminal charges against DiPascali's

colleague JoAnn "Jodi" Crupi, will assert later that she and DiPascali persuaded Madoff to make these payments. In any case, he either initiated the request or approved it and described it to his sons as his own idea.

208 He returns from his street corner meeting and starts following orders: *DiPascali Criminal Information*, p. 20.

208 Frank DiPascali leaves his spacious hilltop home: *U.S.A. v. Daniel Bonventre, Annette Bongiorno, JoAnn Crupi a/k/a/ "Jodi," Jerome O'Hara and George Perez* (hereafter *Second Superseding Bonventre Indictment*), filed on Nov. 18, 2010, as S2-10-cr- 228 (LTS), U.S. District Court, Southern District of New York, pp. 41, 69. This indictment added Bongiorno and Crupi to the indictment pending against Bonventre, Perez, and O'Hara.

209 Crupi tells him she plans on "sticking to my story": Ibid., p. 69.

11. WAKING UP IN THE RUBBLE

211 closed their doors almost immediately: The Robert C. Lappin Foundation also closed immediately, but later reopened with new funding. The Picower Foundation was to be reendowed after Jeffry Picower's widow reached an out-of-court settlement with the bankruptcy trustee.

213 At one breakfast panel, held at the "21" Club in Manhattan: The author's notes from covering the event.

213 The Institute for Jewish Research in Manhattan organized an evening panel discussion: The author's notes from covering the event.

213 "perfect storm for the anti-Semites": Anti-Defamation League press release, Dec. 19, 2008.

215 Roughly a thousand Madoff accounts: SIPC-Garrett Letter, p. 10. Not all of those accounts would file claims. Of the 846 approved claims of less than $500,000, the fictional balances totaled $1.6 billion; the total out-of-pocket cash those victims lost, under the net equity method, was $176.5 million.

215 not "How much did you lose?" but "How much do you have left?": This passage was drafted by the author early in 2010, but the distinction was phrased in similar terms in the eloquent essay by Stephanie Halio, "How Our Lives Have Changed," in *The Club No One Wanted to Join: Madoff Victims in Their Own Words*, ed. Erin Arvedlund, comp. Alexandra Roth (Andover, Mass.: Doukathsan Press, 2010), p. 121.

219 few people in Washington considered SIPC as "insurance" against wall-to-wall fraud inside a brokerage house: See several GAO reports on SIPC, including General Accounting Office, "Securities Investor Protection: A Regulatory Framework Has Minimized SIPC's Losses," September 1992.

220 the GAO was still critical of how SIPC handled its public relations duties: See Letter to the Honorable John D. Dingell, Ranking Minority Member, Committee on Energy and Commerce, House of Representatives, et al., from Orice M. Williams, Acting GAO Director for Financial Markets and Community Investment, GAO, dated July 9, 2004, pp. 5–7.

220 the GAO warned that SIPC was not really prepared: General Accounting Office, "Securities Investor Protection," p. 3.

221 SIPC liquidated 109 firms: These figures are all drawn from the relevant SIPC annual reports, available online at its Web site, www.sipc.org.

224 their first confidential meeting with Bernie Madoff and his lawyers: This passage has been reconstructed from confidential interviews with as many of the participants as possible and from Madoff's own recollections of the event.

226 Madoff could not get four people to sign a surety bond: Letter dated Dec. 17, 2008, to U.S. magistrate judge Gabriel W. Gorenstein from Marc Litt, assistant U.S. attorney, filed in the Madoff criminal case, 08-Mag. 2735, in U.S. District Court for the Southern District of New York.

227 "When I first heard the news that Madoff had been arrested": Kotz Report, p. 363.

227 he armed himself with a shotgun to prepare for the possibility: Markopolos, *No One Would Listen*, pp. 207–8.

227 he provided copies of his extensive documentation to reporters: Ibid., p. 209.

227 "the complicated steps that Mr. Madoff took": SEC press release, "Statement regarding Madoff Investigation," Dec. 16, 2008, Press Release No. 2008-297.

228 "The Commission has learned that credible and specific allegations": Ibid.

228 directing him to open an independent investigation: Interview with H. David Kotz.

229 she met him only a handful of times: Madoff would tell SEC Inspector General Kotz in June 2009 (see Kotz Report, Exhibit 104, p. 9) that Schapiro was a "dear friend," and that she "probably thinks 'I wish I never knew this guy.'" When the Kotz exhibits were released, the SEC immediately put out a public statement denying Madoff's claims of friendship. Kotz confirmed that he found no correspondence between Schapiro and Madoff in her SEC files.

229 sorting through some of their personal treasures: Details in this passage are drawn from court documents and transcripts, auction catalogs, and confidential interviews.

230 She believed she and Bernie would be dead: Ruth Madoff Interview.

230 "in a severe state of depression": E-mail from BLM, Oct. 28, 2011.

230 At some point that day: Ruth Madoff Interview.

230 "We woke the next morning": E-mail from BLM, Oct. 28, 2011. In that message, Madoff also confirmed details of the suicide attempt described by his wife, adding, "Please understand this is very difficult to admit."

230 Ruth began to simply tune out: Ruth Madoff Interview.

12. RECKONING THE DAMAGE

231 "I am supposed to believe that one day he gets up in the morning": Arvedlund and Roth, *Club No One Wanted to Join*, pp. 16–17.

231 "everything had vaporized": Ibid., p. 179.

231 "In the 50 seconds it took to read that fax": Ibid., pp. 35–36.

232 "life-shattering phone call that changed my world": Ibid., p. 160.

232 "I couldn't catch my breath and thought I might be having a heart attack": Ibid., p. 46.

232 "I was hoping that it was all a terrible mistake": Ibid., p. 117.

232 "Everything he worked for all his life was gone—'poof!'": Ibid., p. 99.

232 Steven Norton of Fort Lauderdale had just driven quietly home: Ibid., p. 171.

232 "Kate, we just lost our house": Interview with Gordon Bennett.

233 "The feather doesn't enable you to fly": Confidential interview with victim.

233 Another supposedly came from Harry Markopolos: Markopolos, *No One Would Listen*, p. 99.

233 "A castle of cards falling down in one CNBC news flash": Confidential interview.

234 "It's a complete nightmare": Zachery Kouwe and Michael Wilson, with reporting by Nelson B. Schwartz, "Financier Is Found Dead in a Madoff Aftermath," *New York Times*, Dec. 24, 2008.

234 locked the door behind them: Confidential interview.

236 the judge in the Bayou case ruled: Michael J. Missal, Richard A. Kirby, Rebecca L. Kline Dubill, and Michael D. Ricciuti, "The Madoff Dissolution: A Consideration of the Bayou Precedent and Possible Next Steps," a publication of K&L Gates law firm, Dec. 17, 2008, p. 4.

236 were ordered to return their fictional profits: Although other aspects of this bankruptcy court ruling in the Bayou case were reversed on appeal to U.S. District Court, this conclusion on fictional profits was affirmed. See Judge Paul G. Gardephe, *In the Matter of Bayou Group LLC, et al., Debtors, Christian Brothers High School Endowment, et al., Appellants*, WestLaw 2010, WL 3839277, pp. 42–43.

237 "Mr. Litt, why don't you tell me exactly what we're here for": This passage is based on the official transcript of the hearing before Judge Ellis, a copy of which was provided to the author.

237 the *Wall Street Journal* published an article: Dan Slater, "SEC to Probe Relationship Between Madoff's Niece and Ex-SEC Lawyer," Dec. 17, 2008.

239 The Serious Fraud Office in London was investigating: Katherine Griffiths, "Bernard Madoff's UK Staff Investigated by Serious Fraud Office," Telegraph.co.uk, Mar. 27, 2009, among several other citations from British publications.

239 not getting the cooperation he had expected from the London liquidators: Letter from Joon P. Hong of Richards, Kibbe & Orbe to U.S. district judge Louis L. Stanton, dated Jan. 23, 2009, and First Richards Report.

239 French prosecutors had begun a preliminary inquiry: "Paris Prosecutor to Investigate Madoff's France Businesses for Fraud," *Jurist Legal News & Research*, Jan. 21, 2009, accessible at www.jurist.law.pitt.edu/paperchase/2009/01/dnp-madoff-france.php.

239 Spanish regulators were examining losses in the Optimal funds: Thomas Catan, Christopher Bjork, and Jose de Cordoba, "Giant Bank in Probe over Ties to Madoff," *Wall Street Journal*, Jan. 13, 2009.

239 Austrian officials had begun an emergency examination of Bank Medici: "Austria Regulator Assumes Control of Bank Medici," *New York Times*, Jan. 2, 2009.

239 "I think things are moving a little bit slower": Transcript of the hearing on the *Main Madoff Liquidation*, at this point titled "In the Matter of the SIPA Link," pp. 20–21.

240 "'Denial' is not just a river in Egypt": Notes of the author, who covered the hearing.

240 "The SEC is a group of 3,500 chickens": Ibid.

240 "In order to minimize the risk of discovery": Testimony of Harry Markopolos, Chartered Financial Analyst, Certified Fraud Examiner, Before the U.S. House of Representatives Committee on Financial Services, Wednesday, Feb. 4, 2009, 9:30 AM, pp. 3–4.

240 "each of us feared for our lives": Ibid.

241 armed only with legal technicalities: Notes of the author, who covered the hearing.

241 "We thought the enemy was Mr. Madoff": Diana B. Henriques, "Anger and Drama at a House Hearing on Madoff," *New York Times*, Feb. 4, 2009.

243 As his son Willard Foxton later recounted in a moving BBC documentary: Allan Little, "Banking Crisis Killed My Father," BBC News, Feb. 12, 2009; Roger Corke (producer), Lucy Hetherington (executive producer), and Fiona Stourton (executive producer), "The Madoff Hustle," BBC 2, broadcast on "This World," June 28, 2009.

243 "Dear Will, I will be brief": *Repex Ventures S.A. et al., v. Bernard L. Madoff, et al.,* case number 09-cv-00289 (RMB) in U.S. District Court, Southern District of New York; Declaration of Gregory B. Linkh, Exhibit A, Certification of Proposed Lead Plaintiff Pursuant to the Federal Securities Laws, by Willard Foxton, dated May 2, 2009, p. 2.

244 Shortly after 10:00 AM, Picard and Sheehan walked onto the bare stage: Notes of the author, who covered the meeting.

244 "There are a couple of ground rules": Direct quotations are from a transcript of the hearing obtained by the author.

245 He would serve more than 230 subpoenas: These details are all drawn from the Trustee's Reports to the court, other court filings, and reporting notes by the author, who covered these events.

247 a silver sedan pulled up outside the north entrance: This passage is based on observations and reporting notes from the author's colleagues at the *New York Times*, William K. Rashbaum and Jack Healy, various video segments posted online, and a transcript of the hearing.

249 Two days later, hundreds of victims gathered: This passage is based on notes by the author, who covered the event, as well as a transcript of the hearing.

13. NET WINNERS AND NET LOSERS

254 David Friehling and his lawyer arrived quietly: William K. Rashbaum and Diana B. Henriques, "Accountant for Madoff Is Arrested and Charged with Securities Fraud," *New York Times*, Mar. 19, 2009.

256 Picard had the bank records: Diana B. Henriques, "Court Denies Madoff Aide's Request for Bail," *New York Times*, Oct. 28, 2009; and notes by the author from interviews with Picard.

256 generally known in bankruptcy court as "fraudulent conveyances": New York State's Uniform Fraudulent Conveyance Act involves different standards of proof for nullifying these transfers from those stated in the federal bankruptcy code, but the term *fraudulent conveyance* is typically used to describe withdrawals made in both the two-year and the six-year windows for recovery.

256 But many investors were not familiar with the legalese, and they were outraged: Many victims were in frequent communication with the author about their anger over the form letter sent out by Picard; midway through the claims process, the letter was revised to sound somewhat less accusatory.

257 by the end of June he would file eight of them: All of the figures that follow are drawn from the individual lawsuits filed by Picard, which are enumerated as "Associated Cases" under the main SIPC bankruptcy case against Madoff's firm.

257 for the return of $395 million: "Trustee's First Interim Report for the Period December 11, 2008, to June 30, 2009," *Main Madoff Liquidation* (hereafter *Trustee's First Report*), p. 34.

257 Chais had been honored in absentia: Brad A. Greenberg, "Stanley Chais Targeted in Madoff Suit," *Jewish Journal*, May 6, 2009.

257 He claimed that the brokerage firm had knowingly served as the sales force: *Picard v. Cohmad* First Amended Complaint, p. 3.

257 He sought another $3.5 billion from the Fairfield Sentry funds: *Trustee's First Report*, p. 38.

257 raised to $7.2 billion a few months later: "Trustee's Second Interim Report for the Period Ending October 31, 2009," *Main Madoff Liquidation*, pp. 60–61.

258 as Madoff himself suspected, that Jeffry Picower was shrewd enough: First BLM Interview.

258 Nevertheless, many small investors said they were terrified: Again, this was a common complaint by investors in e-mails and phone conversations with the author, and on victim blogs.

258 The increasing hostility saddened him and frustrated his colleague David Sheehan: Interviews with Picard and Sheehan, and confidential interviews with others involved in the broad effort to respond to Madoff claimants.

259 Picard's team eventually would speed up the claims-paying process: Diana B. Henriques, "It's Thankless, but He Decides Madoff Claims," *New York Times*, May 28, 2009; Diana B. Henriques, "Trustee's Total of Madoff Losses Nears $3 Billion," *New York Times*, July 1, 2009.

260 the only court-tested way to calculate Ponzi scheme losses: It is notable that the K&L Gates law firm memo on the Bayou case's significance for Madoff investors (Missal et al., "Madoff Dissolution") was published within days of Madoff's arrest. Similarly, the receiver in a separate Ponzi scheme, *SEC v. Joseph S. Forte et al.*, acknowledged in a letter on Dec. 2, 2009, to the federal judge in Philadelphia handling that case that "a receiver's right to recover 'net winnings'—the amount by which withdrawals exceed investments—from investors in a Ponzi scheme is *well settled*" (emphasis added).

260 She was a Bryn Mawr graduate: These details are drawn from the biography posted on the Phillips Nizer Web site prior to Chaitman's departure to join another firm, Becker & Poliakoff.

260 a tireless and fiercely tenacious advocate for her clients: On several occasions, opposing lawyers asked unsuccessfully that she be sanctioned by the court for what they considered obstruction of court procedure. Once, she was disciplined by bank regulators for her allegedly overzealous defense of a shuttered bank's owners. See Office of the Comptroller of the Currency, *Quarterly Journal* 24, no. 1 (March 2005): 69.

260 "safe and conservative": Letter from Helen Davis Chaitman to SEC commissioner Mary Schapiro, dated Apr. 2, 2009, p. 2.

261 two separate visits to the appellate court: The two Second Circuit appellate decisions in the *New Times* case are published at 371 F.3d 68 (2004) (hereafter cited as *New Times I*) and 463 F.3d 125, 130 (2006) (hereafter cited as *New Times II*).

261 "Treating . . . fictitious paper profits": *New Times II*.

261 or, indeed, crystal clear about anything: The arguments summarized here were made in hundreds of court filings by Chaitman and Picard in the Madoff bankruptcy case; to simplify the citations, the arguments from both camps are laid out in the ruling in

the dispute by bankruptcy judge Burton R. Lifland, "Memorandum Decision Grant-ing Trustee's Motion for an Order (1) Upholding Trustee's Determination Denying Customer Claims for Amounts Listed on Last Customer Statement; (2) Affirming Trustee's Determination of Net Equity; and (3) Expunging Objections to Determina-tions Relating to Net Equity," dated Mar. 10, 2010, in the *Main Madoff Liquidation*.

261 "there is very little case law on point": The case is *Focht v. Athens (In re: Old Naples Se-curities, Inc.)*, 311 B.R. 607 (Middle District, Fla., 2002); the quotation is at pp. 616–17.

262 nor did it flatly require the trustee to honor customers' final account statements: The statute obliged the trustee to consider final account statements only in determining whether customers had claims for cash, which were limited to a $100,000 advance, or claims for securities, which would be eligible for a $500,000 advance. SIPC had already ruled that the Madoff victims were entitled to be treated as customers with claims for securities, not cash.

263 the Massachusetts School of Law in Andover: The law school had state permission to award law degrees but was not accredited by the American Bar Association.

263 "will have to continue living on welfare or dumpster diving": The quotation is from Velvel's blog, hereafter known as www.velvelonnationalaffairs.blogspot.com.

265 were generally considered fair: See, for example, the editorial "Mr. Feinberg and the Gulf Settlement," *New York Times*, Aug. 29, 2010.

265 a similar approach was taken, with the same special master appointed: Campbell Robertson and John Schwartz, "Rethinking the Process for BP Spill Claims," *New York Times*, Sept. 15, 2010. The program was officially called the Gulf Coast Claims Facility, and it went into operation in June 2010 under an agreement between British Petroleum and the Obama administration.

265 the concept was still generally viewed as a faster route to recovery: "Mr. Feinberg and the Gulf Settlement."

267 Lax & Neville filed a class-action suit against Picard: *Mary Albanese et al. v. Irving H. Picard*, filed as Adversary Proceeding No. 09-01265 (BRL), in the *Main Madoff Liquidation* on June 5, 2009, and amended on June 23, 2009.

267 "I am a human face on this tragedy": Statement of Allan Goldstein, "Assessing the Madoff Ponzi [*sic*] and the Need for Regulatory Reform," before the House Commit-tee on Financial Services, Jan. 5, 2009, p. 1.

268 "I was willing to forgo outsized gains": Ibid., p. 2.

268 "I sit before you today a broken man": Ibid., p. 3.

268 "We are not trust funds, hedge funds or banks": Ibid.

268 a similar complaint by Helen Chaitman: *Diane and Roger Peskin and Maureen Ebel v. Irving H. Picard*, filed as Adversary Proceeding No. 09-01272, in the *Main Madoff Liquidation*.

14. THE SINS OF THE FATHER

270 They came to ask Bernie Madoff: Kotz Report, Exhibit 104.

271 several former top executives at Merrill Lynch and Morgan Stanley: A hedge fund run by a former head of Merrill Lynch's brokerage unit, John "Launny" Steffens, had a stake in Madoff through Ezra Merkin's Ascot Partners, and Madoff's direct investors included the family of Frank A. Petito, a former chairman of Morgan Stanley & Co.

272 "I could see how you might see them as false": Confidential interviews with people familiar with the Kotz-Madoff session.

273 "We seek neither mercy nor sympathy": The letter is filed as Document 84 in the files of *Madoff Criminal Complaint*.

274 a fax machine came to life: This passage is based on court records filed in the government's civil forfeiture agreement with Ruth Madoff.

275 On June 29, spectators squeezed elbow to elbow: This account is based on the author's notes and observations during the sentencing and a transcript of the hearing.

280 The fur coat stayed: Confidential interviews with people familiar with the U.S. Marshals' asset-recovery efforts in the Madoff case.

280 So did her used golf shoes: An inventory of seized property is attached as Exhibit A to Document 121 in the docket for *Madoff Criminal Complaint*.

281 there was no evidence that Ruth had been involved: The Law Blog, "Ruth the Truth? Feds Find No Evidence on Bernie's Wife," WSJ.com, July 1, 2009, 3:36 PM EST; also Amir Efrati, "Evidence to Charge Ruth Madoff Lacking," *Wall Street Journal*, July 2, 2009.

284 investigators had found no evidence linking the sons to Madoff's Ponzi scheme: Alex Berenson and Diana B. Henriques, "Inquiry Finds No Signs Family Aided Madoff," *New York Times*, Dec. 16, 2008.

284 grew leery of including them on playdates: Margolick, "Madoff Chronicles, Part III."

284 Catherine Hooper, an accomplished woman whose background as a fly-fishing guide: Ibid.

284 Andrew exchanged punches with the trader: Ibid.

285 "came out of the experience with a shaved head": Roger Madoff, *Leukemia for Chickens*, p. 132.

285 enjoying each day because "life is short": Ibid.

285 to change her own and their children's last names to "Morgan": Jose Martinez with Alison Gendar, "Take Off My 'Madoff'; Daughter-in-Law Begs Court to Let Her and Small Kids Change Name from Hated Label," New York *Daily News*, Feb. 25, 2010.

287 "perceived as the succubus to Bernie's incubus": Professor Richard A. Shweder, a cultural anthropologist at the University of Chicago, quoted in Lynnley Browning, "The Loneliest Woman in New York," *New York Times*, June 12, 2009.

287 Many lifelong friends shunned her: Browning, "Loneliest Woman."

288 demanded the return of $44.8 million: *In re: Bernard L. Madoff Investment Securities, Debtor; Irving H. Picard, Trustee for the Liquidation of Bernard L. Madoff Investment Securities v. Ruth Madoff*, filed as Adversary Proceeding No. 09-01391 (BRL) in U.S. Bankruptcy Court for the Southern District of New York, p. 3.

288 Her lawyer, Peter Chavkin, was outraged and said so: Public statement from Peter A. Chavkin, released by his law firm, Mintz Levin, July 29, 2009.

288 "had Bernie on a short leash": Sheryl Weinstein, *Madoff's Other Secret: Love, Money, Bernie, and Me* (New York: St. Martin's Press, 2009), pp. 43, 47, 53.

289 "stands as a powerful reminder": Diana B. Henriques and Stephanie Strom, "Woman Tells of Affair with Madoff in New Book," *New York Times*, Aug. 13, 2009.

289 Ruth Madoff had changed her hair color: Initially reported by Anna Schecter and Asa Eslocker, "Ruth Madoff: Summer in the City with No Apologies, Red Dye Job,"

ABC News: Brian Ross Investigates, July 16, 2010. A video posted on the Brian Ross Investigates Web site included telescopic camera footage of her at lunch at a sidewalk restaurant.

15. THE WHEELS OF JUSTICE

292 signing authority for one of the firm's bank accounts until about 1985: Diana B. Henriques, "Judge Freezes Madoff Brother's Assets," *New York Times*, Mar. 25, 2009.

293 he was sued by Andrew Ross Samuels: *Andrew Ross Samuels v. Peter B. Madoff*, Verified Petition-Complaint, Index No. 09-5534, Supreme Court of the State of New York, County of Nassau, Mar. 16, 2009.

293 the subject of a criminal investigation: Letter to the Honorable Madeline Cox Arleo, U.S.M.J., from Charles T. Spada of Lankler, Siffert & Wohl, dated Jan. 26, 2010, filed as Document 40 in *Lautenberg v. Madoff*.

294 In September 2009 the presiding federal judge: Opinion by U.S. district judge Stanley R. Chesler in *Lautenberg v. Madoff*, U.S. District Court for the District of New Jersey, Sept. 9, 2009.

294 "his many years of close association with his brother": Opinion by U.S. district judge Stanley R. Chesler in *Lautenberg v. Madoff*, U.S. District Court for the District of New Jersey, Nov. 18, 2010, pp. 6–7.

294 Irving Picard filed a clawback lawsuit: *Picard v. Madoff Family*.

294 "Simply put, if the family members had been doing their jobs": Ibid., p. 2.

294 "has not taken on the burden of proving criminal complicity": *Picard v. Madoff Family*, Trustee's Memorandum of Law in Opposition to Defendants' Motions to Dismiss, May 21, 2010, p. 1.

295 "the trustee's concession is significant": *Picard v. Madoff Family*, "Defendant Peter B. Madoff's Reply Memorandum of Law in Further Support of His Motion to Dismiss the Complaint," June 21, 2010, p. 1.

297 At 2:45 PM on Tuesday, August 11, 2009: This passage is based primarily on the author's observations and notes, and on a transcript of the hearing in which one of the quotes cited here is slightly garbled.

299 Kohn was questioned privately in a Viennese court: Confidential interviews. A letter filed by Kohn's lawyers in a private lawsuit also confirmed that a member of their firm had represented her in several matters, including "a criminal investigation conducted by the Vienna Public Prosecutor's office." See Letter to the Honorable Richard M. Berman, United States District Court for the Southern District of New York, from Price O. Gielen, of Neuberger, Quinn, Gielen, Rubin & Gibber, dated Nov. 2, 2010, and filed as Document 146 in *In re: Herald, Primeo, and Thema Fund Secs.*, Case No. 09-cv-00289 (RMB), p. 3. Her lawyers acknowledged the investigation was pending as of publication, but said no charges were likely to be filed against Kohn, who denied any role in the Madoff fraud.

299 revoked Bank Medici's banking license: *Picard v. Kohn*, pp. 35, 110.

299 the SFO would quietly announce that it was closing its examination: Diana B. Henriques and Matthew Saltmarsh, "Two Decisions Reshape Inquiry into Madoff Case," *New York Times*, Feb. 2, 2010.

300 those charges would later be dropped: Heather Smith, "Access International's Littaye Charged in Madoff Case (Update3)," Bloomberg news service, Nov. 4, 2009; and

Benjamin Masse-Stamberger and Jean-Marie Pontaut, "Madoff L'heure des comptes," *L'Express*, Sept. 29, 2010.

300 the SEC's assertion simply wasn't enough to sustain the case: *SEC v. Cohmad*, Opinion and Order of Judge Louis L. Stanton, Feb. 2, 2010.

300 "Nowhere does the complaint allege any fact": Ibid., p. 4.

301 roster of important regulatory actions: In February 2009, Halliburton and its subsidiary, Kellogg Brown & Root, paid $177 million to settle the SEC case, without admitting or denying wrongdoing. The KBR subsidiary also paid $402 million to settle related criminal charges filed by the Justice Department. According to the SEC, the combined settlement was the largest ever paid under the Foreign Corrupt Practices Act. See SEC Litigation Release No. 20897A. UBS agreed to pay $200 million to settle the civil charges, without admitting or denying wrongdoing. See SEC Litigation Release No. 20905. The mortgage industry executive was Angelo Mozilo, the former chief executive of Countrywide Financial, who was sued by the SEC on June 4, 2009; without admitting or denying wrongdoing, he paid $67.5 million to settle the case on Oct. 15, 2010. See SEC Litigation Release No. 21068A and Press Release No. 2010-197. The SEC sued Goldman Sachs in April 2010 for allegedly deceiving investors in the sale of complex mortgage derivatives; in July 2010 Goldman paid $550 million to settle the case, neither admitting nor denying wrongdoing but acknowledging that its marketing materials were "incomplete." See SEC Litigation Release No. 21592.

302 "there will very likely be a subpoena on your desk": Robert Khuzami, "My First 100 Days as Director of Enforcement," Aug. 5, 2009, accessible at www.sec.gov/news/speech/2009/spch080509rk.htm.

302 the relationship had not influenced the SEC's handling of Madoff or his firm: Kotz Report, p. 408.

302 "Yet, at no time did the SEC ever verify Madoff's trading": Ibid., p. 23.

303 "When potential investors expressed hesitation": Ibid., p. 25.

303 Mary Schapiro immediately issued a statement apologizing again: Statement by SEC chairman Mary L. Schapiro, Sept. 2, 2009, accessible at www.sec.gov/news/speech/2009/spch090209mls-2.htm.

303 The lawsuit contended that the SEC was liable: *Phyllis Molchatsky and Stephen Schneider, M.D. v. U.S.A.* (hereafter *Molchatsky v. U.S.A.*), filed as Case No. 09-cv-8697 (LTS/AJP) in U.S. District Court for the Southern District of New York. Molchatsky was a disabled retiree who invested her life savings of $1.7 million with a Madoff feeder fund in 2001, and Dr. Schneider had invested more than $750,000 of his retirement savings with Madoff in 1997.

304 "Plaintiffs' losses are undeniably tragic": *Molchatsky v. U.S.A.*, "United States of America Memorandum of Law in Support of Its Motion to Dismiss," pp. 1–2.

304 the final total would be 16,518: See Third Interim Trustee's Report for the Period Ending March 31, 2010, p. 27, *Main Madoff Liquidation*. The figures were updated on Feb. 21, 2011, from the trustee's Web site, www.madofftrustee.com.

306 Judge Burton Lifland took his seat: This passage is based on the author's observations and notes and a transcript of the hearing.

308 "a thorough and comprehensive analysis": *Main Madoff Liquidation*, Memorandum Decision Granting Trustee's Motion, Judge Burton R. Lifland, Mar. 2, 2010, p. 6.

308 "Given that in Madoff's fictional world": Ibid., pp. 10–11.

309 "It would be simply absurd to credit the fraud": Ibid., p. 30.

309 "at no time was I ever aware that Bernard Madoff was engaged in a Ponzi scheme": *Friehling Plea Transcript*, pp. 34–35.

309 The next defendants to come before the court: The original case was *U.S.A. v. Jerome O'Hara and George Perez*, filed as Case No. 09-mj-02484-UA-1 in U.S. District Court for the Southern District of New York. That case was preempted by a subsequent superseding indictment, as noted previously.

310 telling him to "ask Frank": *SEC v. Jerome O'Hara and George Perez*, filed as Case No. 09-cv-9425 in U.S. District Court for the Southern District of New York, pp. 23–24.

310 he stood accused of having conspired to sustain and conceal the Ponzi scheme: *First Superseding Bonventre Indictment*.

310 "I'm saying Dan Bonventre is absolutely innocent": Diana B. Henriques, "Another Madoff Aide Faces Fraud Charges," *New York Times*, Feb. 25, 2010.

311 the senior Picower lawyer, Bill Zabel, balked: Confidential interviews with three people briefed on the negotiations.

312 the worst moment of the entire tortured case: Interview with David J. Sheehan.

16. HOPE, LOST AND FOUND

314 The scene at the firm was like law school finals writ large: Interview with David J. Sheehan.

314 Among the checks Madoff had prepared: *In re: Bernard L. Madoff Investment Securities, Debtor; Irving H. Picard, Trustee for the Liquidation of Bernard L. Madoff Investment Securities v. Irwin Lipkin et al.*, filed as Adversary Proceeding No. 10-04218 (BRL) in U.S. Bankruptcy Court for the Southern District of New York, p. 16. Gary S. Redish, a lawyer for the elder Lipkins, denied the trustee's claims. The fact that the Lipkins used their Madoff accounts to make gifts to their grandchildren showed they "had absolutely no knowledge of the Ponzi scheme," he said. James K. Filan, a lawyer for Eric Lipkin, declined to comment on the trustee's claims.

314 listed as the firm's controller: *In re: Bernard L. Madoff Investment Securities, Debtor; Irving H. Picard, Trustee for the Liquidation of Bernard L. Madoff Investment Securities v. Enrica Cotellessa-Pitz and Thomas Pitz*, filed as Adversary Proceeding No. 10-04213 (BRL) in U.S. Bankruptcy Court for the Southern District of New York. Richard R. Leff, a lawyer for the couple, filed a formal answer denying the trustee's claims. On Dec. 19, 2011, Cotellessa-Pitz pleaded guilty to federal criminal charges; as of Feb. 15, 2012, no charges had been filed against her husband.

314 accused by the trustee of helping to falsify arbitrage trades: *Picard v. Kugel*. Michael V. Blumenthal, a lawyer for the Kugel family, had not responded to requests for comment about the trustee's claims at the time this book went into production.

314 also sued Daniel Bonventre: *In re: Bernard L. Madoff Investment Securities, Debtor; Irving H. Picard, Trustee for the Liquidation of Bernard L. Madoff Investment Securities v. Daniel Bonventre*, filed as Adversary Proceeding No. 10-04214 (BRL) in U.S. Bankruptcy Court for the Southern District of New York.

315 lawsuits filed by Sheehan's team on November 11: *In re: Bernard L. Madoff Investment Securities, Debtor; Irving H. Picard, Trustee for the Liquidation of Bernard L. Madoff Investment Securities v. Annette Bongiorno and Rudy Bongiorno*, filed as Ad-

versary Proceeding No. 10-04315 (BRL) and *In re: Bernard L. Madoff Investment Securities, Debtor; Irving H. Picard, Trustee for the Liquidation of Bernard L. Madoff Investment Securities v. JoAnn Crupi et al.*, filed as Adversary Proceeding No. 10-04216 (BRL), both in U.S. Bankruptcy Court for the Southern District of New York. Roland Riopelle, the lawyer for the Bongiornos, denied the allegations in the trustee's lawsuit. Eric R. Breslin, a lawyer for Crupi, said his client would "absolutely" contest the trustee's allegations and similar accusations made in the civil case filed against Crupi by the SEC.

315 amended in February to include Dan Bonventre: *Second Superseding Bonventre Indictment.*

316 Film crews from local television stations and news Web sites: This passage is based on the author's observations and notes, and auction catalogs available online at www .proxibid.com, the Web site for Proxibid, an online auction bidding service used by the U.S. Marshals Service.

318 the two Madoff auctions raised just under $3 million: The reported total from the first auction was just under $900,000. See Les Christie, "Madoff's Mets Jacket Sells for $14,500," CNNMoney.com, Nov. 16, 2009. The author tallied all the winning bids from both auctions, posted on Proxibid; the first auction total was $854,110 and the second was $2.12 million, for a total of $2.97 million.

318 brought the total from forfeited assets to about $27 million: The Manhattan penthouse sold for $8 million, the Montauk home went for $9.4 million, and the Palm Beach home sold for $5.65 million, considerably below the original listing price of $8.49 million. See Oshrat Carmiel, "Madoff's Home in Palm Beach Sells for $5.65 Million," Bloomberg news service, Oct. 15, 2010. Three boats and a Mercedes convertible brought about $1 million at auction in 2009. See Katya Kazakina, "Madoff's Yachts Bring $1 Million at Florida Auction," Bloomberg news service, Nov. 17, 2009. The French town house had an estimated value of $1.6 million, while the yacht was valued at more than $8 million. See Erica Orden, "Madoff Sell-off," *New York*, Sept. 6, 2009. As of December 2010, there had been no report of either being sold.

318 On November 24, UBS, the giant Swiss bank: *Picard v. UBS.*

318 a second suit involving another set of feeder funds: *In re: Bernard L. Madoff Investment Securities, Debtor; Irving H. Picard, Trustee for the Liquidation of Bernard L. Madoff Investment Securities v. UBS et al. and M&B Capital Advisors*, filed as Adversary Proceeding No. 10-05311 (BRL) in U.S. Bankruptcy Court for the Southern District of New York.

318 "willfully blind" in its dealings: Diana B. Henriques, "Madoff Trustee Sues JPMorgan for $6.4 Billion," *New York Times*, Dec. 2, 2010.

318 The formidable bank said the accusations were preposterous: Ibid.

318 a massive lawsuit seeking $9 billion from HSBC: *Picard v. HSBC.*

319 One was against Tremont Group Holdings: *In re: Bernard L. Madoff Investment Securities, Debtor; Irving H. Picard, Trustee for the Liquidation of Bernard L. Madoff Investment Securities v. Tremont Group Holdings et al.*, filed under seal as Adversary Proceeding No. 10-05310 (BRL) in U.S. Bankruptcy Court for the Southern District of New York.

319 "currently engaged in good-faith negotiations": Press Release, "Trustee for Liquidation of Bernard L. Madoff Investment Securities Files Suit Against Sterling Equities,

Its Partners and Other Related Entities Seeking Recoveries in Ponzi Scheme," Dec. 7, 2010, accessible at www.madofftrustee.com.

319 some key details about the sealed lawsuit: Alison Leigh Cowan, Peter Lattman, Serge F. Kovaleski, and David Waldstein, "Trustee Faults Mets Owners over Madoff Fraud," *New York Times*, Jan. 29, 2011.

319 a case against the directors of Madoff's bankrupt British affiliate: Press Release, "Trustee for Liquidation of Bernard L. Madoff Investment Securities and Liquidator of Madoff Securities International File Lawsuit Against Directors, Officers, Related Entities of London-Based Madoff Securities International Limited," Dec. 8, 2010, accessible at www.madofftrustee.com.

319 a claim for $1 billion against seven major banks: Press Release, "Trustee for Liquidation of Bernard L. Madoff Investment Securities Seeks $1 Billion from Seven Global Financial Institutions in Madoff Ponzi Scheme," Dec. 8, 2010, accessible at www.madofftrustee.com.

319 lawsuits against smaller but notable hedge fund managers: Press Release, "Trustee for Liquidation of Bernard L. Madoff Investment Securities Files Against Tremont Group and Related Entities Including Oppenheimer and MassMutual," Dec. 7, 2010, accessible at www.madofftrustee.com.

320 a $500 million settlement with Union Bancaire Privée: Press Release, "Madoff Trustee Announces Approximately $500 Million Recovery Agreement with Swiss Bank Union Bancaire Privée," Dec. 6, 2010, accessible at www.madofftrustee.com.

320 a sweeping settlement with Carl Shapiro and his family: Press Release, "Madoff Trustee, SIPC Announces $550 Million Recovery Agreement with Carl Shapiro, Robert Jaffe and Related Entities," Dec. 6, 2010, accessible at www.madofftrustee.com. The deal called for the trustee to get $550 million, and for another $75 million to be paid to the Justice Department under its civil forfeiture program.

320 some important charities, including Hadassah: Press Release, "Madoff Trustee, Charities Negotiating Settlements," Dec. 10, 2010, accessible at www.madofftrustee.com.

320 an ambitious 161-page complaint: *Picard v. Kohn.*

321 knowingly pocketing millions of stolen dollars: *Picard v. A&B.*

321 Bernie Madoff's grandchildren: Michael Rothfeld, "The Madoff Fraud: Trustee Sues Kin, Banks for Funds," *Wall Street Journal*, Dec. 9, 2010.

321 "That's why I never believed he knew about the fraud": Confidential interview. The author is also indebted to reporting on the Madoff suicide contributed by colleagues Peter Lattman, Elissa Gootman, and Al Baker of the *New York Times.*

322 "He had always been so proud of his name": Diana B. Henriques and Peter Lattman, "Reopened Wounds: 'Just More Than He Could Bear,'" *New York Times*, Dec. 17, 2010.

322 a suicide note for his father: Stephanie Madoff Mack, *The End of Normal: A Wife's Anguish, A Widow's New Life* (New York: Blue Rider Press, 2011), pp. 148–53. The date of the incident is from Sandell, *Truth and Consequences*, p. 261.

323 "When all of this happened, we decided that we weren't going to sit around": Steve Eder and Mary Pilon, "A Madoff Son Looks Forward," *Wall Street Journal*, Dec. 21, 2010.

324 "combined with our extensive lobbying efforts": Press Release, "NIAP Update on HR 5032," Network for Investor Action and Protection, June 17, 2010, on the Web site of the Network for Investor Action and Protection, www.investoraction.org.

324 promised to introduce a stronger replacement: Press Release, "NIAP President Ron Stein Statement Welcoming Legislation to Protect Investors Defrauded by Bernie Madoff," Network for Investor Action and Protection, Dec. 20, 2010.

325 "Equitable Treatment of Investors Act": Congressman Scott Garrett, a Republican from New Jersey, introduced the bill on Feb. 17, 2011, as H.R. 757, 1st Session, 112th Congress.

330 "recover at least 24 billion in claw backs against 20 billion in valid loss claims": E-mail to author from BLM, Dec. 17, 2010.

331 "banks and hedge funds had reached confidential settlements": Raphael Minder and Diana B. Henriques, "Overseas Madoff Investors Settle with Banks," *New York Times*, May 24, 2010.

331 "I know it's 100% reliable": E-mail to the author from BLM, Dec. 21, 2010.

331 "everyone's principal will be returned": E-mail to the author from BLM, Dec. 19, 2010.

17. THE LONG ROAD FORWARD

333 "treated well by the inmates and staff here": Letter from BLM, dated Oct. 3, 2010; the letter was sent to the author through Madoff's lawyer and was thus not subject to review by prison authorities, lending some credibility to his report of his prison treatment.

333 Ruth Madoff looked out: Ruth Madoff Interview.

334 was once again packed to the walls: Author's notes and observations.

336 The three-judge panel answered: Opinion of the United States Court of Appeals for the Second Circuit, Aug. 16, 2011, in *In re: Bernard L. Madoff Investment Securities LLC*, original docket number 10-2378-bk (L) et seq., pp. 5, 15–17, 23–24, 27.

337 Wilpon had been deeply wounded: See *In re: Bernard L. Madoff Investment Securities, Debtor, Irving H. Picard, Trustee for the Liquidation of Bernard L. Madoff Investment Securities v. Saul B. Katz, et al.* (hereafter *Picard v. Katz*), filed as Adversary Proceeding No. 10-05287 (BRL) in U.S. Bankruptcy Court for the Southern District of New York. Quotations are from *Picard v. Katz* Transcript of Trustee's Rule 2004 Examination of Fred Wilpon, July 20, 2010, pp. 35, 42–43, 64.

337 encouraged a wealthy friend: Details are from *In re: Bernard L. Madoff Investment Securities, Debtor, Irving H. Picard, Trustee for the Liquidation of Bernard L. Madoff Investment Securities v. American Securities Management L.P., et al.*, filed as Adversary Proceeding No. 10-05415 (BRL) in U.S Bankruptcy Court for the Southern District of New York, pp. 3, 51, 58–63.

337 "a waste of money": *Picard v. Katz* Transcript of Trustee's Rule 2004 Examination of Saul B. Katz, Aug. 4, 2010, p. 102.

337 they had repeatedly warned the Wilpons: *Picard v. Katz* Amended Complaint, pp. 165–171. The trustee also claimed that an independent financial–industry consultant hired by Sterling Stamos and the Wilpons told them in 2003 that Madoff's returns "did not make sense." See pp. 176–77.

338 Madoff had misled them: Ibid., pp. 195–96.

338 the Wilpons had invested: Ibid., pp. 196–201.

338 a Merrill Lynch executive had cautioned: Ibid., pp. 172–74.

338 As early as 1996: Ibid., p. 175.

338 Katz had been warned about Madoff: Ibid., p. 176. According to the trustee, a similar warning was made to Katz by "the CEO of a prominent investment management firm" who also chaired the investment committee of the Brooklyn College Foundation, whose honorary governors included Katz and whose board of trustees included Richard Wilpon, Fred's brother. The Wilpons denied this assertion.

338 likely could not pay that sum: The author is grateful for pre-publication access to Howard Megdal, *Wilpon's Folly: The Story of a Man, His Fortune, and the New York Mets* (New York: Bloomsbury USA, 2011), which examines the finances of the extensive Wilpon family enterprises.

338 Picard had no legal right to sue: Opinion and Order dated July 28, 2011, in *Picard v. HSBC*, removed from U.S. Bankruptcy Court, consolidated with a related case against other HSBC entities and filed as 11 Civ. 763 (JSR) and 11 Civ. 836 (JSR) in U.S. District Court, Southern District of New York.

339 there was a "safe harbor" provision: Opinion and Order dated Sept. 27, 2011, in *Picard v. Katz*, removed from U.S. Bankruptcy Court and filed as 11 Civ. 3605 (JSR) in U.S. District Court, Southern District of New York. The disputed "safe harbor" provision is Section 546(e) of the Federal Bankruptcy Code. These issues are described more fully in the judges' opinions and summarized in Diana B. Henriques, "A Lasting Shadow: Three Years After His Arrest, Bernie Madoff Still Haunts His Victims, His Family and Himself," *New York Times*, Dec. 11, 2011.

339 In mid-January 2012: *Picard v. Katz*, Opinion and Order by Judge Jed S. Rakoff, Jan. 17, 2012, p. 2.

339 had come across their wedding album: Sandell, *Truth and Consequences*, pp. 250–51.

340 Then she learned about Sheryl Weinstein's memoir: Ruth Madoff Interview. The book was Weinstein, *Madoff's Other Secret*.

340 "The woman's on fire": Aaron Pressman, "Madoff Whistleblower Markopolos Blasts SEC," *Bloomberg BusinessWeek*, June 5, 2009.

341 He was even more impressed: Stuart Gittleman, "U.S. Whistleblower Program Is on the Right Track, Says Madoff Nemesis Markopolos," *Thomson Reuters* Dodd-Frank Watch Web site: http://www.complinet.com/dodd-frank/news/articles/article/us-whistleblower-program-is-on-the-right-track-says-madoff-nemesis-markopolos.html#top, posted on Aug. 29, 2011.

341 a sterling reputation: Becker was described by more than four dozen members of the bar—including retired U.S. District Court Judge Stanley Sporkin, the legendary SEC enforcement director in the 1970s—as "one of the most talented lawyers of his generation" and a person of "the highest moral and ethical fiber." The letter was sent on Sept. 22, 2011, to the chairmen and ranking members of several House committees and subcommittees.

341 Schapiro had asked Becker: Becker recalled the incident: "When Ms. Schapiro telephoned me, her first words—which she knew I would find impossible to resist—were 'David, your country needs you.' I told Ms. Schapiro that it was a terrible time for me to return to government service, but I agreed to talk to her about it. I accepted her offer a week later. I came back to the SEC because I care deeply about the agency and its people, because my friend Mary Schapiro asked me to, and because I thought it was my duty." Testimony of David M. Becker Before the Oversight and Investigations Subcommittee of the House Committee on Financial Services and the TARP,

Financial Services and Bailouts of Public and Private Programs Subcommittee of the House Committee on Oversight and Government Reform on Sept. 22, 2011, pp. 1–2.

341 the agency's chief ethics officer: Ibid., p. 3.

341 Helen Chaitman speculated: Written Testimony of Helen Davis Chaitman, Mar. 15, 2011, before a Joint Hearing of the House Committee on Oversight and Government Reform, the Subcommittee on TARP, Financial Services and Bailouts of Public and Private Programs and the Subcommittee on Government Organization, Efficiency and Financial Management. (She referred to him as "David I. Becker," but the context made it clear she meant David M. Becker.)

342 would marginally reduce the amount of money: The SEC inspector general calculated the "constant dollar" method would have reduced the Becker family's $1.5 million liability by about $138,500. See U.S. Securities and Exchange Commission Inspector General H. David Kotz, "Investigation of Conflict of Interest Arising from Former General Counsel's Participation in Madoff-Related Matters," Case No. OIG-560, Sept. 16, 2011, p. 6. The Beckers settled with Picard for $556,017 in February 2012.

342 the SEC had voted only once: On Jan. 15, 2009, before Becker returned as general counsel on February 23, the commission and staff met in executive session on Madoff matters but specifically deferred the clawback issue. The minutes of this session stated: "Staff said that they were reluctant to sue customers for return of redeemed funds, and that clawbacks could disadvantage those with few withdrawals." (Ibid., p. 30–31.) The staff said it would study the issue further. At a second closed commission meeting on Feb. 12, 2009, the staff and commissioners "discussed the principles and possible inequities" of clawbacks, and the staff was asked to query SIPC again about them. (Ibid., p. 32.) On Feb. 19, 2009, Schapiro met with SIPC's chairman, general counsel and chief executive. SIPC's chief executive said that Schapiro told them that "three, and possibly four, of the commissioners were in agreement" with SIPC's approach, although Schapiro did not recall that meeting. (Ibid., p. 34.) It seems clear that, while SIPC may have thought the SEC had "reached a consensus" by Feb. 19, an opinion reflected as fact in a chapter heading in the inspector general's report, the SEC's official position on SIPC clawbacks remained unsettled on the day Becker returned to the commission, based on the minutes of the closed-door sessions.

343 "there was no such thing as neutrality": Mack, *End of Normal*, p. 127. Mack recorded that Mark's fury at his father was intense; he threw out every article of clothing his father had given him and would "take detours to avoid driving past" his parents' former penthouse, a cumbersome habit given its location on a major southbound artery in Manhattan. Ibid., pp. 127–28.

343 "I kept e-mailing him": Ruth Madoff Interview.

345 doing clerical chores: *SEC v. Eric Lipkin*, filed as 11 Cv. 3826 in U.S. District Court, Southern District of New York, p. 6.

345 Lipkin confessed that he had conspired: *U.S.A. v. Eric S. Lipkin* Criminal Information, filed on June 6, 2011, as S3 10 Cr. 228 (LTS), U.S. District Court, Southern District of New York (hereafter *Lipkin Information*).

345 seventy years in prison: *Lipkin Information* Transcript of Plea Hearing before U.S. District Judge Laura Taylor Swain on June 6, 2011, p. 22.

345 contained a little bombshell: Letter to Honorable Laura Taylor Swain from Preet Bharara (signed by Julian J. Moore, assistant U.S. attorney), dated Nov. 16, 2011, p. 1.

345 "ready to accept responsibility": *U.S.A. v. David L. Kugel* Criminal Information, filed on Nov. 21, 2011, as S4 10 Cr. 228 (LTS), U.S. District Court, Southern District of New York, Transcript of Plea Hearing on Nov. 21, 2011, p. 31.

345 He admitted he had provided: Ibid., pp. 32–33.

345 her faked trades would always look plausible: Ibid., pp. 36–38.

346 "the rate of return predetermined by Madoff": Ibid., p. 37.

346 "I will do all I can to cooperate": Ibid., p. 31.

346 the third Madoff executive to plead guilty: *U.S.A. v. Enrica Cotellessa-Pitz* Criminal Information, filed on Dec. 19, 2011, as S5 10 Cr. 228 (LTS), U.S. District Court, Southern District of New York.

346 "no clue as to whether they were real trades": Telephone call to the author from BLM, Nov. 29, 2011.

346 "drives me crazy": E-mail to the author from BLM, Oct. 12, 2011.

346 He regretted pleading guilty: E-mail to the author from BLM, Nov. 29, 2011.

347 stage-four chronic kidney disease: Confidential interview.

347 Asked about his health: Telephone call to the author from BLM, Sept. 3, 2011.

347 From his vantage point: E-mail to the author from BLM, Dec. 7, 2011.

347 "My health is as good as can be expected": E-mail to the author from BLM, Jan. 23, 2012.

348 Looking back on the trip: Telephone interview with Ruth Madoff by the author, Nov. 29, 2011.

EPILOGUE

349 his first on-the-record interview: all quotations in this section are from First BLM Interview.

355 "Everyone here always asks me why I never ran": E-mail to the author from BLM, Feb. 23, 2011.

360 Madoff sits for a second interview: Second BLM Interview.

361 a recent *People* magazine article: Liz McNeil and Alex Tresniowski, "The Trials of Ruth Madoff," *People*, Feb. 21, 2011, pp. 78–82.

ACKNOWLEDGMENTS

There are three people without whom this book could not possibly have been written.

The first is my agent, Fredrica "Fredi" Friedman. In the frantic weeks after Bernie Madoff's arrest, Fredi stamped her well-shod foot and waved her bejeweled hands until she finally got my frazzled attention. Then she said, "You were born to write this book." She would not take "I'm too tired" or "I'm too busy" or "I'm too scared" for an answer. The minute a publisher hinted that we should do a "quickie" book, Fredi stood up, smiled, and marched me right out of the building for a fortifying drink. I never would have begun this journey if she hadn't persuaded me I could.

The second is my extraordinary editor at Times Books, Paul Golob. We didn't always agree about the route to follow on this trip. We hit a few rocks in the road, made a few detours, and broke the speed limit repeatedly in the final weeks. But when we finally reached the destination, it was far, far above any elevation I could have reached on my own. And somehow, Paul got us there with most of my original luggage intact—just more neatly, attractively, and logically packed. When I felt I was driving blind, Paul kept us on course. I could not have reached this destination without his help.

The third is my empowering husband, Larry Henriques. Throughout this expedition, he kept gas in the car. He made sure I stopped for coffee. He fixed every flat tire and replaced every dead battery. He kept the road map handy and the windshield clean. He rolled down the windows and told jokes to keep me awake when I was nodding off. He has been my tireless and cheerful companion for every mile of the way, uphill and down, and I will never, ever be able to thank him enough.

Many others made priceless contributions to this project, starting with my researchers: the incomparable Barbara Oliver, from whom no fact or document can hide; the talented Tim Stenovec, who was as deft at hand-holding interviews as he was at finding addresses in phone book archives; and our backstop in Europe, Bernadette Murphy, who was my own French connection.

The entire team at Henry Holt—especially Stephen Rubin, Maggie Richards, Patricia Eisemann, Chris O'Connell, Meryl Levavi, and Emi Ikkanda—has gone above and beyond on my behalf, as has Alex Ward, my trusted liaison in book development at the *New York Times*.

The bricks and mortar of this book are the people, more than a hundred of them from all sides of this scandal, who were willing to share their knowledge and their memories with me. Many did so in confidence, and I am grateful for their trust. Some victims of this crime spoke with me despite despair and disagreements; I am humbled by their generosity. I also want to acknowledge the courtesy of Warden Tracy W. Johns, Associate Warden Deborah Gonzales, and their staff at the Butner federal prison facility, and the cooperation of Bernard L. Madoff and his lawyer, Ike Sorkin, in facilitating my efforts to construct as complete a history of this crime as possible. My thanks are also due to all the professionals at Baker & Hostetler, the Securities and Exchange Commission, the Justice Department, the U.S. Marshals Service, the Financial Industry Regulatory Authority, and the Federal Bureau of Investigation, who responded to my countless queries with unfailing patience, from first to last, even when the only possible response was "no comment."

Earlier drafts were greatly improved by a cadre of trusted critics. Besides Larry Henriques, Barbara Oliver, and Tim Stenovec, they included my dear friend and colleague Floyd Norris, the chief financial correspondent for the *New York Times*; my cousin Dr. Peter R. Henriques, a notable historian and teacher; and Professor Mark Vamos, a gifted editor and journalism educator, whose elegant brushstrokes are here and there in these finished pages. Special thanks to Christine Bockelmann, for her matchless last-minute quality control.

I also owe a huge debt to the family members and friends who patiently suffered through this project and forgave me for all the missed dinners, abbreviated reunions, forgotten birthdays, canceled holiday visits, and boring Madoffian monologues. They include my sister, Peggy van der Swaagh; sisters-in-law Noel Brakenhoff and Teakie Welty; cousins Marsha Wolpa, Sherry Stadtmiller, and Nancy Woodburn; and cherished friends Leslie Eaton, who talked me down from the ledge so often; Jaye Scholl Bohlen, who has endured four of my book projects and still takes my calls; and Jonathan Fuerbringer, who always laughs at all the right places. I am also grateful for the encouragement of Dean Michael Brown and my fan club at the Elliott School of International Affairs at George Washington University, and for the patience and support of my colleagues on the board of the Society of American Business Editors and Writers (SABEW), especially Beth Hunt, Bernie Kohn, Greg McCune, Kevin Noblet, and Rob Reuteman.

I cannot begin to thank all the journalists at the *New York Times* and elsewhere who went out of their way to help. But, with apologies to anyone omitted, I'm going to try: Charles Bagli, Vikas Bajaj, Al Baker, Alex Berenson, Alison Leigh Cowan, Julie Creswell, Eric Dash, Michael de la Merced, Claudio Gatti, Christine Haughney, Jack Healy, Dirk Johnson, Eric Konigsberg, Zachery Kouwe, Steve Labaton, Peter Lattman, Gretchen Morgenson, Joe Nocera, Catherine Rampell, William K. Rashbaum, Nelson D. Schwartz, David Segal, Louise Story, Stephanie Strom, Landon Thomas Jr., Mary Williams Walsh, Ben Weiser, and Julia Werdigier.

I owe an enormous thank-you to my patient and warmhearted newsroom boss, Larry Ingrassia. Add in the other unfailingly supportive *Times* editors: Bill Keller, Jill Abramson, Glenn Kramon, Adam Bryant, Winnie O'Kelley, David Gillen, Dan Niemi, Mark Getzfred, Keith Leighty, Bill Bright, and Kevin McKenna. And top the list off with Cass Peterson's wonderful wizards of truth on the business news copy desk, who saved my bacon countless times and never audibly groaned when they saw me racing up minutes before deadline.

In the months between Bernie Madoff's arrest and his guilty plea, I wrote or worked on about fifty separate stories about the scandal. At least twenty-five other reporters either shared those bylines with me or contributed reporting to those stories. It was the textbook example of a team effort. That is why this book is dedicated not just to my husband, Larry, but also to all the generous and talented people who produce the *New York Times* every day, to all those who came before us and—please, Lord—all those who will come after.

It has been my honor and joy to serve among you for these past twenty-one years.

INDEX